W9-BBA-747

BRITISH
INTERVENTION
IN MALAYA
1867–1877

Hatherley   E. Cardwell   de Grey   Granville   H. Childers   J. Bright   Argyll   Kimberley   Hartington
         Clarendon   C. Fortescue   H. A. Bruce   C. J. Goschen
   R. Lowe   W. E. Gladstone

MR. GLADSTONE'S FIRST CABINET, 1868

From a painting by H. Barraud in the National Liberal Club, London

BRITISH INTERVENTION IN MALAYA 1867-1877

BY

C. NORTHCOTE PARKINSON

KUALA LUMPUR
UNIVERSITY OF MALAYA PRESS
1964

SOLE DISTRIBUTORS

Oxford University Press, Amen House, London E.C.4

GLASGOW NEW YORK TORONTO MELBOURNE WELLINGTON
BOMBAY CALCUTTA MADRAS KARACHI LAHORE DACCA
CAPE TOWN SALISBURY NAIROBI IBADAN ACCRA
KUALA LUMPUR HONG KONG

This edition ● *University of Malaya Press 1964*

First Published 1960
Reissued in Pustaka Ilmu 1964

SET IN GREAT BRITAIN
AT THE UNIVERSITY PRESS, OXFORD.
REPRINTED PHOTOGRAPHICALLY IN HONG KONG BY
THE PENINSULA PRESS, KUN TONG

PREFACE TO THE FIRST EDITION

THIS is the first volume to be published of the Malayan Historical Studies. This is to be a series of histories and historical monographs covering the story of what we now call Malaya from the earliest recorded times down to the year 1957. The series, which will not be numbered, should comprise finally about twelve volumes. The order of publication will follow no chronological order, nor would an exact sequence be possible, the volumes dealing not only with different periods but with different aspects of the subject. Economic history can thus be dealt with in one volume, historical geography in another.

There can be no pretence at finality in the volumes of this series. Much of the work will have been done by authors working somewhat in isolation and without more than occasional access to the archives and libraries upon which their researches should ideally depend. Much of the story will be reinterpreted, no doubt, by subsequent historians for whose monographs and theses there will remain ample scope. But this work of the future will be a less formidable undertaking if there already exists a series of this kind. It will provide the future scholar with a background knowledge, lacking which he might not even know where to begin. The immediate object must be to establish what happened, when and where.

Two problems have been encountered in the compilation of this first volume and they are problems which are likely to recur in others. The first of these relates to the documentary material. The Straits Settlements records preserved in Singapore are those most readily available to the Malayan student of modern Malayan history. Upon these sources much of the work must depend. It is necessary, however, to supplement this archive material by reference to the Parliamentary Papers, as also where necessary to the best source of all, the files preserved in the Public Record Office. The Parliamentary Papers are available in print but arranged in a way which makes them difficult of reference. In the Public Record Office the archives are systematically grouped and numbered, but to give the P.R.O. reference in such a work as this would be misleading, for those were not the archives mainly used. The reader is asked to believe that the transcription has been carefully done. He is further to understand that the dates of the correspondence will lead him most readily to the actual documents, of which the best copies are undoubtedly in London. The author's practice in this volume has been to quote very fully from the sources, leaving the reader free to draw his own conclusions, which may, of course, differ entirely from those reached in the present work.

The second problem concerns the English rendering of Malay and Chinese names. The exact way in which these are represented in English is of concern to the philologist or linguist, who may wish to suggest how the word was originally formed or how it should now be pronounced. The historian is little interested in the word except as a means of identifying a character or place—itself often a matter of extreme difficulty. Some scholars, while conceding this, would urge that there should at least be consistency of spelling throughout. But the difficulty here is that the documents, in this case, reveal no such consistency among those living at the time. To alter the documents would be heresy and would, in any case, give a totally false impression of their authors' erudition. It might even introduce a new source of confusion over identifications already quite difficult enough to establish. To leave the documents as they stand, on the other hand, correcting each spelling in a footnote or subsequent reference would introduce a note of laborious pedantry such as would annoy more readers than it would impress. So, with apologies to the experts, much inconsistency has been retained. In other volumes of the series, less heavily documented, a more consistent policy may well be found practicable.

The author of this first volume is indebted to previous historians, whose works are quoted, as also more especially to former pupils from whose unpublished works he has been glad to draw both for facts and conclusions. Chief of these are Mr. George Bogaars, M.A., whose dissertation on *The Tanjong Pagar Dock Company* has been most useful, and Mr. M. A. Mallal, M.A., whose dissertation entitled *J. W. W. Birch: causes of his assassination* (1952) has proved extremely valuable. The author has also relied on the academic exercises written by Mr. T. Chelliah, Mr. Wee Choon Siang, and several others. Work such as theirs will undoubtedly be of use to other historians contributing to this series. Theirs and other academic exercises are to be found in the Library of the University of Malaya. The author has to make acknowledgement to the following publishers for permission to quote from these works published by them: Messrs. George Allen &

Unwin Ltd., *British Malaya*, by Sir Frank Swettenham; Messrs. Hutchinson & Co., Ltd., *Footprints in Malaya*, by Sir Frank Swettenham; Messrs. John Lane, The Bodly Head, *The Real Malay*, and *Malay Sketches*, by Sir Frank Swettenham; Messrs. John Murray, Ltd., *Life of Sir Andrew Clarke*, by R. H. Vetch, and *About Others and Myself*, by Sir A. E. H. Anson. For assistance with the maps the author is indebted to the Geography Department of the University of Malaya. It was originally hoped to reproduce directly the contemporary maps of the Malay States; maps or sketches made by men involved in the events themselves—McNair, Swettenham, Peyton, and Daly—and reproduced in the Sessional Papers. When reduced in scale, however, these maps were insufficiently legible. Each was accordingly redrawn and is now reproduced in a form which, while preserving the essentials of the original, is no longer an exact copy. While many place-names have been enlarged, no attempt has been made to impose either consistency or modern usage on the spelling. The country here represented was not merely unsurveyed but largely unexplored.

Thanks are also due to the President and Committee of the National Liberal Club for permission to reproduce the frontispiece illustration. This is from the painting by H. Barraud which hangs in the club entrance hall and which portrays, among others, the Rt. Hon. the Earl of Kimberley and the Rt. Hon. Hugh Childer: men who played a leading role in the events with which this book is concerned.

The author must express his thanks, finally, to those who have made this publication feasible: the Asia Foundation, the University of Malaya Press, and the Oxford University Press. Without generous support from all those concerned the Malayan Historical Series would be impossible to publish, or even plan. It is the hope of the historians engaged on this project that the efforts they make will justify all the help that has been given.

C. NORTHCOTE PARKINSON

University of California
January 1960

CONTENTS

LIST OF MAPS

INTRODUCTION

THIS is the story, in some detail, of the ten vital years during which Perak, Selangor, and parts of the Negri Sembilan were absorbed into the British Empire. The interest of this story must centre on the Malay States themselves, but it has for its background the Empire considered as a whole. If we take, for the moment, the broader view, we shall find a vast pattern in which the Malay States have their place. It is a pattern of conquest but neither aimlessly nor boundlessly aggressive. The conquest is that of the main trade route between Europe and Asia and its progress is marked by successive and seemingly inevitable steps, one deliberate stride after another carrying the British flag from the home ports to the upper reaches of the Yangtze-Kiang. A mere recital of chronological sequence must destroy any idea of accident or inconsequence. The old route to and from the East ran via St. Helena, Cape Town, Bombay, Madras, Calcutta, and Penang. To these possessions were added Ceylon, Malacca, Mauritius, and Singapore. The system was extended to Hong Kong in 1841, which was then linked with Singapore by the addition of Labuan and North Borneo. With the opening of the Suez Canal the old Mediterranean route guarded by Gibraltar and Malta was linked with Bombay by additional bases at Cyprus, Alexandria, and Aden.

The development of this vast network was the work of a British aristocracy which, at the time this story begins, was still firmly in power. The British aristocracy was mainly characterized by its peculiar co-ordination of commercial, maritime, naval, military, and colonial policy. This was achieved to some extent through such institutions as Parliament, the Stock Exchange, Lloyds, and the Baltic, but more through social relationships and a pattern of life created and strengthened in public schools, universities, clubs, race-courses, and the hunting field. Society, though stratified, was not so compartmented as to prevent an effective co-operation towards a common aim. Social convention sometimes checked a too open discussion of what the aim was supposed to be but this did little, in practice, to hinder its achievement. It is generally easier to sense the general purpose than to trace the exact means by which it became the accepted policy. The

Map 1. A Map of the Malay Peninsula

connexion between the obvious intention and the desired result is often a little vague. It is reasonable, however, to assume that a connexion there must have been.

When we are told that the British were compelled to intervene in Malaya, after for so long refusing to do so, we must remember that a similar explanation must be found for other events in the same series. If it was a growing state of chaos in Perak which induced the British to interfere, we must suppose that comparable and unprecedented disorders dragged them into Penang, Malacca, Madras, Colombo, Aden, Cyprus, Malta, Gibraltar, Ireland, and Wales. Even were this curious coincidence to be established in every case, we should be left to wonder why this fervent love of order should have brought the flag to those particular places and not to others, like Albania, where British commercial interests were less obviously involved. There is a point beyond which mere coincidence cannot be made to go. It is true, nevertheless, that events seem genuinely accidental to those most nearly concerned in them. A governor exceeds his authority, there is some delay over reproving him, an unpopular decree coincides with a religious festival, a crowd is collected and excitement mounts, the troops are called out but the commandant is ill, a junior officer panics, a volley is fired, the innocent are killed, the situation becomes critical, more troops are sent for, and the whole territory is annexed. Were the story considered merely in isolation (as the local officer sees it) we should have to attribute much of it to accident. The order was ambiguous, the telegram lost, the expert on leave, and the great man sick. With only a small change in circumstance the whole course of events might have been different. This seems plausible until we look at the larger pattern again. Then we realize that accident merely decided the hour and place for the inevitable. On the larger map the sense of coincidence is lost. All we can see are the footprints of a steady and inexorable advance.

Once we have turned, however, from the local gossip to the world atlas we are at once in danger of making the opposite mistake. We see the great trade route, surveyed, charted, lighted, buoyed, and patrolled. We realize that it is flanked by naval bases, frequented by shipping lines, and safeguarded by diplomacy. We conclude that it must have been planned. From this reasonable conclusion we go on to picture a conclave of imperialist warmongers, huddled round a map and deciding what part of it should next be painted red. For a plan to succeed it must first be defined. But such a cartoon as this is palpably false, for the plan must take generations to execute. There are no means by which one generation can bind the next. A plan, therefore, of large-scale maritime strategy can hardly extend beyond the individual's expectation of office. If the plan were merely his, it would die with him. And that, to infer from the results, is exactly what it has not done.

Apart, however, from the logic of the case, we know from both history and experience that no long-term imperialist plan has ever been made in Britain, not at least by those in a position to carry it out. That is not how things are done. The decision to advance or stand fast, made in the light of recent events, is influenced by many things apparently insignificant in themselves. A Colonial Office official is seen to lunch with his friend in the Foreign Office. A letter is written to *The Times*. A retired governor is invited somewhere for the week-end. Certain shares rise or fall. A banker is seen to look grave and an admiral shakes his head. The trend of opinion is suddenly obvious and the Cabinet decision is rarely opposed to it. In the long run it is the trend of opinion which decides the matter, or else it is the trend of events which decides the opinion. The general tendency matters more than governments or individual statesmen. It is by no means easy to oppose.

This book deals with the history of Malaya during a period in which such a trend is very apparent. It will be seen that secretaries of state and governors were powerless beyond a certain point. Instructions issued in accordance with the trend of the period were obeyed, exceeded, exaggerated, and praised. Instructions intended to reverse the trend were queried, shelved, misinterpreted, and forgotten. The people who mattered in the Straits Settlements were resolved to establish British influence over the Malay States, thus opening for themselves a new field for investment and trade. They readily found allies in England who would support their policy. They were consistently opposed by those who saw what their intention was —to conquer Malaya at the expense of the British taxpayer and keep all the profit to themselves. Their motives were repeatedly and bitterly exposed by their opponents. Nor were they consistently supported by the home government, even when that was led by as good an imperialist as Disraeli. But they had the tide under them, the flood-tide of British expansion, and there was little that anyone could do to stop it.

From a first glance at the evidence it would be natural, though mistaken, to trace the whole movement to the Singapore Houses of Agency. But further study will reveal a closely knit system of which commerce formed only a part. Malayan waters were dominated by the Royal Navy, with warships in the Straits, gunboats in the estuaries, and launches penetrating the rivers and creeks. In studying the story of what actually took place, the reader will continually be aware of sea power. Whether in the foreground or background of events, the white ensign is always there. Almost as significant, moreover, at times, is the part played by the red ensign. Troops owed their mobility to the P. & O. and British India Lines and even the local tonnage was taken up when needed. Upon the mail steamships, moreover, depended the regular communication between Hong Kong and Singapore, between Singapore and Penang, between Penang and Colombo. Throughout the whole story of British intervention there is nothing more striking than the effective co-operation of officers and men in the different services, whether military or civilian. They were all soldiers in the last resort.

We find, therefore, on the British side an agreed policy of intervention. What resistance did this arouse? How did Malay patriotism react to this foreign threat? It is clear, first of all, that an effective resistance was almost impossible. Malays and Chinese alike lived on rivers, down which went their produce and up which came their food. The effect of a naval blockade was immediate and decisive. Even were there no actual starvation, food shortage would prevent the assembly of any considerable force in any one place. As a country, the Malay Peninsula proved extremely vulnerable to sea power. Its defenders could never concentrate an army of more than a very few hundred and even that would tend to disperse before anything had been achieved. Although this was not realized when our period began in 1867, it was widely known when the period ended ten years later. It was also known by then that the native inhabitants were divided against each other by race, by geographical barriers, and by mutual dislike. Any hostility there might be between Malays and Chinese was as nothing compared with the hostility revealed by the Chinese towards each other. Nor were the Malays very closely akin as between one district and the next. The aboriginal Malays, the Bugis, the Rawwas, the Mandeelings, and Sumatrans were alike in little save religion. They did not readily combine.

Opposition from the Chinese was most unlikely even had they all belonged to the same province and the same secret society. The resident Straits Chinese were on the British side and fervent in their demands for intervention. The immigrant miners intended only a brief stay in the tin-fields, few residing permanently enough to have any political views or ambitions. All they wanted was peace and order and this the British alone could supply at a reasonable price. As for the Malays, they were vaguely resentful but proved quite unmilitary in character. They had among them known killers, feared by the rest and of legendary prowess. But the Malay royalty had little tradition, it seemed, of personal leadership, and even minor chiefs often preferred to direct operations from a safe distance. Individuals and groups might show considerable courage, but the actual fighting seems often to have been unenterprising and static. Expenditure of ammunition was usually more a matter of noise than marksmanship, and casualties were few.

On the subject of Malay resistance, such as it was, two views have been expressed. It was thought by some at the time that the coincidence of disorders in Perak, Selangor, and the Negri Sembilan pointed to a conspiracy, a concerted movement against Western influence. Such a movement, it was believed, drew inspiration from the Achinese and might well spread to Pahang or even to Johore. Sir Peter Benson Maxwell, by contrast, a stern critic of imperial policy, asks whether there was any such conspiracy and replies in effect that there was not. The truth would seem to be that there was a general movement but that it did not amount to a conspiracy. The Malays lacked organization or even any effective means of contact. What they caught from each other was not a plan but a mood. There was a vague feeling of resentment among the chiefs, a similar reaction in each to the threat which was sensed by all. They lacked the knowledge of how to convert resentment into action. There was among them (as among the British) a trend of opinion but it was too feeble to delay, even momentarily, the general movement of the time.

The only force which might have held up the forward movement was the force of disease. Past invaders of Malaya may have been checked by the local mosquitoes and the British and Indian troops may be counted fortunate to have escaped (as they did) with quite a moderate sick list. Their relative immunity was due, it would seem, to their accidental avoidance of what is now considered the worst time of year. The Perak and Sungei Ujong Wars may be said to have begun on 3 November 1875. On 19–21 March the main body of troops re-embarked for India. Had they been operating on the flat coastal plains, they would have encountered the local mosquitoes at their most active period in November–December. In fact, however, they pushed inland rapidly, moving through inhabited lands at some distance from the coast. These operations would bring them to the territory of *Anopheles maculatus*, the principal vector of malaria in the Malay Peninsula, in later years to be called 'the scourge of the rubber estates'.[1] But the activity of this vector is subject to seasonal variation, the number of mosquitoes reaching a peak at some time between February and June and causing a wave of malaria about a month later. Such waves have been commonly observed in April–May and sometimes again in September–October. If there is a close season it is November–March and that was exactly the period of the campaign. More recently, it was the exact period of the Japanese campaign in Malaya (6 December–15 February). This was purely accidental in both instances and the British of 1875–6 did not even recognize the mosquito as anything more than a nuisance. The malaria parasite was to be first identified by Laveran in 1880 and first traced to the mosquito by Ross in 1897. In the meanwhile, Major McNair feared only the 'miasma that rises from the ground', trusting to his mosquito net to exclude it. Had he but known, his net was even more valuable than his medical armoury, which comprised pyretic saline, chlorodyne, quinine, and brandy—not to mention Lea and Perrin's Worcester sauce, 'a splendid stomachic'.[2]

While the campaign was thus well timed from the medical point of view, this is not to say that mosquitoes would be wholly absent. It so happened, however, that the use of quinine (or cinchona bark), fashionable from 1633 to about 1804, 'forbidden by all authorities' from 1804 to 1840, had become orthodox practice again by about 1850.[3] The result was that the troops of 1875 were liberally supplied with quinine, which remained the standard and effective treatment until about 1932. There can be no doubt that the health of the troops was largely due to the use of this drug, neglect of which was one cause of Penang's heavy mortality earlier in the nineteenth century.

For one cause and another, therefore, there was little resistance to the British, even from the mosquitoes. They were able to establish an effective control. In its political aspect this assertion of influence

---

[1] J. W. Field and others, *The Institute for Medical Research, 1900–1950*, Kuala Lumpur, 1951, pp. 127–77.

[2] J. F. A. McNair, *Perak and the Malays*, London, 1878, p. 419.

[3] Field, op. cit., p. 153.

was characterized by a contrast between the aims and the means. In general policy there was an altruistic element which, if it is over-estimated in books of the past, may well be overlooked in the books of the future. The colonial officials of Victorian days honestly desired to bring justice instead of misrule, prosperity instead of want, health instead of sickness, confidence instead of fear. Many of them were men of private means, demanding little in return. In their desire to abolish debt-slavery they were disinterested, enlightened, and kind. Nor would it be fair to conclude that the merchants were intent only on trade. They had more than economic reasons for desiring to see their customers at peace. As for the British Cabinet, its aims were never more lofty than in the age of Gladstone, Disraeli, and Queen Victoria.

If the aims were pure, the means were not. There were those who, in seeking to spread civilization, order, and law, did not hesitate to prevaricate, conceal, and confuse. In the story which follows it will be found that the British fighting men of this period were not much more honourable than the civilians of that age or any other. As against this, they were genuinely humane. Their opponents, when defeated or outmanœuvred, were treated with surprising generosity and more often pensioned than killed. By the standards of the twentieth century, the conduct of Victorian warfare was almost incredibly civilized. It left remarkably little bitterness among the protagonists and less still among the people at large. It was war as waged by gentlemen.

It should be emphasized, finally, that the Malayan patriot of the future who seeks to identify patriots of old Malaya will seek in vain among the characters of this story. Some of them were admirable in statesmanship, courage, and persistence, but Malaya as we know it did not exist. It remained for the British to invent it.

CHAPTER I

O N 3 April 1867 the Governor of the Straits Settlements was
writing to the Secretary of State for the Colonies as follows:

My Lord

I have the honour to report that on the 1st instant I was sworn in as
Governor and assumed the administration of the Straits Settlements.

The ceremony of reading the Charter and Governor's Commission and
the taking the Oaths was performed in the presence of a very large assem-
blage containing almost every European in Singapore and a great number
of Natives. All places of business were closed and by general consent the
day was observed as a holiday. The Chinese inhabitants went to considerable expense in illuminating their part of the town and in giving a public
display of fireworks and throughout the community there was evinced a
desire to testify in the strongest manner their satisfaction with the change
which has been effected.[1]

Following an official termination the Governor signed his name:
H. St. George Ord.

His term of office had begun, coinciding with the transfer of the
Straits Settlements from the control of the Government of India to
the direct control of the Crown through the Colonial Office. The
fireworks which saluted this event were justified as marking the successful conclusion of an agitation which had begun in 1857 at the time of
the Indian Mutiny. The story of this agitation has often been told and
its causes analysed.[2] Mills has shown[3] that its origins can be traced
back to 1848 or earlier. But the Mutiny, itself discrediting the Indian
Government, was accompanied by a rigid Press control which was
automatically and pointlessly applied to the Straits and followed by
a rumoured likelihood of the mutineers being deported to Singapore.
Worse still was the possibility of these dangerous prisoners being
accompanied by a Sepoy regiment to guard them—such warders
being regarded as even less desirable than the prisoners themselves.

[1] Straits Settlements No. 3, 3 Apr. 1867.
[2] See Parliamentary Papers on the transfer of the Straits Settlements. See also
An Anecdotal History of Old Times in Singapore, by C. B. Buckley, Singapore,
1902, vol. ii, pp. 754–80; and *British Malaya 1824–1867*, by L. A. Mills, Singapore,
1925, pp. 263–75.   [3] Op. cit., p. 263.

Singapore was a convict settlement in any case (the convicts numbered 2,536 in June 1863),[1] but these normally criminal inhabitants were relatively harmless and useful, being employed even as domestic servants; in which capacity murderers were thought preferable to thieves. Worst of all was the probability that such an increase in the size of the garrison might be made the occasion for introducing customs duties as a means of paying for it. This catastrophe, the end of Singapore as a free port, was unthinkable.

The transfer, brought about by a decade of negotiations and dispute, represented not only the averting of a disaster which, by 1867, had become far less imminent, but the opening up of possibilities to which the Petition of 1857 alludes in an isolated but significant paragraph:[2]

The Supreme Government of India has uniformly discouraged the local Government at Singapore from interfering with matters beyond the limits of the Island. The cultivation of friendly relations with Native States and Chiefs has been neglected, and the Government does not possess that influence in the Indian Archipelago which the interests of British commerce require, and which might have been acquired and maintained by a very slight exertion on the part of the Indian Government.

It would be easy to read into this passage more than is actually there. The Petition was drawn up only three years after Sir James Brooke had faced a commission of inquiry at Singapore, itself the result of four years of peisecution. Gladstone, Hume, and Cobden, influenced by an alliance in England of philanthropists and commercial crooks, gaining their information from Mr. R. C. Woods, the irresponsible first editor of the *Straits Times*,[3] brought to an end the movement which Brooke had initiated for extending British influence in Borneo. It is true that the Borneo Company was not formed until 1856, but Sir James had by then resigned his official position and with it all likelihood of official support. So that this reference in the Petition to 'Native States and Chiefs' relates mainly, no doubt, to Sarawak and Brunei. It might not be wrong, however, to see in it some faint hint of a growing interest in the Malay Peninsula itself. The very frustration of Rajah Brooke's hopes and efforts must have tended to deflect elsewhere the energies of his Singapore adherents. But such a tendency would receive little encouragement from the Liberal

---

[1] *Straits Times*, 27 Mar. 1869.
[2] See Buckley, op. cit., p. 756.
[3] See Mills, op. cit., pp. 256-7. The rival *Free Press* was on Brooke's side.

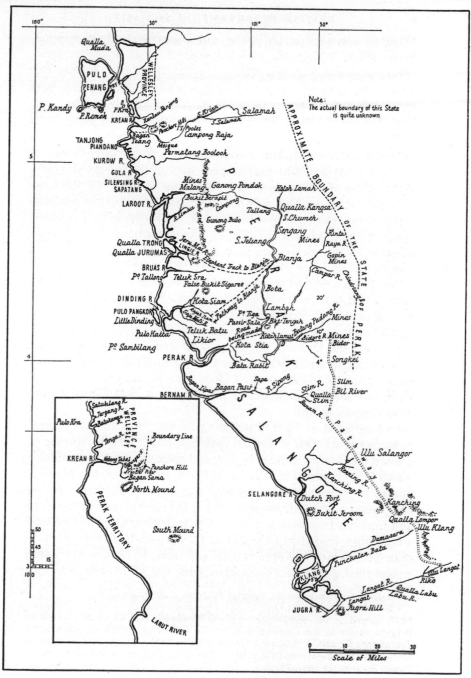

Map 2. Perak and Selangor

Ministers who were to rule in England, almost without interruption, from 1859 to 1874. As St. John observes:[1]

Then came a cool Ministry, to whom Borneo is a bore; and the Rajah, irritated, writes to them in a very improper strain, 'holding them responsible for the lives and properties of British subjects in Sarawak'. They shrug their shoulders and laugh, for they are not responsible, and would not care if they were.

This indifference towards Borneo would certainly extend towards peninsular Malaya. But the moment of transfer coincided with a short period of Tory rule in 1866-8 and no one was then to know how soon it would end. So that there may have been a few who expected the transfer to result, as it eventually did, in a more enterprising policy towards the mainland. They would be far outnumbered, however, by those who rejoiced merely because Indian rule was at an end.

Satisfaction on this score was short-lived for Colonel Harry St. George Ord, C.B., of the Royal Engineers (knighted soon afterwards), proved extremely unpopular almost from the first.[2] His predecessor was found to have been greatly beloved (at least when on the eve of departure) and Ord was considered, by contrast, to be tyrannical, overbearing, quarrelsome, and tactless. At this point, however, it will be more helpful to look at the Colony from the Governor's point of view, to visualize the Straits as they appeared in 1867 and as they would appear to him.

Ord came out in the mail steamship by what was then the normal passenger route. One steamship took him to Alexandria, whence he crossed the isthmus of Suez by rail, embarking in another steamship which brought him then, as it would now, to Bombay, to Colombo, and so to Penang. The Suez Canal was under construction but its completion and its success were still in the future. Heavy cargoes to and from the East went in sailing ships round the Cape and in 1865 a steamship, routed from Macao to Europe, made a longer passage than the slowest tea-clipper of that year's race. In 1867, as Ord's ship passed through the Mediterranean, *Ariel* beat all records in an out-

[1] *Life of Sir James Brooke*, Spenser St. John, Edinburgh, 1879.

[2] Sir Harry St. George Ord, b. 1819, commissioned in the Royal Engineers 1837. Served in the West Indies and at Woolwich and Chatham. Served as Brigade Major in the Crimean War, at the siege and capture of Bomarsund. Transferred for service under the Colonial Office 1855. Lieutenant-Governor of Dominica 1857. Governor of Bermuda 1861-6 (Lt.-Col. and C.B.). Governor of Straits Settlements 1867-73.

ward passage of eighty-three days from Gravesend to Hong Kong—a time never bettered by a sailing ship. On the homeward passage that year *Sir Lancelot* and *Ariel* nearly dead-heated, 102 days from Foochow. Seven of the tea-clippers actually docked in London river on the same day. For mail and passengers the steamships of the Peninsular & Oriental Line had their advantages but, for cargo, the route to the East remained what it had been since Vasco da Gama rounded the Cape in 1497.[1] It did not pass through the Straits of Malacca. It came nowhere near to Singapore.

With the supremacy of the sailing ship still unchallenged on the longest sea-routes, the steamship which entered the Straits was merely on the highway between India and China; and Penang, the first port of call, was a place of obviously limited importance. Colonel Harry Ord had, as his fellow passenger, an officer who was admirably fitted to explain everything for his benefit. John Frederick Adolphus McNair, by this time Major in the Madras Artillery, had first come to the Straits as a Lieutenant in 1853, thereafter serving successively in Malacca, Labuan, and Singapore.[2] From 1857 he had been Colonial Engineer and Superintendent of Convicts. In this dual capacity he was responsible for many of the public works in the Colony, including the present cathedral. His system of management in the Singapore jail, where he had at one time only one European warder, is described in the book he afterwards wrote on this subject.[3] His two daughters married, respectively, partners in Guthrie & Co. and Paterson, Simons & Co., so that he was very much a Straits Settlements man with a grandson serving in Singapore as recently as 1953. It was under his guidance that Colonel Ord first entered the Straits.

Ord landed at Penang on 14 March and learnt that his predecessor, General Orfeur Cavenagh, Governor since 1859, had arranged to leave Singapore on that same day, a fortnight before the transfer was to take place. This left the Hon. Lieutenant-Colonel Henry Man (Resident Councillor at Penang) as Acting Governor and he was urgently needed at Singapore for the purpose of formally surrendering the Colony on behalf of the Indian Government. In the meanwhile he showed Ord round the town of Penang. What this place looked like

[1] See *The China Clippers*, by Basil Lubbock.
[2] Buckley, op. cit., pp. 641–3.
[3] *Prisoners their own Warders*, J. F. A. McNair and W. D. Bayliss, London, 1899. But the deportation of convicts from India stopped in 1860. New arrivals after that (about sixty a year) came from Ceylon. See S.S. No. 108 4 June 1868.

we know from the work of John Cameron, published only two years before:[1]

The point where the European residencies or warehouses are collected together is called George Town; but except in official papers it is seldom distinguished by that name. . . . It is built upon a level sandy point running out on the south-eastern extremity of the island, and separated by a narrow channel of less than three miles from the mainland. The approach to the town from the southward is . . . very beautiful. Between the south-eastern point of the island, which rises in a bold wooded promontory, and the opposite shore of Province Wellesley, the distance is about eight or nine miles; this is some twelve miles south of the town, and the intermediate water has more the appearance of a deep bay than of an open channel. The northern part of the island and the mainland close in together, and shut out the view of the northern outlet.

At the entrance of this bay some pretty green islets are passed, wooded in some parts to the water, and at others encircled by a sparkling beach of white sand. The main island itself towers majestically up on the one hand, and on the other the low mangrove shores of Province Wellesley stretch along, backed in the distance by the blue mountains of the Peninsula. So land-locked is this passage, that as soon as the southern point of the island is passed, the sea assumes a placid lake-like appearance, and indeed it is seldom at any season disturbed by more than a ripple. . . . Between the island and Penang there is a deep though narrow channel, but which is seldom made use of by large vessels. The considerable native village of Jamestown, surrounded by cocoanut and other palm-trees, can just be seen. . . . Further up on the Province Wellesley side the mouths of the Juru and Prye Rivers are passed; on the northern bank formed by the confluence of the latter stands Prye town, the chief village of Province Wellesley.

The shipping of Penang rides at anchor right opposite the town, the chief feature of which is the stone fort. . . . The town, with its suburbs, covers perhaps a square mile of ground, and besides the sea frontage has one principal street, with others branching off from it.

The Resident Councillor could have described (and probably did) how Penang, practically uninhabited in 1786, had now some 70,000 thriving traders and cultivators.[2] He may have remarked, as he was later to do,[3] that:

every Englishman who visits the Straits may be proud to witness the effects of the liberal policy of his country, which has converted two desert

[1] *Our Tropical Possessions in Malayan India*, J. Cameron, London, 1865, pp. 319-21.

[2] The total population amounted to about 150,000 inhabitants according to an official report of 24 Jan. 1868 (S.S. No. 16). This included Province Wellesley.

[3] *Supplement to Correspondence regarding the comparative merits of British and Native administration in India*, Col. H. Man, Calcutta, 1868.

islands, Singapore and Penang, one within half, and the other three quarter, of a century, into world famed ports with a foreign trade of 12 and 5 millions sterling respectively.

To call Penang, or even Singapore, world famed was perhaps at this date an exaggeration, but the Straits Settlements had benefited from recent changes and when (in 1868) the Home Government made a new postal contract by which the P. & O. mail steamer was no longer to touch at Penang the Chamber of Commerce protested that:

from being a place of no importance it [Penang] has risen to the commercial position it now enjoys by the energy and capital of European Merchants, Agriculturalists and Miners, who have devoted themselves to the development of the resources of the country; that these results have taken place only since the opening of a regular packet communication with Europe by the calling here of the P. & O. Mails and that but for this advantage the country would have remained what it was prior to the establishment of this communication.[1]

Watching the bustle occasioned by the arrival of the ship in which he was passenger, Ord must have realized something of the truth of this. He was then told, no doubt, about the mainland opposite the island, clearly visible from the sea-front; Kedah, a friendly Native State, and Province Wellesley, the British territory adjacent. Ord would learn that, whereas Penang was largely inhabited by Chinese, the 80,000 people of Province Wellesley included sixty Europeans and Eurasians, 56,000 Malays, and 10,000 Indians. These had come into the area (the Malays from Kedah, mainly in 1822) since British rule was established, the country having been previously 'a mere tract of jungle and swamp, with little, if any, cultivation in any portion of it'.[2]

In 1860 the cultivated area extended over about 70,000 acres, of which 41,000 were under paddy, 10,000 under sugar-cane, 12,000 cocoanut, and the remainder were divided among spice and fruit trees, tapioca, etc. The progress of this latter cultivation has been wonderful both here and at Malacca, and promises to revolutionise the home trade. The sugar planters are supplied with all the latest improvements in machinery, and afford a highly remunerative employment to a large amount of both capital and labour.[3]

Colonel Man could emphasize the contrast between the contented peasantry of Province Wellesley, where plank houses were replacing attap huts and where 'women now seldom appear abroad without an

---

[1] S.S. No. 16, 24 Jan. 1868.   [2] Col. H. Man, op. cit.
[3] Ibid.

European umbrella or parasol' with the forced labour, casual exactions, disorder, and misrule of the adjacent Native States. He regretted, and probably expressed his regret, that British influence was not more extended. His term of office was at an end and he could afford to speak pretty frankly about the opportunities that were being neglected.

Colonel Ord re-embarked almost at once and the mail steamship went on her way down the Straits of Malacca. The low jungle-covered shores slid by and the distant blue mountains seemed, by comparison, to stand still. Perhaps Major McNair was able to point out the Dindings, the islands ceded to Great Britain in 1826 by the Sultan of Perak—islands which would otherwise have remained the haunt of pirates. Colonel Man had produced a plan for colonizing the Dindings with Malays from Kedah, Perak, and Sumatra and Chinese from Perak, but nothing had yet come of it, perhaps because no tin had been found there. The ship went on past the shores of Selangor, still notorious for the pirates of Bugis origin who lurked there. McNair might have shown Colonel Ord, on the chart, how the shallows contract to form a narrow channel opposite the Selangor coast, with the North Sands and One-Fathom bank as leading features, clearly marked. The navigation of the Straits, never particularly easy, and now, of recent years, far more important, was greatly facilitated by five lighthouses and one lightship. The *Torch*, as the lightship was called, was anchored on the North Sand, although plans for replacing her by a screw-pile lighthouse had been drawn up as far back as 1862. The imminence of the transfer had itself delayed this among other improvements, and the danger remained of a light which had periodically to be removed for the purpose of maintenance and repair. Another likely topic of conversation, as between two engineers, was the light on Cape Rachado, farther north again. McNair had, or was to have, considerable work in connexion with lighthouses, and that on Cape Rachado, with another at Malacca, formed a link in this chain of lights at a point where navigation would otherwise be hazardous. Malacca itself would now be passed in turn and the Governor-elect might learn something of its former importance and its present decay. Traditionally it was called the Fort and Town of Malacca but the Fort had long since been demolished and the settlement comprised, in fact, 658 square miles (as estimated) with a predominantly agricultural population of over 67,000. The port was fairly frequented by local shipping which included a vessel called the *Fair Malacca* on a regular service between there and Singapore.

Malacca was the place of shipment for the tin exported from the Native States in the immediate hinterland but its tin-supply (and indeed its safety) depended upon the complicated politics of the Malays.

So Colonel Ord came at last to Singapore on 16 March, his ship passing on the way that other ship in which his predecessor had sailed thence on the 15th. What Singapore looked like we know pretty exactly, in part from the lithographs made by Vincent Brooks and in part from John Cameron's description,[1] both dating from about 1864. Cameron was a master mariner who lived in Singapore from 1861 until 1881, being a joint proprietor of the *Straits Times*.[2] He describes the approach to Singapore as a seaman would and so tells us how it must have appeared to Colonel Ord:

It is at the western entrance, through New Harbour . . . that the greatest measure of beauty is to be found. This is the side from which Singapore is approached by those who come from home to take up their sojourn there; and no wonder that they enter their new home predisposed in its favour, for the scene is one very rarely to be surpassed in the world, certainly not in the English East Indies. In making this harbour, the steamer enters between the large island and a cluster of little islets, standing high out of the water with rocky banks, and covered to their summit by rich green jungle. . . . As soon as the passage between the main island and these small islets is half-way passed, and New Harbour reached, Mount Faber . . . is seen to the full view. . . . On the very summit of Mount Faber stands a flag-staff, from which vessels approaching from the west can be seen at a distance of sixteen miles.

The P. & O. Company wharves, at which their steamers lie, are situated at the head of a small bay, with the island of Pulo Brani in front. . . .

The mail steamers never come into the roadstead now, but land their passengers, and cargo at these wharves. Most of the passengers, whether their ultimate destination be Singapore or not, land and drive up to town to inspect for themselves the beauties of a place the approach to which is so lovely.

We are not to know whether Colonel Ord was impressed by the beauty of the scenery but we may assume with some confidence that he perceived, as an engineer should, that the original town of Singapore had been built in the wrong place; wrong that is to say, in relation to the eventual position of the harbour. The river mouth around which the first settlement clustered had come to nothing except as a landing place for native craft. The new harbour, where the depth was sufficient for large ships, was remote from the business centre with

[1] Cameron, op. cit.　　　　　　　　　[2] Buckley, op. cit., vol. ii, p. 715.

its offices and godowns. There was talk of attempting to join the old town with its new part by a railway or even a canal. In the meanwhile, however, a distinguished arrival, like Colonel Ord, would approach the town by carriage. His position at the moment of landing was ambiguous. He was not yet Governor of the Straits Settlements nor due to assume office for another fortnight. For people obsessed with problems of precedence the situation bristled with difficulties. Nor were there lacking people who were so obsessed; Ord being one and Sir Peter Benson Maxwell another. The Straits Settlements were still under Indian Government, with Lieutenant-Colonel Man as the officer upon whom the theoretical responsibility devolved and Lieutenant-Colonel Macpherson (Resident Councillor, Singapore) as his local representative. But under Indian Government the Recorder was more especially representative of the Crown, and arbiter besides, on points of procedure. Ord, as Governor-elect, regarded himself as already entitled to be called 'Excellency', even before being sworn in. Sir Peter, as Recorder (and Chief Justice-designate), thought otherwise. It was a relief, perhaps to all, when the day came for the new Governor's inauguration at the Town Hall. Buckley records how, just before noon on 1 April,[1] the Hon. Lieutenant-Colonel Henry Man arrived as Acting Governor, being received with a salute of seventeen guns from Fort Canning. He went round the room and shook hands with the ladies.

Then, under another salute, stalked in Governor Ord, without removing his hat, and sat down on the dais without taking any notice of anyone. The impression thus created was never removed and was justified in the years that he remained in the Straits.[2]

This impression was further emphasized by the arrival immediately afterwards, of Admiral Keppel, naval Commander-in-Chief on the China station. Immensely popular locally since the days of his friend, Sir James Brooke; distinguished alike by ancestry, rank, seniority, war service, and decorations, Keppel bowed to the company and shook hands in turn with the ladies present. Refusing a chair on the dais, Keppel preferred to remain on ground level and among his friends. Taking the oath on the platform, Colonel Ord felt perhaps small, isolated, and lonely. He would evidently have to assert himself.

One difficulty at once apparent to Ord was that the post of

---

[1] The date was chosen because the Indian Government's financial year ended on 31 Mar.   [2] Buckley, op. cit., p. 787.

Governor in the Straits Settlements had not so far been one of any particular dignity. The successive governors appointed by the East India Company, Mr. Fullerton, Mr. Bonham, Colonel Butterworth, and Mr. Blundell, had not been knighted. Colonel Cavenagh, a veteran of the Indian Mutiny, rose by seniority to Major-General, but received no other honour. Nor was he at any pains to maintain the status of his position: a carelessness which extended to his house and office. As Buckley records:[1]

In May [1862], Governor Cavenagh returned from Penang and occupied Leonie Hill House in Grange Road. Complaints were made about the inconvenience of the Governor's office being removed to the house, in place of being in town with the other public departments, as had before that been the case. The Governor's office was for a time at Leonie Cottage, a wooden house with an attap roof. . . . The change led to much of the business which had before been transacted directly with the Governor in town, being passed through the hands of the Resident Councillor; but Colonel Cavenagh could always be seen at any moment in his office at Leonie Hill where he was always to be found without any ceremony, during office hours, working in a room downstairs.

The same homely picture was evidently given to Joseph Conrad (years afterwards) by one in a position to contrast the old days and the new. He thus allows his reminiscent sea-captain to remark on the change since his early days:

No Excellency he—this Mr. Denham—this governor with his jacket off; a man who tended night and day, so to speak, the growing prosperity of the settlement with the self-forgetful devotion of a nurse for a child she loves; a lone bachelor who lived as in a camp with the few servants and his three dogs in what was called then the Government Bungalow; a low-roofed structure on the half-cleared slope of a hill, with a new flagstaff in front and a police orderly on the verandah. He remembered toiling up that hill under a heavy sun for his audience; the unfurnished aspect of the cool shaded room; the long table covered at one end with piles of papers, and with two guns, a brass telescope, a small bottle of oil with a feather stuck in the neck at the other—and the flattering attention given to him by the man in power. . . .

There had been a time when men counted: there were not so many carriages in the colony then, though Mr. Denham, he fancies, had a buggy.[2]

The informality which had surrounded the governorship was reflected in the absence of any permanent and official residence. The original house had been in exactly the right position; on the spot

[1] Buckley, op. cit., p. 690.
[2] *The End of the Tether*, in *Youth*, pp. 193-4 of the Uniform edition of the works of Joseph Conrad, London, 1923.

chosen, in fact, by Sir Stamford Raffles himself. This building was to have been replaced by one rather larger, but news of the Indian Mutiny led to the construction on that site of Fort Canning. Since 1862 the Governor had lived in Leonie Hill House, Grange Road—that property being rented from its owner for £800 a year.[1] A governor so accommodated was the less likely to hedge His Excellence with secretaries and aides-de-camp. He was still definitely approachable.

The ease with which the Governor could be seen resulted, of course, from the relatively small number of the community he had to rule. The population of Singapore was perhaps nearing 100,000 at the period of the transfer, of which total nearly 60,000 were Chinese. This was a smaller population than that of Penang and Province Wellesley and included a fair proportion of country-dwellers, so that the town was of no great size and looked, as now, far smaller (in population) than it was. Apart from the garrison and other impermanent elements, the European residents numbered less than a thousand. Cameron considered (in 1864) that 'Europeans and their immediate and unmixed descendants do not, I think, number 800'.[2] With even more confidence does he number those of any social pretensions.

Society in its restrictive signification in Singapore is not unfrequently the subject of remark and sometimes of animadversion. . . . The community is a very small one. There are not, I think, over forty families who aim to form a part of society, and if I might offer an opinion on so very delicate a subject it would be that, among so few, a more general, even though less intimate, intercourse should spring up.

Whatever it may be under the new regime, the official world has certainly not hitherto taken a prominent lead in social affairs. But this is doubtless accounted for by the expensive nature of hospitality as practised in these parts. To Government officers who receive fixed salaries, the cost of housekeeping must be a more serious consideration than to the merchants whose profits on a single venture may outbid the highest salary in the land. . . .

It is to the merchants chiefly that Singapore is indebted for the introduction of its very expensive, though very pleasant style of hospitality. . . .

But even the ordinary style of living in Singapore may be set down as luxurious. . . . The tables of the wealthiest are to be distinguished from those of the poorest rather by the lavish supply of European preserves and condiments—and, of course, by a draft from a choicer and more extensive cellar—than by any greater abundance or variety of dishes. Again, every one has his stable—though the poor man may have but one steed, and the rich man a dozen.[3]

[1] S.S. No. 67, 3 Aug. 1867.   [2] Cameron, op. cit., p. 109.
[3] Ibid., pp. 285–9.

Society, 'in its restrictive signification', comprised officials, bankers, lawyers, physicians, and army officers, but centred on an aristocracy of merchants. Some of these claimed a sort of 'Pilgrim Fathers' descent from men who had come to Singapore in 1820–2; men who had spoken with Sir Stamford Raffles himself. These original settlers had included A. L. Johnston, José d'Almeida, Alexander Guthrie, C. R. Read, John Purvis, and Dr. Alexander Martin. Mr. C. R. Read had come, on Raffles's advice, from Bencoolen and Dr. Martin was said to have come with Raffles himself.[1] Soon afterwards, in 1823, came Mr. Hugh Syme, and (in 1824) Mr. W. Spottiswoode and Mr. F. Maclaine. In 1827 arrived Mr. E. B. Boustead and in 1828 landed Mr. W. W. Ker, whose clerk was Mr. William Paterson. These early settlers were the founders of the chief houses of agency. These were now (in 1867) Guthrie & Co., A. L. Johnston & Co., John Purvis & Sons, W. Spottiswoode & Co., Boustead & Co., Maclaine, Fraser & Co., Paterson, Simons & Co., and Syme & Co. A sort of seniority was given to José d'Almeida & Sons because Mrs. d'Almeida (wife of the firm's founder) was still alive; at the installation of Governor Ord it was Mrs. d'Almeida that the Admiral greeted first. Of rather more recent vintage were Behn, Meyer & Co., W. R. Paterson & Co. (called the Borneo Company since 1857 and managed in about 1859 by S. Gilfillan) and the retail firm of John Little & Co. The brothers Little were very much of the aristocracy, being nephews of Dr. Alexander Martin, but the most prominent of the family was Dr. Robert Little, a physician with interests in land. The rival retail firm of Robinson & Co. was of more recent origin, beginning no earlier than 1858. Of the older firms, John Purvis & Sons had an added importance from being the agents of the famous China firm of Jardine, Matheson, founded in 1832.

Not all these firms were managed by their founders' sons and nephews, but Singapore still contained members of the original families: W. H. M. Read, R. B. Read, Joachim d'Almeida, E. d'Almeida, W. d'Almeida, John Purvis, Mathew Little, and others. The representatives, moreover, of the older firms—Thomas Scott (of Guthrie & Co.), W. R. George (of d'Almeida & Sons), W. Manford (of Spottiswood & Co.), Thomas Shelford (of Paterson, Simons & Co.)—had the prestige either of office or family connexion or both. On the fringe of this inner circle stood the lawyers, headed by J. G. Davidson (nephew of James Guthrie), John Simons Atchison (a relative of

[1] Buckley, op. cit., p. 212.

H. M. Simons of Paterson, Simons & Co.),[1] J. R. Logan (the author), Thomas Braddell, who was formerly partner with Abraham Logan, and W. Rodyk, who founded, with Davidson, a firm which still exists. The more official families contained a proportion of gentlemen who had married daughters of Governor Blundell—his daughters had been numerous, although his term of office had been relatively short. Outside the social circle in the narrower sense stood a few foreign merchants—Rautenberg, Schmidt & Co., Puttfarcken, Rheiner & Co., and the American firm of Hutchinson. A partner in this latter was Mr. G. H. Dana, author of satirical contributions to the *Straits Times* under the *nom de plume* 'Extinguisher'. Some of the merchants with teutonic names were fairly assimilated—Adolf Schmidt had even married a Miss Blundell. There was no question, however, of assimilating the Parsee, Indian, and Chinese business men. One English-speaking Chinese, and a notable local character, was Hoo Ah Kay (1816–80), always called 'Mr. Whampoa'. Another leading Chinese was Tan Kim Cheng, son of Tan Tock Seng, after whom the hospital is named.

According to Cameron[2] the Europeans, who had long since deserted their original mansions in Beach Road, lived in bungalows about two miles out of town, but within sound of the 68-pounder gun which was fired each morning from Fort Canning at 5 a.m. Then or soon afterwards everyone rose and went for a ride or walk at sunrise (5.15 to 5.45, according to the time of year). Returning from exercise, gentlemen would don pyjamas and have tea or coffee with biscuits or fruit, reading or talking on the verandah until 8.30. After a bath and a shave, gentlemen would breakfast at 9.0 with their ladies; then visible for the first time. As Cameron observes:

A little fish, some curry and rice, and perhaps a couple of eggs, washed down with a tumbler or so of good claret, does not take long to get through and yet forms a fair foundation on which to begin the labours of the day.

After breakfast the vehicles were at the door and people were in their offices from about 10 to 1. They had a light tiffin, apparently in town, and then worked until 4.30 or 5. The more active then

---

[1] Editor of the *Straits Observer*. The other local newspapers had been the *Free Press*, a weekly founded in 1835, and the *Straits Times*, another weekly, founded in 1845 and edited by Mr. R. C. Woods. In the 1850s they were respectively for and against Sir James Brooke.

[2] Cameron, op. cit., pp. 289 et seq.

played fives or cricket except on nights (twice a week) when the band played on the esplanade.

The band plays from half-past five till half-past six, at which hour it is all but dark, when the carriages make for home in a long string, gradually falling off one by one as the various residencies are reached.

Except on band nights however, most of the commercial and all of the official world retire home a little before six o'clock. Arrived there, probably a glass of sherry and bitters will anticipate the refreshing process of dressing for dinner.

Dinner followed at 6.30 or 7 and was not, as Cameron thoughtfully observes, 'the light airy meal which might reasonably be imagined from the nature of the climate'. Soup and fish preceded beef or mutton, turkey or capon, with side-dishes of tongue, fowl, and cutlets. Then followed curry and rice in the Straits fashion, which was followed in turn by pudding or preserves, cheese and butter, pineapple, bananas, mangoes, rambutans, pomeloes, and mangosteens.

During the progress of the substantials and of the curry and rice, the usual beverage is beer, accompanied by a glass or two of pale sherry. The good folks of Singapore are by no means inclined to place too narrow restrictions on their libations, and it has been found in the experience of older residents that a liberality in this respect conduces to good health and long life. Besides this the American Tudor Company keeps up a tolerably regular supply of ice, and as it is sold at three cents, or less than 1½d per lb., it is within the reach of all and is an invaluable adjunct to all beverages. . . . A cigar and a glass or two of sherry after the ladies are gone, and dinner is over.

Dinner rarely ended before 8 and everyone was in bed by 10, the intervening time being spent in reading, conversation, or billiards.

Advertisements of this period show that civilized life in Singapore depended upon regular importations by sea; the heavy goods round the Cape, the butter and cheese by the overland mail. Advertisements for the products made by Crosse & Blackwell, Lea & Perrin, Bryant & May, and Keatings look tolerably familiar. There is also something sternly British in the offer by John Little & Co. of 'Railway Rugs, Scotch Maudis, Shetland Shawls' together with the 'Light Buggy Springs' for which a readier sale might have been foreseen. Most advertising space was taken, as a rule, by Holloway's patent medicine firm, undeterred by the rumour that one of their remedies had killed the King of Siam. As orders reaching the Borneo Company in 1862 from that quarter included an Armstrong cannon, six bottles of cough lozenges, and an English schoolmistress guaranteed not to teach Christianity,[1] the story was not wholly improbable. But what is that to a vendor of patent medicines?

From India the European residents had learnt their way of life. They thus resolutely refused to have any social relations with 'all who are descended in any way from the people of India, no matter how remote the descent'. As part of the same general policy they sent their children back to England at a certain age, retiring there themselves as soon as their means would admit. The children might come out in their turn, but there was nothing like a permanent establishment. One result of this was that it was possible to assemble in London the representatives of the leading (or formerly leading) families—the Napiers, Bousteads, Guthries, Patersons, Simons, Littles, Gilfillans, and the rest. This was to have its importance. As against that, there was no established practice of going home on leave. That, as we shall see, was to come later and was to be important in its turn.

From all this it will be seen that Colonel Ord had to impose his rule on an organized community with its own hierarchy and habits, its own leaders, and its own opinions. And the transfer for which local opinion had clamoured—under conditions which had since altered—was to have two immediately significant results. On the one hand, the Governor was to claim a viceregal dignity which set him apart from the other residents and made him extremely unpopular. On the other hand, he brought with him a new colonial constitution by virtue of which the local leaders were to be given some real, if rather loosely defined, political powers. There had been talk at one stage of these powers being far more extensive. But the idea of anything like self-government had been rejected at the Colonial Office 'because the colonists would then be able to interfere in the problems of native states, and thus become involved in wars, from which they would have to be extricated at the cost of Great Britain'.[2] The result was that the Charter under the Great Seal, of which Ord had seen a draft, together with his letter of appointment dated 6 February,[3] provided for a Legislative Council comprising both official and unofficial (but nominated) members. Lord Carnarvon had further emphasized that, whereas government officers might not obstruct in Council the settled

---

[1] Letter to Wm. Adamson, Manager of the Borneo Company; original in the Company's possession.
[2] *The Colonial Office, a History*, H. L. Hall, London, 1937, see p. 238.
[3] C.O. No. 2, 6 Feb. 1867.

policy of the Government, the unofficial members might say what they liked.

I need hardly point out first that, as a general rule, the assistance which the Governor derives from the Debates in the Legislative Council will be in proportion to the freedom with which each Member of it is encouraged to express his opinion on all the questions which will come before them. Secondly that the obligation to support the Governor is much stronger in the case of Executive Officers than in the case of the Judge from whom a general support may fairly be expected by the Governor, but can scarcely be enforced without injuring that character for independence which it is of the first importance that he should preserve.

To Unofficial Members the fullest possible latitude must be allowed in discussing and voting upon all questions brought before the Council, and when they are absolutely or nearly unanimous, great deference should be paid to their opinion, especially in regard to all new ideas of Expenditure or Taxation.

[Lord Carnarvon to Colonel Ord.]

Ord was thus instructed to give a political voice, a right of criticism, to the very people to whom he was, by his viceregal pretensions, giving most offence. These circumstances did not foreshadow the most peaceful and harmonious relationships between Governor and governed. In fact, as things turned out, these relationships were to be very bad indeed. People disliked Governor Ord and were not, in those days, afraid to say so.

CHAPTER II

S IR HARRY ST. GEORGE ORD, Knight (as he now became) and
Companion of the Most Noble Order of the Bath (as he had
been before), had first of all to form a government. When formed
it appeared somewhat as follows in the *Straits Almanac and Directory*
(1867):

Sir Harry St. George Ord	Colonel, R.E.	Governor
Henry Frederick Plow	Clerk of Council and Private Secretary	
J. F. A. McNair	Major, Madras Artillery	A.D.C. (Acting)
Hon. Archibald E. H. Anson	Lt.-Col., R.A.	Lieut.-Governor of Penang
Hon. William W. Cairns		Lieut.-Governor of Malacca
His Honor Sir Peter Benson Maxwell		Chief Justice
Hon. W. J. Cooke	Col., Madras Staff Corps	O.C. Troops
Hon. R. Macpherson	Lt.-Col., Madras Artillery	Colonial Secretary (absent)
Hon. F. L. Playfair	Captain, Madras Staff Corps	Colonial Secretary (acting)
Hon. Thomas Braddell		Attorney-General
Hon. W. W. Willans		Treasurer
Hon. John Irving		Auditor
Hon. J. F. A. McNair	Major, Madras Artillery	Colonial Engineer
Daniel Logan		Solicitor-General
Thomas Dunman		Commissioner of Police
D. F. A. Hervey	Cadet	Colonial Secretary's Office
Henry Burn	Lieutenant	Master Attendant

The principal changes brought about by the transfer were the
appointments of Ord himself, Anson, and Cairns. Lieutenant-Colonels
Man and Macpherson,[1] with Mr. Burn, were to be retained for only

[1] Lt.-Col. Macpherson had been employed in the Straits Settlements for
twenty-five years, and had been Resident Councillor at Singapore before the
transfer. After Ord's arrival he was Colonial Secretary and Surveyor-General.
Ord thought very highly of him and attributed to him 'the rapid and satisfactory

three or four months. Certain other officials—Dunman, Vaughan (the police magistrate, Singapore), and Cuppage (post master)—were due for fairly early retirement, so that it would be possible within a few years to introduce more civil servants with a colonial (as opposed to an Indian Government) background. Retained from the old establishment were Plow, Willans, Irving, McNair, and Logan. Braddell had been Crown Counsel and was now made Attorney-General. Captain H. St. G. Ord of the 78th Light Infantry, brother of the Governor, came out as police magistrate, Malacca. Of the old regime, the chief representative was the former Recorder, now Chief Justice, Sir Peter Benson Maxwell. As A.D.C. the Governor had asked for Lieutenant Carpenter of the 60th Rifles, but was told that his A.D.C. must be recruited from a unit stationed in the Colony. The garrison was to comprise six companies of Ceylon Rifles and two batteries of Artillery with two more companies of the Ceylon Rifles in Labuan. Singapore was to have, in addition, the headquarters of a European battalion stationed principally for service 'in China and Japan'.[1] The European regiment was the 73rd,[2] later replaced by the 1/10th. It does not appear that the Ceylon Rifles materialized, their place being taken by the 7th Madras Native Infantry.[3]

In addition to these paid appointments on the civil establishment, Ord had to choose his Unofficial Members of Council. In practice he was bound to appoint men who were already important in the Colony and those first chosen, on 3 April, were more or less inevitable. These were W. H. M. Read (partner in A. L. Johnston & Co. and president of the Chamber of Commerce), F. T. Brown ('head of one of the oldest and wealthiest firms at Penang' and 'perhaps the largest landholder in the Straits'[4]), T. Scott (senior resident partner in Guthrie & Co.), and Dr. R. Little 'representative of the agricultural interest'.[4] To these four Ord later added C. H. H. Wilsons, Captain of the Singapore Volunteers, making five temporary members whose names had, however, to be submitted to the Secretary of State. As the Secretary of State wanted ten names, from which to choose six, Ord then added to his list[5] J. Weis (partner in W. Spottiswoode & Co.),

manner' in which the transfer was carried out. He was retained, accordingly, as Colonial Secretary but died in 1869 (see S.S. Confidential Dispatches, 22 Apr. 1867).   [1] P.O. No. 5, 7 Feb. 1867.
[2] Transferred to Ceylon in Mar. 1869 (*S.T.* 20 Mar.).
[3] This unit served in the Straits Settlements from 1867 to 1871 (S.S. No. 179 6 Sept. 1870).   [4] S.S. No. 3, 3 Apr. 1867.
[5] S.S. No. 135, 21 Nov. 1867.

L. Nairne (a Penang planter), G. Lipscombe (senior resident partner in Boustead & Co.), J. F. Crockett (Singapore representative of Jardine, Matheson & Co.), and Charles Dunlop (senior resident partner in Maclaine, Fraser & Co.). The members actually approved were the five first named and no more were nominated until 1869.[1]

In the description given of these first-nominated members it will be noted that Thomas Scott was described as senior *resident* partner in Guthrie & Co. just as G. Lipscombe was the senior *resident* partner in Boustead & Co. This may serve to remind us that in these and other instances the actual senior partner was in London. An important result of the transfer was that these former residents, still with important interests in the Straits, were able to organize political pressure on the Colonial Office. They had been unable, formerly, to bring any direct pressure to bear upon the Governor-General of India, if only because they were in England and he was at Calcutta. But a Secretary of State for the Colonies, directly responsible for the welfare of the Straits Settlements, could be petitioned, persuaded, pestered, and threatened. The result was the prompt formation in London of the Straits Settlements Association. Discussions, obviously begun in 1867, led to an inaugural meeting in January 1868.

On Friday the 31st day of January, 1868, a Meeting was held at Mr. Boustead's Office, Newman's Court, Cornhill, by a numerous body of former residents in Singapore and Penang, to take into consideration the advantage of forming an Association to guard against any legislation that might prejudicially affect the interests of the Straits Settlements, and, in particular, that might be calculated to check or interfere with their commercial prosperity as free ports of trade; to use means to prevent unnecessary expenditure by the local Government and otherwise to watch over the general interests of the Settlements.

Mr. William Napier was called to the Chair when Resolutions to the following effect were put and unanimously carried. . . .

That Mr. John Crawfurd should be requested to accept the office of President.

That Mr. William Napier should be Chairman, and Mr. James Guthrie, the Deputy-Chairman of the Association.

---

[1] Dr. Little resigned in 1869 and Ord had difficulty in finding a successor. He reported that the resident partners of English houses numbered thirteen, of whom six were ineligible from youth or inexperience. Of the remainder, five refused to serve. Ord said that this was due to their belief that time not spent in money-making was wasted. He was able to report, further, that Boustead's would not even allow their members to hold public office, even as Justices of the Peace. But this reluctance to take office was attributed locally to Ord's unpopularity. (See Confidential S.S., 26 Apr. 1869.)

That the Committee should consist of the following gentlemen, viz.—

Mr. Edward Boustead	Mr. Jonathan Padday
Mr. William Paterson	Mr. William McTaggart
Mr. John Harvey	Mr. Edward John Leverson
Mr. James Fraser	Mr. John James Greenshields
Mr. Henry Menchin Simons	Mr. William Wardrop Shaw

The meeting did not end its labours there, but its further deliberations are perhaps less significant than the names of the committee. Crawfurd was the former Governor (1823–6) to whom Raffles had entrusted the colony in June 1823. Mr. William Napier, 'Royal Billy', was an almost legendary character, a lawyer who edited the *Free Press* from 1835 to 1846, was Lieutenant-Governor of Labuan in 1848, and retired to England in 1857. Edward Boustead had been a resident partner of his firm from 1828 to 1849. William Paterson had been in Singapore from 1828 until 1862 at least and was later to become chairman of the Chartered Bank. More than that, William Paterson, William McTaggart, and John Greenshields had been among those foremost at Singapore in demanding the transfer from the period of the Indian Mutiny.[1] Initially, the Straits Settlements Association lacked representation in Parliament, but by 1872 it comprised ten Members,[2] the beginning of quite a useful 'pressure group'.

A first object of the Straits Settlements Association was, as we have seen, to ensure that Singapore and Penang should remain free ports. The second object (closely connected with the first) was to oppose any needless expenditure by the colonial government as now established. The difficulty about limiting expenditure, from the Governor's point of view, lay in the very nature of the transfer which the members of the Straits Association had done so much to bring about. For the British Government had been emphatic throughout the long negotiations that the change, if it were sanctioned, should place no fresh burden on the British taxpayer. Deficits previously incurred by the settlements had been set against a surplus of Indian revenue, partly in recognition of the settlements' usefulness (until 1860) as convict stations. As Cameron admits:

at no time has the Indian Government sought to derive a profit out of the Straits. The most it has done was to endeavour to raise the revenue to a sum sufficient to cover the military as well as the civil expenditure [and this was not attempted until 1863–4]. . . . During the long years that preceded

[1] Buckley, op. cit., vol. ii, p. 771.
[2] *One Hundred Years of Singapore*, Makepeace, Brooke, and Braddell, 2 vols., London, 1921, vol. ii, p. 297.

this last [attempt] India has suffered and suffered patiently a yearly drain upon her treasury on account of the Straits Settlements of over 30,000. . . .

When the Indian Government hands over the Straits Settlements to the Crown, it will deliver a trust honestly kept and well deserving the solicitude of its new guardian. It has shown, too, an example of high-minded forbearance in abstaining to check the growth of a promising colony to save its own treasury. . . . With the new colony, the Indian Government will also hand over to the Crown a revenue ready made, ample in all respects, and gathered in a manner that leaves trade and industry unburdened, and lays the pressure chiefly upon native vice and luxury.[1]

Those who had most loudly demanded the transfer had necessarily been emphatic on the sufficiency of the revenue; and the Colonial Office had taken them at their word. This is apparent from the instructions issued to Ord by Lord Carnarvon:

Revenue and Expenditure

You will not fail to bear in mind that the Lords Commissioners of the Treasury have only assented to the transfer on the condition that the Colonial Revenue shall be able to cover all its Expenditure both Military and Civil: and I must impress upon you as an imperative duty that you should not submit any new Items of expenditure, whether for Establishments or Public Works, without conclusive proof that the funds necessary to cover such charges will be forthcoming when required.[2]

Ord was thus made to realize during his first year of office that no funds were to be expected from the Colonial Office; that no duties were to be imposed without meeting the almost fanatical opposition of the Straits Settlements Association; that any increase of expenditure would meet with the criticism of the Unofficial Members of the Legislative Council; and that he might nevertheless be blamed as inert if his policy (as regards, say, the Native States) were not more spirited than that of previous governors.

For these various reasons, financial problems loomed large. There were, to begin with, the inevitable bickerings with the Indian Government over the apportionment of the public debt, the transfer of government property, the valuation of stores and the liability for pensions to be paid to officers on the eve of retirement when the transfer took place. The Indian Government also demanded the return of a steamship, which had in fact been condemned as unseaworthy and found to be unsaleable.[3] But the amounts involved in all these disputes were small. The Colony's heavy liability was the military con-

---

[1] Cameron, op. cit., p. 206.　　　　　　　[2] C.O. No. 2, 6 Feb. 1867.
[3] S.S. No. 76 of 17 Aug. 1867.

tribution of £59,300 a year, the assessed value of the Colony's local defence.[1] This was, as Ord complained, a serious drain on a total colonial revenue of about £200,000. He wanted to dispose of the garrison, except for the artillery, and replace the troops by Indian police (400 at Singapore, 250 at Penang, and 150 at Malacca) costing only £25,000 a year. This proposal was discussed on a high level and the report of a committee formed at the War Office to go into this and allied questions came finally before His Royal Highness the Duke of Cambridge.[2] Ord's proposals were not approved and he came to recognize himself that they were impracticable.[3] The problem was complicated by the discovery that the barracks at Penang were in need of repair, while those at Tanglin, Singapore, had never even been completed. And while it was urged locally that £59,300 was more than the Colony could afford, it had also to be recognized that the force which such a sum would provide was insufficient for security. But, complain as it might, the government of the Straits Settlement was held to its bargain.

The obvious solution to the financial problem was to introduce direct taxation and Sir Harry Ord mentioned this possibility in the speech with which he closed the Legislative Council's Session for 1867:

I am glad to state that to meet the proposed expenditure for the year, there is every prospect of a more than adequate revenue, and that it will be raised without its being necessary to resort to additional taxation.

On this head it may be as well that I should state, that, although unable to concur in the opinion, which is so extensively professed in the Settlements, that the establishment of Import or other duties affecting shipping resorting to our ports, would have a most disastrous effect upon our trade, and consequently upon the prosperity of the Colony, I should be extremely unwilling to try an experiment, the result of which is certainly not free from doubt, except under the pressure of a necessity which can hardly arise so long as another and equally legitimate, but less objectionable mode of raising revenue remains open to us, by the imposition of direct taxation.[4]

It was evidently typical of Ord thus to disclaim a present intention while hinting at a future possibility. Without actually increasing his

---

[1] S.S. No. 23 of 20 Apr. 1867.
[2] S.S. No. 203, Military, of 8 Oct. 1868.
[3] S.S. No. 76 of 5 Apr. 1870. Maj.-Gen. Hodgson considered the idea of enlisting Malays but did not expect many to volunteer: 'It would appear that the taste for Military life has passed from amongst them, there being so many more advantageous ways of advancing themselves.' Besides, Malay troops might refuse to act against Malays. (Report No. 20, dated 23 Apr. 1867.)
[4] Singapore Government *Gazette*, 27 Dec. 1867.

revenue he thus made himself just as unpopular as if he had. To merchants of the Straits any talk of customs duties was flat heresy and an insult to the memory of Sir Stamford Raffles; and to anyone at all familiar with the Straits the fair collection of a direct tax seemed as impracticable then as it has been proved since.

If Ord was merely testing opinion he certainly achieved his object, and not merely locally. One prompt reaction was from the Colonial Office, the Duke of Buckingham and Chandos wording his official reproof as follows:

I observe that in that Speech you refer to the possible imposition of Import Duties. I regret that you should have used any language which was calculated to raise the impression that so vital a change would be authorised in the Commercial policy of the Government except under express instructions from home.[1]

In a reply of 21 May Ord rather protested against this strict control. He then received a further reproof in a confidential dispatch which is worth quoting fairly extensively, as showing what the Colonial Office view was:

I have for some time apprehended that your difficulties in undertaking the administration of the Straits Settlements during a period of transition from the state of an Indian Dependency to that of a Crown Colony have been somewhat increased by the circumstance that you have never yourself administered the Government of such a Colony, and have not at hand any official who has taken a leading part in such an administration. I am confirmed in this apprehension by some passages in your despatch . . . [quotations follow]. . . . But my reason for quoting your language is that it seems to indicate a misconception, not perhaps unnatural under the circumstances, of the relations which subsist between the Home Government and the Government of a Crown Colony.

In a Colony possessing Representative Institutions the powers of the Governor are circumscribed by the necessities of that form of Government. . . . In Crown Colonies the powers of Her Majesty and Her Representatives are far greater. But the effect of this is not to create an irresponsible power in the Governor, but to transfer to Her Majesty's Advisers in this country the form of supervision which is exercised in other Colonies by the Representatives of the Community through the powers of legislation and of the purse. In proportion as the Governor's power is increased, it becomes the duty of Her Majesty's Advisers to exercise a closer supervision over measures for which they are responsible. In proportion as the Community is imperfectly represented in the Legislation so it is necessary for the Home Government to be fully informed by the Governor of the feelings

[1] C.O. No. 49, 1 Apr. 1868.

and interests of that Community and of any measures of importance which he may contemplate. . . . And there can be no reason why those principles of Government generally adopted in the administration of such Colonies should be relaxed in the Straits Settlements. Indeed the circumstances of those Settlements, in so far as they are exceptional—their recent changes of Government and their relations to neighbouring States—seem to require from the Home Government an exceptionally careful supervision of their administration. . . .

Your apprehension that by submitting [the question of municipal reform] . . . say to a Committee of the Legislative Council, you will appear to acknowledge your own inability to deal with it, arises, I am confident, from your want of familiarity with the exact form of Government which you are now administering. It is a course of proceeding to which the ablest and most experienced Governors never hesitate to resort. . . .

With regard to your insertion in an official document of a reference to Import Duties, I think it was unfortunate. The language used was not unlikely to be interpreted as a threat. . . . I give you every credit for your desire to secure an equitable apportionment of taxation between Europeans and Natives. . . . But you cannot be unaware of the extreme sensitiveness of Commerce. You cannot be unaware of the very prevalent opinion that the prosperity of Singapore is based on its character of a free port—an opinion which, whether right or wrong, is widely held and by high authorities—it is certainly held most tenaciously by those who are most nearly interested in the prosperity of the Straits Settlements. Such an announcement of opinion, unaccompanied, moreover, by careful argument, exposes you to the charge of hasty judgment—is likely to force on the Home Government a disavowal of your opinions detrimental to your authority—and it has some share in calling into existence an organization in this Country under the title of the Straits Settlements Association—which may not be without its use in informing the Secretary of State—but which even while so doing, may also prove a source of much embarrassment to the Governor.

I have thought it necessary to write this despatch in order to remove a misconception which while it exists is calculated to interfere with the confidence which should subsist between a Colonial Governor and Her Majesty's Government. But I have marked it Confidential because I think that it should not be placed on record in the office of the Colonial Secretary.[1]

The reaction of the Straits Settlements Association was less immediate but more emphatic. In a letter dated 22 April 1868 the Chairman, Mr. William Napier, pointed out that as the existing revenue exceeded the expenditure (on the Governor's own admission) this talk of additional taxation could only foreshadow further expense.

With regard to raising revenue from duties on imports or exports, it is,

[1] Confidential, C.O. to S.S., 31 July 1868.

I believe, unnecessary to remind your Grace that, ever since their incorporation in 1826, the three stations in the Straits have existed as free ports of trade, without either duties on goods or tonnage dues on shipping, and open on equal terms to the flag of every nation without exception. It was not out of deference to the opinion of the inhabitants that this policy was adopted, but in obedience to the principles on which Singapore, the chief port in the Straits, had been founded in 1819.[1]

For what sort of object, asked Napier, could these time-honoured principles be violated? The expense which loomed largest at the moment was the Governor's plan for building himself an official residence.

A Government house on a large and costly scale has been ordered, and ground to form an enclosure for it, to the extent of about 100 acres . . . it will not be going too far to estimate the combined cost at 150,000 dollars, or somewhat over £37,000.[2]

Expenditure on the present Government House was a sore point locally from two points of view. It might lead to further taxation and, apart from that, it symbolized just those pretensions to dignity which the local families resented. The building was on an ambitious scale and the original estimate omitted the cost of its stables, necessitating supplementary estimates to a considerable amount. It was built by convict labour under the direction of Major McNair, and 'Extinguisher' was able to make effective play of the design, the cost, and the speed of execution.[3] Its completion was said to have been hastened through Ord's desire to offer adequate hospitality to the visiting Duke of Edinburgh.[4] Wrote 'Extinguisher' in the *Straits Times* of 20 March 1869:

Chronicles of St. George, Book 2, Chap. 3
1. Now the Chief Ruler was a generous man, for he stinted not of the money of his subjects.
2. And the people had given him one hundred thousand shekels of silver that he might build himself a palace.
3. And some of the Government officials, even the convicts, had labored upon it for many months, and it approached completion.
4. Then went the Chief Ruler to gaze upon the work, and, when he had looked he said: Lo! I have used up the money that was given of my

---

[1] Straits Settlements Association to Secretary of State, 22 Apr. 1868. It is perhaps worthy of note that Mr. W. H. Read was on leave at this time and in London, a guest of Mr. Seymour Clarke.
[2] Ibid.   [3] *Straits Times*, 20 Mar. 1869.
[4] The Governor wanted to entertain His Royal Highness handsomely, according to 'Extinguisher', 'so that I may be rewarded of the Queen'.

subjects and I have none wherewith to build a place for my oxen and asses.

5. Then called he his chief workman, even him who was called Makan Angin [McNair].

The writer goes on happily to describe the new approach to the Legislative Council and concludes with the result:

11. Then answered one of the Council and said. We thought that the asses were to live in the palace,—but since we are wrong, *and have no choice in the matter*, we give the money unto thee.

In fact there was a further expenditure of over $7,400 over and above the supplementary estimate of $40,000.[1] This did not escape the notice of the critics.[2]

Whatever exception might be taken to the cost of building Government House, no one could question that a residence for the Governor must be provided. Still less could anyone deny that the Straits Government needed at least one steamship to maintain communication between the settlements and for the relief of four lighthouses scattered over 300 miles. Of the two existing vessels, one was worn out, 'her bottom being worn so thin that holes could be knocked in it with a hammer',[3] and the other needed a new engine. Ord therefore ordered from England a steamship, a steam-cutter, and the engine for a steam-launch. As these could not arrive for over a year, he purchased a small screw steamship called the *Pei Ho* for $62,000, for use until the others arrived. The new government steamship *Pluto* did not reach Singapore until 4 January 1871 and there was heavy expense in the meanwhile over providing and repairing various obsolete and inefficient substitutes. Fresh controversy raged over the expenses of the Marine Department.

[1] S.S. No. 201 of 8 Oct. 1870.

[2] Government House, it was stated in the leading article of 20 Mar., 'looms in imposing dimensions over the whole island, reminding one of the towering castles of Fairyland which Doré can so graphically depict. Its cost however will do full justice to its size.' There was in fact constant criticism of government in the *Straits Times* editorials. Ord was stung by these into pointing out (S.S. No. 242 of 9 Dec. 1868) to the Secretary of State that the *Straits Times* contained 'unfounded and foolish statements . . . made by the Editor in the full knowledge of their incorrectness'. He added: 'I have on several occasions made efforts to induce him either to allow himself to be furnished with correct information, or to contradict the errors which he has put forth but usually without effect, and he has lately stated openly that he publishes what he knows to be acceptable to his supporters, and has no desire for better information than he has.'

[3] S.S. No. 56 of 6 July 1867.

The necessity for the means of rapid communication between the settlements—and the need as well for a military garrison—was demonstrated by events which took place a little over three months after Ord's arrival at Singapore. These were the Penang Riots of July 1867; a conflict between the two main groups of Chinese in the settlement, the Ghee Hin Society of about 20,000 members, and the Toh Peh Kong Society of about 9,000. This particular outbreak was short-lived but a part of the garrison was then withdrawn ('A' Battery, R.A., and some native infantry)[1] and this was the signal for a new outbreak of violence. Although 'every soldier and policemen and every European inhabitant' was called out, the riots spread from the suburbs to the country and led to the destruction of the village of Jellutong.[2] The troops managed to prevent a battle in the town itself and suffered only two casualties in the process.

This result is the more extraordinary when it is considered that not only was there a promiscuous fire of musketry throughout the Town but that several pieces of cannon afterwards captured were mounted by the Rioters on roofs of houses and fired at intervals. . . . It is impossible to form an estimate of the loss sustained by the rioters as they invariably carried off the bodies of all who fell on their side and interred them secretly afterwards.[3]

At the time of these disorders Colonel Anson was Lieutenant-Governor with his predecessor, Colonel Man, still there. Anson sent a message to Ord, which reached him on 11 August. The Governor left Singapore on the afternoon of the 12th, following an emergency meeting of the Legislative Council, and reached Penang on the 14th together with H.M.S. *Rifleman*. H.M.S. *Wasp* had returned to Penang from the Nicobars on the day before and H.M.S. *Satellite* on the day after. Even with these naval reinforcements, order was not easily restored, and Ord discovered that the suppression of the Chinese societies was 'a task altogether beyond the power of the Government'. Some of the rioters were tried at the Penang Sessions in September, six being sentenced to transportation for twenty-one years.[4] Some drastic legislation was also passed, authorizing, in one instance, sentences of up to a hundred lashes with the cat-o'-nine tails, but Ord returned to Singapore without any certainty that these troubles

---

[1] Sent on an expedition to the Nicobars, occupied at this time but not placed (as Ord would have liked) under the control of the Straits Government.
[2] S.S. No. 79 of 19 Aug. 1867.   [3] Ibid.
[4] Four Chinese were convicted of murder and sentenced to death but the sentence was eventually commuted to imprisonment (S.S. No. 44, 23 Mar. 1868).

were at an end. His and Anson's actions were approved in Downing Street and Colonel Man was thanked for his services.[1] The lull at Penang lasted until 1871 and left Ord free to continue his reorganization of the Straits Settlements as a whole. There was much to do and his first task was to organize the civil service on 'a practical, efficient, and at the same time economical system'.[2] It was in future to comprise all administrative, magisterial, and revenue appointments, being recruited by a system of cadetships designed 'to induce educated English gentlemen to accept appointments in the Colony at an age at which they would easily acquire the native languages'.[3] This initial inducement was fixed at £200 a year with lodging allowance. Questions of establishment led to questions of finance and there can be no doubt that Ord did good work in both fields.[4] He it was who introduced the telegraph into government service. Nothing he did, however, seems to have added to his popularity. He faced continual criticism and was forced, in the end, to reply formally to a memorial sent to the Secretary of State from the Straits Settlements Association.

This memorial was dated 10 March 1869 and a copy went to Ord with the Secretary of State's dispatch of 3 April. This memorial was strongly supported, as the *Straits Times* observed, 'by most of the representatives of the better days of Singapore'. 'The phalanx', added the editorial, 'is a strong one'. The *Singapore Daily Times* was also hostile to the Governor and complained that 'the whole Colony has been placed, tied hand and foot, practically in the power of one man'.[5] The gist of the Association's complaint was that the expense of government in the Straits was far more in 1868 than it had been in 1865. In his reply of 20 May,[6] Ord showed that the comparison drawn by the Association was to some extent fallacious, but admitted that there was an increase ($92,000 over two years) which the Colonial Office had sanctioned. 'I have shewn', he claimed, 'beyond a doubt that there was a necessity for providing a Government House, and a new Steamer, and that they have been provided for on a reasonable

[1] A Commission of Inquiry produced a full report on these riots, completed by Jan. 1869.   [2] S.S. No. 101, 12 June 1869, Lord Granville.
[3] S.S. No. 58, 5 Mar. 1869.
[4] 'From my assumption of the administration of the Colony nothing has demanded or occupied more of my attention, than the condition and working of the Departments of the Treasury and Stamps.' S.S. No. 110, 10 May 1869.
[5] *Singapore Daily Times*, 4 Jan. 1869. The *Singapore Daily Times* was the daily version of the *Straits Times*, a weekly, and under the same management.
[6] S.S. No. 122, 20 May 1869.

and suitable scale.' That did not end the dispute however. The Straits Association continued the campaign with complaints about the official majority in the Legislative Council,[1] about the insecure position of the Chief Justice, about the Deportation Act, and about the Governor's salary. They referred again to their former complaints concerning the Quarantine and Pilotage ordinances. They urged that the Governor should study the customs and temper of the natives. So far, so they said, 'it would hardly appear that he had given himself that trouble.' From specific complaints they went on to a more general criticism which amounted to little more than a reiteration that they did not like Sir Harry Ord.

The Governor denied the various charges made and was able to show that the complaints made against the colonial government could all be matched by former complaints against the Indian Government —and complaints, moreover, coming from the same people. He was able further to counter-attack by pointing out that nearly all the taxation fell on the native population. The Europeans, he stated, paid no taxes except for a house-tax of 10 per cent. on rental, a tax on spirits, and a tax of 50s. on each horse and carriage. The rest of the revenue (and nearly the whole of it) came from taxes on opium, toddy, and pawnbroking.

For instance, taking as fair examples the leading partners or managers of the twelve largest European firms in Singapore, I find that the greatest amount of assessed taxes paid by any one of these gentlemen is £28 and the lowest £10. 10.—the average being £17 a year and this with the addition of a payment of 6d per bottle on such spirits as he may consume constitutes the whole contribution which a Merchant doing business to the extent of hundreds of thousands of Pounds is required to make towards the revenue of the Colony.[2]

[1] The Legislative Council tended to split into two parties:

Lieutenant-Governor	Chief Justice
Colonial Secretary	
O.C. Troops	and
Attorney-General	
Treasurer	five Unofficial
Auditor-General	Members
Colonial Engineer	
Total 7	Total 6

Ord suggested the appointment of another Unofficial Member, which would have made the parties equal. But he would still have had the casting vote (see S.S. No. 196, 16 Sept. 1869).

[2] S.S. No. 181, 27 Aug. 1869, the substance repeated in No. 196 of 16 Sept. 1869.

Ord also denied the general unpopularity of his government and alleged that opposition to him was confined to a small group, to dissatisfied officials headed by the Chief Justice, and to the junior members of the European community.[1] The opposition of this party was intensified in August when an open quarrel developed between the Governor and the Hon. W. H. Read. There may have been a period of truce before and during the visit of H.R.H. the Duke of Edinburgh in December[2] but feelings were running high again in the early months of 1870 and led to a public meeting called on 8 April. About 150 persons attended, but no Chinese, Malays, or Germans.[3] The organizers of the meeting were:

The Hon. W. H. Read, Partner in A. L. Johnstone & Co.
Mr. B. Read   „   „
Mr. Buckley   Clerk in A. L. Johnstone & Co.
Mr. Lipscombe   Partner in Boustead & Co.
Mr. José d'Almeida   Merchant.
Mr. Dunlop   Partner in Maclaine, Fraser & Co.
Mr. J. D. Vaughan   Formerly Police Magistrate, Singapore.
Mr. Carmichael   Manager of the Chartered Mercantile Bank.
Mr. Atchison   Legal Practitioner.

These proposed or spoke in favour of three resolutions, the first to thank the Straits Settlements Association in London, the second to deplore the waste of public money, and the last to assure the Governor of his unpopularity. The first two resolutions were carried but the third was opposed and carried only in an amended form. The opposition party had gone too far, being opposed by Dr. Little, Mr. W. Adamson, Mr. Thomas Scott, and others, and no longer supported consistently by the *Straits Times*.

Before this controversy was at its height, on 6 December 1869, Colonel Macpherson, the popular Colonial Secretary, died of 'a local complaint'. Ord added to his own unpopularity by failing to cancel the sports then being held in Johore, and also by giving inadequate notice of the time and place of the funeral, so that few were there of all who would have wished to attend. This loss left the Governor with a vacancy to fill, if only temporarily. He received two prompt

---

[1] Ord was never invited, however, to the Tanglin Club and was instrumental, according to 'Extinguisher', in preventing the Duke of Edinburgh going there without him.
[2] See *The Cruise of H.M.S. Galatea, Captain H.R.H. the Duke of Edinburgh, 1867-68*, John Milner and Oswald W. Brierly, London, 1869.
[3] S.S. No. 79 of 9 Apr. 1870.

applications, one from the Auditor-General, Mr. C. J. Irving, and the other from the Lieutenant-Governor of Malacca, Captain E. W. Shaw, R.N. Ord inclined to favour Captain Shaw, whom he appointed as Acting Colonial Secretary,[1] but the Secretary of State very naturally preferred to appoint an officer with Crown Colony experience and no association with the party disputes of Singapore.[2] He chose Mr. James Wheeler Woodford Birch, the government agent of the Eastern Province of Ceylon. Captain Shaw was bitterly aggrieved and began an acrimonious correspondence which continued until Birch arrived in June 1870. Neither Shaw nor Irving was ever promoted, the one remaining at Malacca until 1880 and the other remaining Auditor-General for just as long. Birch was obviously, and from the beginning a far more efficient man. It was evidently his coming that enabled Sir Harry Ord to turn (with relief, perhaps) to foreign affairs.

It would, of course, be wrong to suppose that all foreign relations had been in abeyance during the worst period of domestic strife at Singapore. Two separate negotiations were in progress and both of importance to the future of Malaya. One was with the Dutch and the other with the Siamese. The discussions with the Netherlands Government hinged on the Dutch plans for the conquest of Sumatra. The Dutch had occupied the east coast of Sumatra, from Cape Timiang to the River Jambi as early as 1824, with British trading rights secured by treaty. They had also controlled the pepper ports of Siak since 1857, and subsequently all of Sumatra except Acheen, with some loss of trade to Britain. By 1868 the Dutch were openly claiming the whole of Sumatra despite the treaty of 1819 between Britain and Acheen. There was no serious intention of resisting this Dutch encroachment, but it was felt at the Foreign Office that the Dutch ought to purchase British recognition by some trade concessions at least. Sir Harry Ord was consulted and expressed the opinion (9 December 1869, Closed Dispatches, S.S. to F.O.) that the Dutch conquest would be an advantage to British trade, then hampered by the internal disorders of northern Sumatra. This view was accepted and the Dutch policy led on logically to a declaration of war against Acheen in 1873. Ord went through the motions of preventing the Achinese obtaining arms and

---

[1] As 'Extinguisher' put it: 'Then the Kapitanshaw sent unto Singapore that he should fill the place of the loved departed one.'

[2] Lord Kimberley had no very high opinion of the Straits officials. In a Minute of Dec. 1872, he wrote: 'Is there a satisfactory public officer at the Straits? I begin to doubt it.' *The Colonial Office*, M. L. Hall, 1937, p. 240.

ammunition from Singapore, with the result that they probably obtained these essential supplies instead from Penang.[1]

Ord's relationship with Siam turned on the total eclipse of the sun which took place on 18 August 1868. The King of Siam wanted to view the eclipse from Whae Wan, a village on the Malay coast in latitude 11° 29' N.—the most favourable place in Siamese territory and, indeed, it was thought, in the world. He invited Ord to join him there and Ord accepted the invitation, arriving in his colonial steamship *Pei Ho* on the 16th, to find there a motley collection of French, British, and Siamese men-of-war, steam vessels, and yachts.[2] A meeting on the 17th was cordial and another, after the eclipse, still more so. The King was then, as Ord reported, in excellent spirits 'it having proved, as he informed me, that his calculation of the time of the occurrence of the eclipse was more correct than that given by the French astronomers'. Nothing passed on this occasion but mutual protestations of friendly feeling but Ord felt encouraged to pay subsequent visits to Trengganu and Pahang, both States being in some degree under Siamese influence. The visit to Pahang was to negotiate a settlement of the boundary between that State and Johore, which was actually accomplished with both rulers present. Messrs. Paterson, Simons & Co. thought this a good moment to press a claim of their own against the Bandahara of Pahang but were told that any governmental interference would be inexpedient. The visit to Trengganu had a rather embarrassing sequel in the embassy which the Sultan of that State sent to England in 1869.[3] This was the result of the Maharajah of Johore visiting Queen Victoria in 1866; a visit which seemed likely at one time to inspire several imitations.[4] The Sultan of Trengganu seems to have mentioned this idea to Sir Harry Ord, who did all he could to discourage the proposal. An envoy was actually sent, however, and the Governor's first knowledge of the fact came from

[1] Some 80,000 lb. of gunpowder and 4,049 stands of arms were exported from Penang to Acheen in 1872–3 before the prohibition came into force. See S.S. No. 101 of 9 Apr. 1873.

[2] According to 'Extinguisher', Ord 'took with him a Cockatoo, two monkeys, an aide-de-camp, and a parrot, besides other animals' (*Letters, &c.*, chap. xix. Ord was afterwards an Honorary Fellow of the Royal Zoological Society.

[3] The actual envoy was a young Malay called Mohamed Arafin, whom Ord afterwards described as 'this rascally intriguer' (S.S. No. 79 of 24 Mar. 1873).

[4] The Maharajah had been 'warmly received by many Royal and noble personages and was finally honoured by being Her Majesty's Guest at Windsor where he was made a Knight Commander of the Star of India' (S.S. No 22, 10 Feb. 1868).

the Colonial Office.[1] In his reply[2] Ord was apprehensive about the results.

It is difficult to foretell what will be the effect on the Siamese Government when it learns that one of its tributary Princes has sent an Envoy to England without its knowledge, but from the suspicious character of the people I am apprehensive that it may not be easy to persuade them that our Government has not been accessory to the step, and that it does not conceal something adverse to Siamese interests.

No permanent damage resulted, however, to Anglo-Siamese friendship, which was cemented in March 1871 by the visit paid to Singapore by the King of Siam in person. He was the son of the king Ord had met at Whae Wan in 1868, and he was accompanied by his two brothers. Anson (who was acting as Governor), 'at great personal inconvenience', had them all to stay at Government House and reported afterwards that the effect of the visit would be to 'strengthen the present good understanding between Great Britain and Siam and tend to the opening up and advancement of the latter country'. Anson, the Chief Justice, the Colonial Secretary, the Assistant Colonial Secretary, and the Colonial Engineer all received the Siamese Order of the White Elephant.[3]

If one dared to generalize so far, it would probably be true to say that the period of Ord's governorship witnessed a gradual increase of foreign rivalry in Southeast Asia. Relationships with Spain had been bad since the incident affecting the ship *Queen Victoria* in 1866. They grew worse with the further activities of the Spanish in the Sulu Archipelago in 1870, which led to the Sultan of Sulu's appeal to Ord in May 1872 and a further incident involving a trading vessel in 1873. The French were still more active and news came in 1867 of Vice-Admiral de la Grandière occupying the western provinces of Cochin China and threatening to seize and destroy any vessels carrying arms to those provinces or to Cambodia. The rule of Napoleon III in France was associated with ideas of French aggrandizement and even the defeat of France by Germany in 1870, which allayed one anxiety, was also suggestive of another. The rumours that Italy or the U.S.A. were about to intervene in Sumatra were baseless, but they illustrate the mutual suspicions which were current.

[1] C.O. to S.S. Nos. 195 and 198 of 19 Nov. 1869.
[2] S.S. No. 268, 22 Dec. 1869.
[3] Which they were not allowed to wear. Singapore itself, however, received a bronze elephant, cast at Bangkok, which is still there as a memento of the occasion.

While this increasing European pressure dates from before 1869 there can be no doubt that it was intensified by, and that it partly originated from, the opening of the Suez Canal. The great project of De Lesseps had been opposed by Britain from the beginning, but the British attitude was one of resignation from 1862. The ultimate success of the scheme was by then regarded as so certain that the new naval base at Malta, designed to protect the new route, was actually begun in 1863.[1] Policy in the East was being reshaped in terms of the canal from that date at the latest. Not all the implications, however, were foreseen and it was the vast increase of traffic in 1872 which set the seal of success on the new highway.[2] From the beginning, British ships predominated, amounting to 71 per cent. of the total up to June 1872 and rising to 80 per cent. over the next decade. But, apart from the increased flow of shipping through the Straits of Malacca, which thus regained a world importance lost in about 1620, the whole of Southeast Asia was now brought into closer contact with Europe. The distance saved was about one-third, but the time saved was greater still for the new route was (for all practical purposes) restricted to steamships. Thus the best passage from London to Singapore in 1867 was made by the *Eileen Radford* in 116 days, whereas the *Shantung* steamed from Glasgow to Singapore in 1870 in forty-two days, allowing for stops at Port Said, Suez, and Penang.[3] Singapore was connected with England by telegraph in 1871; not an unmixed blessing to the administrator but a powerful aid to commerce.[4] The effect on Singapore was immediate and profound. Trade there had been going through a depression since about 1859. The statistics show improvement in 1870 and still greater improvement in 1872.[5]

[1] *The Suez Canal, its History and Diplomatic Importance*, C. W. Hallberg, New York, 1931, p. 207 footnote.
[2] Ibid., p. 379. See also *Seaways of the Empire*, A. J. Sargent, London, 1918, chap. iii, and *The Suez Canal in World Affairs*, H. J. Schofield, London, 1952.
[3] The whole subject of the Suez Canal and the Singapore Trade has been the subject of an essay by G. Bogaars of the University of Malaya. To this I have referred extensively, as also to his M.A. dissertation on 'The Tanjong Pagar Dock Co.', in the Library of the University of Malaya.
[4] 'In the eyes of the men who do their country's work on the outskirts, telegraphy, seen in the light of bitter experience, is the most abominable of human inventions . . . by its aid a centralisation is created which, had it existed from the beginning, would infallibly have choked the life out of our eastern empire while it was still a puling thing in swaddling clothes. . . .' *Bush Whacking*, Hugh Clifford, London, 1929, p. 120. There is some truth in this. On the other hand, however, it was by telegraph that the British Government bought the Khedive's Suez Canal shares in 1875.   [5] Bogaar's academic exercise, appendix 5.

With the introduction of steam and telegraphy and the completion of the Suez Canal the trade of Singapore underwent a complete revolution. The Tanjong Pagar Dock Company, which had been a struggling concern, upon which the Banks looked askance, and with its shares down to $80, now came to the front.[1]

This Company had been formed in 1864[2] and by 1869 its principal shareholders included T. Scott, P. Joaquim, Dr. Little, Wm. Adamson, and Mr. Whampoa. The purpose of the Company had been to repair ships, but the lessening number of wooden sailing vessels made this business less profitable. The graving-dock had become unremunerative by 1871 but the cargo-handling business increased rapidly, with congested godowns in February 1870, a 12 per cent. dividend in 1872 and more wet docks being planned in 1874.

While the Suez Canal thus brought a new prosperity to Singapore, it also brought with it a new pressure of foreign competition. French trade with Indo-China now passed through Singapore, French ships entered showing an increase from twelve in 1870 to thirty-four in 1873. By this latter year German competition was also being felt, with eleven German ships entered from Hamburg via Suez. With the unification of Germany and the recent triumph over France, it could be reported with accuracy that 'The Germans are pushing their way irrepressibly in the East'.[3] German business firms in Singapore had numbered only three before 1867, but two more were opened in that year and one in 1868. Five more German firms started business between 1870 and 1871 and the transactions of the older firms were extended. These inroads, however, were into the entrepôt business, and there was growing up at the same time an expanding trade in which foreign competition was negligible. This was the export of the Malayan products: tin, sago, pepper, and gambier. In the 1860s the world's tin came very largely from Cornwall, which produced about 10,000 tons a year, but with additional supplies from Banka and, especially after 1853, from Billiton. Straits tin had always been exported, for the most part, to China, but by the period 1859–64 some 3,000 tons were going each year from Singapore to Britain and a smaller amount (less than 1,000 tons) to America.[4] The opening of the Suez Canal and the lowering of freights stimulated this trade and the export to Eng-

---

[1] *Capital of a Little Empire*, John Dill Ross, Singapore, 1898.
[2] General Meeting reported in *Straits Times*, 21 Jan. 1864.
[3] *Straits Observer*, 6 Aug. 1875.
[4] G. Bogaars, op. cit., p. 14. Singapore handled only 970 tons a year in 1826–8. See *Dictionary of Commerce*, McCulloch, 2 vols., 1834.

land jumped by 1,000 tons in 1870. The export of tin to China had been declining from 1862 onwards and amounted to 796 tons only in 1865. But the American market absorbed any surplus after 1870 so that, by 1871, North America was importing 2,465 tons as compared with Great Britain's 2,079 tons.[1] The great expansion of the tinplate industry did not begin until 1879, but the world demand for tin was on the increase before that and the effect in Malaya was profound.

Sago-flour was another important export, of which 3,513 tons were shipped to England in 1864 and only a negligible quantity to North America. In 1870, 6,798 tons went to England with an increase to 9,949 tons in 1871, 13,407 tons in 1872, and 15,158 tons in 1875. Again about 10,000 tons of gambier, a dyestuff, went to Britain in 1869; and no less than 21,371 tons in 1870. The export trades were on the increase, leading to a greater interest in the Malayan hinterland. Not for nothing was William Adamson known locally as 'Gambier Bill'. The actual cultivation was done, however, by Chinese, partly on Singapore island and partly in Johore. Dr. Yvan wrote a description of this cultivation[2] which dates from an earlier period but is true, no doubt, of the period after 1867:

In the environs of Singapore are a great number of small farms, industriously cultivated by the Chinese, consisting chiefly of plantations of sugarcane, rice, pepper, gambier etc. The pleasant aspect of their little wood-built houses, and the excellent condition of their land bespeak the order, industry and prosperity which prevail throughout. . . .

I paid several visits to these little establishments, particularly to one which took my fancy more than the others, and was managed by six Chinese, who cultivated the gambier, and also made the extract which bears its name.

Yvan states that the six Chinese were all of twenty-five to thirty years of age and lived in common, drawing equal profits. He continues:

By far the greater number of the Chinese at Singapore live in a state of celibacy, and it seems as though, when they arrive in the country, they made a sort of vow to renounce all the pleasures for which they generally manifest a considerable inclination. Their laborious lives are consequently uninterrupted by anything which might distract their attention from the one sole

---

[1] The figures are for Singapore only. If Penang exports are added, the totals would be larger.

[2] *Six Months Among the Malays, and a Year in China*, Dr. Yvan, London, 1855, p. 128.

object which they always appear to have in view—that of acquiring a fortune sufficient to enable them to go and live quietly in Malacca or some part of the celestial empire.

To such migratory cultivators it mattered little that the gambier plants should cause soil erosion, even if they were aware of it. Gambier cultivators were welcomed by the enlightened ruler of Johore and many of them settled along the rivers in that State.

One cynical observer of the local agricultural enterprise was John Dill Ross, who lived at 'Woodneuk', Tanglin, in a park of 36 acres (afterwards sold to the Sultan of Johore). Ross asks, with great detachment, whether the local products were of any real use to anyone.

It is rather strange to think that our Commerce in the Straits consists largely of products which are really of no great use. Millions of money have been spent on pepper, for instance. It would be interesting to know who first introduced the use of pepper, but except for the purposes of trade he might as well have left it alone. Supposing there was no pepper, what then? Would anybody in this world be much worse off? Yet the stuff is shipped from this place in thousands of tons. The taste for all spices such as cloves, nutmegs and mace must necessarily have been artificially cultivated at enormous expense. Take sago flour again; this goes home in shiploads to be converted into glucose and put into beer. Well, there are people who prefer the old fashioned beer which is not made of glucose. I never saw the alleged British workman mopping up his ale without thinking that the unfortunate man was putting down a decoction of sago flour without in the least knowing it. Except for the purposes of trade sago flour would appear to be a rather doubtful blessing.[1]

Few Singapore merchants of that day (or this) would care to follow Ross in his doubts as to whether trade does any good. Trade was for them an object in itself and they could not but realize that Malaya itself, the hinterland of Singapore and Penang, was coming to play a greater part in their transactions. In strictly entrepot business the British merchants might find it hard to compete with their German rivals, but in trade with the Malayan mainland their position was more secure. They were themselves the agents for Malay rulers, who turned also to British lawyers for legal advice. The ruler of Johore lived in Singapore itself and the ruler of Larut had his house in Penang. With the Native States there was, definitely, business to be done.

It would be quite untrue to say that a local demand for an extension of British influence in Malaya was any novelty in 1868. There had been suggestions and proposals long before that and the idea had been

[1] Ross, op. cit.

present, to some small extent, in the minds of those who demanded the transfer of the Straits Settlements. But one particularly urgent plea is worthy of record. It came from Mr. W. H. M. Read and was addressed to the Duke of Buckingham and Chandos on 9 May 1868, being dated from King's Cross just before Read's return to Singapore. He asked for new treaties to be made with the Native States, with which a 'valuable trade . . . is still in its infancy'. Then he goes on:

I do not apprehend that any political complications are likely to follow from the formation of new treaties with the different Rulers, of the independent Native States, but, on the contrary, I am led to believe that they will gladly avail themselves of an opportunity which would enable them to derive revenues from the increasing trade which must follow on treaties, which while protecting the lives and property of British Subjects, would ensure to these Native Princes the valuable countenance of the British Authorities and such good counsel and advice as would enable them to govern their Subjects upon more enlightened principles than at present prevail.[1]

He concludes by urging the Secretary of State to consult Lieutenant-Colonel Macpherson, John Crawfurd, G. T. Knox (H.M. Consul at Bangkok), and William Napier. In forwarding this memorandum to the Governor, the Duke concluded a brief covering letter with the words 'I wish you to understand clearly that the policy of Her Majesty's Government in the Malayan Peninsula is not one of intervention in Native affairs'.[2]

It is manifest that many factors were combining to persuade Ord to intervene in the Malay States. The foreign rivalries of the Dutch, the French, and even the Germans had created a general feeling that any advantage neglected by one would certainly be seized by another. These rivalries had been intensified by the opening of the Suez Canal, the commercial changes which had resulted in the Straits, and the growing export of tin, no longer to China but to Europe. Ord was thus under considerable pressure and, being personally unpopular, must have been the more tempted to pursue a policy which would have been widely acclaimed. But he was in no position to do this. The instructions issued by the third Duke of Buckingham and Chandos were not to be ignored. Nor was a different attitude to be expected from his successor, the fifth Earl Granville, appointed in December 1868; nor indeed from the first Earl of Kimberley, appointed in July

---

[1] Forwarded to Sir H. St. G. Ord under cover of C.O. No. 77 of 20 May 1868.
[2] C.O. No. 77, 20 May 1868.

1870.[1] They all voiced a settled Colonial Office policy: that there was to be no intervention in the Native States.

[1]

Prime Ministers		Secretaries of State for the Colonies	
Earl of Derby	28 June 1866	Lord Carnarvon	6 July 1866
Benjamin Disraeli	27 Feb. 1868	Buckingham	8 Mar. 1867
W. E. Gladstone	3 Dec. 1868	{ Lord Granville	10 Dec. 1868
		{ Lord Kimberley	6 July 1870
Benjamin Disraeli	20 Feb. 1874	{ Lord Carnarvon	21 Feb. 1874
		{ Sir Michael Hicks Beach	4 Feb. 1878
W. E. Gladstone	23 Apr. 1880	Lord Kimberley	28 Apr. 1880

CHAPTER III

THE Native States in which successive Governors had been forbidden to intervene can be said to have comprised three groups: those under the influence of Siam, those under British influence, and those nominally independent but subject to occasional British advice or admonition. The States owing admitted allegiance to Siam were Kelantan and Trengganu. Kedah and Perlis owed the same sort of allegiance to Siam, but were, in practice, so near to Penang as to fall within the British sphere. Johore was virtually under British control, the astute Maharajah Abubakar preserving a close alliance with each Governor in turn and also with Queen Victoria herself. As Ord pointed out:

> The present Maharajah of Johore . . . was born in his father's house at Singapore where by Treaty the family have considerable landed property adjoining the town and was educated by an English Clergyman. . . . In his tastes and habits he is an English Gentleman. As a Ruler, he is anxious to promote in everything the advancement and civilization of his people and is the only Rajah in the whole Peninsula or the adjoining states who rules in accordance with the practice of civilized nations.
>
> He is deeply attached to the British Government and nation and, feeling that with their support and encouragement he is most likely to benefit his country, he takes no step of importance in administration without the advice of the local Government, whilst he is ready at all times to place the whole resources of his country at our disposal. . . .[1]

As he was a British subject by birth, a resident of Singapore, a man who played cricket and could quote Tennyson, he was clearly a man to be relied upon.

The independent States were, on the west coast, Perak, Selangor, and the small States near Malacca; on the east coast, Pahang. Perak falls geographically into two parts; the Perak river and its tributaries, and the district of Larut. Perak (and Larut especially) was closely connected with Penang, the port at which the Perak tin was shipped. Selangor was closely connected in the same way with Singapore. Sungei Ujong (one of the small States) was closely connected with Malacca and, indirectly, with Singapore as the final place of shipment.

---

[1] S.S. No. 22, 10 Feb. 1868.

Pahang had less economic importance, producing little at this time and being inaccessible by sea for about half the year and inaccessible by land for the whole of it. Perak and Selangor were monarchies of a feudal character in which the Malay office of 'Yang di-pertuan' had been overlaid by the Hindu rank of Rajah and this in turn covered by the Islamic title of Sultan. Sir Richard Winstedt points out that the constitutions of these States were founded, like those of Burma, Siam, and Cambodia, on the astrological numbers 4, 8, 16, and 32.

In all those countries there were 4 chief ministers and 4 chief consorts for the king. In most Malay countries there are not only 4 chief ministers but 8 major chiefs and 16 minor chiefs, and, below the last, medieval Malacca and modern Perak have had also 32 petty chiefs. Thirty-two chiefs plus a king made up the number of gods in Indra's heaven, and a Malay kingdom was conceived as 'an image of the heavenly world of stars and gods'.[1]

To impartial observers this likeness was not always immediately apparent. Least of all was it apparent in Selangor, where civil war had been endemic since 1825, the year in which the State's boundary had been fixed. Selangor had actually split into five petty States during the period 1826–58, namely, Langat, Bernam, Klang, Lukut, and Selangor proper. Sultan Abdul Samad came to the throne in 1859 and was visited by Captain Macpherson, the Resident Councillor of Malacca, in 1860. He reported that the new ruler was 'an opium-smoker and a debauchee' and that a murrain had killed most of the Selangor buffaloes, throwing the rice-fields out of cultivation and driving the hungry people to piracy and disorder. At that period Raja Jumaat was ruling Lukut so effectively that his district had attracted Chinese miners and was flourishing.[2] Elsewhere was misery and a situation which deteriorated steadily over the next seven years. The Sultan had no control over the chiefs nor over his sons. Of these, the Raja Muda Mahmud, 'a very intelligent and interesting boy', had been disinherited in favour of Raja Musa, 'an ill-looking lad'. Several chiefs, notably Raja Mahdie and Raja Ismail, were at war with each other a few years later for the possession of Klang, and other chiefs (including the Sultan's other sons) were encouraging piracy on the coast. There was always a tendency among the Selangor chiefs to engage in piracy, partly because the position of the sandbanks drove the

---

[1] *Malaya and its History*, R. O. Winstedt, p. 85.
[2] See *The Chinese in Malaya*, Victor Purcell. The Chinese had been numerous in Selangor in 1834 and earlier and arrived in greater numbers after 1850.

traffic over to their side of the Straits and partly because they were mostly of seafaring stock, being Bugis from Celebes by origin. The Sultan needed someone to govern the country for him.

In the light of subsequent events there are certain features of Malay government which are especially worthy of note. In the first place, the succession to the throne was not automatic. The theoretical principle has been expressed as follows:

Thus, suppose A, a son of the last Sultan but two, to be Sultan of Perak; B, Raja Muda, son of the last Sultan but one; C, the Bendahara, son of the last Sultan; and D, a Prince, the eldest son of A; now suppose A dies, then
B becomes Sultan
C   „   Raja Muda
D   „   Raja Bendahara, and so on,
and thus the Sultan is always a man of considerable age and experience; and yet always the eldest son of a Sultan.[1]

In other words, the Sultan, Raja Muda (or heir apparent), and Bendahara (Chief Minister) were all royal and the successors by rotation. The other Ministers, Orang Kaya Besar (Treasurer), Temenngong (Chief Judge), Mentri (Adviser), Maharaja Lela (General), Laxamana (Admiral), and Shahbandar (Harbour Master) were Chiefs also of particular districts, but were not necessarily of royal birth.

This principle of succession was not as simple as it sounds. For the actual appointment of the Sultan was by election and the chiefs who had a voice in it could exercise a limited choice. They could decide which son was the eldest—or the eldest rather for the purposes of the succession. They could follow the wishes of the late Sultan, as for example in setting aside a certain candidate. They could also follow their own interests by preferring a weak ruler to one whom they might have reason to fear. These possibilities apart, the Raja Muda or the Bendahara (or both) might die before the Sultan, giving the latter some influence, and perhaps a decisive influence, in replacing them. It must also be remembered that any Sultan was likely to have had a number of wives, those of royal birth having the preference when it came to deciding the succession. But in setting aside one son on account of his mother's birth there was room again for disagreement about which mother was, in fact, of better descent. The result was that

[1] See *Some Account of the Independent Native States of the Malay Peninsula*, F. A. Swettenham, Singapore, 1880; and also *Perak and the Malays*, Major J. F. A. McNair, London, 1878, pp. 348 et seq.

the succession was often doubtful. More than that, the rulers were weakened by the fact of their election and the real powers which the chiefs still retained. As a consequence, moreover, of marrying so often, a ruler was apt to have many children and many relatives by marriage. His rule was anything but absolute.

Sultan Abdul Samad of Selangor tried to rule in person for eight years and then turned for help to Tunku Kudin.[1] This was in 1867, the year of the transfer. Tunku Kudin, or Tunku dia Oodin, was the brother of the Rajah of Kedah, and had just married a daughter of the Sultan of Selangor. Tunku Kudin was 'a needy adventurer with his wits about him', according to the *Straits Observer*.[2] He had received a more or less European education in Kedah and was blamed for his laxity in drinking wine and eating with Europeans. He was, at least by Malay standards, energetic and competent and it was to him, his son-in-law, that Abdul Samad now turned for advice and help. Receiving both in good measure, he appointed Tunku Kudin his Viceroy in 1868 and assigned him the revenues of Langat. He could not assign him the revenues of Klang and Selangor because he had no effective control of either. Tunku Kudin's European friends never-

---

[1] The relationship of the various claimants for power can be shown thus:

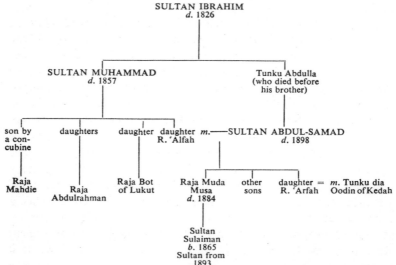

See also *A History of Selangor* by R. O. Winstedt, *JMBRAS*, vol. xii, part 3, Oct. 1934.

[2] 26 Apr. 1875.

theless expected the dawn of a golden age in Selangor with peace, prosperity, and a new field for investment.

Tunku Kudin's success was neither immediate nor complete, and the Sultan, who had lived at Klang, withdrew to Langat and left the former place the scene of conflict between Rajas Ismail and Mahdie. If, moreover, the Sultan's sons and relatives agreed in anything it was in their common detestation of Tunku Kudin, an upstart from Kedah. The Viceroy felt unable to cope with all this opposition and returned to Kedah in 1870 to ask his brother for help. The Sultan of Kedah, a strict Muslim, rather disapproved of Kudin than otherwise but was willing to assist up to a point, partly to please the British and partly to annoy the Maharajah of Johore. Tunku dia Oodin was encouraged at this period by Sir Harry Ord, probably on Colonel Anson's advice. Ord visited Langat in May 1870 and apparently persuaded the Sultan to continue his support of Tunku dia Oodin. The latter returned to the fray with 500 men from Kedah and, taking Ismail's side, drove Raja Mahdie out of Klang.[1]

This campaign seems to have centred on Raja Mahdie's stockade on the Klang river, ten miles from the river mouth and just below Pangallon Batu. Tunku dia Oodin's artillery was commanded by Mr. de Fontaine, a former midshipman of the French navy, and it was he who dragged two 18-pounder carronades to the summit of a neighbouring hill, and opened fire from there. Mahdie's guns were more numerous and mounted on earthworks forming a square enclosure, thirty feet above river-level. These cannon:

. . . like many at Salangore, in Mahdie's time were without means of elevating, being either laid upon two parallel timbers placed in the desired direction, or when on a carriage lashed down with rattan in a fixed position. It was the custom of Mahdie's men before firing a gun to assemble round it and pray for a successful result. . . .[2]

Divine intervention would have been essential to obtain much result from guns that would not elevate, but no such favour was shown. A shot from one of Mr. de Fontaine's 18-pounders hit and dismounted one of Raja Mahdie's guns while its crew were at their

---

[1] The character of these Kedah men is perhaps indicated by the fact that some of them, being left idle after the capture of Klang, turned pirate and captured a small vessel from Penang. Thirty-nine of them were caught by H.M. Gunboat *Algerine*, early in 1871, and taken to Malacca where they were tried and sentenced by the Chief Justice, Sir Peter Benson Maxwell, very shortly before his retirement.

[2] Report of Commander Bloomfield, 6 Aug. 1871. Quoted in P.P. C. 466 of 1872.

devotions, killing many and discouraging the rest. The stockade was captured together with two others near the river mouth and Tunku dia Oodin was able to establish his own custom-house on the river with Raja Ismail in charge and Mr. Langlois as Assistant Collector of a revenue amounting to $4,000–$5,000 a month. Mahdie withdrew to Selangor town, which he occupied despite the presence there of Raja Musa.

The year 1871 began auspiciously in the Straits with the long-expected arrival of the Colonial steamship *Pluto*. She reached Singapore on 4 January after calling at Malacca for fuel. There she procured billets of mangrove wood to fill her empty bunkers and, burning these, just managed to complete a rather tedious voyage. The *Pluto*, replacing an older 400-ton vessel of the same name, had been originally designed as a blockade runner in the time of the American Civil War. She had seen her best days before the Crown Agents bought her for $60,000 and, when docked and surveyed, seemed hardly worth what had been paid for her. The officers who inspected her advised that essential repairs and alterations would cost another $6,000 or $7,000. It was agreed, furthermore, that her plates were thin, her engines obsolete and wasteful of fuel, and her probable life very limited.[1] The *Pluto* might have been sold there and then but for doubts expressed as to whether she was even saleable. She was taken into the service, with some reluctance, and two other vessels, the *Rainbow* and *Pei Ho*, were disposed of. The *Pluto*, despite her defects, was to have a distinguished career and a definite place in Malayan history. She became historic, indeed, on this, her outward voyage to the Straits, via the Suez Canal. For she carried two colonial cadets, her only passengers, and one of them was Frank Athelstane Swettenham.

The significance of this reinforcement was wasted, however, on Sir Harry Ord, who was just about to leave for England on furlough. His departure occasioned no excessive grief on either side. He sailed early in March 1871 and his place was taken by Colonel A. E. H. Anson as 'Administrator'. It was a peculiarity of Anson's appointment that he was Lieutenant-Governor not of Penang, but of the Straits Settlements and so succeeded automatically to the Governor's authority in the latter's absence.[2] He moved into Government House, Singapore, just in time to play host to the King of Siam.

---

[1] S.S. No. 265, 8 Nov. 1871.

[2] Sir Harry Ord had recommended in Nov. 1867 that Macpherson, not Anson,

Like Ord, Anson was a veteran of the Crimean War. He differed from the Governor, however, in other ways and especially in this: that we know more about him. To judge from his autobiography,[1] he was quite able, rather self-satisfied, a little too fond of his own wit. As compared with Ord, however, he was popular. Having so far, moreover, been in far closer touch with people at Penang than with the policy of the Colonial Office, he was far more receptive to representations made about the need for intervention in the Native States. One of his first acts was to appoint a committee to inquire into British relations with the States not tributary to 'any country having a recognized Consul or other representatives accredited to this Government'.[2] This committee comprised the Hon. Arthur Birch (Acting Lieutenant-Governor, Penang),[3] Commander Robinson, R.N. (Senior Naval Officer), and Major McNair, R.A. (Colonial Engineer). This committee expressed the view in its report that a Commission of Officers of Rank should visit Acheen, Perak, and other States; also that a political agent should be appointed to visit them regularly and carry on all correspondence with them. In forwarding the report to the Colonial Office, Anson agreed with those recommendations but added:

I also consider it desirable that there should be frequent communication between this Government and these Native States but I do not think the Colonial Legislature would be prepared to vote the salaries of Resident Officers for them, and I am quite certain that Native Governments would not be prepared to incur any expenditure on that account.

Nor do I think the time has yet arrived, having regard to the present barbarous state of these countries for making such appointments. . . .

I shall defer any measures as in connection with the report of the Committee until I receive Your Lordship's instructions.[2]

Before any such instructions could arrive, Anson had found cause to take more positive action than merely forming a committee. This action concerned a case of piracy which took place, apparently, in

should be his deputy. This may have been the foundation for the dislike which Anson always felt for Ord (Confidential, S.S. 7 Nov. 1867).

[1] *About Others and Myself*, General Sir Archibald E. H. Anson, London, 1920.

[2] S.S. No. 144, 3 June 1871.

[3] This Mr. Birch was from the Colonial Office and must not be confused with his namesake, the energetic Colonial Secretary at Singapore. The experiment of sending out a Colonial Office man for a short tour of duty in substitution for an officer needed elsewhere or on leave was not a success. He was relieved eventually by Mr. G. W. R. Campbell, who held the acting appointment until Anson's return.

June. A Chinese junk called the *Kim Seng Cheong* belonging to Penang owners sailed from that port for Larut, where she should have arrived in about a day and a half. Instead, the rumour came, over a week later, that the junk had been seized by pirates, embarked at the last moment as passengers, who had murdered the crew and the genuine passengers (thirty-four men, women, and children) and carried off the junk and her cargo, valued respectively at $1,500 and $7,000, including $3,000 in specie. The owners came in distress to Birch, who sent a letter to Anson at Singapore, accompanied by one of the owners.

This Chinaman came to Government House late on Sunday afternoon, and informed me that he had on his way down the Straits seen his junk sailing along inshore to the South of the *Torch* Lighthouse, that being far off he could not see the hull, but he knew the junk by the sails, one of them being new and white.

As this was about ten days after the junk had left Penang and there were many other junks constantly about that part of the Straits, I put very little credence in this man's story. . . .

My own opinion was that a few bad characters from Perak, some perhaps of those who had from time to time committed gang robberies in Province Wellesley, having grown confident, had extended their operations in this new form to Penang, and taken possession of the junk.

I considered it almost certain that they would have taken the junk to some out of the way place up one of the rivers or creeks, and, after securing the money and valuables, have abandoned or more probably scuttled or burnt it.

I confess I never myself expected that the junk or the Pirates who seized it would be heard of again; at the same time I considered it right to do what I could. . . .[1]

Anson now ordered the *Pluto* to leave next morning for Malacca, pick up some armed police there under Inspector Cox,[2] and proceed up the coast to Langat, Klang, and, if necessary, to Delhi in Sumatra. It was for just this sort of work that the *Pluto* (drawing only six feet of water) was to prove well suited; provided, of course, that there was no opposition.

The *Pluto* went, as ordered, to Malacca, Langat, Klang, and Selangor, where on 28 June the missing junk was found at anchor with six of the pirates on board. The junk was seized and the men on

[1] S.S. No. 238, 19 Oct. 1871.
[2] The Malacca police comprised 'a better class of Malays than are in the Police, Singapore', and so more likely to be useful.

board arrested. Mr. Cox and Captain Bradberry (master of the *Pluto*) then went ashore to recover the stolen cargo. Raja Musa, the Sultan's son and heir, the appointed governor of the place, 'received them very kindly and gave them encouragement and assistance in recovering the goods that were in the shops and in removing them down to the beach'.[1] Cox reported the subsequent event as follows:

My troubles and difficulties here commenced—a large party of Malays and Bugis surrounded us, with a determined opposition to resist us to the utmost of their power; one Malay went so far as to hold up his fist in my face, and only withdrew it after some remonstrance—the crowd at this time was increasing, and another Malay chief, whose name I have since ascertained as that of Syed Mashahoor, came up with a retinue of armed followers; I went to meet him and received him cordially but he treated me . . . with the utmost contempt. . . . His language to me was also highly insulting. . . .[2]

Undeterred by this, Cox went on to arrest three of the pirates, identified with the aid of Raja Musa's followers. Then a fourth was found.

. . . on capturing the fourth—evidently one of the head pirates, he having a belt round his waist, and as we supposed, full of money—whilst trying to get him into the boat, he laid hold of one of the Malay Chiefs by the leg, at the same time whispering something in his ear, on which the chief told us to give him over to his charge, and he would be responsible for him: we did so, and the prisoner escaped and ran into one of the huts, where he was pursued by Mr. Cox; this excited the Malays, who immediately drew their krisses and threatened our party, causing most of us to take to the boats, which shoved off to the ship, leaving a few of us, including Captain Bradberry and Mr. Cox still on the beach.[3]

According to George Cox, it was Raja Mahmood who helped the fourth pirate to escape, and his version of the story ends:

another Chinese pirate was also arrested . . . [but] was rescued by a Malay Chief named Rajah Mahmood, through whose instrumentality he got away, although pursued by me into a stockade. . . . Rajah Mahmood collected a large body of armed Malays, who drew their weapons, and yelling to murder us all outright: and it was with extreme difficulty and hazard that we managed to reach the vessel with safety, as numbers of the police and crew of the steamer were obliged to swim off to the ship. . . . We

[1] S.S. No. 238, 19 Oct. 1871. See also No. 172 of 14 July.
[2] Cox to Lieutenant-Governor of Penang, 1 July 1871. P.P. C. 466, 1872.
[3] Bradberry to Lieutenant-Governor of Penang, 1 July 1871, P.P. C. 466, 1872.

B 6911   E

left Salangore at noon, the 29th, and on passing Rajah Mahdie's stockade, were fired at seven times; none of the shot took any effect.[1]

The devotional school of gunnery had failed again and Cox and Bradberry were wounded only by an insulting message from Mahmood, received before they weighed anchor. Raja Musa came on board that morning to explain that Rajas Mahdie, Syed Mashor, Mahmood, and Berkat were acting in opposition to him. The *Pluto* returned to Penang with the recaptured junk and there Cox and Bradberry reported to Birch, Acting Lieutenant-Governor. They stated that Selangor town was held and fortified by Raja Mahdie. Birch telegraphed the news to Anson at Singapore.

On receipt of a telegram . . . informing me of what had occurred I immediately placed myself in communication with Captain Robinson commanding H.M.S. *Rinaldo*, Senior Naval Officer of the Division of the China Squadron, and requested him to proceed to Selangore and endeavour to secure the remainder of the Pirates and to obtain possession of the stolen property. At the same time I telegraphed for the *Pluto* to meet the *Rinaldo* at the *Torch* Light Vessel on the North Sands 200 miles from Singapore, 160 miles from Penang, and about 30 miles South West of the Selangore River. This arrangement was carried out. . . .[2]

The *Rinaldo* anchored at the bar of the Selangor river at 4.15 a.m. on 3 July and Commander Robinson sent his boats, manned and armed, to the *Pluto*, which he had met the previous evening. He commanded them in person from the *Pluto*, which at 7.30 began to tow them up the river. The *Pluto* anchored off Selangor town at 2.0 and the boats were sent to search the river banks. One armed party under Lieutenant Stopford went in search of Raja Mahmood and eventually found him, a mile from where they had landed. They induced him to return with them to the beach, where Lieutenant Maude had another armed party drawn up. What happened then is best told in Robinson's own words:

. . . The Rajah went between the boat and the small arm men, with about twenty men round him. He was told that the boat was ready, when he replied that he would not go now [to the *Pluto*], as he wanted to cross over to the other side. Maude told him if he did not go willingly, he must force him. Immediately afterwards a shot was fired at our men from the nearest house, at a distance of only ten yards. The Rajah and his men instantly fled into the jungle, and heavy firing immediately followed from huts and

[1] Cox to Lieutenant-Governor of Penang, 30 June 1871. In C. 466 of 1872.
[2] P.P. C. 466 of 1872.

jungle. One of our men fell mortally wounded at once, and Maude was obliged to make the best of his way back to the *Pluto*, followed by a continuous fire, which did not cease until he got alongside.[1]

Robinson was in a difficult position. He had left the *Rinaldo* at the river mouth from doubt as to whether the river was navigable for a ship of *Rinaldo*'s class. He had ninety-five officers and men with him, crowded in boats and exposed to fire from unseen opponents in the jungle. He decided to make a fresh landing at the river entrance.

But Captain Bradberry of the *Pluto* then made such a strong remonstrance to me—that his vessel had only half-inch plates, that I reluctantly changed my mind and determined to take *Rinaldo* in next day, if possible. I am very glad now that I did change my mind.[2]

Commander Robinson now withdrew his forces to the river mouth. Once more on board *Rinaldo*, he sent the *Pluto* to Penang with the wounded and a letter to the Lieutenant-Governor asking for a surgeon. 'I also advised that some troops should be sent to assist in jungle fighting.' He did not, however, wait for these troops to arrive. Instead, on the 4th, at 4.45 a.m. he proceeded up the Selangor river under steam.

I knew that it was touch and go whether we could get over the bar (more than two miles in width) at the top of high water; that we had no chart of the river; that we had no surgeon on board, that it would be twelve hours before we could get out again and that for the whole of that time we might be under fire: yet took the responsibility of incurring all risks for the sake of punishing the pirates for their treacherous attack of the previous day, and for the sake of teaching them to respect the flag for the future.[3]

Firm in this intention and armed with some knowledge of the river, gained on the previous day, Robinson took the *Rinaldo* into battle.

At 6.15, when about 400 yards from the forts on the southern entrance of the river, fire was opened upon us from those forts, and from those on the northern bank. It was a hot and well-directed fire, and was, of course, immediately answered by the *Rinaldo*; in less than five minutes we had three men wounded, and had suffered severely in hull and rigging, but by steaming past their batteries into the river their position was turned, and before they could get most of their guns round we had either dismounted them or rendered their chief defences untenable.

[1] Commander Robinson, R.N., to Acting Governor Anson, 6 July 1871, quoted in C. 466 of 1872.
[2] Ibid.
[3] Ibid.

The *Rinaldo* anchored off Selangor town at 6.40 and engaged the batteries there. By 8.0 these too had been silenced. Robinson decided, however, against landing until the troops arrived. This was at 4.30 p.m. on 5 July, when the *Pluto* returned with Lieutenant-Colonel V. Shortland, 113 officers and men of the 19th Madras Native Infantry and an artillery detachment of 1 officer and 21 gunners, all from Penang. The *Rinaldo* had withdrawn again on the 4th and now entered the river again at 5.30 a.m. on the 6th with the *Pluto* close astern. The forts were bombarded afresh but there was no reply. So the troops and seamen landed at the lower fort at 8.0. It was deserted. Fire was switched to the upper fort, but that too was deserted. The lower fort had thirteen 32-pounder guns on carriages. There were eleven guns mounted in the upper fort, two being 32-pounders and the rest of varying calibre. These guns were spiked and their carriages burnt, all gunpowder removed and the stockades destroyed. Five armed native prahus were burnt.

Commander Robinson evidently expected the leading inhabitants to appear at this stage, contrite and ready to hand over the remaining pirates. They had all, however, fled, and Shortland proceeded to blow up the chief's house, burn the huts in the stockades, and finally burn Selangor town itself. As Robinson puts it: 'We spent the day in utterly destroying this nest of pirates.' Owing to the 'splendid precision of the fire' the town was unharmed in the bombardment and so deserted when set alight. There must have been casualties in the forts but only one body was found. On the British side there were the three sailors wounded and one gunner dead—of sunstroke. The *Rinaldo* withdrew on the 6th, grounded on the bar, was floated again without damage, and returned to Singapore on the 8th.[1] A chartered steamship sent by Anson from Singapore with the Master Attendant, more troops, some 12-pounder howitzers, and a surgeon, came too late for the fray. The campaign was over.

Locally, Colonel Anson was thought to have done rather well. He was criticized, however, for sending the *Pluto* in the first instance, with no guns and few men.[2] The same criticism came from the Secretary of State, the Earl of Kimberley, who pointed out that a ship of war should have been sent, and could have been sent

[1] Commander Robinson afterwards committed an error of judgement in asking or allowing the colonial government to publish his dispatch in the *Straits Times* before it had been received and approved at the Admiralty. He was suitably admonished by his Commander-in-Chief (S.S. Confidential Dispatches, 1872).

[2] *Penang Gazette*, 1 July 1871, quoted in C. 466, 1872.

without loss of time.[1] The *Pluto* was not to be sent on such errands again.

At the time of the bombardment of the Selangor forts, Tunku dia Oodin was apparently at Pangallon Batu on the Klang river, possibly meditating his own future operations against Mahdie. On hearing the sound of the *Rinaldo*'s guns, he promptly embarked 150 men (probably sepoys) on board his schooner *Fair Singapore*, commanded by Mr. Pennyfather, and sent them to the Selangor river. These were not under the orders of Mr. de Fontaine, who remained in command at Pangallon Batu, but were led by Tunku Chi. He and Pennyfather found the forts deserted and peacefully occupied them. Raja Musa should have been there but, being threatened by Mahdie (perhaps before the bombardment took place) had fled overland to Klang, where he arrived safely after a perilous journey. He was regarded as 'a young man of weak capacity and little influence'[2] and all we know of him seems at least consistent with this description. Mahdie was reported to have fled at an early stage of the *Rinaldo* affair, possibly to the Bernam river or to Perak. It was Raja Mahmood who had fired on the warship until driven from his guns. All accounts agree in giving him the credit for such resistance as was shown, and he was believed to be still in the neighbourhood when the landings were made. He was the most formidable of the rajas and far more so, in particular, than Mahdie. The latter went first to Sumatra and then eventually to Johore.

On receiving Robinson's report, Anson expressed his satisfaction with what had been done.

There can be no doubt from the frequent complaints which have from time to time reached Penang of interference with and piratical attacks upon vessels in the neighbourhood of Selangore and the Klang Straits that Rajah Mahdie has for a very long time been carrying on depredations of this nature undiscovered and undisturbed and it is to be hoped that the chastisement he and his followers have received at the hands of Captain Robinson together with the destruction of their War Prahus and Fort will produce a very salutary effect not only upon themselves but upon all other native chiefs on both sides of the Straits of Malacca who connive at such lawless transactions.[3]

Anson resolved to reap the benefit of this affair while the memory of it was still fresh. When the *Pluto* returned from Penang, Anson

[1] Kimberley to Acting Governor, 6 Sept. 1871.
[2] C. J. Irving to Acting Governor Anson, July 1871, quoted in C. 466, 1872.
[3] S.S. No. 172 of 14 July 1871.

resolved to bring pressure to bear on the presumably terrified Sultan. The *Rinaldo* having been ordered elsewhere, Anson now requested Bloomfield, Commander of H.M.S. *Teazer*, to proceed to Langat on 14 July with a letter to the Sultan, calling upon him to arrest and hand over the remaining pirates and 'to appoint some person to govern the town and district of Selangor in whom this Government can have confidence'.[1] The *Teazer* evidently sailed before the *Pluto* arrived and Anson, having decided to take stronger action, sent Birch and Irving (the Auditor-General) to overtake Bloomfield and perform the diplomatic part of his mission. 'I further instructed the Colonial Secretary to urge upon the Sultan the appointing of Tunku dia Oodin or some other person in whom this Government would have confidence as the responsible Officer of his Government.'[2] This was the sort of mission for which Birch was well qualified.

In all these proceedings during Anson's term of office at Singapore it is difficult not to suspect Birch's influence at work. But others felt as he did, including the members of the committee appointed by Anson (see above, p. 47). One of these was Captain Robinson of the *Rinaldo*, whose action at Selangor certainly erred not at all on the side of leniency. Birch, an energetic officer who believed in a policy of great firmness with the natives, now had the possibly congenial task of frightening the Sultan into a policy which would gain Anson's approval. The Sultan was terrified before Birch even appeared and had already sent five of the remaining pirates to Malacca, together with the pigtail of the sixth (who died at Langat). He later, and rather pathetically, sent a pair of elephant's tusks as a gift for Queen Victoria.

The *Pluto*, with Birch and Irving, joined H.M.S. *Teazer* in the Selangor river, where they found the lower forts garrisoned by a hundred of Tunku dia Oodin's men, who had unspiked several of the guns. Tunku dia Oodin himself appeared on the 18th in his steamship *Rainbow*, accompanied by his principal native adviser, an Arab called Syed Zein. The *Rainbow* was presumably the old colonial yacht sold on 24 May 1871 after the arrival of the *Pluto* and now finishing her days on the Selangor coast. The Tunku was on his way to see Anson at Singapore, but was induced to come on board the *Teazer*. Then the *Teazer*, with Birch, Irving, and Tunku dia Oodin went up the Klang river on the 20th, piloted by Mr. de Fontaine, and visited the Viceroy's fort, held by Raja Ismail and Raja Abdulrah-

---

[1] S.S. No. 172 of 14 July 1871.   [2] S.S. No. 176, 28 July 1871.

man. On the 21st *Teazer*, followed this time by *Pluto*, steamed up to the Sultan's Istana at the mouth of the Jugra river. She dropped anchor some 400 yards from the landing-place and the subsequent negotiations took place 'with the *Teazer*'s guns bearing upon the Sultan's palace' at a range of under 600 yards. The hint was underlined by some previous 'gunnery practice' in the presence of the Sultan's younger and favourite son, Raja Yacoob.

After a salute had been fired there was a landing in some force, Birch, Irving, and Commander Bloomfield being accompanied by Tunku dia Oodin and Raja Musa. 'The Sultan', reported Birch, 'met us at the entry of the stockade and, taking me by the hand, escorted me to his Audience Hall, where he had chairs arranged for us all.'[1] The Governor's letter was read and then the conference began. Birch's first object was to ascertain whether Tunku dia Oodin was really Viceroy. He held a written authority from the Sultan dating from 1868 but Mahdie claimed that it was a forgery. The Sultan declared at once that it was genuine. Birch now asked him to confirm it but over this the Sultan hesitated. Birch gave him twenty-four hours in which to answer—that is, until 5.0 p.m. next day —and abruptly took his leave. He and his party re-embarked.

Very early the next morning Birch wrote the Sultan a letter in which his demands were made more explicit. He required the Sultan to hand over the pirates and also the chiefs who supported them, and that he should 'appoint one man who the English Government could trust to act as our friend's Vakeel and conduct the affairs of the whole country between Malacca and Perak'.[2] With this written demand there was conveyed a verbal message, by Raja Yacoob, threatening that, failing a satisfactory answer, Birch would 'take all the tin in the place and require an indemnity'. By 3.0 p.m. two replies came from the Sultan, one outlawing Mahdie, Mahmood, and Syed Mashor, the other confirming Tunku dia Oodin's appointment but in collaboration with Raja Bot and Raja Yaya. Tunku dia Oodin was asked his views on this proposal and at once declared it impracticable. Irving attributed this proposal to Raja Yaya's influence over the Sultan—'the poor weak old man seems always to be under the hand of someone or other'.[3] There was a fresh meeting at which the Sultan immediately gave way and

---

[1] Birch to Anson, 26 July, C. 466, 1872.
[2] Birch to Anson, 26 July 1871, quoted in C. 446, 1872.
[3] Irving to Anson, ibid.

reappointed Tunku dia Oodin with full powers, as 'Wakil Yamtuan'—
the title being suggested by Irving. It was he who noticed that Raja
Yaya had brought the small seal and insisted that the great seal
should be used. The document was sealed, witnessed by the Europeans,
and handed to the Viceroy. The *Pluto* sailed on the 23rd for Malacca,
leaving H.M.S. *Teazer* on the Selangor coast. Birch collected the
pirates at Malacca and arrived back in Singapore on the afternoon
of the 26th.

Irving felt particularly satisfied with the results of this mission:

As regards the future prospects of the country, Tunku dia Oodin said
that now the English Government had pronounced itself on his side, he
felt no doubt whatever of his power soon to establish his authority over
the whole country. When this was done, he said that it was his wish to establish a regular system for the collection of the revenue and administration of
justice in the several Rivers. For this purpose he stated that he should
require the services of European officers. I represented this to Mr. Birch
and, with his concurrence, I told him that we thought he had been singu-
larly fortunate in his choice of the two principal European officers at present in his service, M. Langlois and M. de Fontaine . . . [but he might do
well to ask the Governor's advice before choosing any more].[1]

Irving was impressed with Selangor's great economic possibilities
and pointed the example of Johore where '. . . the East India Company's Government selected the most intelligent of the Native Chiefs,
the present Maharajah, and supported him by their advice and their
influence . . .'.[1]

Birch and Irving were agreed that the most intelligent chief in
Selangor was Tunku dia Oodin.

As news of these events in Selangor reached England, there were
some who said that Birch had gone far beyond his brief. But there
were others disposed to criticize even Cox's attempt to arrest the
pirates, subjects as they were of an independent State. These doubts
were voiced in a letter to *The Times* from Sir Peter Benson Maxwell,
retired Chief Justice, who said that Inspector Cox had no more right
to arrest pirates in Selangor than 'a French Police Agent has to
arrest a Communist in the streets of London'. Colonel Anson could
not ignore this, coming from the man who had so recently tried and
sentenced the pirates caught by H.M. Gunboat *Algerine*: pirates
belonging to the other side in the Klang War. He told the Secretary
of State that Cox had done no more than assist the Raja Musa, who

[1] Irving to Anson, quoted in P.P. C. 466 of 1872.

had since been rewarded by the gift of 'a handsomely finished gilt revolver' sent by the hands of Mr. Birch. He admitted, nevertheless, that Birch had gone too far.

I regretted, however, to hear from Mr. Birch on his return that he had been so peremptory in his manner to the Sultan when arranging about the appointment of a proper Governor for Selangore and I expressed to Mr. Birch my disapprobation of this on his return. . . . The proverbial dilatoriness and 'Shilly-Shallying' of the Malays may . . . be taken in justification of Mr. Birch's active and vigorous opposition to . . . [the Sultan's proposal] but still it is a pity that under the circumstances an empty threat should have been made use of when in all probability patience and perseverance would have gained the same object. . . .

I was much pressed to call upon the Sultan for an indemnity but I could see no sort of excuse for doing so . . . because he was as much interested in the overthrow of Mahdie as was this Government.[1]

'Much pressed', one wonders, by whom? By Birch? Apart from that, Anson's assumption that the Sultan desired Raja Mahdie's overthrow was incorrect. Anson believed, or chose to assume, that the Sultan whole-heartedly supported Tunku dia Oodin, whose interests were identical with his own. There may have been a period in 1868–9 when this was true. Since then, however, the position had changed. From the time of his Viceroy's return with his Kedah followers in 1870 (if not from an earlier date) the Sultan had begun to fear that Tunku dia Oodin was aiming at the Sultanate; intending to succeed in place of his weak (and, by one account, 'half-witted') brother-in-law, Raja Musa. To this plot, as he believed it to be, the Sultan was naturally opposed. And while he may not have approved Raja Mahdie's men turning pirate, he knew that Tunku dia Oodin's men had done the same. As for Raja Mahdie, Raja Mahmood, and Syed Massahoor, they usefully counterbalanced the now excessive power of Tunku dia Oodin. Without them, he would be powerless, in the Viceroy's hands. With them in the field he could play off one party against the other and so safeguard Raja Musa's succession. The Sultan might pretend to welcome the news of Mahdie's discomfiture but he realized that the guns of the *Rinaldo* had given Tunku dia Oodin possession of Selangor as well as Langat and Klang; had given him control in fact of the whole coast. From this period, and probably from an even earlier period, he began to favour the other side.

Looked at from one point of view, the *Rinaldo* had merely punished

[1] S.S. No. 249, 24 Oct. 1871.

some pirates; and that was the official version of the affair. But the echoes of the gunfire had been heard farther afield. Some trouble over the theft of cattle in Rembau suddenly settled itself. The Raja of Larut (of whom more presently), as suddenly handed over some persons who had committed gang robbery in Province Wellesley. The British were regarded with a new respect, even in Sumatra. But the interpretation put upon the *Rinaldo* affair in Malaya was that the Straits Government was backing Tunku dia Oodin, with force if necessary, and even possibly as the Sultan's successor. Nor was this conclusion entirely wrong. Anson, through Birch, had insisted upon Tunku dia Oodin's being made the 'responsible officer' in the Selangor government. Birch had been 'peremptory' and had used threats to gain this end; and the Sultan, for his part, had agreed. It is relevant, however, to recall that the Sultan would agree to anything, even without a preliminary naval bombardment. He was far from being the feeble person described by Irving. His own fighting days were over, it is true, and he preferred his ease; *opium cum dignitate*. But if every chief claimed to have the Sultan's approval, Frank Swettenham explains how this came about. He was in a position to do this, having asked the Sultan himself.

He promptly pointed out that each of these Rajas in turn came to him, stated his case, and asked the Sultan if that was not correct. His Highness always replied, 'Quite correct,' but, as he explained to me . . . [meaning] 'correct in their view, not in mine'. He was evidently tickled by this happy inspiration and laughed heartily at his own ingenuity.[1]

The local interpretation of the '*Rinaldo* affair' must also be seen in the light of events which followed Birch's return to Singapore. For H.M.S. *Teazer* was still on the coast and Commander Bloomfield's further proceedings are especially significant. He proceeded to an anchorage on the edge of the bank off Bukit Tergon, accompanied by the Tunku's steamship *Fair Singapore*. He then sent his boats to visit Sungei Sulo, where Mahdie had had a stockade. 'I also took about sixty of the Tunku's Sepoys.'[2] The stockade was deserted but with its guns still there. The trunnions were knocked off these cannon, which were then rolled into the river. Ashore in company with Tunku dia Oodin and Mr. Langlois, Bloomfield now told the local inhabitants that the British Government was supporting Tunku dia Oodin. On the 26th he gave a vivid demonstration of this by returning

---

[1] *Malay Sketches*, F. A. Swettenham, 2nd edn. 1895, p. 104.
[2] Admiralty to Colonial Office, 16 Dec. 1871, quoted in C. 466, 1872.

to Selangor town with the Viceroy on board and 'flying the Tunku's flag'. He co-operated in a further hunt for Raja Mahdie at Passang and afterwards reported that 'unless some practical aid is given by us matters will gradually lapse into their original condition'. The sooner, in his view, that Tunku dia Oodin was firmly established, 'the less trouble we may have hereafter'.[1]

Bloomfield had gone far beyond his brief and was promptly forbidden by Vice-Admiral Sir H. Kellett (Commander-in-Chief, China Station) to engage in any further operations of the kind.[2] In his reply, excusing himself, dated from Singapore on 20 September, he wrote as follows:

His Excellency the Administrator has given me verbally to understand that it is contrary to the policy and instructions of Her Majesty's Government to interfere with the management of the various Governments of the Malay Peninsula, and consequently no further steps will be taken. I therefore deem it my duty, as I have been to a certain extent mixed up with the appointment of Tunku dia Oodin to his present position . . . to acquaint my Commander-in-Chief with the circumstances. . . .

He goes on to do so at some length. But while advocating support for Tunku dia Oodin, he clearly considered (as Birch and Irving did not, or at least not openly) that such an arrangement could be only temporary. Of the Tunku he wrote:

He is no doubt much involved in debt at present, in a great measure the consequence of his wars with the rebel Rajah, and partly perhaps, of his own extravagance, but as the revenue from tin alone of the Kallang and Salangore Rivers is expected to bring in near 100,000 dollars a year when the country has recovered from its present alarm, and the rivers are freely open, the Tunku would have no difficulty in paying his debts provided that his revenue and expenditure were properly assessed by a trustworthy European whose services at a proper salary he could have no difficulty in obtaining. At present I believe Tunku dia Oodin is entirely ignorant of both revenue and expenditure, his financial affairs being in the hands of an Arab of doubtful character,[3] whose business seems to provide him with funds when he requires them and who is believed to look well after his own interests.

The Tunku has European tastes, and professes to be desirous of taking the Maharajah of Johore as his model, and no doubt is sincere, but his natural good-natured indolence will probably, without firm advice and

---

[1] Commander Bloomfield to Commander Robinson, 6 Aug. 1871, quoted in C. 466, 1872. See also Bloomfield to Sir H. Kellett, ibid.
[2] Admiralty to Colonial Office, 16 Dec. 1871, quoted in C. 466, 1872.
[3] Presumably Syed Zein. See above, p. 54.

assistance, allow matters to relapse into their original condition under the old system of squeezing and extortion by petty Rajahs, which paralyses the trade of the country, and a few years might see his own displacement by one of the many envious Rajahs or relatives of the Sultan, and a repetition of the cause of the late Salangore affair.

[Proper police are needed to keep order] but I believe he has neither the energy or determination to enable him to undertake it without a helping hand, and I think that leaving him to shift for himself with many enemies, whilst his affairs and country are in a state of chaos, the moment the Sultan has been induced to appoint him, would be productive of no ultimate good. Moreover, the knowledge, if such be the case, that we have ceased to interest ourselves would be sure to give fresh encouragements to the rebel Rajahs over whom the Sultan appears to have no control whatever.[1]

It is doubtful whether Vice-Admiral Sir H. Kellett was much interested in all this. His only concern was to prevent the vessels of his squadron penetrating these Malayan mangrove swamps in further-ance of a policy which the Colonial Office did not approve. After all, the *Teazer* had been hard aground in the Langat river and might easily have been lost. But Bloomfield's assessment of Tunku dia Oodin, and indeed of the whole situation, is interesting and probably accurate. The policy of helping the Viceroy up to a point and then, in effect, deserting him was, of course (and inevitably), the policy that government pursued. Bloomfield had reported that the bombard-ment of Selangor town 'had been of very material service in aiding the Tunku's cause all over the country',[2] and this was clearly true. But events were to show that the gunfire made a more lasting impres-sion in Singapore, Malacca, Penang, and even in London than it did among the Selangor chiefs.

Following the withdrawal of H.M.S. *Teazer*, the immediate prob-lem in Selangor was to determine whether authority on the Selangor river was to rest, as it had nominally rested before, with Raja Musa, or whether the Viceroy was to reap all the benefits of a bombard-ment which had cleared his enemies from the scene. Urged or led by his more energetic friends, Musa returned and, by 10 September, had built a fort for himself at Permatang. To this in itself Tunku dia Oodin had no objection. But he was desperately short of money and would not resign to Musa the revenues—or, anyway, the whole revenues—of the Selangor river. Tunku dia Oodin persuaded the Sultan to replace Musa by his half-brother Yacoob,[3] but the latter

---

[1] Bloomfield to Vice-Admiral Sir H. Kellett, 20 Sept. 1871, C. 466.
[2] Bloomfield to Robinson, 6 Aug. 1871, C. 466.
[3] Winstedt, *History of Selangor*.

proved equally reluctant to administer Selangor on those terms and the disagreement between Tunku dia Oodin and the Sultan's sons gave encouragement to the Viceroy's enemies, who were still at large. Nor were these enemies convinced that Tunku dia Oodin was likely to have consistent and effective support from the Government of the Straits Settlements.

As against that, investors were now hastening to speculate in Selangor mining concessions. 'The mineral and agricultural resources of the territory of Selangor are enormous'[1] it was believed, and miners flocked into territories where peace had been apparently established. In a few months the number of Chinese miners on the Klang river had risen to 12,000, with a monthly output of 3,000 piculs, all destined for Malacca, Penang, or Singapore. Output had doubled since the 'Rinaldo affair' and there was now a regular steamship service between Malacca and Klang and another between Klang and Singapore. It was realized that this commercial development was possible only with capital provided by Straits Settlements or British investors and efforts were made to convince Government of the potential importance of a trade 'which must ultimately tend to increase the prosperity and the revenues of the Colony'.[2] Behind these efforts were the Singapore Houses of Agency and, connected with these, were the London firms with which they were associated. The establishment in power of Tunku dia Oodin was to be the prelude, it was hoped, to the development of Selangor as a profitable field for investment. It might become, in effect, another Johore but with far greater possibilities. These expectations would have been better founded if Birch's mission to Selangor had been authorized by the Governor. In fact, however, Birch had been sent by Colonel Anson, acting as administrator in Ord's absence. Ord was due to return early in 1872 and much would depend on his attitude towards Tunku dia Oodin. Just as Anson had almost disowned the peremptory tone of Birch's embassy, so Ord could now disown even the general policy of which it was the expression. And this is practically what he did.

Ord was back in Singapore early in 1872 and Anson returned to his duties at Penang. Ord, as we know, had urged on the Colonial Office the policy of intervention in the Malay States. He had met with a very cold response.

The Secretary of State, whilst acknowledging to some extent the force

[1] Petition from Malacca Merchants, 27 July 1872, C.P. 465 (cont.).
[2] Ibid.

of my statements, expressed in the most decided terms his objection to extend in any way the Governor's authority to deal with native affairs. . . .

With these peremptory instructions for my guidance, I returned to the Straits at the beginning of 1872.[1]

The idea of the Straits Settlements merchants was that the Colonial Office should authorize a policy which could lead only to military and naval expense. The profit would go to Straits investors (who paid practically nothing in taxation) and the cost would fall on the British taxpayer. A policy having this effect would have no support from Mr. Gladstone or the Earl of Kimberley, and Ord was evidently made aware of this. On his return, he was greeted with accounts of fresh disturbances in Selangor and with suggestions for further aid to be given to Tunku dia Oodin. He was disinclined to give any such aid and the rumour of his attitude soon made the disturbances worse.

The question of further intervention turned on the problem presented by Raja Mahdie. After the 'Rinaldo affair' Mahdie had fled to Bengkalis in Sumatra, where he was collecting arms and men early in 1872.

On hearing of this, I wrote to the Dutch Resident at Bankalis, telling him who Rajah Mahdie was and requested that he might be prevented from effecting his object. The Dutch Authorities then took steps to arrest him with the view of handing him over to me, but Mahdie, obtaining information, fled from the Country leaving behind him his family and people and 2 vessels with a large quantity of arms and gunpowder. He landed on the west coast of Johore near Malacca where he remained concealed for some days, but was at length discovered by some of the Maharajah's people who reported it to His Highness. The Maharajah at once called on me and asked what steps he should take with him. After careful consideration I came to the conclusion that if he were allowed to take refuge in Johore, it might be possible to make some terms between him and Tungku Koodin, which would secure the latter from being further troubled by one of the most crafty, energetic and mischievous Chiefs in the Peninsula.[2]

The obvious alternative to this plan was to ask the Maharajah to arrest Mahdie and hand him over to the Singapore police. Ord considered that possibility but first, and properly, consulted the Attorney-General, Mr. Thomas Braddell. In Braddell's opinion, it appeared, there was no real evidence against Mahdie. He was believed to have been engaged in piracy but there was no proof of it. The *Pluto* had been fired upon from Mahdie's stockade but there was no witness to

---

[1] P.P., *Further Correspondence etc.*, 6 Aug. 1875. In continuation of C.P. C.1111 of July 1874, p. 3.   [2] S.S. No. 174 of 24 Oct. 1872.

swear that Mahdie had been present. There was evidence to show that Mahdie had resisted arrest when detained by Lieutenant Stopford, but it was doubtful whether that arrest was legal and Sir Peter Benson Maxwell would certainly hold that it was not. So Ord decided against taking Mahdie into custody, and wrote afterwards:

although I am satisfied that Rajah Mahdie is a thoroughly bad man capable of any treachery, I am bound to say that having gone carefully into all the statements which have been made regarding his conduct in the Selangore affair, I have satisfied myself that we possess no evidence which would secure his conviction in our Courts on any charge that could be preferred against him.

Having this fact in view I requested the Maharajah to tell him that he might come to Johore and that so long as he conducted himself quietly and took no part in the quarrels at Selangore, I would not ask the Maharajah to give him up or send him away. He at once accepted this offer and came with some half dozen followers and took up his abode in a house belonging to one of the Maharajah's Officers.

I then sent for Tungku Koodin and pointed out to him the importance of offering this man such terms as would secure his neutrality in future. Tungku Koodin expressed his willingness to agree to any terms which I might think it right he should offer and it was finally settled that the Maharajah should propose to Rajah Mahdie that he should be guaranteed the payment of a Pension of $350 a month and a free asylum in Johore on condition of his pledging himself to abandon all claims against Selangore and never in any way to engage in any quarrels or intrigues against that Country.

The Maharajah made repeated efforts to induce Mahdie to accept these terms, but without success. I then went to Johore and sending for him I pointed out that he was without money or friends, a refugee in a foreign Country and indebted to the forbearance of its ruler and the British Government for his existence. I urged on him the propriety of accepting the very liberal offers which have been made to him by Tungku Koodin, but equally without effect. He steadily refused all terms and in reply to enquiries as to what he proposed to do in future fell back on the usual formula that he trusted in God.[1]

In describing these negotiations, which took place in May 1872, Ord was something less than candid. To begin with, he says nothing of the possibility (which he quietly rejects) of handing Mahdie over to the Sultan of Selangor, by whom he had been outlawed. He also makes it seem that the Maharajah of Johore was bringing pressure to bear upon Mahdie in the interests of Tunku dia Oodin. But it is far from clear that the Maharajah was well disposed towards the

[1] S.S. No. 174 of 24 Oct. 1872.

Viceroy, who was brother-in-law of Sultan Ali's daughter—Sultan Ali of Muar being the dispossessed claimant to the kingdom of Johore. In fact the Maharajah was rather friendly than otherwise towards Mahdie as a useful obstacle to Tunku dia Oodin's ambitions. The Maharajah was clearly on the side of Raja Musa, with whom the Viceroy had quarrelled. More than that, the Maharajah had friends in Singapore who were of his way of thinking. Mr. J. G. Davidson might sponsor the Malacca petition but Mr. Thomas Braddell (whose advice Ord had followed) was in the Maharajah's pay. There were people in Singapore who favoured the cause of Raja Musa and their views were reflected in the columns of the *Straits Observer*,[1] the paper founded by J. S. Atchinson, Davidson's rival at the Singapore Bar. There were also people in Singapore who were providing Raja Musa and even Syed Massahoor with arms, provisions, and money. Ord was induced by the Maharajah and by Thomas Braddell to consider that there were two sides to the question and that the Viceroy was not always in the right. Anson and Birch had perhaps unduly ignored the claims of others.

After his unsuccessful interview with Mahdie, Ord sent for Tunku dia Oodin and warned him that Mahdie was still dangerous and that his friends in Selangor were still at large. The Governor suggested that Mahdie might escape from Johore and return to Selangor:

I explained to Tungku Koodin how easily he might prevent this by keeping a couple of rowing boats at either end of the Johore Straits and warned him if he did not take proper precautions he might rest assured that I should learn some morning by an express from Johore that Mahdie had left the country during the night.

Tungku Koodin agreed entirely with me and promised to take every precaution to prevent Mahdie's escape, but as I fully anticipated no such precautions were taken and very shortly afterwards I had the unpleasant duty of communicating to his Agent in Singapore the Maharajah's report to me that Mahdie and two or three followers who were safe in Johore the night before were no longer to be found there the following morning.

I have since ascertained that he got away in a small boat and proceeded up the coast until he reached the Linghy River on the Northern boundary of Malacca, from whence he found his way into the interior of Selangore, where he joined his friends.[2]

It was in July 1872 that Mahdie left Johore and returned to Selangor. His doing so began a new phase in the Selangor War, a phase in which Tunku dia Oodin was faced with the hostility of Raja Musa

---

[1] See, e.g. the issue of 26 Apr. 1875.   [2] S.S. No. 174, 24 Oct. 1872.

in addition to that of his former enemies. On 17 July Raja Mahmood collected 300 men at Lukut and Langat and led them to attack Batu and Gomback. Mahmood and his friends were aided by the Dato Bandar of Sungei Ujong and it was in his territory, up the Linggi river, that Raja Mahdie now rejoined his allies. Rumour had it that Mahdie was supported by the Maharajah of Johore and it was also rumoured that the Viceroy no longer had British recognition. One of Tunku dia Oodin's chief adherents, Raja Asal, now deserted to the other side.

It was this turn of events which produced the Malacca petition of 27 July, signed by Theo Siong Chwee and thirty-three other merchants. They complained that it had been publicly announced in 1871 that the British Government would support Tunku dia Oodin and secure the arrest of Mahdie, Syed Massahoor, and Mahmood:

Having full confidence in the administration of Tunku dia Oodin, and believing that the Colonial Government would carry out the views above expressed, and that the trade of Salangore would consequently prosper, we (being British subjects trading at Malacca) and other British subjects have invested large sums of money in the trade of Salangore, and more particularly in the mines in which that country abounds, and large sums of our money still remain invested there. It would appear, however, that the policy of Government has since been changed, for we now find that disturbances have been renewed in the territory of Salangore by Rajah Mahdie, Syed Masahoor, and Rajah Mahmood and others acting with them, and that the Colonial Government has done nothing to assist Tunku dia Oodin or to obtain the custody of the three men above named, though the most notorious of them, Rajah Mahdie, might easily have been arrested at Siak or Johore or Singapore. . . . Syed Masahoor is now on the Salangore River with an armed force, and Rajah Mahmood is on the Langkat River also with an armed force, and they are killing the inhabitants and burning and destroying property. Some of their friends have succeeded in penetrating to Klang and the works of two tin mines have already been burnt. Our money is principally invested in Klang, which is situated between the Salangore and Langkat Rivers, and is now threatened with an attack from both sides, and our property, therefore, is in great jeopardy and the lives of the servants and agents whom we have sent into Salangore are in great danger. What has the Colonial Government done to put down these noted pirates and robbers, or to support Tunku dia Oodin in his Government?

This appeal went to Mr. J. G. Davidson, Chairman of the Singapore Chamber of Commerce, and it was he who forwarded it to the Colonial Secretary. Birch was himself largely responsible for raising the hopes that he was now officially bound to discourage. For Sir

Harry Ord only one reply was possible and Birch now made it in his name:

Colonial Secretary's Office, Singapore
August 21, 1872

Sir,

In reply to your letter of the 30th July, I am directed by the Governor to state, for the information of the Chamber of Commerce, that His Excellency has learnt with great regret that, notwithstanding the efforts made to induce the Native Princes of Salangore to submit to the authority of the Sultan and his Viceroy, and allow peace to prevail in that country, fighting and disturbances are still going on and that, there being no security for life and prosperity, trade is paralysed, and persons, like the petitioners, who have embarked in it are ruined and great sufferers.

2. At the same time I am further directed to point out that it is the policy of Her Majesty's Government not to interfere in the affairs of these countries unless where it becomes necessary for the suppression of piracy or the punishment of aggression on our people or territories; and that, if traders, prompted by the prospect of large gains, choose to run the risk of placing their persons and property in the jeopardy which they are aware attends them in these countries under present circumstances, it is impossible for Government to be answerable for their protection or that of their property.

I have etc. etc.

J. W. W. Birch[1]

This reply was fully approved by Lord Kimberley[2] but gave cold comfort to the investors of Malacca. As for the Singapore Chamber of Commerce, it could protest and did. Its new Chairman, W. H. Read, replied on 17 September, that Government had largely caused the trouble in Selangor through failing to arrest Mahdie. He expressed the fear that 'all confidence in British protection will be lost'. He demanded 'a straightforward and well-defined policy', not only in Selangor but in the other States as well. These appeals were in vain. To be strictly accurate, the Colonial Office *had* a well-defined policy; and it was one of non-intervention.

Meanwhile, in Selangor Tunku dia Oodin's position had become difficult. He was confronted by Raja Mahdie and his adherents, opposed by Raja Musa and by the Sultan himself, deserted by the British, and disliked by the Maharajah of Johore. Fighting in Selangor now hinged on the mining village of Kuala Lumpur where Tunku dia Oodin had a fort at Bukit Nanas. It was besieged by Raja Asal, his former supporter, and cut off from the coast by Syed

[1] P.P. In continuation of C.P. 465 of 1872, presented 31 July 1874.
[2] Ibid. 28 Dec. 1872.

Mashor. Kuala Lumpur was little known before this time, being described as 'a place in the neighbourhood of the tin mines', known to be ruled by its Capitan China, Yap Ah Loy. We gain an idea of the village from Mr. Frank Swettenham, who visited the place early in 1872. He went in company with Mr. J. G. Davidson, whose firm (Rodyk & Davidson) were legal advisers to Tunku dia Oodin. Davidson was on a legal mission, Swettenham merely travelling to see the country. They reached Klang in the steamship from Singapore and stayed there as guests of the Viceroy. It then took them three days to cover the twenty miles to Kuala Lumpur by boat. They were hospitably received by Yap Ah Loy, who even supplied spoons and forks for the use of those unskilled with chopsticks. These, of pure silver from melted dollars, bent under the slightest pressure, so the guests found that chopsticks were preferable. Of Kuala Lumpur Swettenham wrote:

With the exception of the Capitan China's own house—which was more pretentious and solidly built—the place consisted of thatched hovels with earth flooring, some of them unoccupied. The next day, while Davidson was making his enquiries, I wandered round Kuala Lumpur and went into what appeared to be an empty hut: it was quite empty, except for a dead Chinese, with a bullet hole in his chest, who was sitting on the red earth floor with his back against the wall.[1]

Davidson's legal mission was a failure and he and Swettenham returned to Klang. Impatient of the three days of rowing and poling which they had spent in arriving there, they rashly decided to return on foot through more or less virgin jungle. The twelve hours' effort left Davidson prostrate for two or three days, after which he and his friend returned to Singapore in a badly manned sailing boat. One fact that emerges from this episode is that Kuala Lumpur was geographically isolated. This difficulty of access was to be proved again to the garrison's cost.

Tunku dia Oodin's men at Kuala Lumpur would have had a better chance had they been Malays. But the Viceroy had tried to westernize his forces, which partly consisted of Indian sepoys under European officers. At Kuala Lumpur the sepoys numbered over eighty, the officers numbered two. These last had been recruited in Singapore, where Swettenham had met one of them.

Not many months after my first arrival in the East I met, in a club in Singapore, an Italian called Cavaliero. He was quite young, tall, dark, and

[1] *Footprints in Malaya*, F. A. Swettenham, London (1942).

good-looking, of a pronounced Italian type. What his occupation was I have no idea; I suppose he had some sort of business, but it could not have been very attractive or profitable, for one day I was told that he and a Hollander named Van Hagen had collected about a hundred natives of all sorts and conditions and had accepted service with the Viceroy of the Sultan of Selangor.

Selangor was then an absolutely independent Malay State, so independent in fact that the principal and almost only employment of its inhabitants was fighting.

. . . the Viceroy's party, being in funds, conceived the plan of raising a force in Singapore with which they hoped to deal an effective blow to their enemies.

I have said I knew little of Cavaliero, but of Van Hagen, who took command of the recruits, I know less. I was told that he had been an officer in the Netherlands army, and that he lost his commission owing to some breach of discipline, but that he was a man of birth, character and courage.

His heterogeneous force, composed of natives of half-a-dozen nationalities, went by sea to Klang, disembarked and made its way with guides through the jungle to Kuala Lumpur. There they stockaded themselves on a hill above the town and did valiantly in its defence.[1]

This 'foreign legion' (as Swettenham calls it) had apparently been raised and armed in Singapore with a measure of connivance from the Government and by means of borrowed money. The money had been borrowed through, and partly from, Mr. J. G. Davidson. In the event of Tunku dia Oodin's victory, the loan would be repaid with interest from the revenue on tin. In the event of his defeat, the debt would be obviously irrecoverable. So the Viceroy had some firm supporters in Singapore, Mr. J. G. Davidson being the chief. They were now to learn with consternation that the 'foreign legion' had been completely annihilated. Cut off from supplies, Van Hagen and Cavaliero tried to return to their base at Klang. This, as Swettenham observed with feeling (from his own experience), was no easy task. There were many stragglers but what remained of the force marched unknowingly in a circle and ended at Petaling, only four miles from Kuala Lumpur. They may have been deliberately misled by a guide. At any rate, they walked straight into an ambush. Cavaliero and twenty of his men were killed. Van Hagen and forty others were taken prisoner and publicly slaughtered at Kuala Lumpur. The total casualties, there and at Kuala Selangor (which fell soon afterwards to Syed Mashor), came to 119, including three European officers,

---

[1] Swettenham, *Malay Sketches*, pp. 103–11.

eight probably Eurasian N.C.O.s, and 108 sepoys. Tunku dia Oodin was left holding Klang and very little else.[1] The Viceroy now had to resort to diplomacy. He had, in fact, played his trump card before Kuala Lumpur fell. He had appealed for help to Bandahara Ahmad of Pahang, sending a message by the hands of Wan Pa. This latter chief, a relative of Ahmad, returned to Klang in company with the Bandahara's envoy, Haji Muhammad Nor, who carried letters to Tunku dia Oodin and also to Governor Ord. In these letters Ahmad offered his help (on certain terms), provided the Governor had no objection. One reason why he offered assistance was because Raja Mahdie had invaded Pahang in 1870. When the Pahang envoy reached Klang, Tunku dia Oodin was in Singapore, presumably borrowing more money. Haji Muhammad Nor followed him there and they interviewed the Governor together. Ord not only expressed his approval of Ahmad's plan but went by sea to Pekan to assure the Bandahara that his intervention would be welcome.[2] Ahmad concentrated his forces at Bentong and their advance began in August 1872. One column was actually moving towards Kuala Lumpur at the time of its capture. Another column was attacking Raja Asal in Ulu Klang. The campaign was indecisive and a part of the Pahang forces were withdrawn to Pekan in order to go round by sea and join Tunku dia Oodin's troops at Klang.

It was at the end of October that Sir Harry Ord decided to intervene in person. He went by sea to Sempang where the Dato of Sungei Ujong promised to prevent supplies reaching Raja Mahdie by the Linggi river route. Then, on 1 November, the Governor visited the Sultan of Selangor:

I accordingly went to Langkat on the 1st instant, accompanied by the Tunku Koodin and knowing that Mahdie was in the neighbourhood and that some of the Sultan's relatives and people were ill-affected towards the Tunku, I thought it prudent to ask to be accompanied by the armed boats of H.M.S. *Zebra* and an escort of a few of the 80th Regiment.

Before landing, I had a long interview with Tunku Koodin. I pointed out to him the apparently precarious nature of his position, that although he had the nominal support of the Sultan, and was well backed up by people who were satisfied with his ultimate success and who readily advanced him money merely on the prospect of his eventually restoring peace to and

---

[1] See Winstedt, *History of Selangor.*

[2] *A History of Pahang,* W. Linehan, *JMBRAS,* vol. xiv, part 2, Singapore, 1936, pp. 93–100.

opening up the trade of the country, yet that he had immense difficulties to contend with in the open hostility of the rebel chiefs and lukewarmness, if not treachery, of the Sultan's sons. I reminded him that he was then in a worse position than he was 12 months since, and that although I had given and was ready to continue to give him all the support in my power, it must evidently be very questionable whether he could hope eventually to drive out his enemies. . . . I suggested to him that if he did not feel very sanguine of success it would be better for him to retire from the contest while he could do so without loss or disgrace and that if he decided on this, I would in our interview with the Sultan pave the way for his doing so in an honourable and satisfactory manner.

Tunku Koodin, while acknowledging the justice of much that I have said, stated that he did not consider his situation desperate so long as he had the prospect of the aid which had been promised him from Pahang. He admitted that this was his last chance and stated that, if that failed, he was quite ready to hand back to the Sultan the trust he had given him, asking only to be recouped the expenses he had incurred in endeavouring to carry it out. He said that if I wished it, he would adopt this course at once, but that he would prefer having a chance of making one more effort for success.

I did not think it necessary to accept this offer and was glad to find in our interview with the Sultan that he professed the greatest trust and confidence in Tunku Koodin. . . .[1]

I have been neither so ignorant nor so unmindful as has been alleged of the bearing which the internal condition of these States has upon certain important interests in the Settlements and that notwithstanding the little actual power I have, I have done what I could to protect those interests . . .[2]

Reading this account, it is difficult to decide what Ord was trying to do. He began by telling Tunku dia Oodin that his position was hopeless and that he might do well to retire, despite the 'support' which he, the Governor, was still ready to promise. When Tunku dia Oodin replied that he preferred to continue the struggle, the Governor agreed to his doing so and ascertained from the Sultan that Tunku dia Oodin was still in favour. Afterwards, Ord claimed that he had done what he could to protect the interests of those who had lent the Viceroy the funds by means of which he was fighting.

In trying to understand Ord's conduct it is important to remember what his own relations were with the investors of whose interests he professed to be mindful. Chief of these was Mr. J. G. Davidson. He had not been one of the group which censured the Governor in 1870, nor had Guthrie's been represented in it at all. As against that, however, he had quarrelled publicly with Ord's brother, being finally

---

[1] The Sultan was actually on Mahdie's side but still gave verbal support to everyone.   [2] S.S. No. 189, 6 Nov. 1872.

awarded damages against him as the result of a long and acrimonious lawsuit.[1] If not identified with Ord's sternest critics, he came of one of the old Singapore families, the group which Sir Harry Ord had so bitterly offended. It is difficult to believe that Davidson's impending bankruptcy would give the Governor any sleepless nights. As for the other investors, they were mostly the very people who grumbled at the expense of government and refused to pay taxes. It might be that Birch had given them reason to expect active intervention in Selangor and that Anson had done nothing to disavow his measures. Well, they might realize now that the Governor was back and that *his* attitude might be different. Besides, there was no recent case of piracy which could justify the *Zebra* in bombarding the Selangor forts afresh. In encouraging the Bendahara of Pahang to assist Tunku dia Oodin, the Governor had given the Davidson syndicate all the help that was proper and more, perhaps, than they deserved.

The Viceroy's refusal to abandon hope was more than justified. The Pahang forces were on the move and Tunku dia Oodin timed his own operations accordingly. He retook Petaling on 18 November.[1] The Pahang sea-borne expedition arrived in time to give impetus to a further attack on Kuala Lumpur. The other Pahang column now attacked Raja Asal afresh in Ulu Klang, defeated him on 23 March 1873, and drove his forces into Ulu Selangor. Fighting continued throughout the year, Syed Mashor being defeated in November and forced to retreat into Perak. Soon afterwards the Pahang men, who had suffered from dysentery and smallpox, returned to their own country. Haji Muhammad Nor remained, however, in temporary control of Ulu Selangor, with power to collect the revenue. The revenues, moreover, of Klang were assigned to pay the expenses of the campaign in which the Pahang forces had intervened so decisively. Apart from these debts, Tunku dia Oodin now controlled all Selangor, with the Sultan's sons his only remaining enemies, his other opponents having all fled into adjacent States.

It was while the war still continued, although after Tunku dia Oodin's prospects had considerably improved, that the Viceroy gave the Davidson syndicate some security for the money they had advanced. This took the form of a concession dated 8 March 1873, granted on extremely favourable terms. By it, Tunku dia Oodin granted Count Charles Maur de Seloes of Java and James Guthrie Davidson mining rights in Selangor, Klang, and Bernam for ten

[1] Linehan, op. cit., p. 96.

years, with royalties payable of only 5 per cent. on the gross produce and $3 per bahara of tin exported. As 10 per cent. was the usual royalty, this concession presumably cost the syndicate a premium in cash or in cancellation of debts or indeed in both. It also raised the interesting question of whether such a concession, made by the Viceroy and not by the Sultan, was valid. There was no urgency about this, however, until after the Viceroy had won the war. In the meanwhile, and as the Viceroy's party gained their last successes in 1873, Davidson had no difficulty in transferring his concession to a new group which now formed the Selangor Tin Mining Company with a nominal capital of £100,000. There were members of this group in London, headed by Mr. Seymour Clarke, whose activities we shall presently have occasion to note. The Viceroy's stock, at a discount in 1872, was rising on the Singapore and even on the London market. Something might be made of Selangor after all.

CHAPTER IV

WHILE observing events in Selangor, Sir Harry Ord was equally bound to watch developments in Perak. These came particularly to his notice after the death of Sultan Ali on 25 May 1871, when there seemed every likelihood of a disputed succession. For the usual practice had been broken on the death of Sultan Abdullah Muhammad Shah, the Raja Muda (Ngah Jaffar) succeeding in the usual way but a favourite (Raja Ismail) being made Bendahara instead of the eldest son of the late Sultan (Raja Yusof). This was because Abdullah Muhammad Shah had been at war with most of his chiefs, with Yusof as his principal and ruthless commander. Yusof was therefore passed over as being too unpopular to become Sultan. When Jaffar died, however, being succeeded by Sultan Ali, the Bendahara Ismail was not made Raja Muda. Instead, Raja Abdullah (son of Ngah J'affar) was elected Raja Muda and Yusof again passed over.

The result was that, in 1871, Abdullah could claim the normal succession as Raja Muda, Ismail could claim as having been Bendahara during the two previous reigns, and Raja Yusof could claim as one who would have been Raja Muda had the proper succession been observed. Abdullah was unpopular, an opium-smoker and a coward.[1] Ismail was old, inoffensive, and weak. Ismail was elected Sultan.

Why? Because, among a rather feeble set of men, one of them knew what he wanted. This was the Mantri of Perak, Ngah Ibrahim, who had ruled the district of Larut since 1862 and who now aspired either to independence in Larut or to ultimate succession as Sultan of Perak. He had no claim by law to either but he had the revenues of what had become the richest mining area in Perak. More than that, Larut is cut off geographically from the Perak river and was just

---

[1] Abdullah was invited to attend Sultan Ali's funeral, the necessary preliminary to his own installation, but not in the proper form. He dared not go to Sayang for fear of being attacked by Raja Yusof at Senggang on the way up the river. The chiefs waited thirty-two days and then installed Ismail. Abdullah's wife was so disgusted by his cowardice that she ran away with Raja Daud of Selangor. Abdullah attempted no revenge and was still further discredited. At this period his only supporter was the Laksamana but the Shahbandar later joined forces with him. See *A History of Perak*, R. O. Winstedt and R. J. Wilkinson, *JMBRAS*, vol. xii, part 1, Singapore, 1934.

the sort of area in which an independent State might be established. Chinese miners had flocked into Larut since about 1860, financed by Chinese merchants in Penang, and it was from these that Ngah Ibrahim's large income was derived. He had been promoted Orang Kaya Mantri in 1863 and henceforth played a dual role as Rajah of Larut and as court official under Sultan Jaffar. It was largely through his influence that Ngah Ali came to the throne and it was through his influence again that Ismail was proclaimed Sultan in 1871.[1] The Mantri's motives were twofold. Ismail, having to rely upon his support against Abdullah, might be induced to grant him his independence as ruler of Larut. But Ismail's succession was also a useful precedent for the election of someone outside the royal family. On Ismail's death, the Mantri might become Bendahara and so only two removes from the throne itself and with a claim no worse than Ismail's had been. With a revenue of perhaps $200,000 a year from tin alone,[2] the Mantri in 1871 was at the height of his power.

Unfortunately for him, however, his ambitions were checked in two directions, by the party which supported Abdullah and by the dissensions among the Chinese upon whom he relied for his income. Abdullah still asserted his claim and the Mantri's wealth and success rather drove the other chiefs to side against him. Ismail himself was weak and his only supporters, apart from the Mantri, were the Bendahara Oosman and the Temonggong, and a few chiefs in upper Perak. The excluded Abdullah had or soon attracted the support of the Laksamana, the Shahbandar, the Maharajah Lela and Dato Sagor, the chiefs of lower Perak. As, moreover, Abdullah was hostile to Raja Mahdie of Selangor (whose brother had abducted his wife) he had the approval of Tunku dia Oodin and, more remotely, of the Rajah of Kedah. Abdullah sought to strengthen his position by calling himself Sultan and recognizing the excluded Yusof as Raja Muda.

Dissensions among the Chinese in Larut arose from the fact that the miners came, in part, from the Five Districts immediately round Canton and in part from the Four Districts which lay farther afield, although still in the Province of Kwang Tung. The hostility between the Five and the Four Districts had caused war in Kwang Tung in 1855-68 and the enmities remained among the Chinese emigrants. The See Kwans (Four Districts) were Cantonese members of the

---

[1] The story has been told in some detail in an academic exercise entitled 'Ngah Ibrahim in Larut, 1858-1874', Wee Choon Siang, University of Malaya, 1952.   [2] Wee Choon Siang, op. cit., p. 35.

Ghee Hin or Triad secret society. The Go Kwans (Five Districts), with Hakka or Kheh allies, formed the Hai San or Tokong secret society.[1] The first conflicts between Hai San and Ghee Hin men in Larut occurred in 1861 and ended with a Hai San victory. Ngah Ibrahim had to pay compensation to such of the sufferers as were British for the expenditure incurred in blockading the Larut river. His title of Orang Kaya Mantri was his reward for paying an indemnity which might otherwise have been charged to the Sultan. He tried to recover the money by increasing the export duties on tin and was probably still doing so when fresh trouble broke out between the Chinese in 1865. This outbreak (the Second Larut War) was of shorter duration, however, and Ngah Ibrahim managed this time to evade having to pay compensation. It was apparent, however, that the Mantri lacked power to keep order by force or even mediation. All he could do was to support one Chinese faction against the other and this in fact was all he did. Having so far supported the Hai San or Go Kwan party, the Mantri went over to the Ghee Hin (or Triad) side after their victory in the Third Larut War. So Abdullah came to Penang in July 1872 and began secret negotiations with the defeated Hai San leaders. This intrigue could only lead to a fresh invasion of Larut and the Mantri, hearing of it, wrote in August to Mr. G. W. R. Campbell, Acting Lieutenant-Governor of Penang, asking him to prevent the expedition sailing. The Hai Sans launched their attack nevertheless on 14 October and at once gained the victory and the Mantri's alliance. There was evident danger that the conflict in Larut would spread to Penang and produce a repetition there of the riots of 1867.

On 16 October, after the expedition had sailed, the Superintendent of Police, Captain T. C. S. Speedy, reported to the Acting Governor of Penang that he had searched a Chinese junk in the harbour which, 'from information received', he suspected of infringing the Gunpowder Licensing Act. His suspicions were groundless (the powder being in another vessel outside the limits of the port) but he could not fail to notice a hundred Chinese on board with 200 muskets, leaden bullets, 8 pieces of small ordnance, iron shot, and 400 spearheads. The Nakoda (or skipper) stated that the junk belonged to Ah Chocy. The export of arms was a normal feature of Penang business and Speedy allowed the junk to proceed. He reported, however, that over a thousand 'Chinese fighting men' were rumoured to have

[1] For more accurate details of these secret societies see Appendix F.

gone to Larut during the week. He concluded his report as follows:

The Agent of the Rajah of Laroot, a Chinese merchant named Ho Ghee Sew, whose life was lately attempted in the streets of Penang, asserts that within the last four days upwards of 2,000 muskets and 10,000 lbs. of gunpowder have been forwarded to Laroot.

I would, therefore, solicit your orders regarding the exportation of arms and ammunition to Laroot, as I am assured that quantities of gunpowder and fire-arms are daily exported to the said native State.[1]

Mr. Campbell's conclusions on this point were strengthened by other evidence. He received on the same day a petition[2] from Mohamad Zein and Ho Ghee Siew, attorneys of the Tunku Mantri, stating that junks had gone to Larut flying British colours and carrying over 1,000 men. The Mantri's gunboat *Batara Bayou* could not interfere, being detained under a writ of sequestration at the instance of Ken Ah Chooi. They asked for the intervention of British men-of-war.

At much the same time Mr. D. C. Presgrave, the police magistrate, in the presence of the Lieutenant-Governor and the Solicitor-General, received the information and complaint of Chin Too Sen and Lim Foh Sew:

The said Chin Too Sen for himself states—That, last night, I arrived from Laroot and saw Chong Quee, Lew Sam and Fong Meng Choey shipping a quantity of arms on board a vessel in the harbour. I saw the arms in four boats, and taken from them and put on board the vessel. I also saw the above mentioned persons on board the vessel to which the arms were taken. The vessel is owned by Fong Meng Choey, and it was bound to Laroot. I was at the back of Beach Street in the ground of the Hysan Kongsee at the time. I saw the muskets and bundles of arms and also small cannons. There is a disturbance in Laroot, and I believe the arms are shipped to a party who are fighting against the authorities at Laroot. The vessel has now left the harbour.

The said Lim Foh Sew for himself states—That I am a resident of Penang. That the day before yesterday I saw three men named Lew Sam, Chong Quee, and Fong Meng Choey go into a shop opposite to my shop in Oojong Passier, about 10 A.M. and I saw there [these?] three persons buy a quantity of arms, about 70 or 80 pieces.

They were fire-arms, and some were to be used on carriages. I don't know the name of the shopkeeper. The next day about 6.30 P.M. I saw Chong Quee and Lew Sam at the back of the same shop on the beach at

[1] P.P. in continuation of C.P. 465 of 1872, presented to Parliament, 31 July 1874 (Speedy to Campbell, 16 Oct. 1872).   [2] Ibid.

the back of Beach Street ordering coolies to put arms into boats, there were three boats. The boats were well loaded, and they went to Fong Meng Choey's vessel.

I saw them put on board. I was at the time on board of my vessel, which was close to the vessel into which the arms were put. The vessel has since sailed for Laroot. I was on board the same vessel (Fong Meng Choey's) with Captain Speedy last night, and saw it well loaded with arms. There is fighting now going on in Laroot and I believe the arms were shipped to certain Chinese who are now waging war with the Mantri of Laroot and Perak.[1]

All this evidence relates to a well-planned Hysan invasion of Larut with Penang as base. The Hysan or Tokong leader in Penang was Chan Keng Kwi, with Lew Ah Sam as leader in Larut. But Chan Keng Kwi took care not to make himself conspicuous. It is not he but Ken Ah Chooi that makes the first move, detaining the Mantri's gunboat. Nor in fact does the real leader appear at all. It is Lew Sam, Chong Quee, and Fong Meng who are seen openly purchasing firearms on the morning of the 14th. It is they again who are seen loading arms into boats at the back of Beach Street on the evening of the 15th. It is to Fong Meng Choey's junk that the arms are taken but even he is not on board when Captain Speedy arrives.

What was the Triad or Ghee Hin reaction to this? Ho Ghee Siew, leader of the party actually in control of the mines, was agent for the Mantri and could claim to be acting, with Mohamad Zein, in the Mantri's name. He was, of course, in fact, far more powerful than his Malay ally, whose friendship was temporary and whose preference (if he had any) was for the Hysan Society, to which indeed he probably belonged. This show of legality nevertheless allowed Ho Ghee Siew to appear more openly as a law-abiding citizen, shocked to observe the lawless behaviour of his opponents. The actual observing was done by Chin Too Sen (presumably a spy, lurking round the Hysan Kongsee), by Lim Foh Sew (a shopkeeper in the gunsmith's area of Penang), and no doubt by other people who do not appear as witnesses. On receiving the news, the Triad leaders pondered over the matter for two days and then lodged their official complaint. Before doing so, on the evening of the 15th, they sent Lim Foh Sew to fetch Captain Speedy to witness the fact that Fong Meng Choey's junk was loaded with arms. By an odd coincidence, Lim Foh Sew's own vessel was close at hand. So Ho Ghee Siew was able to prove without difficulty that something unusual was going on.

[1] P.P., ibid.

One thing apparent from the evidence and proved, in any case, by the sequel, is that the junk which Captain Speedy boarded was among the last of a fleet. The remainder had sailed 'within the last four days'—i.e. 13th–16th—and the fighting in Larut had begun on the 15th at latest. What is surprising about all this is the slowness of the Triad to take action in Penang and the failure of the British authorities to take action by themselves. As regards Ho Ghee Siew's delay, it cannot have been due to ignorance. It may have been due to a general reluctance to invoke British help in a Chinese quarrel— even the Triad witness, Lim Foh Sew, professed ignorance of the name of the gunsmith whose shop was opposite his own!—coupled with a fear that investigation would reveal other illegalities besides those of the rival Society. It might also be due to a desire to let the expedition actually sail and arrange for a British intervention which would lead to the Hysan men returning under escort and with considerable loss of face. If the latter motive were uppermost, Ho Ghee Siew mistimed his complaint.

But what about Campbell and Speedy? They can hardly have been ignorant of all that was going on. The Nakoda of Fong Meng Choey's junk actually held a port clearance for his 200 muskets, and the embarkation of a thousand men or more could not have been unnoticed. It is relevant, however, to observe that fighting in Larut had begun as far back as 1861 and that both parties were based on Penang. Each campaign had begun with a departure from Penang and each had concluded with the return there of the defeated side. It was no unusual matter to find wounded and destitute Chinese in the Penang streets. It was an expedition from Penang which gave the Triad its victory earlier in 1872 and it was a similar expedition which would give them the victory again in December. The process was at least familiar. Nor was it easy to define the point at which illegality began. The export of arms was a normal branch of business and one in which the founder of Penang had himself been engaged. The departure of miners from Penang to Larut was a normal migration, without which there could have been no trade in tin. Who was to say at what point the simultaneous departure of men and weapons began to constitute an armed expedition against a neighbouring State with which Britain was at peace? That such an offence had taken place was apparent as soon as the fighting began but the intention might have been difficult to establish beforehand.

On receiving Speedy's report, Mr. Campbell's first action was to request Commander Chimmo, R.N., of H.M. Sloop *Nassau*, to delay his departure for a day or two. On receiving the Triad petition, stating that a thousand men, 'secretly despatched from Penang', were already burning and ravaging in Larut, Campbell issued warrants for the arrest of the Chinese who had equipped the expedition— and who had now disappeared. He then borrowed a local steamship, the *Fair Penang*, which sailed on the evening of the 16th with the Solicitor-General, the Superintendent of Police, the Harbour Master, an interpreter, and a party of police. The *Fair Penang* was escorted by the *Nassau*, in which Campbell himself embarked. In his subsequent report the Acting Lieutenant-Governor defined his purpose in proceeding to Larut as follows:

> I decided to do this, firstly, in order to bring thoroughly home to the persons who had sent the junks already mentioned, the grave offence of which they had been guilty; and, secondly, to prevent, if possible, by the appearance of an English man-of-war at Laroot, the turbulence of the Chinese in Laroot being in any degree imitated by their numerous sympathisers in this settlement.[1]

It could have been objected that the absence of the Lieutenant-Governor and of H.M. Sloop *Nassau* might have created the ideal background for a repetition of the Penang Riots of 1867. Campbell's absence was, however, short. He arrived off the Larut river at 10.0 a.m. on the 17th and, at noon, sent Captain Speedy up the river in the *Fair Penang*. He himself remained in the *Nassau* at the mouth of the river. Speedy and the other officers found three junks at a point eight miles up from the river mouth, one being the vessel boarded on the 16th:

> They had on board 200 picked Chinamen, armed with muskets and bayonets. They had thirteen 4 pounders ready for action, and they had powder, and ball, and bullets in plenty. They had, moreover, a large number of spears and the apparatus for using stink-pots. . . . The leading captain was armed with a loaded revolver.
>
> The *Fair Penang* anchored close to the junks, and Captain Speedy and a few of his men boarded them. Every information they asked for was given, except as to the business of the junks in the river, and their evident preparation for fighting. All the explanation given in these points was that they were trading, and that in such dangerous times it was necessary to be

---

[1] P.P., ibid., Campbell to Ord, 18 Oct. 1872. The gist of this report was contained in a telegram of the same date asking permission to detain the *Nassau* and ending 'Chinese here greatly interested in Laroot struggle'.

on the defensive. The junks' people were stout fighting-looking men, many of them belonging to Penang. They were civil in their manner, but seemed very determined.

Two Chinamen caught by the junks that day on their way down the river from Laroot were found battened down in the hold. Their limbs were cut and bruised by the tightness with which they had been bound and by blows. At Captain Speedy's request they were at once given up to him. They seemed half dead with fear, and told him that they were to have been decapitated that night. Captain Speedy, with these men and with his party, rejoined the *Nassau* at 2 A.M. this morning, and now, at noon, while I write we are steaming to Penang, which I hope we shall reach in time to send this report by to-day's mail.[1]

Whether promptly delivered or not, this report had only a sorry tale to tell. If the Chinese in the armed junks had been made aware of their grave offence, they showed no signs of penitence. All, in fact, that was gained was the rescue of the two prisoners. From one of these men fairly definite information was gained about the fighting. This was Ong Ah Ya, whose sworn statement was taken down by Speedy on the 18th.

I am a tailor by trade and went over to Laroot about four months ago. I lived at Permatang near the Tunku Mantri's house. About a week ago, I went up country a day's journey to a place called Tangkang. Three days after, upwards of 1,000 armed Chinese of the Goh Tay Kwan[2] tribe entered the village and attacked Ho Ghee Sew's men, who are all Khong men.[3] The latter being beaten, those who could ran away, about 400 of the Khay tribe were killed. I saw their bodies. I also ran away to the jungle and made my way to Permatang. The evening before last I took my passage in a Hokien boat bound for Penang. I paid 70 cents for passage; about half-an-hour afterwards, as we passed three armed junks a sampan put off to us and having boarded us searched our boat. They discovered me and another man named See Ah Kwee to be of the Khay tribe, on which they took us out of the boat and brought on board one of the three junks; they tied us hand and foot and beat us. They said we had killed some of their men and burnt their houses, so they would have revenge, and that as soon as dark they would cut off our heads; some said no, better wait till our Chief arrives, and then we will kill you: we were then thrown down the hatchway.

Yesterday afternoon I heard them saying a steamer is coming up, let us get ready; I heard them preparing for action: one man said are we to fight, and several said of course we will if they show fight or want to take us

---

[1] P.P., ibid.
[2] Go Kwans of the Tokong or Hysan Society.
[3] See Kwans of the Ghee Hin or Triad.

prisoners. They seemed to be divided as to whether they would fight. Soon after I heard a man say 'Oh, it is a Government vessel, but still be ready to fire;' then they shut down the hatches over us, I could hear no more. I think it was an hour after that the hatches were opened, and I saw the Commissioner of Police looking down at me; I got up and knew I was saved.[1]

The evidence of Ong Ah Ya provided further proof, if any were needed, that a war was being waged in Larut and that the Hysan side was winning, 'helped', as Campbell said, 'by the richest merchants in Penang'. Having established these facts, Campbell brought his dispatch to its lame conclusion:

The course of action I prescribe for myself is simply to watch carefully the state of feeling amongst the Chinese in Penang, and to look sharply after the export of arms and ammunition and the departure of vessels from the island. I fancy the presence in the harbour of the *Nassau* has, in some degree, a tranquilising effect.[2]

In this last surmise Campbell may have been right. If he imagined, on the other hand, that his dispatch would have a tranquilizing effect on the Governor, he was doomed to disappointment. He received a cold reply from Mr. Birch, who had been desired by His Excellency to draw his attention to Clauses 125 and 126 of the Penal Code, which at least one of the junks had infringed:

his Excellency cannot understand how, with such a force to support you, you should not have at once required the vessel or vessels to desist from their illegal proceedings.

It would also appear that the police and harbour authorities were cognizant that these vessels were preparing to commit a breach of the peace, and his Excellency is at a loss to understand how they could have permitted their departure.

I am to request that the fullest explanation may be afforded of the reasons for these proceedings.[3]

This rebuke crossed with a further letter from Campbell, reporting the Hysan victory and repeating the rumour that Ghee Hin casualties had amounted to 2,000, probably an exaggeration. There were that number of refugees, however, in Penang, 200 of them being wounded and some hundreds believed to have perished on the way there. 'The Rajah of Laroot is reported to have joined the victorious faction this

---

[1] P.P., ibid.
[2] Campbell to Colonial Secretary, 18 Oct. 1872. P.P.
[3] Birch to Campbell, 24 Oct. 1872. P.P.

time, as he did their opponents when the latter were victorious.' A Chinese concerned with the fitting out of the junks had been arrested but could now claim that he was acting for the Mantri, not against him. The only remedy was to intervene in Perak. '. . . a leading and very representative Chinaman said to me: "When the British flag is seen over Perak or Laroot, every Chinaman will go down on his knees and bless God." '[1]

It now lay with Sir Harry Ord to decide on a policy. His immediate adviser, so far as Perak was concerned, was Mr. C. J. Irving, Auditor-General, who had visited the Native States in April. Irving had then seen Abdullah, but not Ismail, and reached the tentative conclusion that the latter was the more influential and had, in addition, the Mantri's support. He had been sent back in May with letters urging that the succession question should be settled at a conference of chiefs, to be attended by a British 'Officer of rank'. Neither visit produced any tangible result, but Ord learnt of the cessation of fighting which followed the Ghee Hin victory and 'trusted that matters would soon settle down and mining go on as before'.[2] Towards the middle of the year came news of renewed fighting and now, in October, came the dispatch from Campbell with all its indications of wavering indecision and possible bribery. The time had come for resolute action.

But Ord showed no inclination to interfere. While visiting Selangor at the end of October, he went no farther north at that time but returned to Singapore. He was compelled to return there because, on 1 November, news reached him in the Langkat river of riots which had broken out in Singapore itself on 29 October. He reached Singapore on the night of 2 November, to find the riot over. It had been caused by a police notice warning the Chinese not to obstruct the streets with their stalls. 'The hawkers, especially those carrying cooked food by which a very large part of the Chinese population supports itself, imagined that it was intended to prevent them from plying their trade', and the assembly of a riotous mob had been the result. The Singapore problem of street obstruction by hawkers remains unsolved to this day and so perhaps needs no particular description; nor were these riots particularly serious. Ord was concerned, however, to discover that the authorities on the spot—Birch being away with the Governor—had acted with insufficient vigour.

---

[1] P.P., Campbell to Birch, 24 Oct. 1872.
[2] S.S. No. 189, 6 Nov. 1872.

Little harm had been done on this occasion because the secret societies were not involved. But what if there were a repetition of the riots of October 1871 between the Hokkiens and Teochews? Campbell had expressed concern lest the Larut War should spread to Penang. It now seemed possible that the Larut War would spread to Singapore as well. It was against this possibility that Ord had now to provide. Thinking none too highly of Mr. Plunket, the Superintendent of Police, he called on Captain Dunlop to reorganize the police force in the light of the evidence which the inquiry produced.

That the Larut War might spread to Penang was obvious. With armed Chinese sailing from there as reinforcements to either side, it was a small transition for them to begin fighting before they embarked rather than to wait until after they had landed. Both headquarters were in Penang and the actual organizers were bound to meet each other in the streets of what was, in those days, a relatively small town. There had been severe fighting in Penang as recently as 1867. More recently still, there had been plots and counter-plots, the plan for murdering the Mantri, the actual attempt on the life of Ho Ghee Siew, whose house there had been blown up in June. It needed only a small incident to produce a fresh outbreak of war between the rival societies. But these societies drew their recruits ultimately from China; recruits who came via Singapore, where the same societies were again strongly represented. It was once more a small transition for the reinforcements to begin fighting each other before they left Singapore. Anticipating trouble of this kind, Ord put into force the 3rd section of the Dangerous Societies Ordinance of 1869.[1] Then at last he left for Penang in early December, only to have to return to Singapore at once. The crisis this time was the arrival on 12 December of their Serene Highnesses Prince Philip and Prince Augustus of Saxe-Coburg and Gotha.[2] They came in the French mail steamer from Galle and departed on the 13th, leaving Ord free to return to Penang, which he did a few days later.

Ord's departure seemed to be the signal for the very outbreak he had feared. The trouble began on 17 December between societies which were known in Singapore as the Ghee Hins and Gee Kees. This riot was soon suppressed and the aggressor, Lye Seng, headman of the Gee Kee society, was tried and sentenced to seven years' penal servitude. The Ghee Hins were members of the Hung League or Triad, the Gee Kees were the Singapore branch of the Han League or

[1] S.S. No. 14, 18 Jan. 1873.   [2] S.S. No. 208, 13 Dec. 1872.

Hysan. Their enmities were therefore deep, and fighting began again on 23 December, the Ghee Hins now being the aggressors. The police, however, under Captain Dunlop and Mr. H. Plunket, 'exhibited a steadiness and determination very much greater than they had hitherto displayed'.[1] Order was restored with some difficulty and Ord informed of what was happening. He was a sick man by this time and badly in need of a holiday on Penang Hill. So he left Birch to cope with the situation and with the further strife in the dockside area between Macao shipwrights and Hokkien coal-heavers. Birch, on his telegraphed instructions, proclaimed what was virtually martial law under the Preservation of the Peace Ordinance. The military forces actually available were insignificant, the Singapore garrison comprising only 389 officers and men of the 1st Battalion of the 10th Regiment, the remainder of that unit being at Hong Kong.[2]

Because of these distractions and because of his illness, Ord arrived finally at Penang in no mood for settling the problems of Larut. They presented themselves, nevertheless, as soon as he landed. They presented themselves in the form of a petition and statement from R. G. Jeremiah and S. Whate, captain and owner respectively of the steamship *Fair Malacca*. They stated that their ship arrived at the bar of the Larut river at 2.30 p.m. on 12 December. Jeremiah observed eleven junks approaching from the south-east and a mile and a half distant. He then tried to enter the river so as to land his passengers, fifty-three in number. He was prevented, however, from entering the river by five war-junks, in the Mantri's service but belonging to Ah Qwee, being told that Matang had been taken that morning at 11.0 a.m. by Ho Ghi Siew's men. Captain Jeremiah was advised to return to Penang and decided to do so. His narrative continues:

I then turned the steamer round and returned down the river and cleared the mouth the first time at 4 P.M., when I saw the eleven junks, about a mile distant, guarding the entrance of the river. They were all anchored in line. I then returned and anchored near the five junks in the river. During the time I was at anchor the Rajah's gun-boat called the *Indra Bayoo* steamed out, and when passing the eleven junks they fired at her and she returned the fire. There being lots of smoke, I am unable to state if the steamer was sunk or not, but I never saw her afterwards.[3] I am informed that the eleven junks belong to Ho Gee Siew's society. I asked the five junks to give me

[1] P.P., Petition dated 17 Dec. 1872; S.S. No. 14, 18 Jan. 1873.
[2] S.S. No. 207, 10 Dec. 1872. This detachment had relieved a slightly larger detachment of the 80th Regiment in November.
[3] She actually survived.

assistance for passing out. They said they would do so at 8 o'clock; but after remaining at anchor until midnight, and finding there was no chance of the junks rendering me any assistance, I weighed anchor at 2 P.M. on the 13th, being high water at that time, and steaming full-power, I proceeded towards the junks. As soon as I got near the eleven junks they all opened fire on the steamer, hitting the vessel in about 35 places, wounding a Chinese passenger in the head. I was unable to fire more than three guns, as I was going at full speed. After passing the junks about half an hour I sighted two more junks at the outer end of the channel near the fishing stakes; these also fired on me about forty or fifty times, without hitting the steamer. I then returned to Penang with all despatch. I met the Rajah's steamer the *Batara Bayou Sree* near No. 9 buoy this morning at 8 A.M.; after informing the master of that vessel of what had taken place, she returned with me to Penang, where we anchored about 10 A.M.

The five junks which I stated were anchored in the river, and belonging to Ah Quee's Society, are drawing all their expenses from the Rajah. The eleven junks which I saw yesterday morning were coming, I believe, from a river about 5 miles south of the Laroot river, which is named Trong. The Rajahs of that place are named Kulop Oondoab and Allung, and from the appearance of the shot which remains on board the steamer, these junks must have been armed partly with Lelas.[1]

These Rajahs are cousins to the Rajah of Laroot, and are in favour of Ho Ghee Siew's Society; and from information I received from a fishing boat off Laroot, I believe these junks are vessels which are regular traders on the coast, having the appearance of wood-boats and coasting junks, and have been fitted out by the Rajahs at Trong against the Rajah of Laroot. These young men being anxious to take the life of the Rajah of Laroot, I believe the reason of the hatred of these young men against the Rajah formerly arose, through the Rajah of Laroot not paying them their tribute money of 200 dollars each per month. I have never passed any junks with large numbers of Chinese on board, nor have I seen any armed junks before this trip; and all the men who have proceeded to Laroot have done so overland. I have heard that money was subscribed here and sent to Singapore and other ports for the purchase of arms which have been taken from these places direct to Laroot.[2]

[Signed] R. G. Jeremiah

Dec. 13, 1872

The *Fair Malacca* was visited by Mr. T. A. Fox, Acting Harbour Master at Penang, who heard from the chief engineer that the eleven junks were 'regular piratical boats' from China. She was also visited by Speedy, who counted thirty to forty shot-holes and ascertained that the crew and the captain were telling the same story. On the 15th

[1] A Lela is a Malay cannon.
[2] P.P., ibid. Statement by R. G. Jeremiah, 13 Dec. 1872.

there arrived a survivor of the junk *Kim Hoab* captured in the Larut river by eight junks flying the 'Gehum flag'. The rest of the crew had been killed but Ah Lok had swum ashore and made his way to Penang. If his story were accurate, Speedy pointed out on the 16th, there was 'danger that the rivalry between the leading secret societies' might 'spread to Penang'.

Campbell was glad to be able to refer this case to the Governor. Ord realized that the *Fair Malacca* had been employed by the Hysan party, her owner well knowing that Larut was the scene of a war between the Hysans and Ghee Hins. Jeremiah and Whate knew perfectly well what the risks were and had no claim for protection. It might of course be a case of piracy, but Commander Denison of H.M.S. *Zebra* could decide that for himself when he arrived. Ord replied more or less on those lines and then apparently went off to Province Wellesley for a few days. There he saw large numbers of Chinese, ostensibly landed as labourers but actually fighting men on their way via Krian to Larut.[1] By the 23rd Ord was in Penang again and so by then was H.M.S. *Zebra*.

Neither Campbell nor Denison felt able to decide whether firing at the *Fair Malacca* constituted an act of piracy. They referred the question to David Logan, the Solicitor-General, who gave opinion, on 22 December, that it was not piracy because it was not on the high seas. Ordinarily that would have decided the matter, Campbell especially being anxious not to go beyond his powers,[2] but Ord (to whom Logan's opinion was submitted) suggested that the deed, if not piracy, was sufficiently unlawful to justify detaining the vessels concerned until further evidence had been found. Logan agreed that the attack was unlawful and detention of the vessel justified, even if there was no proof as yet of piracy. Ord, who was spending Christmas on Penang Hill, wrote from there to Denison on 25 December, giving him this later legal opinion and asking him to proceed to Larut. The *Zebra* was presumably kept at Penang for some days by one of those technical mishaps which are liable to keep H.M. ships in port over Christmas; for she did not sail until the 30th. The *Zebra* was too large a ship for the Larut river, so Denison telegraphed

---

[1] S.S. No. 216, 24 July 1873.
[2] One of his motives for caution on the previous occasion in October had been the knowledge that Mr. Bond, the leading lawyer in Penang, had been retained with a fee of $2,000 by the owners of the junks which Speedy had boarded. P.P., ibid. Campbell to Ord, 27 Oct. 1872.

orders to Commander Osborn to bring the *Hornet* from Singapore to a rendezvous off the Larut river early on the 31st. With Denison came a Malay interpreter (English), a Chinese interpreter, and the second mate of the *Fair Malacca* as one able to identify the junks. At daylight on the 31st the *Hornet* steamed up the river with the boats of the *Zebra* in tow. Five miles from the mouth Denison found the river blocked by a barrier, guarded by eleven junks. The *Hornet* could not have gone any farther in any case and had already gone too far for safety. Of the junks, two were identified as having fired on the *Fair Malacca*. Denison's report[1] continues:

> On boarding the junks we found them full of men well-armed, and with stink pots at their mast-heads and boarding nets ready. In one we found a red British ensign, but no one knew anything about it, and we could find no English papers. They all denied having fired on any English vessel. They all owned they belonged to Hoo-Gee-Sew's party, and wanted to know why we did not take Lew Ah Sam's junks. In the evening, when their excitement had cooled down, a man acknowledged that they had fired at the *Fair Malacca*, but that she had fired on them first. Next morning, the 1st January, I proceeded up the river with the boats to the town . . . and there found three more armed junks none of which the man from the *Fair Malacca* could recognise. Commander Osborn and myself, with the interpreters, then went to the Rajah's house, in order to communicate with him and the head men of the Chinese factions. I found it impossible to speak to the Rajah himself, or to the leader of Lew Ah Sam's faction, as the Rajah was on the other side of Lew Ah Sam's men and they would not trust themselves in the neighbourhood [of] Hoo-Gee-Sew's people.

It is apparent from this account that the Ghee Hin invasion had led to the capture of Matang town and that the Mantri was still within the fortification which surrounded his house, and which is still there. The Mantri afterwards explained in a statement dated 26 August 1873 that the Ghee Hins had attacked his house, killed ten of his police, and stolen his tin. He was also virtually a prisoner in the hands of the Hysan party. Fighting had ceased for the moment under some form of truce. Denison was thus able to explain that he sided with neither faction and that his sole concern was with piracy. He came 'as a policeman of the seas, to seize a pirate, and did not, and would not, interfere in their dissensions'.

I then addressed the head man of the Rajah, and told him that we were all very sorry there was such trouble in his dominions; that I did not come

[1] P.P., Report from Commander Denison to Vice-Admiral Charles F. A. Shadwell, C.B., Commander-in-Chief, 3 Jan. 1873.

from the Governor, but as I said before, I only came to seize the junks that happened to be in his [i.e. the Mantri's] dominions, as he could not help us. I believe the Governor had already warned him of what would happen if he would not trust him and let him know his policy; that the Governor never knew which were his friends, and that his prophecy had come true. I did not know the Governor's feelings on the subject; but as a friend of the Rajah, I would advise him to communicate with the Governor and, if possible, see him; but it was no use hearing his advice unless he followed it out. I then repeated to him about my being perfectly impartial in the affair; that I could not help either side, as that would require authority from the English Government. I only came as a naval officer to seize pirates. The Rajah's man said he was very glad we felt friendly, and that probably the Rajah would consult the Governor. Hoo-gee-Sew's man made no answer, but said he understood.

They all seemed in great fear of one another, although nominally friends, and mistrusted one another in every way.[1]

The upshot of this affair was that the *Zebra* took the two identified junks back to Penang. Towing in heavy weather, one of them capsized and sank, without loss of life. The Chinese on board them were released for lack of evidence. The other junk was condemned in the Admiralty Court.

Ord thus demonstrated to Campbell how he and Speedy should have acted in October. A naval officer could act without fear of reprimand from the Colonial Office, and on his own responsibility. At the same time, he was open to suggestion. In this instance Ord, while asserting the sanctity of the British flag, had contrived to give his advice to the Mantri; and the advice was 'Come to Penang and talk it over'. Denison's admission of ignorance as to what the Governor felt must be read, of course, in the light of circumstances. He had presumably dined with Ord during the previous few days.

The Mantri does not appear to have taken Ord's advice about coming to Penang. It is doubtful whether he was a sufficiently free agent to do that immediately. He did, however, make a move in that direction, for he fled to Krian and came therefore to the borders of Province Wellesley. Krian was controlled by Abdullah and a meeting now took place between him and the Mantri. On one thing they were readily agreed and that was the undesirability of allowing Larut to fall into the hands of the Chinese. The only obstacle to such a conquest was the failure of the Chinese to agree among themselves. Irving had pointed this out in April 1872:

[1] Denison's Report ibid.

. . . If ever the Chinese chose to combine and turn the Malays out altogether, I do not see what is to prevent them. In such a case there would be seen an entirely unprecedented political combination, groups of Chinese republics, with governments of secret societies tempered by faction fights.

But if the Chinese were disunited, so were the Malays. It was at this point, however, that an effort was made by the chiefs to reach agreement among themselves. Abdullah had already recognized Ismail as Sultan, and now Ismail, the Mantri, and other chiefs recognized Abdullah's claim to be Raja Muda and heir presumptive. It has been stated that Abdullah was actually recognized as Sultan in this agreement,[1] which would account for his afterwards recognizing Raja Yusof as Raja Muda in April. The Mantri, on the other hand, denied having recognized Abdullah as more than prospective Sultan. The conference would seem to have been one of those confused discussions from which each party emerges with a different idea as to what has been agreed. Unanimity sufficed, however, for the Malay chiefs to cross over to Penang in January—using the *Fair Malacca* the *Indra Bayou*, and *Moulmein*[2]—and there attempt to reach agreement with the Hysans and Ghee Hins. The negotiations broke down and Abdullah, on 28 February, made an alliance with the Ghee Hins, who proposed to recapture Larut with his financial help. So far, however, was Abdullah from being able to aid them in this way that he fled from his Penang creditors in March and took refuge in Krian. His debts had been incurred, according to Anson, 'during a course of extravagance, dissipation and folly'. The Mantri remained for a time in Penang applying unsuccessfully to the Governor for permission to import arms. By May, however, he was living in a boat in the Krian river, enlisting men and arming them with the muskets he had managed to smuggle in despite the proclamation. The Malay chiefs were as far as ever from agreement either with the Chinese or with each other.

As things in Larut went from bad to worse, with the Ghee Hin blockade turning into piracy, Colonel Anson returned to his post at Penang. It now lay with him to succeed where Campbell, his deputy, had failed. All Ord had done was to prohibit the export of arms and ask Denison to keep H.M.S. *Hornet* at Penang. The prohibition may have been effective, for the arms dealers in the Straits hastened to

---

[1] Winstedt and Wilkinson, op. cit., p. 86.
[2] *Triad and Tabut*, M. L. Wynne, Singapore, 1941, p. 272.

export their surplus to Acheen for use against the Dutch,[1] but it did little towards ending the Perak War. It was for Anson to devise a better policy. In trying to do this, he was evidently advised by the Mantri, from whom he gained a certain impression of what the situation was.[2] He was also, no doubt, advised by Captain Speedy, who was much in the Mantri's confidence. He seems to have concluded that the best policy (short of annexing the whole of Perak) would be to recognize the Mantri as independent ruler of Larut and retain Ismail as Sultan. To Abdullah's pretensions he was and remained utterly opposed. It was perhaps with Anson's advice that the Mantri now appealed to Sir Harry Ord for help. But Ord refused to do more than he had already done:

> I have also pointed out to him that if he will only abandon his former vacillating policy and decide which of the two factions has a right to the mining privileges they are fighting about and should receive his acknowledgement and support, I will on hearing from him to this effect at once give instructions that the existing restrictions as to the export of arms etc., shall be relaxed in favour of the body whose claim he recognises and that then under his guidance they ought to be able in a very short time to drive out the opposite party and to allow of his re-establishing himself with the others in peaceable possession of the Country.
>
> This is, however, far too energetic and summary a proceeding to meet the views of, or be adopted by an ordinary Malay Chief and he is content to remain an exile from his country without making an effort for himself except by intriguing alternately with the Rajah Mudah of Perak and his disaffected subjects in the hope that by promising to throw his influence into the scale on this side he may induce one or the other to come to his aid; a hope altogether delusive since neither the Rajah Mudah nor his opponent the Bandahara have any force of their own nor the money which alone would enable them to procure it.[3]

The Mantri did not respond at once to this invitation. Neither, however, did he wholly limit himself to alternate intrigue with Ismail and Abdullah. He began to intrigue instead with Captain Speedy, who, as from 29 July, resigned his post as Superintendent of Police at Penang in order to enter the Mantri's service.

There can be little doubt that Speedy's transference arose from

---

[1] S.S. No. 101, 9 Apr. 1873.

[2] Anson had once asked the Mantri whether Malay elephants were of the Indian or African species. The Mantri had replied 'I do not know—I will send you one', and did so. Anson, op. cit.

[3] S.S. No. 188, 10 July 1873.

discussions with Anson and even represented Anson's attempt to pacify Larut. Anson admittedly opposed Speedy's going, as he wanted to do, at four days' notice but was otherwise resigned to losing him and hopeful of what he might achieve on the Mantri's behalf. Ord was kept fully informed and evidently acquiesced in the plan, concluding perhaps that the Mantri, with Speedy as his adviser, would adopt such a policy as might earn him more official support. Speedy, for his part, was to receive both a salary and a share of the revenue—totalling, by one account, £10,000–£15,000 a year.[1] From the nature of this arrangement it would be fair to assume that Speedy had been the originator of this plan, which Anson had then proposed to Ord. From the sequel it is equally apparent that the Mantri had managed to borrow some money, presumably from Chang Keng Kwi and the other Hysan merchants in Penang. At any rate, Speedy left for India on 27 July with money enough to recruit sepoys in India.[2] Since Abdullah's alliance with the Ghee Hins, the Mantri's Hysan connexions had been, no doubt, strengthened.

Tristram C. S. Speedy, the Mantri's new Commander-in-Chief, was a slightly improbable character. Born in 1836 in India, he obtained an army commission in 1854 but relinquished it while still a junior officer in 1860. He had adventures in Abyssinia and New Zealand and then took a prominent part in the Abyssinian campaign of 1867. He returned to England in charge of King Theodore's son Alamayn, married Miss Cornelia Cotton, and spent three years as a district superintendent of police in Oudh. He came to Penang as Deputy Superintendent of Police in April 1871 and had since become Superintendent. He was six feet five inches tall, broad in proportion, and sported a bushy fair beard. He was to be one of the three 'Long Men of Larut' mentioned by Rudyard Kipling. Of Speedy, Swettenham wrote:

He was a very unusual character with a great fondness for 'dressing-up', and he had a reputation for speaking many languages—of which modern Greek was one, and various Indian dialects others—but for good cause I had reason to doubt whether this knowledge was very profound. He claimed

---

[1] Governor's Dispatches, Confidential, 18 Oct. 1876. But see also *The Tin Mines and the Mining Industries of Perak*, L. Wray, Taiping, 1894; and *Miscellaneous Papers*, F. Swettenham, 1875, p. 167.

[2] *Captain Speedy of Larut*, J. M. Gullick, *JMBRAS*, vol. xxvi, part 3, Singapore, 1953. See p. 32.

acquaintance with Burton and Speke, and told us strange stories of a journey made with those travellers in some remote regions of Hindustan or Arabia.[1]

If, as there was reason to suspect, Speedy's knowledge of languages (Chinese included) was bogus, so was his boasted friendship with Sir Richard Burton and so was his assumed title of 'Captain'. There were some queer characters in the Straits in those days (as indeed there still are) and Speedy was not the least queer of them. At thirty-seven he was still young enough to carve out a kingdom for himself. Earlier in the century he might have succeeded in doing so. It was perhaps his misfortune to be born fifty years too late.

On 2 July the *Fair Malacca* was once more involved in the fighting. She had again been chartered to carry supplies to the Hysans and was attacked accordingly by the Ghee Hins. At Anson's request, H.M.S. *Midge* appeared off the Larut river on 7 August. Two days later, Abdullah was complaining to Anson, who thereupon decided to call a meeting of the chiefs and headmen, apparently without allowing any to know that the others had been invited. With still more originality, he called in Tunku dia Oodin to assist in arbitration. His diplomacy succeeded to the extent of assembling together Abdullah, the Mantri, Ho Ghee Siew, and Chang Ah Kwi. He even persuaded them to sign an armistice.[2] But to make it effective the essential step was to make the Ghee Hins withdraw from the coast of Larut. The Hysans, in possession of the mines, were, of course, ready to make peace and needed little persuasion. The Ghee Hins would cease fire only on orders from Ho Ghee Siew, to whom Abdullah was allied. But Anson's position as mediator had already been gravely compromised. With Speedy in the Mantri's employment and the Mantri in alliance with the Hysans, it was becoming obvious that Anson meant to support the party in actual possession of the mines. There was every reason for mutual distrust and the sole result of the agreement reached on 10 August 1873, was that Abdullah issued a proclamation calling upon the Ghee Hins to come out of the Larut rivers and creeks. But Ho Ghee Siew stayed behind in Penang, leaving Abdullah to embark in the *Midge* without him. With the *Midge* sailed two other steamships laden with rice for the blockaded Hysans but the Ghee Hins would not let them pass without an order from Ho Ghee Siew. By the 14th the *Midge* was back at Penang, having

---

[1] Swettenham, *Footprints in Malaya*.   [2] Winstedt and Wilkinson, op. cit., p. 87.

achieved nothing, and Abdullah was professing to be unwell. Anson, wrote afterwards:

It was owing to the failure of the Raja Muda to carry out the agreement he had signed with the rest that my efforts failed. In consequence of this, and his notorious bad conduct, I told him he should never, so far as I had any influence, become Sultan of the country.[1]

Abdullah protested to Sir Harry Ord against Speedy's employment by the Mantri, whom he now 'deprived' of his title and office. The breach between them was complete.

Anson evidently felt that he could do no more. He telegraphed to Singapore (20 August):

If Laroot disturbances are not stopped considered certain riots will break out at Penang before many days can do nothing without Man of Wars boats can Thalia come here further complaint of Piracies.[2]

It was obvious that the Governor would have to go to Penang in person. Captain Woolcombe having agreed to sail with *Thalia* on 21 August, Ord decided to go with him. He reported this intention in a dispatch to Lord Kimberley dated on the 21st and then realized that he would himself reach Penang before it. So he kept the dispatch for the present and added a postscript after his arrival:

P.S. I arrived at this Settlement on the night of the 23rd instant, and found that Colonel Anson's anticipation that the proceedings of the rival Chinese factions in Laroot might lead to serious disturbances in Penang had been well founded. He had, however, ordered the arrest of some of the leading Chinese in the Settlement under the provisions of sections 125 and 126 of the Penal Code, and they have been held to bail by the Magistrate to answer the charge.

This, coupled with the knowledge that I was on my way to the Settlement with a large ship-of-war, has not been without its effect on the contending parties, who appear to be waiting to see what the action of the Government will be.

I am engaged in considering the best way of securing the Settlement against the danger with which it has been, and is even now threatened, and if possible, of preventing the recurrence of such danger in future, and I trust to be able to make a satisfactory report to your Lordship on the subject by the next mail.[3]

It was probably true, as Ord reported, that the various protagonists were waiting to see what the action of the Government would be.

[1] Anson, op. cit., pp. 321–2.
[2] Ord to Kimberley, S.S. No. 248, 21 Aug. 1873.
[3] Postscript to S.S. No. 248, P.P.

What *was* its action to be? Broadly speaking, Ord could either follow Anson's advice or go directly against it. And Anson, if unable to make the decision himself, was now quite definite as to the policy he advised. He proposed to recognize the Mantri as independent ruler of Larut, Kurau, and Krian, appointing Speedy to be his unofficial adviser and using force if necessary (and practicable) to support his authority. This implied supporting also the Chinese faction with which the Mantri happened, at the moment, to be allied. What was the alternative? The only obvious alternative was to replace Ismail by Abdullah, and allow the latter to replace the Mantri in turn by another chief—one more capable perhaps of keeping order in Larut. This policy would imply supporting the Chinese faction to which the Mantri happened, at the moment, to be opposed. A third possibility, the removal of both Ismail and Abdullah, was not discussed and may not even have been feasible.

While Sir Harry Ord may well have been influenced by Colonel Anson, whose local knowledge was respectable and whose prejudice against Abdullah was now permanent, he may have been at least equally influenced by his own knowledge of the facts. And the central fact, the fact he could not overlook, was that the Hysans were in possession of the mines, the Ghee Hins operating merely on the coast, little farther inland than Matang. It was therefore possible to accuse the Ghee Hins of piracy, allowing the Navy to deal with them at sea or in the rivers. Ord had used H.M.S. *Rinaldo* against pirates in Selangor and so given valuable aid and recognition to Tunku dia Oodin. He could now use H.M.S. *Thalia* or H.M.S. *Midge* in Perak to prop the Mantri in position as Rajah of Larut. But he could not have used the Navy to evict the Hysans from mines which were not on the coast. If he was to use force it could only be against the Ghee Hins. They might or might not be in the wrong. It was more important that they seemed to be, at least relatively, within reach. To operate inland, Ord would have needed troops; and he had barely troops enough to keep order in Singapore. He would also have needed permission from the Secretary of State, who would certainly never give it. Whatever was to be done had to be done at sea and against pirates. Both the word 'sea' and the word 'pirate' could be given, of course, a wide interpretation.

Advised perhaps by Anson and belatedly realizing his opportunity, the Mantri announced, on 26 August, that the Go Kwans (or Hysans) were the rightful occupiers of the tin-mines and the Ghee

Hins merely lawless intruders. He also produced for the Governor's inspection the various documents upon which he based his claim to independence; the charters drawn up and sealed in 1850, in 1858, in 1863 and again in 1864. These documents certainly invested Long Jaffar and Ngah Ibrahim with exceptional powers, but they stopped short of transferring sovereignty and could therefore be revoked by the same authority from which they had derived. The Mantri had not himself claimed independence until this moment nor had the government of the Straits Settlements ever recognized more than one responsible ruler in Perak. The documents could be considered, nevertheless, as evidence leading to a convenient conclusion and the Mantri was at hand to draw attention to the words which seemed most emphatic and final and explain as merely formal the words by which the Sultan's sovereignty was still upheld.[1]

While thus swayed by both circumstances and arguments, Ord made one last effort to reach an understanding with Abdullah. Between Abdullah and the Mantri one outstanding difference was that the Mantri was there and Abdullah was not. In a letter dated 21 August Abdullah complained to the Governor of the Mantri: 'He has left Larut and is now living in Penang where he hatches deep-laid schemes aiming at dominion over all Perak.' This may have been substantially true, but Abdullah's obvious remedy was to live in Penang himself and hatch even more deeply laid schemes of his own. Ord replied to his letter by inviting him to a conference at Penang. Abdullah may have felt safer where he was in Krian, if only safer from his creditors. He replied evasively on 2 September, referred to a slight sickness, and offered to send, as his representatives, his Panglima Besar and his lawyer. Ord, with Anson at his elbow, had no hesitation in refusing to receive Abdullah's views at second-hand. He came to a decision on the 3rd and gave Anson written instructions to recognize the Mantri as independent ruler of the Larut district of Perak.

As I am satisfied, from the various documents which the Orang Kaya Mantri has produced, that he is the lawful ruler of Larut and, as such, independent of the Sultan or any authority in Perak, he will now be recognised by the Government as the independent ruler of Larut.[2]

This decision taken, the logical consequences followed. Without

---

[1] 'Ngah Ibrahim in Larut, 1858–74', academic exercise by Wee Choon Siang, Singapore, 1952, appendix ii. Winstedt and Wilkinson, op. cit. p. 88.

waste of time, on the 5th, Ord repealed the proclamation of 21 February 1873, forbidding the export of arms, ammunition, and food, to either party. He replaced it by a proclamation forbidding such export to the Mantri's enemies but legalizing the supply of munitions to his friends. On the same day he informed the Mantri of his new status, made arrangements for denying supplies to the Ghee Hins and embarked for Singapore in the *Thalia*:

Instructions were given by the Lieut.-Governor that all applications for clearances by boat to proceed to any part of the West Coast near Laroot should be carefully enquired into, and that they should not be issued unless it was satisfactorily established that they were made in good faith, whilst those for Laroot should only be issued where it was found that the terms of the Proclamation had been complied with.

Commander Grant has proceeded in the *Midge* under orders to cruise off the Laroot Coast, to board passing junks and boats and ascertain that their clearances are in form, to send his boats on shore, whenever practicable, to search the creeks for piratical boats and to use his best exertions to prevent these Marauders from receiving that assistance without which it will be impossible for them to carry on their depredations.

I have authorised the temporary establishment of an additional Marine Police Station on Pulo Kraw at the entrance of the South Channel by which all junks and vessels passing out by that route will be readily overhauled, the ordinary Marine Police being thus left free to attend to the North Channel Passage. By these means I anticipate that an effective control will be afforded over the movements of these junks and boats which have hitherto, notwithstanding all the efforts of the local authorities, been able through the agency of the Penang Chinese to keep alive their feuds in Laroot until they have at length culminated in the piratical depredations which have rendered our interference necessary.[1]

At Singapore, on 9 September, the Governor told the Legislative Council (in answer to a question from Thomas Scott) that Anson's apprehensions for the internal security of Penang had been well founded but that his arrest of some leading Chinese had averted an actual outbreak of violence. Then Ord explained his own policy as follows: 'The Orang Kaya Mantri having produced satisfactory evidence that the Government of that country had been bestowed upon him by the late Sultans of Perak, with the consent of the great men of their country, I have recognized him as a Ruler. . . .' He did not explain why the Mantri had not asserted his claim to independence before.

[1] S.S. No. 253, 5 Sept. 1873, dated on board H.M.S. *Thalia* in the Straits of Malacca.

Whereas the *Midge* was now left to patrol the Perak coastline unaided, the Navy had not been idle during the previous week. While the Governor was ashore at Penang the *Thalia* and *Midge* had swept up and down between the Dindings and the Krian to the terror of the lawless and the relief of the law-abiding. The larger junks having put to sea and the war-boats and prahus withdrawn up the creeks, the craft captured numbered no more than two. The other pirates waited patiently for the men-of-war to go.

Back at Singapore on the 6th, Captain H. B. Woolcombe of the *Thalia* (Senior Officer, Malacca Straits) made his report to the Admiralty.

As matters now stand in the Larut and District, the Orang Mantri is kept out by the See Lings,[1] who have two stockades, and (it is said) a strong fort on the river, and he is consequently prevented from sending rice to the miners (the Yo Quangs)[2] and also from bringing down the tin. In this strait, rice has been landed at the Korrow River,[3] some 15 miles to the northward. The See Lings then threatened the Hokeens, who have a small settlement at that place, with destruction, if they allow rice, etc. to pass to the Yo Quangs. Upon this, the Hokeens, who are very strong at Penang, said 'If one of our men are hurt at Korrow, we will kill you all at Penang, where we are much stronger than you.' Hence the cause of alarm at Penang.

Hogi Sew, a resident of Penang, and a British subject, is one of the great supporters of the See Lings, and owns most of the piratical craft. He has been arrested, and will be tried at Penang for his offence.

The piratical junks and row-boats are now dispersed; the former, I presume, have gone to Sumatra, and the latter hidden in creeks, almost unknown to anyone except the natives.[4]

Woolcombe's fears about a renewal of disorder in Penang were aptly illustrated within a matter of days. The Ghee Hins' reply to the Mantri's diplomatic success took the form of a spirited attempt to assassinate him at his Penang residence. Finding the Mantri constantly protected by the police, they resorted to the use of gunpowder. This was a commodity of which there was always plenty in Penang. According to the Acting Harbour Master the marine police were so busy superintending the landing and shipping of gunpowder that they had no time for anything else—hence the ease with which armed expeditions could leave Penang unnoticed. Gunpowder came from England in consignments of up to a hundred tons at a time. So

---

[1] Woolcombe was evidently confusing (and small blame to him) the See Kwans and the Sin Engs. The general sense of his dispatch is clear.

[2] The Go Kwans.   [3] Kurau river.

[4] P.P., Woolcombe to Admiralty, 6 Sept. 1873.

the explosion on the night of 15–16 September which blew up the Mantri's house may have attracted less notice than it would have done in a town where explosives were less commonplace. However satisfactory as a spectacle, this demolition was disappointing in results. For one thing, the Mantri was not there. For another, the conspirators (or some of them) were caught and identified. The incident showed, nevertheless, that the Ghee Hins were far from regarding Ord's policy as necessarily fatal to their cause.

The Hysans, however, had better grounds for optimism. Their hopes now centred on Captain Speedy, who was in India recruiting men for the Mantri's army. He had left within about three weeks of his appointment and was at Calcutta on or before 15 September. Mystified officials in India wired their queries back and forth and it was not until about the 24th that a final telegram from Ord secured for Speedy the permission he needed to embark the army (110 strong, Punjabis and Pathans) which he had contrived to enlist. Meanwhile, in his absence, events were all tending to favour his and the Mantri's cause. It was merely a question of time before the Ghee Hins fired on the white ensign and so exposed themselves to vigorous retaliation. The trouble began soon after the *Midge* returned to Larut from Penang on 12–13 September. On the evening of the 13th the Mantri appeared in his steam-vessel, out from Larut, and Commander John F. G. Grant proposed to him a joint search of the creeks. Bad weather prevented immediate execution of this plan and the Mantri returned to Penang 'where he had important business to transact'. He left with the *Midge*, however, a small decked schooner which Grant expected to find useful in shoal water.

With his gig and with this schooner, Grant ascended the Larut river on the 16th, intending to seize all boats carrying supplies and without a pass from the Mantri.

We then proceeded slowly up the river with our ensigns and pendants flying, and, on arriving within 2,500 yards of the stockade, two large row-boats with about 50 to 60 men in each came out of a creek and pulled fast towards us. I immediately prepared to receive them, and attempted with my boat to try and drive them to seaward, they then opened fire, but unfortunately, directly after the firing commenced, the native pilot dropped the tiller and went into the hold; the schooner flew up into the wind and grounded on a mud bank.[1] I, therefore, returned to her in my boat and, after a great deal of trouble and laying out her anchor, succeeded in getting afloat. During the time she was aground a smart fire of rifles was kept up by

[1] On a falling tide.

Sub-Lieutenant William Rooke Cresswell (belonging to Her Majesty's ship *Thalia*, lent to do special duty) and two marines, the seamen also firing whenever they had a spare moment from their duties in getting the boat off. I also used rockets to check their advance, which finally caused them to retreat and take shelter under the stockade, who also fired on me; the firing lasted for about an hour, the firing from the row-boats being well directed, chiefly muskets and with occasional rounds of grape from the guns, repeatedly hitting our boats, and I have great regret in reporting that Sub-Lieutenant A. H. Lindsay and Sub-Lieutenant W. R. Cresswell of *Thalia* were both dangerously wounded. . . .[1]

It is difficult not to see in this affair a deliberate provocation. Grant was at pains, it would seem, to display the white ensign in open alliance with the Mantri[2] and yet with a force so small as to encourage resistance (three officers and fourteen men). The Navy could now take steps to punish an insult to the flag.

From other evidence it appears that the Ghee Hins had twelve or thirteen of these rowing-boats in the Larut river, each with fifty to sixty men and rowing twenty oars a side, thus having men to spare besides the oarsmen. When the *Midge* was sighted, the Ghee Hins blew up a tongkang which they had captured—a timber vessel of a type still in common use—and two other captured craft. The tongkang was identified by two witnesses (a Malay called Deen and a Chinese shrimp-catcher, Sin Sew) as the property of a Penang merchant called Chew Teowt. All the other row-boats, apart from the two which attacked Grant, had fled up the river. Meanwhile Nacodah Kullam was among the Ghee Hins as Abdullah's representative, asking them to accept the latter's authority as Sultan and that of Yusof as Raja Muda. The arrival of the *Midge* had ended these discussions besides terminating the process of looting the captured tongkang.

With the case for retaliation established, Grant took his time over the next move. It was a period of neap tides and it would be some days before the *Midge* could cross the bar. When he regained his ship, therefore, at 7.0 p.m. on the 16th, he sailed at once for Penang, partly to see whether he could borrow a steam-launch and partly, no doubt, to land his wounded men.[3] At Penang he found that the

---

[1] Grant to Anson, Penang, 17 Sept. 1873.

[2] His schooner presumably flew the Larut colours, as did the Hysan junks regarded by the Mantri as in his employ—even when he could not recognize them except by questioning the crew.

[3] The two officers were invalided home, returning to England in Holt's steamship via the Suez Canal, which had made sick-leave, or even ordinary leave, a relatively simple matter to arrange.

evidence of piracy had come to hand and that the Solicitor-General had ruled (16 September) that 'a piratical attack of a serious nature has been made on the Tongkang'. In his report, written at Penang on the 17th, Grant outlined his future programme in these words: 'It is my intention, as soon as I can cross the bar in the *Midge* to proceed up the river and destroy the stockade for having fired on me.' He would, no doubt, have preferred to do this unassisted. The result, however, of his telegraphed report to Woolcombe, received by that officer on the afternoon of the 17th, was that H.M.S. *Thalia* sailed from Singapore at daybreak on the 18th, signalling the *Midge* to be off the Larut river on the following day.

On this occasion Grant had supplied the want of a steam-launch by conscripting the Mantri's yacht and arming her for the occasion with a 20-pounder Armstrong gun. With this vessel and the *Midge* he joined *Thalia* off the Larut river on the 19th. Although Woolcombe was now in command, *Midge* remained the largest man-of-war capable of entering the Larut river. On the 20th, therefore, it was the *Midge* which crossed the bar, preceded by the Mantri's yacht and followed by the boats of the *Thalia*.[1] The stated object of the operation which followed was to avenge 'the insult offered to the British flag'. For this purpose the *Midge* was placed in barely sufficient depth of water at 1,800–2,000 yards range from the stockade. As she took up this position fire was opened from the stockade with seven guns. The *Midge* replied and the boats dashed in under cover of her fire. The Mantri's yacht was to have gone in to give still closer support but her crew showed reluctance to close the range despite the curses of Lieutenant the Hon. F. C. Lascelles. The stockade was captured, nevertheless, by assault, and with only two casualties. The guns were dismounted and spiked, three large war-junks destroyed, and the stockade burnt. A second stockade, undefended, was next destroyed, by which time the Ghee Hins (3,000–4,000 in number) had retreated to their settlement. From there Nacodah Kullam sent Woolcombe an obscure message which was taken to convey the Ghee Hins' wish to surrender. Woolcombe accordingly visited 'the town of Laroot' (presumably Matang) where the inhabitants 'surrendered to the English Government, and requested protection from the Orang Kaya Mantree'.[2] Woolcombe later went on to bombard the stockades at Selinsing.

[1] Woolcombe to Vice-Admiral Sir Charles Shadwell on 4 Oct., P.P.
[2] Woolcombe reported to Anson, to Shadwell, and to the Admiralty, P.P.,

At this juncture Abdullah's fortunes were at a low ebb. His rival, the Mantri, had full recognition. His associates, the Ghee Hins, had been defeated. Speedy was known to be on his way with troops raised in the Mantri's name. And Abdullah's only Malay supporters in the vicinity were on the Kurau river, just south of the Krian, and these too few to achieve anything. Concluding that his only hope lay in an appeal to the chiefs of the Perak river, he left Krian in a small steam-ship and headed down the Straits. How he came to have this vessel is something of a mystery. The likelihood is, however, that this craft changed hands during the negotiations between the Malay chiefs in January. The Mantri had at one stage made him an offer which included a steam-vessel for his own use and it is not unlikely that the *Indra Bayou* was actually handed over as part, perhaps, of an agreement which was not otherwise fulfilled. It was in her, finally, that he now embarked. The Mantri, on the other hand, still regarded the *Indra Bayou* as his, and had said as much to Woolcombe or Grant. When sighted, therefore, from the *Midge* on 23 September, she was promptly captured. As Woolcombe reported to Anson on the 26th:

On Tuesday Commander Grant captured a small steamer which required shotted guns to bring her to: on board this steamer we found the Rajah Muda, bound for Perak. As the Orang Kayah Mantri claimed that the steamer was his property, but had been taken from him, I have brought her to this port for your investigation. The Rajah Muda has received all the respect due to his rank.

That Anson should have now returned the vessel to the Mantri seems more than probable. In any case, Abdullah realized that he was not to be allowed to return to Perak. He gave up the struggle for the moment and went to Singapore, where he arrived on 3 October accompanied by two Malay chiefs, the Shahbandar and Raja Dris, together with his lawyer, Mr. Charles Rodyk. He was leaving the Mantri in possession of the field.

At this juncture Captain Speedy returned from India with his sepoys. He does not seem to have landed at Penang but merely to have assembled there the flotilla in which his troops, munitions, and supplies were to be embarked.[1] With two steam-vessels and fifteen

25 26 Sept. and 4 Oct. Ord reported to the Secretary of State (S.S. No. 288 of 27 Sept. 1873) that: 'At Laroot 4,000 Chinamen surrendered saying they saw they had been very foolish men.'

[1] Speedy was authorized by Ord to proceed to Larut, a telegram to that effect having been sent to India on 24 Sept. S.S. No. 24, 28 Jan. 1874.

small sailing craft, he left Penang on 29 September,[1] landed in Larut and joined the Hysan forces, not in the actual area of the mines at Klian Pao and Assam Kumbang but in an area farther to the south towards Bukit Gantang, where he was joined by Kulop Rhee with a hundred Mandeelings from Kampong Gaja in Kinta. It was evidently his intention to threaten Simpang and so check the Ghee Hins' further advance towards the mines. Speedy was accompanied by his brother, James Havelock Speedy, and their immediate concern seems to have been in manufacturing gun-carriages for their cannon. They were in no great hurry. Their opponents wer blockaded and driven from the coast. Time was on their side and starvation would soon drive the Ghee Hins into a tactical error if not into actual surrender.

The Ghee Hins were nevertheless, at this stage, undefeated. Their 'surrender' to Captain Woolcombe had been an empty formality and they still held the Larut river from Teluk Kertang to Ah Oon, above Simpang. With Abdullah gone, their only ally was Yusof, a brave man, but with only fifty Malay followers. Earlier in the year (on 10 July) Yusof had tried to enlist Inspector Philip Jeremiah into his service. That negotiation had failed, but a Mr. J. Irving joined the Ghe Hin forces as an artillery expert.[2] The only hope of the Ghee Hins now lay in a final effort to capture the mines. Some such effort they made and it brought them as far as Kota. There, however, the Mantri and the Hysans blocked their further progress. They were distracted, in any case, through having to watch Speedy and Kulop Rhee, who advanced, still without fighting, to Padang Lalang. Speedy paused there long enough to acquire for the place the nickname of Kuboo Sija[3] but his threat was real. Partly through lack of supplies and partly, no doubt, because of this threat to their communications, the Ghee Hins were driven out of their position at Kota on 29 November. By then Speedy was entrenched within a few hundred yards of Simpang. In the artillery duel which followed, Speedy and Irving were each said to have been 'closely shadowed by a standard-bearer carrying a large gaudy flag'. This display of banners was not for the greater majesty and terror of the enemy but arose from a private agreement not to fire at each other.[4] On 7 December the Mantri felt able to report progress to Anson. He claimed to have defeated the Ghee Hins,

---

[1] Winstedt and Wilkinson, op. cit., p. 89.
[2] *Sunday Times* article of 20 May 1951.
[3] Perak Enquiry Papers, III, Kulop Rhee's statement, 29 June 1877. Kuboo Sija means 'a place of inactivity'.   [4] *Sunday Times* article of 20 May 1951.

driving them back 'nearly to the place where my people are posted by the tin mines', but asked for naval assistance against the people on the coast.[1] Anson replied expressing his disappointment with the Mantri's failure to suppress piracy. The Mantri retorted[2] that he could not suppress it without naval help.

From Anson's point of view, things were going badly. It was on his advice that the Mantri had been given official countenance and indirect help. But there had been as yet little useful result. Indeed, Speedy's success had driven the Ghee Hins to gain by piracy the supplies they could acquire in no other way. Some junks were attacked off Pulo Pangkor on 4 November and a Malay trader at the same place on the 10th. Of three junks attacked off the Dindings on the 13th, two were sunk. On the 14th a sampan was attacked off the south coast of Penang, and a Chinese schooner on the following day. On instructions from Singapore, Anson established a police station on Pulo Pangkor, leaving there a European sergeant and fifteen police on 22 November. This created a sort of lull, which was prolonged during the cruise (2–12 December) of H.M.S. *Avon*. But her return to Penang was the signal for fresh activity, beginning with an attack on three traders off the Dindings on the 13th. Fresh incidents were reported on the 22nd and 24th off the Krian and Pulo Pangkor respectively and Anson telegraphed in despair that one gun-vessel was insufficient. This was true. Apart from that, however, a gun-vessel was unsuitable for the work. She could not approach within miles of the shore and her boats pulled more slowly than the pirate craft. Frank Swettenham (who had tried this pastime between 29 September and 2 October) wrote afterwards of these operations that the net result was that 'about fifty per cent. of the crews of the gun-vessels were invalided' without loss to the pirates of any kind.[3] It was not apparent that Ord's policy had been a success.

Ord's period of office was now at an end and he can hardly have been sorry. Earlier in the year there had been a period of truce between him and his critics but this ended in September 1873 when he introduced legislation for abolishing the Grand Jury and controlling Chinese immigration. This led to a public meeting being held on the 15th. 'It is understood', wrote the Governor, 'that this Meeting was the work of Mr. Read and the party who both here and at home

---

[1] P.P., Mantri to Anson, 7 Dec. 1873.
[2] P.P., Mantri to Anson, 24 Dec. 1873.
[3] *British Malaya*, Sir Frank Swettenham, rev. edn., 1929, p. 126.

so persistently oppose every act of the local Government.' Resolutions were passed condemning these measures as 'impolitic and unnecessary' and Sir Harry was at pains to explain why:

The Mercantile community which constitutes the society of the place takes hardly any interest in anything beyond their own immediate business. Most of them openly avow that they come here solely to make money and in some of the most important firms it is made a stipulation that its Singapore Members take no part in public affairs. It is not therefore to be wondered at that upon political and even social questions not immediately and apparently affecting their own interests, they are seldom found to have formed any fixed convictions. The paucity of communications to the Newspaper on public matters of moment and the poverty of the few that do appear is an evidence of this. Its result is that they are easily led to follow a cry raised by any one in whom they have confidence. Only let them be assured that they have rights and privileges, and especially if it be trusted that it is only another instance of the tyrannical and despotic action of the Government under which they suffer, and there is not the least difficulty in rallying a public meeting to express its disapprobation of a public measure, even though the majority of those present may be entirely ignorant of or utterly indifferent to it.[1]

Sir Harry Ord remained unpopular to the end, and resentment at his efforts to push through his immigration bill led to the resignation of Messrs. T. Scott, W. R. Scott, and Dr. Little. The bill was passed, but referred back by the Secretary of State. Ord sent home, however, in October,[2] the last annual account of his stewardship which showed a credit balance of over $240,000. This was perhaps his main contribution to the later extension of British influence.

An article in the *Hong Kong Times*, quoted in the *Straits Observer*,[3] states clearly what the local opinion of Ord remained to the end.

Sir Harry was a man who consulted his own whims first and the interests of the Straits Settlements afterwards, whenever he chose to take into consideration the latter at all, and the consequence was, the residents of the Settlements felt, and said, they were treated in a manner sufficiently bad to call down the most severe strictures possible from the Secretary of State for the Colonies. The Colonists were of one opinion and the Secretary of State on the whole of another, and instead of having his worst acts placed under a most sweeping condemnation, they were either supported or glozed over. Singapore worked itself up, on more than one occasion, into a frightful frenzy—and small blame to it.

In point of fact, Ord had not escaped censure from the Secretary

---

[1] S.S. No. 291, 1 Oct. 1873.   [2] S.S. No. 318, 5 Oct. 1873.
[3] *Straits Observer*, 11 Mar. 1875.

of State, but the admonitions had been (and very properly) a confidential matter. Ord was allowed to complete a normal period of office but the sequel shows that his failings were not unnoticed. He was offered no other colonial appointment for a period of four years, and then served as Governor of South Australia for only two years (1877–9) before his final retirement.

During Ord's governorship of the Straits Settlements he made one friend, however, in Abu-Bakar, the Temenggong of Johore, raised to the rank of Maharajah in 1868. Ord had defended the Maharajah against criticism in 1872. 'In every communication written or verbal . . . I have invariably expressed the strong sense I entertained of his high character. . . .'[1] The strongest supporter in Singapore of the old Johore dynasty was Mr. W. H. Read, Ord's inveterate opponent; while Ord's most trusted adviser, Thomas Braddell, was actually in the Maharajah's pay. The propriety of this last circumstance had been queried in the Legislative Council but officially defended. Finally, when the Maharajah wished to pay off his debts by means of a loan from Government on the security of his opium and spirit farms, Ord agreed at once and gained the unanimous support of the Executive Council.[2]

Of these past favours Abu-Bakar was not unmindful. He was among the few who were genuinely sorry to bid Sir Harry Ord good-bye. When the news came of Ord's death in 1885, it was the Maharajah who came forward to preserve his memory. From 1879 Sir Harry Ord had lived in retirement at Fornham House, near Bury St. Edmunds. The Maharajah had a village institute built at Fornham in Ord's memory. It was fitting that the memorial should have taken this form. There would be no public monument to Ord in Singapore.

[1] S.S. No. 174, 24 Oct. 1872.
[2] S.S. No. 119, 24 Apr. 1873.

CHAPTER V

W HILE Sir Harry Ord ruled, a twofold agitation had been in progress directed towards intervention in the Malay States. Pressure was brought to bear upon the Straits Government, culminating in a petition dated 28 March 1873 and signed by 248 'Chinese merchants and traders, British subjects and inhabitants of Singapore, Penang, and Malacca'. Pressure was also brought to bear on the Colonial Office, beginning in June 1873 and intensifying throughout the remainder of the year. These two movements might have been found to have a common source in the Singapore Houses of Agency. Whatever their origin, however, they had gained a measure of success by the autumn of 1873.

To earlier requests for intervention the response in Whitehall had been an invariable prompt and emphatic refusal. Proposals to annex the Malay States had been current in Singapore and heard in Whitehall long before 1867 and opposition to them had centred all along on the Permanent Under-Secretary, Sir Frederic Rogers. It was he who, in 1858, minuted that:

Settlers and merchants are always ready to call for operations of which they are to reap the benefit in the shape of security of commerce etc., and Government to bear the cost in the way of military proceedings, embassies etc. And Governors are only too apt to fall in with a policy which gives interest and importance to their proceedings.[1]

Ord was told that no protection could be offered to persons who ventured into the Malay States. More than that, Rogers disallowed the estimates for steamships in 1869, partly because the possession of such vessels might tempt the Straits Government to meddle in adjacent territories. Rogers, however, retired in 1871, to be replaced by Sir Robert Herbert, a former Governor of Queensland, whose opposition was less consistent. The Parliamentary Under-Secretary, moreover, E. H. Knatchbull-Hugessen, went so far as to advise a policy of annexation in 1872. But Gladstone and his colleagues were guiltless of imperialism. Their sole venture in this field had been to purchase the Dutch possessions on the Gold Coast in 1872, part of the general

---

[1] *The Colonial Office, a History*, H. L. Hall, London, 1937, p. 240.

agreement by which the Dutch were given a free hand in Sumatra. The immediate and discouraging result had been the Ashanti War and the commonly expressed belief that Britain had had the worst of the bargain. Generally speaking, Gladstone was the last man to authorize any extensions of territory; and if Lord Kimberley had any dreams of conquest, he would certainly have had to keep them to himself. Knatchbull-Hugessen had spoken of the misgovernment which prevailed, but was reminded by Kimberley that the annexation by Britain of all misgoverned territory in Asia would involve dividing that continent with Russia. Imperialism was out of fashion while Gladstone ruled.

But Gladstone's rule, in 1873, was tottering. His government had been defeated in March and had resigned, only to resume office when Disraeli declined to accept it. Subsequent by-elections had further reduced a barely sufficient majority and there were disagreements in the party and even in the Cabinet. It was as a member of a defeated and divided government that Lord Kimberley now appointed Sir Harry Ord's successor. His choice fell upon Colonel Andrew Clarke of the Royal Engineers, aged forty-nine but not, like Ord and Anson, a veteran of the Crimean War. Clarke had served in New Zealand and Australia and had held a seat both in the legislature and Cabinet of Victoria. There served with him Mr. Hugh C. E. Childers, Auditor-General, with whose career his own was henceforth to be linked. Childers became Agent-General in London for Victoria but was elected to Parliament in 1860, making Clarke his successor as Agent-General. A recognized expert on the Colonies, Childers was made a Civil Lord of the Admiralty in 1864 and chose Clarke as the Admiralty's director of engineering works. In 1865 Childers was given the key post of Financial Secretary to the Treasury, serving under Gladstone, who was then Chancellor of the Exchequer.[1] He was regarded henceforth as a follower of Gladstone, with whom he went out of office in 1866. Childers showed great interest in the Suez Canal, sending Clarke and Captain G. H. Evans, R.N., to inspect it in 1870. They reported that the canal should be wider and that it should be under British control. Now, in May 1873, Clarke was offered the governorship of the Straits Settlements, having been made K.C.M.G. in April, and a full Colonel the previous year. Childers resigned office during the year and may well have taken this opportunity of obtaining

---

[1] Childers played a part in the process by which the Straits Settlements were transferred to the Crown.

the promotion of an adherent. But Clarke had other important friends, including Lord Henry Gordon Lennox, who offered to introduce him to the Duke of Cambridge.[1] Nor was the appointment in any way unreasonable in itself.

Patronage apart, Andrew Clarke was a proper recipient of any colonial appointment which the Liberals still had it in their power to bestow. His knowledge of fortifications, railways, and canals, his experience of the Gold Coast and Australia, his acquaintance with official procedure and his known abilities: all these told in his favour. And if Ord had failed politically through being too much the disciplinarian, Clarke was far more fitted to succeed. He was, to begin with, an ardent Radical, an advocate of universal suffrage, a democratic politician, and a believer in progress. While thus acceptable to the Liberals as a follower of Gladstone, he was by no means unfitted to implement a policy which only the Tories would approve. There were Liberals, and Childers was one of them, who would have favoured a more active colonial policy. Gladstone's desire for national economy amounted, it has been said, to a passion. It was a passion, however, which not all his colleagues shared.[2] To those with their own ideas on this subject, the appointment of Clarke would seem especially appropriate.

That Sir Andrew was fully alive to the political situation is apparent from his letters. He was in close touch, moreover, with both parties. He had even discussed election prospects with (of all people) Mr. Montagu Corry—with 'his elbows on the iron railing in Rotten Row'. As Corry was Disraeli's closest friend and adherent, in the very centre of Tory affairs—just as Childers was in the innermost circles of Liberalism—Clarke may be said to have had all the inside information obtainable. On the basis of all he could learn he apparently expected the ministry to fall in February 1874—Parliament was to meet on the 5th of that month. 'I remember your telling me before you left that by February we should all be out of office.' So wrote Admiral of the Fleet Sir William Houston Stewart. Disraeli himself predicted a dissolution of Parliament in March.[3] This must have been the general expectation long before the end of 1873, falsified only by Gladstone's

---

[1] *Life of Lieutenant-General the Hon. Sir Andrew Clarke*, R. H. Vetch, London, 1905. See p. 114.

[2] *Life of the first Viscount Goschen, 1831–1907*, Hon. A. D. Elliott, 2 vols., vol. i, p. 125.

[3] *The Life of Benjamin Disraeli*, G. E. Buckle, 6 vols., London, 1920, vol. v, p. 269, letter from Disraeli to Lady Chesterfield, 13 Dec. 1873.

impulsive decision of January 1874 which brought about his downfall so much the sooner.

It is against this background that we must see the efforts of the Straits Settlements Association and the Selangor Tin-Mining Company. Mr. Seymour Clarke was writing in July 1873 from Northcotts, Walthamstow, to hint at the likelihood of Tunku dia Oodin seeking help elsewhere, and probably in Germany, if no British help were forthcoming. The Colonial Office was not unduly impressed by this, Sir Robert Herbert merely observing, in reply, that Her Majesty's Government 'have hitherto made it their practice to abstain, as far as possible, from interference in the internal affairs of those States'.[1] An optimist might have found something hopeful in this use of the word 'hitherto', more especially if he recalled that Herbert was cousin to Lord Carnarvon, Kimberley's probable successor in office. There was, it is true, no absolute certainty that Carnarvon would accept office, but then Disraeli was himself an imperialist and had discovered as long ago as 1866 that 'England is the metropolis of a great maritime empire. . . . She interferes in Asia because she is really more of an Asiatic than a European power.' Nor had Disraeli lost sight of the Straits Settlements themselves, as the sequel was to show. So if Sir Andrew Clarke wished to ascertain when the Liberals would go out of office and what difference that would make in colonial policy, he had the opportunity as well as the motive.

In point of fact the policy changed slightly even while Gladstone remained in power. The crucial date was probably 21 August, the date of arrival of the Chinese petition signed on 28 March but not forwarded (for some reason) until 10 July. The conception and wording of this petition was both European and astute. Ord had blackened the character of the British merchants in the Straits, describing them as selfish, greedy, and mean, contributing little to the revenue and caring nothing for the Colony's welfare. But this petition came not from them but from the Chinese, equally British subjects (as they reminded the Governor) and the providers, beyond question, of most of the revenue. In this document the petitioners described the prosperity they had enjoyed under the British flag and then continued:

Hitherto there has been a large trade with the Native States of the Malayan Peninsula, but, owing to internal dissensions this has in some cases entirely ceased. Laroot, Perak, and Selangore have been and are in a state of such disturbance that all legitimate trade with them is at an end,

[1] P.P., 5 Aug. 1873.

and unless the British Government interfere to restore order and peace, these rich countries will be impoverished, and their inhabitants ruined.

This spirit of disorder has extended to Langkat, Rambow and Sunghy Oojong, so that nearly the whole of the West Coast of the Peninsula from Malacca to Province Wellesley may be said to be in a state of anarchy, and anything like regular trade is altogether at an end.

The petitioners then drew a contrast between the disordered States and the enlightened State of Johore, and a further contrast between the present and former days. They then continued:

Your Excellency is well aware that the large mining operations which it had been proposed to commence in some of the adjoining States, and which would have largely benefited the country in which they were carried on as well as all concerned, have been abandoned solely on account of the want of protection which the promoters sought to find from this Government.

In conclusion, we would add that we are aware of the unceasing efforts your Excellency has made to cultivate the friendship of the native Rajahs of the Peninsula. . . .

We are, however, sensible that more success would have attended your Excellency's efforts had it been your Excellency's duty to carry out a different policy, and we are persuaded that, if your Excellency had the liberty to protect your fellow subjects, and the legitimate traders residing under your Excellency's Government, and to preserve the peace and order of the adjacent States, not by expeditions and aggressions, but by a moral intervention, and a determined attitude . . . the disastrous spectacle which now presents itself . . . would never have been exhibited.

Much of this petition concerns the trade actually lost and it contrasts, in this respect, with earlier petitions. The Malacca Traders in July 1872 emphasized the great possibilities of Selangor and added that 'The yield of tin has doubled' [since 1871]. The Singapore Chamber of Commerce was begging the Straits Government in September, 1872 'to promote the development of an important commerce, which must ultimately tend to increase the prosperity and revenues of the Colony'. In other words, the complaint in 1872 was of a new branch of trade failing to develop as expected, while in 1873 the traders were deploring the interruption of a trade which had been the source of their prosperity for years. The Chinese petition covered both these aspects of the subject, the latter complaint applying chiefly to Penang. Reference to the large mining operations that had been planned and since abandoned could relate only to Selangor and one is tempted to suspect Davidson's influence in the drafting of that paragraph. Nor is it impossible that he wrote the whole document.

Its effect, in the political circumstances of the day, may have been considerable. On 5 August Herbert is repeating that it is not government policy to interfere in the Malay States. This petition arrives on 21 August and on 20 September Sir Andrew Clarke is being handed the instructions (as we shall see) which authorize a departure from the policy as previously laid down.

In the month or six weeks during which the trend of policy was so strikingly reversed, more had happened than the perusal of a petition. The Government was quickly losing support, having alienated in turn the country gentlemen, the public-house keepers, and the dissenters. Goschen, Cardwell, and Kimberley were pursuing policies of their own somewhat at variance with the Prime Minister. And Disraeli, at Hughenden, was watching with amusement 'the fast-drifting incidents of the political scene'.[1] By 8 September he felt able to say of the Liberal ministry: 'The firm is now insolvent, and will soon be bankrupt.'[2] So indeed it was and the members of the Straits Settlements Association organized a banquet for Sir Andrew Clarke. Taking heart from the political changes impending, they made their own ideas fairly clear; nor was Clarke unresponsive. We are not to know, however, exactly what was said to him at the Colonial Office by Lord Kimberley and Sir Robert Herbert. Did Kimberley, amid his worries over the Gold Coast, find time to suggest verbally to Clarke what he dared not place on record? Apparently not. Did Herbert hint gently at the sort of policy to be expected under Tory rule? There is no means of knowing. All we do know is that Clarke was handed written instructions on 20 September, the day of his departure. Enclosed with these was an exhaustive memorandum on past relations with the Malay States.

The more important paragraphs of the instructions read as follows:

It is an important part of the duties of the Governor of the Straits Settlements to conduct the relations between the British Government and the States of the Malay peninsula which are not tributary to Siam.

The anarchy which prevails and appears to be increasing in parts of the peninsula, and the consequent injury to trade and British interests generally, render it necessary to consider seriously whether any step can be taken to improve this condition. . . .

Her Majesty's Government have, it need hardly be said, no desire to interfere in the internal affairs of the Malay States. But looking to the long and intimate connection between them and the British Governments and

---

[1] Buckle, op. cit., vol. v, pp. 257-9.   [2] Ibid.

to the well-being of the British settlements themselves, H.M. Government find it incumbent upon them to employ such influence as they possess with the native princes to rescue, if possible, these fertile and productive countries from the ruin which must befall them if the present disorders continue unchecked.

I have to request that you will carefully ascertain, as far as you are able, the actual condition of affairs in each state, and that you will report to me whether there are, in your opinion, any steps which can properly be taken by the Colonial Government to promote the restoration of peace and order, and to secure protection to trade and commerce with the native territories. I should wish you especially to consider whether it would be advisable to appoint a British officer to reside in any of the States. Such an appointment could, of course, only be made with the full consent of the Native Government, and the expenses connected with it would have to be defrayed by the Government of the Straits Settlements.[1]

As for the Chinese petition, Lord Kimberley acknowledged the receipt of it in a letter to Sir Harry Ord of 23 September, admitting that:

The dissensions prevailing in some of the native States not tributary to Siam, and the consequent interruption to trade, are matters calling for early and serious consideration. But as you will be so soon returning to England, I propose leaving them to be dealt with by your successor.[2]

That successor had by then left London. The Liberal Government survived his departure by about four months, resigning in January 1874. As Justin McCarthy wrote:

On the night of January 23, an astonishing rumour began to fly through various limited circles of London politicians. Men were mysteriously beckoned away from dinner-tables, and drawing-rooms and club-rooms. Agitated messengers hurried to ministerial doors seeking for information. There was commotion in the newspaper offices; the telegraph was set in constant action. Next morning all the world read the news in the papers. Mr. Gladstone had suddenly made up his mind to dissolve Parliament.[3]

By 30 January experts at the Carlton Club were sure of a Tory majority. By 6 February there was despair at Brooks. And in the speeches made by the two party leaders there was emphatic and rather surprising reference to the Straits of Malacca. The point at issue was the ceding of British rights in Sumatra. A letter on this subject, written by Captain Sherard Osborn, R.N., had appeared in *The*

---

[1] P.P., Kimberley to Clarke, 20 Sept. 1873.
[2] P.P., Kimberley to Ord. 23 Sept. 1873.
[3] *A History of Our Own Times*, Justin McCarthy, vol. iv, p. 201.

Times in July 1873.[1] Osborn drew attention to the unprotected state of British commerce following the withdrawal of British influence from Sumatra. An article by Bowles in *Fraser's Magazine* emphasized the same point. Seizing on this issue, Disraeli made use of it in his address to the electors of Buckinghamshire:

By an act of folly or of ignorance rarely equalled, the present Ministry relinquished a Treaty which secured us the freedom of the Straits of Malacca for our trade with China and Japan. . . .[2]

Gladstone replied to this, denying that the transaction of 1871 affected the navigation of the Straits. The damage, if any, was done when the Dutch occupied Siak in 1868—when Disraeli was in office. Disraeli retorted on 31 January that his reference had been not to Siak but to Acheen. Gladstone said that the Straits of Malacca were not opposite Acheen but opposite Siak. Disraeli's speech at Aylesbury gave rise to the verses:

> The farmers of Aylesbury sat down to dine
> They'd plenty of cheer and very good wine;
> And after the dinner they took to their bacca
> And the gist of their talk was the Straits of Malacca.

On 1 February Disraeli told Lady Bradford: 'I think the Malacca Straits will now be pretty well understood by all England—and Mr. Gladstone too.'[3]

It is unfortunately open to doubt whether the problem of the Straits was understood by England, by Gladstone, or even by Disraeli. There was, in fact, no further mention of the Straits after the General Election was over. What is significant, however, about this brief episode is that Disraeli refrained from announcing any policy of his own for securing the passage of the Straits—by an extension, for example, of British influence in the Malay Peninsula. There is little reason, indeed, for supposing that Disraeli knew much about it. Lord Carnarvon, who was to be his Secretary of State for the Colonies, would have known more, but it was uncertain at this time whether he would even accept office. He had resigned with Lord Cranborne (by this time Marquis of Salisbury) in 1867 and it was doubtful whether either would work with Disraeli again. In fact, as we now know, Carnarvon

---

[1] Sherard Osborn had served in the Straits and was author of *My Journal in Malayan Waters*, London, 1837.
[2] *Annual Register*, 1874, pp. 6–9.
[3] Buckle, op. cit., vol. v, p. 278.

was foremost among those who urged Lord Salisbury to accept office.[1] As against that, he was not in close touch with Disraeli. They met indeed at Bretby Park on 19–23 January, but Disraeli's letter of the 20th to Lady Bradford in which he wrote 'I ought not to forget Carnarvon, whom I absolutely did not recognise . . .'[2] does not reflect any close relationship at that period. Nor did Disraeli form his Cabinet until 18 February.

Much had happened in the meanwhile. Sir Andrew Clarke landed at Singapore on 4 November 1873. He had already decided to go beyond the letter of his instructions. He had been told to inquire and report. But, as he explained in his old age, 'Reporting alone scarcely seemed to meet the grave urgency of the situation. It was necessary to act in the first place, and to report afterwards.'[3] This necessity might not have been apparent to anyone in the permanent employment of the Colonial Office. But Clarke's colonial career was to be merely an interlude in a career mainly devoted to railways, canals, and coaling-stations. As soon as his friends returned to power (in 1880) he became Inspector-General of Fortifications. He was not dependent (as Ord had been) on the good opinion of the Colonial Office.

If Sir Andrew Clarke had already, before his arrival, decided upon a vigorous policy, all that he needed was evidence of continual unrest. There was evidence and to spare. It came to light, moreover, before Clarke had even reached Singapore. At Penang he had found two British men-of-war (presumably the *Midge* and the *Avon*), the commanders of which told him frankly that there were pirates about and that there was no chance of catching them. Sir Harry Ord had assured the Legislative Council on 9 September that order had been restored and that trade was reviving. But was this true? It was far from true, as was soon to be obvious. On 16 November 1873 at 1.0 p.m., a vessel described as a 'Malacca scotchie' laden with rattan left Langat for Malacca. She was registered at Malacca and carried six Malay sailors and three Chinese passengers. When waiting for a favourable wind or, more probably, for the tide, outside the Jugra river at Marif or Merib, at 5.0 p.m., the tongkang or 'scotchie' was overtaken by two boats coming out, it was stated, from Langat. She was boarded by about twenty men, who killed five of the crew and all the passengers.

---

[1] *Life of Robert, Marquis of Salisbury*, 2 vols., London, 1921, by Lady Gwendolen Cecil, vol. ii, pp. 43–51, covering the events of Feb. 1874.

[2] Buckle, op. cit., vol. v, p. 272.

[3] *India, Ceylon and the Straits Settlements*, 1906, chapter by Clarke, p. 449.

One Malay, a youth called Mat Syed (aged twenty), jumped overboard and, holding on to the rudder chains for an hour or more
(perhaps until after dusk), swam the 600 yards to the shore. There he
took hold of a pile, one of those supporting the jetty of the 'Qualling'
Fort, and clung to it. His evidence continues:

I remained quiet in the water[holding on for a quarter of an hour, when
I heard the voice of a Bugis. I was up to my neck in water. After a short
time I heard a man come to the pier from the fort; then the pirates' two
boats came up to within two fathoms of where I was. The man on the pier
said 'What news?'[1] 'Good news' was the reply from the men in the boats.[2]
'Have you finished them all?' said the man on the pier. 'All but one,' was
the answer from the boat. 'We searched but could not find him.' 'Where
are you going now?' was the next question from the man just over my
head. They answered, 'Up the river;' and went away, returning again in
about an hour, when they landed at the steps close]to where I was. I
heard them regretting that they had lost one of us to the friends from the
fort. If they had not lost one no news could have reached Malacca. When
I heard all quiet I swam to the Bugis boat, which was near the pier. I asked
the men on board . . . to save my life.[3]

The Bugis seamen, trading at Langat but not resident there, were
well armed (as they needed to be) and were unafraid of the Langat
people. They protected Mat Syed but took him ashore next day to
the fort. The panglima in charge there, Marsah or Moosah—afraid,
shall we say, to commit murder in daylight before witnesses?—told
the Bugis to take Mat Syed to the Sultan.

Yeam Tuan [the Sultan] was asleep and they took me to Dato Banda,
who asked me if I knew who had committed the murder. I said I did and
he told me to stop quiet. Then I was taken to Yeam Tuan, who examined
me. I told him everything. He asked me if I knew the men. I said I did not
know them. . . .[4]

The chief to whom Mat Syed was taken was none other than Tunku
Allang (Raja Yacoob alias Raja Kaha), whose men were supposed to
have been the murderers and at whose house the plundered vessel
remained.

The owner or a part-owner of the scotchie was Mohammad bin
Hassan of Malacca, brother-in-law of the murdered nacodah (or
master), Hadji Abdul Rahman. He heard of the affair on 18 November and made a statement before Mr. E. E. Isemonger, the magistrate.

[1] The conventional Malay greeting, not a deliberate question.
[2] Again, a formal reply.   [3] P.P., evidence of Mahomed Syed.
[4] P.P., evidence of Mat Syed.

Captain Shaw, the Lieutenant-Governor of Malacca, reported the complaint to the Colonial Secretary and furnished Mohammad bin Hassan with a letter to the Sultan of Selangor, asking him to release the survivor and arrest the pirates. The Sultan duly released Mat Syed, replying to Captain Shaw in a letter which read thus in translation:

Regarding the letter written by our friend on the 27th Ramillan, it reached me safely, and we have read its contents. Regarding the man remaining, the friend of those who were attacked, he is given to Mahomed, the bearer of this letter; also there are three men of mine dead together with those who were attacked; this we inform our friend.[1]

Once safely back in Malacca, Mat Syed professed his ability to identify the murderers. He deposed that the stolen specie had amounted to 2,000 dollars[2] and had been handed to Abdul Rahman by a Muslim Chinese called Ah Kim. A brother of Ah Kim, Chow Ah Yang, explained that Ah Kim had been prevented by the Sultan and Tunku Allang from coming to Malacca to give his evidence on this point.

On 10 December Mat Syed saw a Langat boat in Malacca river and recognized four of the murderers on board. They were arrested on the 12th by Sergeant-Major Mahomed on the orders of Mr. Hayward, one of them resisting arrest.[3] Mat Syed recognized others on the 13th—four in another Langat boat and another at the police station—and these were arrested by Inspector Warne. In the boats concerned Mat Syed identified property from the plundered scotchie. He gave his evidence on 29 December and made further statements on 2 January and 9–10 January, all these taken down before A. R. Ord, Esq., as Justice of the Peace. One of the accused was Moosah (headman at the fort) and another was a man called Daga, who turned Queen's Evidence and incriminated the rest. Daga, by his own account, had on 14 November demanded payment from Tunku Allang for some fish. The Tunku had no money at that time but learnt by inquiry that there was specie on board Abdul Rahman's vessel. He told his men to capture her and Daga was himself a witness of all that took place and explained how Tunku Allang divided the spoil or (to be more accurate) kept most of it for himself.

One puzzling feature about this affair was the apparent lunacy of the pirates in coming to Malacca. They knew that Mat Syed had sur-

[1] P.P., Sultan to Capt. Shaw.
[2] The amount lost tended rather to increase. Mohammed bin Hassan mentioned 600 dollars in his complaint of 18 Nov.
[3] The delay was due, no doubt, to some expectation that the others were coming later, as they did.

vived the massacre, to be brought before the Sultan afterwards. They knew that he had been taken to Malacca at the Lieutenant-Governor's request. And yet, barely three weeks later, they are in Malacca harbour. Why? According to Daga, 'We came to buy betel and cocoanuts.' No one, surely, could be in such frantic need of betel (or of coconuts) to run such a risk for them as that. The only possible explanation—or the only explanation so far put forward—is that Mat Syed identified the wrong men. Frank Swettenham, who was living soon afterwards at Bandar Langat, was told that this was so.

> I ascertained that the men who had been executed were not responsible for this particular crime, though the punishment must have been deserved on general principles. The evidence of the Malacca witness was positive and unshakable, but it is probable that his own state of mind would not allow him to take very careful note of the features of the assailants at the moment of attack, and from the rudder he would not, on a dark night, have a very clear view of the subsequent proceedings.[1]

This theory, that Mat Syed was mistaken, is obviously untenable. To begin with, he must have known the Langat people perfectly well. The scotchie probably traded there regularly. She had been there on this occasion, probably, for days; for long enough anyway to dispose of one cargo and load another. Indeed, according to the Sultan, three of the murdered men were his subjects; perhaps from Langat itself. Mat Syed would know the Langat people by sight and by name and it would be light enough at 5.0 p.m. to recognize them. But, quite apart from his identification of the accused, Mat Syed also identified *property* from the vessel to which he had belonged; gear he had seen and handled and could recognize again. This would seem to obviate any idea of his being mistaken. We are rather left to decide whether he was telling the truth or lying. It should be emphasized in this connexion that the whole case was to rest on his assertions alone. For the court which tried the accused found no evidence to implicate Tunku Allang, thus dismissing the testimony of Daga. But if Daga was lying about Tunku Allang's complicity, he might equally have lied about everything else. The suspicion is bound to dawn that the actual pirates were never arrested and may, for example, have been the same men responsible for another attack (on another scotchie from Malacca) on 6 January.

Were that the truth it would become necessary to account for the

---

[1] Swettenham, *British Malaya*, p. 184.

lies which were told and believed. Nor would this be difficult, for Tunku dia Oodin's adherents had every motive for throwing discredit on Tunku Allang. They had ample opportunity, moreover, for persuading Mat Syed to identify as murderers the men he had seen at the fort on the morning after the crime. That they were given to piracy is likely enough. That they committed it in their own home port is far less probable. There are other doubts, moreover, aroused by Mat Syed's story. His Bugis friends, while protecting him, take him into the very fort which is the murderers' headquarters. The panglima there (a pirate chief) makes no attempt, apparently, to detain the vital witness to his crime. He sends him instead to the Sultan, although admittedly at an hour when that potentate would certainly be asleep. From the Sultan's house, Mat Syed is taken to Tunku Allang, the man who is supposed to have organized the massacre. Again, there is nothing to prevent him from taking custody of the witness with a view to his quiet dispatch. Instead, he sends him back to the Sultan, at a more hopeful hour, and allows him to tell his story. This story told, Mat Syed lives quietly among the murderers until Mohammad bin Hassan arrives to take him home to Malacca. He knows the men who killed his shipmates. They know that he knows them, for he has said as much to Tunku Allang. And what do they do? They let him return safely to Malacca. Then, after about three weeks, they go to Malacca themselves, carefully equipping their boats with stolen property which he can identify. The story makes no sense except as part of a plot to discredit Tunku Allang. That he did in fact encourage piracy is more than likely. That there were people in Selangor who might wish to convict him of it is certain.

News of the piracy of 16 November was reported to Singapore on the 18th. Nor was this the only news of piracy to be received. For H.M.S. *Thalia* left Penang on 2 December on a routine cruise, partly to show the flag and partly to deliver stores for the police station on Dinding Island, and reported finding a pirate camp on Pulo Tallong. Commander J. C. Patterson decided to remain in the vicinity, sending his boats in to search the creeks. He was rewarded on the night of 11 December when he found three trading vessels being attacked by six pirate boats near the north entrance of the Dinding Channel. He opened fire but the pirates escaped in shallow water towards Pulo Tallong. The *Thalia* reached Penang on the 13th and Patterson reported to Captain Woolcombe at Singapore, concluding significantly: 'I am sorry to add, we have had and still continue a large sick list.'

In the few weeks, therefore, after his arrival, Sir Andrew Clarke had ample evidence of continual disorder on the coasts of both Selangor and Perak. He was armed with instructions which he could interpret as permission to intervene. He had reason to conclude that his predecessor's policy had been a failure, and a failure for which Anson was partly responsible. He had to devise a new policy, turning to such advisers as were available and conciliating the people Ord had offended. From the first he and Lady Clarke dispensed an open hospitality, and not merely to Europeans. The Chinese visitors to Government House were numerous and well received, and everything was done to make Government House 'the social centre of the community of Singapore'.[1] Invitations went forth to Sir Harry Ord's enemies, like Mr. W. H. M. Read, and Lady Clarke avoided any appearance of favouring any particular group or clique. For advisers there were Birch, Braddell, McNair, Irving, and Willans. Without initially asking for their formal views, Clarke evidently discovered what their opinions were about his main problem. The professed expert among them on native affairs was Mr. C. J. Irving, Auditor-General, whom Ord had employed in various negotiations. He stood alone in opposing any active intervention in the Malay States and was later to urge that their independence should be 'encouraged by a wholesome neglect'. He was eventually found to panic in an emergency. Opposed to him were the two strong personalities, the Attorney-General and Colonial Secretary. Thomas Braddell, with thirty years' experience in the Straits, was at no pains to conceal his contempt for Irving and for half-measures. He was strongly supported by Birch, who, with far less local knowledge, was emphatic in urging intervention or even annexation. As experienced as Braddell was W. W. Willans, the Treasurer, whose views in fact were much the same, and McNair (Colonial Engineer), who voiced the same opinions in a minor key.[2]

Clarke did not, however, consult only the members of his Executive Council. He discussed matters with Mr. W. H. M. Read. He talked with Mr. Kim Cheng. He asked the views of Mr. W. R. Scott. He also tried to discover, but with far less success, what had been the policy of his various predecessors in office. The secretarial archives were ransacked for relevant memoranda, but with only meagre results. Ord had kept his information to himself and the East India Company had

---

[1] Vetch, op. cit., p. 131.
[2] P.P., pp. 212 et seq., Minutes submitted to Clarke on the subject of the Secretary of State's dispatch dated 20 Sept. 1873.

rarely displayed much interest in the Straits. As Clarke afterwards explained to the Legislative Council (on 15 September 1874):

And here I may say, with respect to what was the previous course of dealing with these matters, that I had to grope everywhere in the dark, from the unconnected and inconsistent, and incongruous character of the policy which had guided us in the Straits, there was no record, no system, no authority to which I could turn; and had it not been for the gentleman I have alluded to before, who had in the earlier period of his life here studied, and has since given himself to studying the Malay customs and traditions,—I mean, your Attorney-General—I do not know how I could have accomplished what has been done. . . . I had several conferences with him, and . . . he was enabled to bring out of the chaos which existed as to the affairs and relations of the native States something like a consistent result.

Ord had relied upon Irving for information and upon Birch for action but Clarke preferred Braddell to either. He was not, for one thing, implicated in Ord's policy of upholding the Mantri; a policy which Clarke intended to reverse. Braddell was not weak, like Irving, nor inexperienced, so far as the Straits were concerned, like Birch. He was to be the man upon whom Clarke chiefly depended for advice and help; and for part of November Birch and McNair were not even available for consultation.[1]

While the Governor was thus seeking to master the facts of a complex situation, certain other people in Singapore were preparing to influence his ultimate decision for their own benefit. Abdullah, the defeated candidate to the Perak throne, had arrived in Singapore in October with a small group of adherents. His case would have seemed hopeless had not the Mantri, by allying himself with the Hysans, won for Abdullah the friendship of the Ghee Hins; that is, of the Triad. The head of the Triad in Singapore was Tan Kim Cheng, a Hokkien merchant of almost Whampoa's respectability whose influence among the Chinese was only vaguely realized among the government officials.[2] With an introduction from the Ghee Hin leaders in Penang, Abdullah saw Kim Cheng, who offered to put him on the throne. His terms (as

---

[1] They had been sent to attend the coronation at Bangkok. See S.S. No. 371 of 30 Nov. 1873.

[2] Tan Kim Cheng was son of the Tan Tock Seng, after whom the hospital is named—one of the very early Chinese merchants in Singapore. At the time of the Chinese riots in 1854 Tan Kim Cheng (or Seng) was one of the recognized headmen. He contributed £13,000 towards the cost of the Singapore waterworks in 1858. For his Triad position, see *Triad and Tabut*, M. L. Wynne, Singapore, 1941, p. 275. See also *The Golden Chersonese*, Isabella Bird, p. 268.

offered to a penniless fugitive) were stiff; five-elevenths of all duties collected between Telok Serah and Krian for the next decade. Abdullah then had interviews (no doubt by arrangements made through Mr. Charles Rodyk) with Thomas Scott and Major McNair. Clarke had not yet arrived and both these gentlemen advised him to wait until after the new Governor's installation. A man known both to Kim Cheng and Rodyk was Mr. W. H. M. Read, to whom Abdullah had written previously and with whom he now held discussions. In so far as Ord had shown favour to the Mantri, there were certain to be people in Singapore opposed to his pretensions and Read no doubt was one of them. Abdullah, besides, was a supporter of Tunku dia Oodin in Selangor and an assured enemy of Raja Mahdie, and this was enough to gain him the favour of the Davidson group. What other interests were involved it is difficult now to say.

What followed is best told in the words of W. H. M. Read:

On December 13th, dining at Government House, his Excellency, when the guests were leaving, asked me to stay behind and have a talk; and, as was natural, the conversation turned upon the unfortunate position of affairs in Perak. I asked him whether he intended moving quickly in the matter. He said: 'I am ready, at a moment's notice, if I can get the key to the door.' I said: 'Give me a fortnight, and I will get it for you.'

I immediately drew up, and had translated into Malay, a letter [for signature by Abdullah and others].

A special messenger was at once despatched with this letter for the signature of the said parties, and he returned on January 9th, 1874. On Sunday, the 11th, Sir Andrew Clarke and suite left for the scene of the disturbances.[1]

Although this story is, no doubt, essentially true, it misleads somewhat by over-simplification. Read, born in 1819, was about fifty-four at the date of the dinner-party to which he refers. In 1901, when his memoirs appeared, he would have been about eighty-two and writing with gusto about what happened over a quarter of a century before. He tends to exaggerate his own part in everything (even maybe in his claim to have introduced horse-racing in 1843). That he and Kim Cheng drew up the letter for Abdullah's signature is fairly certain but it would be wrong to conclude that his was the only influence at work or that this letter was the determining factor in all that afterwards took place.

The letter runs as follows:

We and our great men request the Governor, who is now arbitrator and

¹ Play and Politics, By an Old Resident, London, 1901, p. 25. For his connexion with Tan Kim Cheng, see pp. 91–116.

mediator, to aid us by enquiring into these disturbances with authority so that they shall cease, and be settled properly and with justice. And if all these dissensions are brought to an end and set right, and the country is restored to peace, we and our great men desire to settle under the sheltering protection of the English flag.

Further, we and our great men wish to make a new treaty of lasting friendship with the English Government, which will benefit both sides, and we, together with our great men, to show our good faith, ask of our friend, Sir Andrew Clarke, for a man of sufficient abilities to live with us in Perak, or at any fit place not far from us, and show us a good system of government for our dominions, so that our country may be opened up and bring profit, and increase the revenues as well as peace and justice. . . . [Dated 30 December 1873.][1]

Without friends, money, or credit, Abdullah was in a weak position to bargain. To secure his accession he would offer half his power to the Straits Government and nearly half his revenue to Tan Kim Cheng. Having done this, he returned to Perak and is next heard of at his house at Bandar, near the mouth of the Perak river. As regards the Chinese, the basis of the agreement was that neither party should be excluded from Larut and that their claims should be settled by arbitration. This was Sir Andrew Clarke's decision—completely reversing his predecessor's policy—and Kim Cheng agreed with it and wrote in that sense to the Ghee Hins of Penang.[2]

Sir Andrew's decision to favour neither of the Chinese factions was an essential preliminary to any mediation between them. It implied, however, an equally open mind over the Perak Succession and the Mantri's claim to sovereignty in Larut. To consider the mining rights of the Ghee Hins, it was necessary to withdraw recognition of the Mantri's independent position, for the Mantri had denied that the Ghee Hins had any rights at all. But if the Mantri was not the ruler of Larut, save as the Sultan's deputy, it became all the more important to decide who the rightful Sultan was. And the objection to Ismail was that he and the Mantri supported each other. There was thus a logical case for reviewing Abdullah's claim even apart from his willingness to accept a measure of British control. For the reversal, moreover, of Ord's policy there was the further argument that it had failed. The Mantri and Speedy had not gained the complete victory which would have pacified Larut, nor would a more striking success have prevented the Ghee Hins from renewing the conflict at some more

[1] P.P., C. 1111, No. 39, encl. 12, 30 Dec. 1873.
[2] P.P., Pickering to Governor, 5 Jan. 1874.

favourable opportunity. Speaking afterwards of Ord's policy, Clarke said: 'Whether that policy was right or wrong, I do not now propose to consider. There may have been certain reasons which led to it.'[1] His condemnation could hardly have been more explicit. It was, moreover, justified. For Ord, while sacrificing the impartiality which might have allowed him to arbitrate, had lacked the force to make his partisan intervention a success.

Following his discussions with Read and Kim Cheng, Clarke's first move was to send Mr. W. A. Pickering in the S.S. *Johore* to interview the Ghee Hin leaders at Penang, 'as if acting on his own responsibility'.[2] Pickering was the only civil servant who spoke Chinese, a man who had great influence among the Chinese at Singapore. He spoke four dialects, having lived in China from 1862 to 1870, and had joined the Straits Civil Service as interpreter in 1871. His being sent to Penang was perhaps a first intimation that Anson's help was not required. Arriving on 3 January, Pickering presented his credentials to Anson, who drove him to the jail, the present abode of those (or some of those) he wished to see.

> On our way to the gaol, Colonel Anson handed me a letter which he had received from the Sin Nengs' [i.e. Ghee Hins'] party dated 11th December, begging the Government to interfere in the Larut troubles, and put an end to the great misery and loss of life.
>
> It was signed by Chin Ah Yam in the name of seventeen headmen; men who had given him full power to carry out whatever orders the Lieutenant-Governor might give him.[3]

Anson intended, no doubt, to show that his policy had succeeded and that the situation was well in hand. But Chin Ah Yam, when interviewed, told a different story:

> He told me that all his party had been anxiously waiting for the new Governor to take the matter up, and to make the settlement which they had in vain begged from the Lieutenant-Governor and the former Governor so many times. He said Colonel Anson had told him that, before anything could be done, the Sin Nengs must turn out of the country, and leave the Raja Mantri's party in possession. He also said that their three former petitions had never been listened to, that his people were ready to do anything and everything your Excellency might order, and that he would call a meeting of all the Chiefs that night, and bring them to me the next morning, [4th].

---

[1] Speech in Legislative Council, 15 Sept. 1874. P.P., p. 249.
[2] S.S. No. 14, 26 Jan. 1874.
[3] P.P., Pickering to Governor, 5 Jan. 1874.

Pickering gave Chin Ah Yam the letter he had brought from Kim Cheng, adding his own advice, and then went to see Ho Ghee Siew, whom he presumably had released to attend the meeting. The result was that twenty Ghee Hin headmen met that evening in the Kongsee House and spent all night in considering Kim Cheng's letter. In the morning a deputation led by Chin Ah Yam came to Pickering at the Police Office and agreed that their forces should surrender in seven days' time, stipulating only that Speedy should be restrained from attacking them.

The Sin Nengs say that they hate the Raja Mantri, and that the Muda is the rightful Lord, but that he is no better than the other, and they humbly beg and pray the British Government to take the country in hand. I told them that was neither my nor their business; I could only advise them to leave everything in your hands, whose only object was to deal fairly, and give them a chance to save themselves before it was too late. The headmen continued to say that neither Sin Nengs or Go Kwans were fighting for the sake of fighting; that, under good Government, both were men to make a country flourish, being all men of some trade or handicraft, and only fighting because all they possessed was being ruined by the rapacity of Malay Chiefs. They say that Speedy is a good man, and does not want to kill them; but that, if he were ordered to stay his hand and the Government take charge of the country till at least the disputes are arranged then everything would go all right, and all parties of Chinese would be delighted and thankful.[1]

Pickering on 4 January informed the Governor by telegram of the gist of an agreement which was not actually drawn up and signed until the 8th.

To have persuaded the Ghee Hins to lay down their arms was an important step. It was easier, however, than to induce their opponents to do the same. For the Ghee Hins, as they told Pickering, had 2,700 men in Larut 'but they say that they cannot hold out much longer, as they are starving and cooped up in a few places'. The Go Kwans or Hysans were in a stronger position and to that extent less amenable, but Pickering cajoled their Penang headmen into agreeing to a cease-fire. It seems, however, that their real leaders were in Larut. When, therefore, Major McNair and Captain Dunlop (the Singapore Chief of Police) came to join Pickering in his mission, their first task, on or about 9 January, was to meet Ah Kwee and the other Hysan head-men at the mouth of the Larut river and persuade them in turn to accept arbitration. The Hysans were initially hostile and might have

[1] P.P., Pickering to Governor, 5 Jan. 1874.

fired on the *Johore* had not four of their headmen been on board her as hostages.[1]

On receiving Pickering's telegram, Sir Andrew Clarke had decided that the next step was to summon all parties (Malay and Chinese) to a conference. For this meeting he chose the island of Pangkor for the place and 14 January for the opening date. It remained to contact all concerned. The Ghee Hins were easily found, their leaders being in Penang. The Hysans agreed more reluctantly to a meeting and did not consent at first to an armistice. The Mantri was more difficult to find and the task of fetching him was entrusted to Frank Swettenham. He was taken to Larut in H.M.S. *Avon* and made his way thirteen miles inland to Captain Speedy's stockade near Simpang. Commander J. C. Patterson accompanied him with three marines; an unhappy arrangement, as Swettenham detested Patterson.[2] Kulop Rhee, in command there, afterwards described how:

One evening I was in Captain Speedy's stockade. Captain Speedy was at Bukit Gantang. We were collecting rice. Nobody was on the look out. All of a sudden in the dusk I saw Mr. Swettenham crawling through the embrasure in front of one of the guns. Three Europeans stood outside with an English flag. We were all taken by surprise. A few seized their arms. Mr. Swettenham said, 'Where is Captain Speedy?' I said, 'He is not here. He is at Bukit Gantang.' Mr. Swettenham then asked who else was there. I told him that Mr. Speedy's brother was at the stockade at Padang Lalang. It went by the name of Kuboo Sija, because there was no fighting going on there. I then pulled away the cannon and Mr. Swettenham and his friends came inside. After some conversation I took them to the stockade at Padang Lalang.[3]

It would seem that the Mantri was with Speedy at Bukit Gantang, together with the Temenggong and Dato Sagor. He also had with him his lawyer, Mr. R. C. Woods.[4] The Mantri agreed to attend the conference at Pangkor, although it is doubtful whether Swettenham told

[1] Perak Enquiry Papers, II, Haji Hussein's statement, 25 Aug. 1876.

[2] Swettenham afterwards professed to have heard enough of Patterson's doings 'to have tried him by Court Martial ten times and hanged him ten times if once was not enough'. *Sir Frank Swettenham's Perak Journals 1874–76*, ed. C. D. Cowan, *JMBRAS*, vol. xxiv, part 4, Dec. 1951, p. 39.

[3] P.E.P. III, Kulop Rhee's statement, 29 June 1877. See also Swettenham, *Miscellaneous Papers*, p. 167; Swettenham, *Footprints in Malaya*, p. 32.

[4] Mr. Robert Carr Woods (1815–75) had reached Singapore via Bombay in 1844 and edited the *Straits Times* from 1845, being prominent among those who opposed Sir James Brooke. He qualified as a lawyer and practised in the Supreme Court, being called to the Bar (Gray's Inn) in 1873. He was Acting Puisne Judge when he died.

him (or even himself knew) its precise purpose. Swettenham also handed to the Mantri a letter to Ismail, which he undertook to forward. It was Clarke's policy to summon the various parties individually without telling them who else was to be there, or why. Sultan Ismail and Raja Yusof 'were too far away, and made no effort to attend'.[1] After returning to the *Avon*, Swettenham and Patterson then went up the Perak river in the *Fair Malacca*—until then towed by the *Avon*—and found Abdullah at his house. He was readily induced to attend, together with his neighbours the Laxamana and Shahbandar. All was ready now for Sir Andrew Clarke to intervene decisively.

Had the Governor already decided on his policy, virtually on the advice of the Triad? In this connexion, a significant document is that of 7 January in which McNair and Dunlop were given their instructions.[2] They were told that it would be premature to decide at that moment on the Perak succession, although also assured that Ismail and Abdullah were the only candidates and that 'the Raja Muda is at present unsupported by any of the principal Chiefs'. They were instructed to collect information about the amount of support upon which either candidate could rely. Then the letter continues:

It may be as well that you should privately sound the Raja Muda as to whether he would peacefully relinquish his claim on receiving a pension, and if so, what pension it is probable he would accept.

In the event of its appearing plain that the Bandahara (the *de facto* Sultan) is to be elected and confirmed, certain fixed incomes will be required to be guaranteed to the Laksamana and other high officers. . . etc.

The tendency of this letter is to anticipate Ismail's continuance in office. The writer was not, however, the Governor but the Colonial Secretary, and there is reason to suppose that Clarke and Birch thought differently on this question.

What the Governor was inclined to decide is apparent from the names of the officers he took with him when he sailed in the *Pluto* from Singapore on 11 January. It is still more evident from the list of those he significantly left behind. With him embarked Mr. Braddell, Mr. A. M. Skinner and his A.D.C., Lieutenant Brackenbury. Ahead of him had gone Major McNair and Captain Dunlop, who had enlisted the help of Frank Swettenham and Commander Patterson. Ahead of them, in turn, had gone Mr. Pickering. Left in Singapore

---

[1] Swettenham, *British Malaya*, p. 176.
[2] P.P., Birch to McNair and Dunlop, Singapore, 7 Jan. 1874.

were Birch and Irving. Left in Penang was Colonel Anson. To have taken Anson would have been consistent with the policy which Birch inclined to support, and Anson was the officer most closely concerned with Perak affairs. But how could the Governor decide against the Mantri's claim to independence with Anson—the man who had persuaded Ord to recognize it—beside him? How could he decide in favour of Abdullah with Anson there, who had sworn to use his influence against such a decision? Birch was also inclined to favour Ismail and Irving had been Ord's adviser on Perak affairs. Irving, it is true, regarded Abdullah as the legitimate claimant[1] but he doubted whether he were strong enough to succeed, Abdullah being an opium-smoker and 'a man of feeble constitution'. So Clarke's advisers then were Thomas Braddell, Allan Skinner, and John McNair; and McNair had been in touch with Abdullah already. Skinner was the author of a long memorandum on Perak affairs, completed on the day before the *Pluto* sailed. Pickering and Swettenham were needed mainly as interpreters, Dunlop as an expert in Chinese customs, and Brackenbury to be generally useful.

The *Pluto* reached the Dindings early on 13 January, to find H.M.S. *Avon* at anchor there, with the Hysan headmen on board. Patterson was not there, having gone with Swettenham up the Perak river in the Mantri's vessel *Fair Malacca*. At 11.0 the *Johore* arrived with McNair, Dunlop, and Pickering, together with two Ghee Hin headmen. They had just returned from the Larut river, having delivered rice to the Ghee Hins and received their promise to be at Pulo Pangkor on the 14th. Clarke had little faith, evidently, in Swettenham's mission to fetch Abdullah, for he now sent the *Johore* to the Perak river with letters to Abdullah and the Laxamana. On board this vessel, at Pickering's instigation, went Ching Ah Kwee and Ah Yam, leaders on opposite sides, who were thus brought together. Off the Perak river the *Johore* met the *Fair Malacca*, returning without Abdullah. So the *Johore* went on, reached Abdullah's house at 9.30 p.m. and was boarded by Abdullah and his retinue at 11.0 p.m. McNair and Dunlop were evidently at pains to persuade Abdullah to come, which he promised to do on the following day. They had been shown, on their arrival at Pangkor, Abdullah's letter of 30 December, and they could be sincere enough (in the light of its contents) in assuring him that it would be to his advantage to come. Come he did, on the 14th, but the *Johore* ran aground and it was not until the 15th that she

[1] See his report of 24 July 1872. P.P.

reached Pangkor again, bringing not only Abdullah but also a number of other chiefs including the Laxamana and Shabandar.

It may be that McNair and Dunlop used their opportunity to some purpose. Part of the 14th they spent in writing a memorandum in Abdullah's favour, and part (possibly) in telling him how to play his cards when the time came. The most significant paragraphs of their memorandum read as follows:

There can be no doubt that the Mantri, lowest in rank of the four principal officers of the Perak Government, has, owing to his long residence and intercourse with Europeans in Penang, and to the support he has always received from the British Government, assumed in Perak a position of independence which his office and rank do not justify. This position has been recently considerably strengthened by the action of the Government in the issue of the Proclamation of August last.

Perceiving all this, and believing him to be recognised by us, as the alone chief authority in Laroot, the most important part of Perak, the Goh Kwans, the most numerous faction of the contending Chinese, have supported him liberally in men and money, to carry out what we believe to be his ultimate object, viz., by keeping back the Raja Muda from the sovereignty of the country on the death of the aged Bandahara now temporarily installed, to proclaim himself the chief ruler in Perak. The Raja Muda is by Malay custom and by long usage in Perak, the legitimate heir to the throne. Up to the death of the late Sultan no question appears to have been raised, as far as we can ascertain, as to his right to succeed as heir apparent, and had it not been for the contrary influence exerted in the country by the Mantri, there can be no doubt that in due course he would have been installed with the general approbation of the people. The reasons assigned by the Mantri and those who have acted, with them, for this departure from the line of proper succession, seem to us to be frivolous.[1]

The Mantri's claim to independence in Larut they considered 'weak and doubtful'. Braddell noted afterwards that McNair's and Dunlop's report 'placed matters in a clearer light'. It did indeed. The mishap to the *Johore* might well have given the Mantri his opportunity, for he arrived at noon on the 14th before Abdullah had appeared. But he was given no chance to see the Governor on that day. Nothing happened, in fact, apart from the arrival of the *Luzon* with rice from Singapore. On the 15th, however, the *Johore* reappeared with Abdullah and the other chiefs on board. On that day, moreover (at 3.0 p.m.), the Chinese headmen from both sides came on board

---

[1] P.P., p. 77. Report dated on board the steamer *Johore*, 'Perak river, 14 Jan. 1874'.

the *Pluto* and reached a verbal agreement with each other in the Governor's presence, with Pickering as interpreter. They agreed, in fact, to accept British arbitration in Larut. It only remained to disarm their war boats, as a preliminary to a written agreement. As only three of the Ghee Hin boats had so far surrendered, Commander Patterson took the *Avon* (at his own suggestion) to look for the rest at Selinsing, with Skinner as Malay interpreter. Two more boats were found and removed. The *Johore*, meanwhile, under a sub-lieutenant, armed for the occasion with a naval gun, and flying the white ensign, took Dunlop, Pickering, and the Hysan headmen up the Larut river. There they found and removed two junks and five more boats. The *Avon* and *Johore* did not return to the Dindings until the morning of the 19th. Both Skinner and Dunlop must have been absent during the decisive negotiations, responsibility for which must rest therefore with Braddell and McNair.

If there is much of significance in the absence on the British side of people who might well have been there, there is even more of significance in the absence on the Malay side of people who certainly should have been there. Chief among these was Ismail, the Sultan *de facto*, who had been invited but who never came.[1] Second only in importance to him, however, was Raja Yusof. His absence is further emphasized (to the historian) by a tacit agreement to ignore his existence altogether. There were other absentees, but none of comparable importance, for Yusof (see p. 73 above) had the strongest claim by birth and was incidentally, as it came to be recognized, the ablest man available. Nor would it be true to say that those present were altogether representative, for the chiefs of the 'Kuala' (the lower reaches of the Perak river) were proportionately more in evidence than the chiefs of the 'Hilir' or upper reaches, partly perhaps because it was easier for them to attend.

It was on 16 January that the business of the conference began, with visits of ceremony paid to the Governor by the chiefs. These first interviews and the subsequent discussions seem all to have taken place on board the *Pluto*. It was the Chinese who collected on shore and it is nowhere stated that the Governor landed at all, although he may well have done so. On this first day Sir Andrew Clarke opened actual negotiations with the Mantri, who was with him alone from 3.30 p.m.,

---

[1] By his own account, Ismail received the invitation on 15 Jan., set out for Pangkor, but received news on the way that the conference was over and everything settled and so returned home again.

after the visits of ceremony had ended. The Mantri would have wished, no doubt, to have his lawyer with him but Clarke refused to hear Mr. Woods on the grounds that the other chiefs were without their legal advisers. At the same time, the Mantri was presumably coached by Woods and Speedy beforehand and this makes it the more surprising that he had no inkling, apparently, of what the Governor's attitude was likely to be. It seems that Clarke had so far kept his ideas to himself.

The Governor naturally began the interview by asking for an assurance that Ismail had duly received his invitation. On the Mantri asserting that he had (which was strictly true—Ismail had received it the day before), the Governor evidently felt entitled to regard the Mantri as the leader and representative of Ismail's party; as indeed he was. So he went on, after some further discussion, to ask the Mantri whether he would accept his (Clarke's) arbitration. The Mantri agreed to this but would at first give no direct reply to the next query: whether he was prepared to disarm the Hysans.

The Mantri fenced with this question, and said that if the Government would restore tranquillity by driving out the Ghee Hins, he was strong enough to deal with the Hye Sans himself; on this the Governor said—you quite misunderstand my views—I do not wish to favour either party, or to drive out either, but to do justice to all. It is by your policy, of attempting to play off one party against the other that you have lost your influence, caused difficulties, and prevented a settlement. The headmen of both parties have agreed to accept my arbitration; are you willing to disarm the Hye Sans?[1]

The Mantri, after some hesitation, assented. His hesitation was natural. He had been, until quite recently, in a strong position, with his forces led by a British officer, raised in India with governmental approval and ready to exterminate the starving Ghee Hins amidst the decorous applause of his European friends at Penang. His independence had been acknowledged, his opponents blockaded, his supporters supplied. Now he was confronted by a new Governor whose attitude was bewilderingly different. The next question came while he was still seeking a clue to the implications of the last:

It has been suggested to place a British Officer in Larut to assist and advise you. Do you agree to this?
The Mantri appeared at first to have some objections to this proposal, but at last agreed that a British Officer should be appointed.

[1] Braddell's report. P.P., pp. 160 et seq.

The Governor then explained, as regards the Perak succession, that it was a British responsibility to ensure that the proper heir should be chosen unless obviously unsuitable.

On this the Mantri professed his readiness to give his allegiance to the Sultan who might be preferred by the British Government, but asserted his claim to the territory of Larut . . . he claimed to hold it now independent of the Sultan.

On this it was pointed out to him that no Sultan had a right to give away territory in this way . . . [the Mantri cited the case of Johore as a precedent] . . . This, however, was declared to be quite inadmissible . . . the agreement made with the Sultan of Johore, by which a new sovereignty was created, was sanctioned by the Government on grounds not at all applicable to the case of Larut. During this discussion the Mantri, persisting in claiming sovereign rights in Larut, was asked if he wished to become Sultan of Perak, as had been suggested, but he repudiated such an intention.[1]

The interview ended and Clarke compared the impression made on him by Abdullah and by the Mantri. He described them afterwards as follows:

It was gratifying to me to find myself disappointed in the opinion I had formed of the Rajah Mudah who, to my surprise, I found a man of considerable intelligence and possessing perfect confidence that he should be able to maintain his position if he were once placed in Perak as its legitimate ruler.[2]

His previous opinion, derived no doubt from Irving and Skinner, is again emphasized in these words:

It may be here stated that the Raja Muda had been represented as a person of such debauched habits, and bad health, mental and bodily, as to be unfit to rule: but it was only necessary to be in his company for a few minutes to see that this was an erroneous opinion. The Raja Muda not only looked well in health, but was alert, and for a Malay Prince, more than ordinarily sharp and intelligent. . . . He was frank and ready in his answers to all questions; in this respect forming a very favourable contrast to the Mantri. The impression left by the Mantri's behaviour was not favourable. He fenced with the questions put to him, and inspired but little confidence in his truthfulness, sincerity, or courage.[3]

This contrast in impressions would have been more relevant had Clarke been trying to decide between Abdullah and the Mantri. In fact, however, he was to decide between Ismail and Abdullah: and of

---

[1] Braddell's report, ibid.
[2] S.S. No. 14, 26 Jan. 1874.   [3] Braddell's report, ibid.

Ismail he could have no impression at all, for Ismail was not there. Apart, however, from these personal impressions which Clarke could assess for himself, he had also to compare certain legal claims and in this comparison rely upon others. It was primarily a question as to who was the rightful Sultan; essentially a question for the expert. So Clarke turned that evening to Haji Mahomed Syed, who undertook to produce a genealogy of the Perak royal house showing what the proper succession was. He produced a memorandum in Malay which Frank Swettenham translated into English. It was submitted to the Governor next day (the 17th), countersigned by J. F. A. McNair as a testimony to the truth of its text, vouched for by Swettenham as to the accuracy of the translation.

This memorandum is remarkable chiefly in that it hardly mentions Raja Yusof. It is not merely that his claim was set aside; it is not even mentioned. His name is misspelt 'Raja Oossoo' and he is otherwise quietly ignored. So Clarke had no difficulty in deciding that Abdullah had a better claim than Ismail; which, in one sense, he had. It was as easy for him to decide that the Mantri, because of his wealth and his position at Penang, and 'through the want of proper information on our part', had been allowed to assume an authority in Larut to which he had no right. It has been suggested[1] that Clarke, at this stage, was unaware that the Mantri's independence had been recognized by Sir Harry Ord; and it is certainly true that copies of Ord's letters to the Mantri (of 3 and 5 September 1873) were sent to the Colonial Secretary on 23 January by Anson. But, even supposing that there were no copies of these already in the Secretariat files, Ord had explained his recognition of the Mantri to the Legislative Council on 9 September; to a Council, that is to say, of which both Braddell and McNair were members. To have denied this vital information to Clarke would have been culpable negligence in either of these officers, and such a neglect (or deliberate suppression of facts) as we can hardly attribute to them without proof. It would be fairer to assume that Clarke knew all about Ord's policy and fully intended to reverse it.

Briefed thus by his advisers, Clarke held his general conference with the Malay chiefs on the afternoon of Saturday, 17 January. Abdullah arrived at 1.0 p.m. with the Bandahara and other chiefs. From Braddell's account of the discussion which followed, it is obvious that the Governor's main decision was already made. He was merely considering its implications. With Abdullah as Sultan, who would be the new

[1] Winstedt and Wilkinson, op. cit., p. 98.

Raja Muda? What position would Abdullah accord to the Mantri? And to Ismail? Braddell reports Abdullah as denying that he wished to displace the Mantri provided he could be brought more under control. He then went on to assert:

that he should like to have a British officer, not only at Larut, but also in Perak, at his own place, and he would gladly pay the expense; and that, if installed, he would agree to the Bandahara Ismail having the title of ex-Sultan, with a small territory to govern, and a proper income; that he was not unfriendly to Ismail, as his father had made him Bandahara. . . .[1]

Negotiations had reached this point before the Mantri arrived and it was with some difficulty that he was made to come at all. To quote Haji Mohamed Syed's narrative:

We were kept waiting for the Mantri. Mr. Swettenham and Mr. Pickering were sent to call him, but he refused to come. Mr. Pickering was then sent a second time with some twenty soldiers, and returned with the Mantri, Dato Sagor, Captain Speedy, and Temenggong. When they came on board, Raja Abdullah, the Bendahara, and Raja Ngha were seated on chairs. All the other Chiefs were seated on the deck. The Mantri wanted to be given a chair also. Captain Speedy asked that he might be given one. The governor was very angry and told him to sit down at once. Major McNair took him by the waist and forced him to sit down. The Mantri said, 'Very good. I will submit.'[2]

His fall from power could hardly have been more vividly illustrated. Braddell's report touches more lightly on the same incident:

On coming on deck, and seeing all the other great officers sitting on the deck, according to Malay custom, the Mantri seemed disinclined to go near them; but on the Tumongong, who is his superior in rank, and his friend, taking his place, the Mantri followed his example.[3]

After the Mantri's arrival (under escort) Sir Andrew ascertained from the chiefs that enough were present for a lawful election, that precedent existed for the title of ex-Sultan and that all those present would agree to Abdullah's coronation. The Mantri's consent was admittedly grudging—'If the people like it I have no place, I of course follow them'—nevertheless, it was given. There was no dissentient. It remained only to draw up the agreement in writing, for which purpose representatives were chosen: Abdullah, the Bandahara, the Laxamana, Mantri, Shahbandar, and Temenggong. The Mantri was given a final opportunity to voice his objections but merely said: 'As

---

[1] Braddell's report. P.P., pp. 160 et seq.
[2] P.E.P. III, Haji Mohamed Syed's statement, 16 Dec. 1876.
[3] Braddell's report, ibid.

to the succession I have nothing further to say.' And so the conference ended. The Mantri remained for a further interview with the Governor but perhaps words failed him, for 'nothing of importance was done'.

Sunday was observed so that it was on the following morning, the 19th, that the Pangkor Engagement, was drawn up—the day on which the *Avon* and *Johore* returned from Larut. The various articles of the Engagement were agreed that afternoon without much discussion and Tuesday, the 20th, fixed for the signing and sealing of the document; as also of the agreement between the Chinese. It was the Chinese headmen who concluded their agreement first, at 11.30; and the Malay chiefs came on board again at 3.0. The Engagement (with a last-minute amendment to Article XI, at Abdullah's request) was signed with due formality and the new Sultan saluted with eleven guns.[1] The coronation was fixed for a month hence, at Bandar on the Perak river, the Governor to be present. A letter was written to Ismail, informing him that he had been deposed and that he should surrender the regalia, without which the coronation could not take place. Dunlop, Swettenham, and Pickering were appointed commissioners to settle the mining dispute and release all prisoners. Speedy was asked to accept office, provisionally, as Assistant Resident, to advise his former employer, the Mantri. He was directed (after he had accepted the appointment) to disband his sepoys and re-enlist them as the Resident's Guard.

The Commissioners left for Larut with the *Johore* and *Luzon*, and the *Pluto* sailed for the Perak river, reaching Bandar on the following day, where (after salutes) the new Sultan was received by his people 'apparently with great affection'. The *Pluto* then returned to Singapore, where the Governor landed on 23 January after an absence of eleven days.

[1] A photograph exists which has been supposed to represent the Europeans present at the signing of the Pangkor Engagement. It was taken ashore, presumably at the police station, and represents a group of nine men (standing) and one—evidently the Governor—seated. The two most easily identified are Speedy and Swettenham. The men present at Pangkor on this occasion were Sir Andrew Clarke, Braddell, McNair, Dunlop, Skinner, Swettenham, Brackenbury, and Speedy, with Commander Patterson on the 20th but not during the previous negotiations. If the Governor was ashore on the 18th (the most probable date, if indeed he landed at all) his possible companions would have been Braddell, McNair, Swettenham, Brackenbury, and Speedy. The number could have been made up from the ship's company of the *Pluto* but the names of those known to be there do not fit in with any previous attempt at identification. It is practically certain that the photograph was taken in Sept. 1875 and that the Governor shown is Jervois.

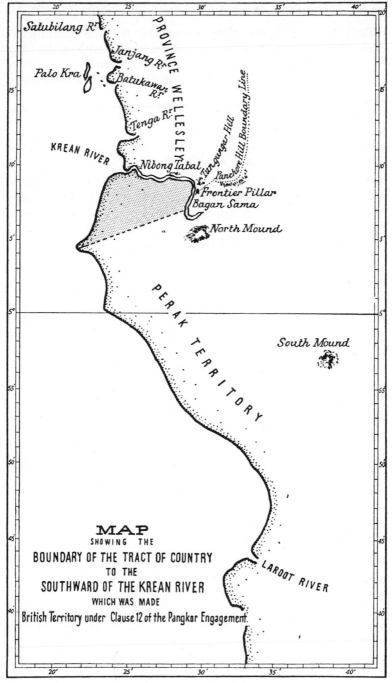

Map 3. The Perak Boundary

The terms of the Pangkor Engagement are set forth in Appendix A. Their effect was to make Abdullah Sultan, reduce Ismail to the status of ex-Sultan, retain the Mantri as ruler (but not independent ruler) of Larut, and subject both Abdullah and the Mantri to British advice. Article VI provided specifically:

That the Sultan receive and provide a suitable residence for a British officer to be called Resident, who shall be accredited to his Court, and whose advice must be asked and acted upon on all questions other than those touching Malay religion and custom.

Article VII gave the Mantri an Assistant Resident as adviser, with similar powers but subordinate to the Resident. Article VIII empowered the Government of the Straits Settlements to determine the cost of the Residents and their staffs, which would be a first charge on the revenues of Perak; and Article X provided:

That the collection and control of all revenues, and the general administration of the country, be regulated under the advice of these Residents.

Other articles concerned the Civil List, the mines dispute, the expenses of intervention (all debited to the Mantri) and the adjustment of the Province Wellesley and Dindings boundaries in favour of the Straits Settlements.

Although subsequent references to the 'Treaty of Pangkor' have been frequent, Sir Andrew Clarke himself was careful to explain that it was *not* a treaty but 'a voluntary arrangement on the part of the Chiefs' involving no obligation on the British side from which government could not honourably withdraw.[1] This was not strictly true of the frontier adjustments, which might seem very proper subjects for the text of a treaty. As regards the more important provisions, however (and more especially those by which Abdullah became Sultan), it could be argued that they recorded the decisions of Malay chiefs made in the presence of the Governor as mediator. This argument was afterwards used by Birch and Swettenham in discussion with Ismail.

we took the greatest care to explain *several times* that the Governor had never chosen a Sultan of Perak, but that having summoned the chiefs to a conference, and they having unanimously selected Abdullah to be Sultan, the Governor had acknowledged him as Sultan.[2]

This is, of course, a fiction, but one which the text of the agreement could be used to sustain.

---

[1] Sir Andrew Clarke's speech to the Legislative Council, 15 Sept. 1874. P.P., p. 249.   [2] *Sir Frank Swettenham's Perak Journals*, p. 62.

The Engagement was drawn up in English but translated into Malay by Frank Swettenham and Munshi Mahomed Said (or Syed). 'Both English and Malay Versions were then signed and sealed by the parties.'[1] The original English version has survived in the Public Record Office; the Malay version has not. Mr. M. A. Mallal, however, who has thoroughly investigated the whole incident,[2] has photographed and had translated a Malay version of the Engagement in the possession of Raja Rayman of Kuala Kangsar and said to be a true copy, written by Sultan Idris himself. This Malay version differs from the English in one vital respect, as the following comparison shows:

ENGLISH VERSION	MALAY VERSION (*translated*)
VI. *Sixth.*—That the Sultan receive and provide a suitable residence for a British Officer to be called Resident, who shall be accredited to his Court, and whose advice must be asked and acted upon on all questions other than those touching Malay Religion and Custom.	*Item* 6—The Sultan should accept and build a suitable residential house for one officer who is under the British Government whose title shall be British Resident of Perak State and who is to be trusted by the British Government. The Sultan of Perak shall have to consult with him on all matters and the working of Perak State except that he cannot interfere with Muslim religious affairs and Malay custom.
X. *Tenth.*—That the collection and control of all Revenues and the general administration of the Country be regulated under the advice of these Residents.	*Item* 10—The Administration, collection of all revenues as well as the order governing rules and regulations of the State should be with the consultation and advice of the British Resident.

Reading this, a Malayan patriot might hastily conclude that Swettenham had deliberately deceived the Malay signatories by omitting from the Malay version of Article VI the significant words 'and acted upon'. It was not quite as simple as that. To begin with, Article X (which was translated more successfully) comprises much of the sense of Article VI. Apart from that, however, the translation of diplomatic and legal terms into Malay is not a particularly easy task. To illustrate this, the reader should examine a third version of Articles VI and X.

---

[1] Swettenham, *Footprints in Malaya*, p. 33.

[2] 'J. W. W. Birch: Causes of his Assassination', unpublished dissertation by M. A. Mallal, 1952, in University of Malaya Library. See p. 43.

This results from asking a modern Malay scholar to translate the official English text into Malay; his Malay text being then put into English by a different and equally competent scholar who had not seen the original. This third version reads as follows:

ARTICLE VI

The Sultan shall accept a British official, to be known by the title of Resident, and shall have a suitable residence constructed for him. This official shall be installed in his office by letters of appointment, in the Sultan's palace. His advice shall be sought and acted upon in all matters except matters concerning Malay religion and custom.

ARTICLE X

The collection and supervision of revenue, and the general administration of the country, shall be organized according to the Resident's advice.

It will be seen from this alternative rendering that the English admits of more than one version in the Malay. The phrase 'accredited to his court' is thus so impossible to translate that the efforts to find a Malay equivalent are likely to differ from each other. And while it is manifest that the words 'and acted upon' could and should have been translated, and that even Article X might have been more accurately rendered, the final effect is more one of confusion than of deceit. For the significant exception as regards Malay custom could have been taken, on the Malay side, to cover almost everything, revenue included. The 'Engagement' was not, let us admit, a masterpiece of lucidity, even in English.

In view of the inherent difficulty of putting precise and legal terms into Malay, it would be wrong to lay too much stress on any failure there may have been in the literal translation of the words used. The culprit, if there was one, was perhaps Haji Mohamed Syed, who might easily have softened the Malay version so as to avoid giving offence to Abdullah. But the real flaw in these negotiations was more fundamental than that, and lay in the speed at which the business was done. Even had Sir Andrew Clarke gone about the affair with what seemed to him maddening deliberation, the Malays would have been dazed by the hectic whirl of events. In fact, however, he rather prided himself on the brisk way in which matters were handled. This is apparent from the letter he wrote to his patron, Childers:

[From Singapore]

I have nominated Captain Speedy Acting Resident of Larut. In doing this I went, no doubt, beyond my instructions, but all I had done would have come to nothing had I not left someone in the country to see the engagement carried out and a proper police organised. I feel I have done a good stroke; in short, all the people here say that nothing has been done so complete and equal to it since Raffles's time. . . .

The Colonial Office may say that I might have submitted my scheme to them for their approval before putting it into force, but the only chance of success I had was to do what I did rapidly, so that not a soul knew my plans until I had almost pulled them through. The Chinese were moving and had no idea who was moving them. I had got hold of the heads of both parties, and neither knew that I knew the other.

I sent a steamer for the Malay chiefs telling them to come to see me at the Dindings, giving them no time to hesitate, nor telling them what I wanted them for, nor affording them time to send for their lawyers—nearly all Malay chiefs have Penang or Singapore lawyers retained by them. I was assured I could not get them together under six weeks or two months. I collected them in a week, and they were without their lawyers. One alone, the Mantri of Larut, had one; but as none of the others had, I would not assent to his putting in an appearance.[1]

Clarke's achievement was due, in his own opinion, to secrecy and speed. He had rushed the Malay chiefs into an agreement upon which he had decided beforehand.[2] Nor had he any illusions about what he had done and why. As he wrote afterwards in 1875:

I believe in every way I was right in putting up Abdulla. Had I taken the other man, I could not have secured the peace of the coast, or the lower parts of the rivers, my first object, as Abdulla and his party are strong there, while Ismail and his followers are high up the river where we have no trade, and where we need not go for years. . . . No doubt Abdulla is a weak, vain fool in some things, but he was ten times better than old Ismail.[3]

His was the decision, on the advice of Braddell and McNair, and the Malay chiefs were hustled (as Malays can usually be hustled) into apparent agreement. The first to perceive the unreality of this agreement was, naturally, Colonel Anson, the man whose opinion had not been asked.

There can be little doubt that these chiefs did not fully realise what they were asked to agree to; or if they did, had no intention of acting up to it. One of them, with whom I was well acquainted,[4] and whom I had always

---

[1] *Life of General Sir Andrew Clarke*, R. H. Vetch, p. 154.
[2] The same could not be said of the Chinese. He rather underestimates their finesse in supposing them to be puppets. It is at least arguable that the Triad was the moving force and Clarke the puppet.
[3] Vetch, op. cit., p. 189.
[4] Obviously the Mantri.

found very willing to comply with any request I made to him, came to me a few days after the affair at Pankor, and said he was so confused and upset at that meeting, that he did not rightly know what the Governor wanted him to do.[1]

Anson adds, on a later page of his memoirs:

Sir Andrew Clarke seemed to think that in his short interview with Abdullah at Pankor, on the 20th Jan., 1874, he had sounded his character better than I had in my seven years previous knowledge of him. Of course, on the occasion of the engagement at Pankor, when the chiefs were all on board the Government steamer, with a man-of-war close by, they appeared to agree to everything that was proposed to them.[2]

Elsewhere he remarks 'Malays cannot be dealt with hurriedly. One must obtain their confidence. . . .' This is true, and while we may not be impressed by the Mantri's bewilderment (which may well have been assumed for Anson's benefit) we can readily believe that others present at Pangkor were genuinely muddled. As Sir Harry Ord remarked long after the event:

It was natural that Sir A. Clarke, seeing the readiness with which his terms were agreed to by the natives, should have taken it for granted that they understood what was required of them, and were really prepared to accept our assistance in governing their country according to our views. But a more intimate acquaintance with Malay character would have prevented this misconception. The Malay is essentially slow to receive new impressions, and it is not possible that these people could have realised at once what was expected of them.[3]

It was clearly one of those conferences which different parties leave with a different idea of what has been decided and some with no idea at all. Such things have happened even more recently than 1874.

To be fair to Sir Andrew, however, he met with little criticism in Singapore, even from those who had the longest experience in the East. He landed amid a chorus of congratulation and, heartened by this applause, sat down to report progress to the Secretary of State. He did so, first of all, in a telegram dated 23 January.[4] This was followed by a long dispatch sent on the 26th,[5] with a full account of all that had happened and a further dispatch of the same date[6] enclosing a copy of the Pangkor Engagement. In the first of these he referred carefully to the instructions he had received and remarked that both

[1] Anson, op. cit., p. 322.   [2] Anson, op. cit., p. 355.
[3] P.P., Ord to Secretary of State, 3 Jan. 1876.
[4] Text given in S.S. No. 23 of 28 Jan. 1876.
[5] S.S. No. 14, 26 Jan. 1874.   [6] S.S. No. 15, 26 Jan. 1874.

the newly elected Sultan and the Mantri 'had actually foreseen the course pointed out by your Lordship's despatch and had asked me to appoint British Residents to their States'. Odd as this coincidence may have been, Clarke had still to explain why he had chosen to act when he had been told merely to inquire. He explained in some detail, adding the assurance that the Residents would be paid from Perak revenues and ending with the frank admission:

I am perfectly aware . . . that I have acted beyond my instructions and that nothing but very urgent circumstances would justify in the eyes of H.M. Government the steps I have taken, but I have confidence that your Lordship will feel that the circumstances at the time, the utter stoppage of all trade, the daily loss of life by the piratical attacks on even peaceful traders and by the fighting of the factions themselves, and the imminent peril of the disturbances spreading to the Chinese in our own Settlements justified me in assuming the responsibility I have taken.

In the second dispatch he had to justify both the decision to fill the post created at Larut and his choice of Speedy as the first Assistant Resident to hold the office.

The difficulty to be overcome was the selection of a person to whom so grave a responsibility could be entrusted. For it was necessary that he should enjoy the confidence of this Government, of the Chiefs, of the Malay Government and of the Headmen of both rival Chinese factions.

Captain Speedy essentially fulfils all these conditions. During his tenure of office in Penang he had great opportunity of making himself acquainted with the character both of the Chinese and of the Malays, and although his services have recently been enlisted by the Mantri of Laroot against the See Kwans, he has nevertheless in no way forfeited the ascendancy which he formerly exercised amongst them. . . .

I would suggest that this officer should receive an annual stipend of two thousand pounds a year, an amount that will be a first charge on the Revenues of Perak as arranged in the Agreement.[1]

How were these dispatches received? They reached the Colonial Office on 2 March, the Government having fallen on 17 February. They were opened, therefore, not by Lord Kimberley, but by his successor, Henry Howard Molyneux Herbert, fourth Earl of Carnarvon. This statesman, dignified representative of an extremely wealthy family, was in the happy position of being able either to claim the credit for Clarke's success or else to disown the consequences of any failure due to Lord Kimberley's inept direction. He had merely to decide whether success or failure were the more likely to result. He

[1] S.S. No. 15, 26 Jan. 1874.

may still have been pondering this question when there came an enthusiastic letter from the Straits Settlements Association, signed by Mr. W. Napier himself.

They consider that the negotiations of Sir Andrew Clarke with the Authorities of Perak, so long a prey to anarchical confusion, constitute the most important step that has for many years been taken by the British Government in the Straits of Malacca, to introduce order and security for life and property into the native States of the Peninsula. Your Lordship is fully aware that, without these indispensable guarantees the important resources of that extensive region cannot be developed; and they therefore confidently appeal to your Lordship for a confirmatory approval of Sir A. Clarke's proceedings in the establishment of new relations with the State of Perak, as not only valuable in themselves but as involving principles capable of a wide and beneficial extension in the neighbouring territories.[1]

This appeal was dated 6 March and presumably received the same day. Whether as a result of this encouragement or not, Lord Carnarvon replied (on the same date again) to Sir Andrew Clarke and without censure of his temerity. At the same time, his reply was as non-committal as can well be imagined.

As far as your explanations enable me to judge, I am disposed to hope that, without unduly compromising Her Majesty's Government in the internal affairs of these States, your proceedings may have the effect of allaying disorders and promoting peaceful trade.

With an official approval expressed in these guarded terms Sir Andrew had to be content. He was to have praise enough from private persons and a letter to *The Times* of 11 March expressed the thoughts of many in predicting of the Governor that, 'He will before long find it necessary to turn his attention to the affairs of Salangore, Sungei-ujong and Rambau, which are in a very unsatisfactory state.' In point of fact, this prediction came after the event and corresponded so closely with what Sir Andrew Clarke had already done that it is difficult to resist the conclusion that the writer, who signed himself 'Malacca', knew something in advance of what the Governor intended. It is clear that, had Sir Andrew faltered at this time, there were people and there were interests ready to urge him on.

[1] P.P., Napier to Lord Carnarvon, 6 Mar. 1874.

CHAPTER VI

SIR ANDREW CLARKE landed in Singapore, returning from Perak, on 23 January. Had he intended all along to follow up his Perak mission with a similar visitation to Selangor, events certainly played into his hands. To the stories of piracy received in November there were now added reports of the crimes committed since. On 1 January, the very day on which the *Pluto* sailed from Singapore to the Dindings, pirates had attacked—of all things —the lighthouse at Cape Rachado. As an operation this raid was not a brilliant success, the four thieves being fairly chased off by the irate lighthouse-keeper (Mr. G. Lucas) with a carbine. Mr. W. D. Bayliss of the Marine Department was sent from Malacca to investigate. He reinforced the lighthouse with two policemen and four rifles, returning to Malacca on the 16th. It was believed that the pirate boat belonged to Raja Mahmood of Langat, Raja Bote of Lukut, or Tunku Allang. Captain Shaw reported this to the Colonial Secretary on 17 January and then reported again on the 22nd that the boat hired to relieve the men on the *Torch* light-vessel had returned for fear of the pirates. As a tale of bloodshed this might seem to fall short of the sensational, but it came aptly to hand. It almost coincided with Sir Andrew Clarke's return from Perak and that almost coincided with the arrival at Singapore of Vice-Admiral Shadwell and his squadron. He came into harbour on the 22nd from Bangkok, with H.M. ships *Iron Duke*, *Frolic*, *Midge*, and *Salamis*, finding *Thalia* there at anchor in the roads. It was an unusual concentration of naval strength and Sir Andrew decided to take full advantage of this temporary situation, laying stress on the threat to the safety of the North Sands and Cape Rachado Light.

It is unnecessary to trace the various acts of piracy which had lately been committed off the coast of Salangore. A number of prisoners had been arrested at Malacca and recognised as having been parties engaged in an atrocious case of piracy at the mouth of the Jugra River. It was at first determined to have these prisoners tried for their offence at Malacca; but, when the Governor had decided on taking up the case of Salangore, it was arranged, as part of the plan of operations, that these prisoners should, on the requisition of the authorities of Salangore, be given up for trial at the scene of their crime.

It happened that, when this last piracy was under enquiry, the Rachado Light House was attacked by men supposed to be from the same River Jugra. The Admiral in command of the China Station was expected with a large force. The Governor determined therefore, while informing the Admiral of these piracies, and thus securing the co-operation of the fleet, to undertake to deal with the Government of Salangore on land, and thus to combine the action; in the hope, not merely of being able to check actual present piracy, but to be enabled to exercise a strong influence on the Sultan, his family and dependants up the Langat River, where they lived secure, as they thought, from active interference on the part of our Government.[1]

It is clear, from this and from other documents, that Clarke intended to make these piracies the occasion for establishing British influence over Selangor. His plans were fully discussed, no doubt, with the Admiral on and after 23 January. As a result of these discussions, Sir Andrew wrote to the Admiral on 1 February, making an official request for his help. In this letter the Governor mentioned the former reputation of the Selangor chiefs for encouraging piracy, and then continued:

It is a matter of regret to notice that these *bona fide* acts of piracy by Malays (which must be looked upon as very distinct from the lawless attacks by Chinese, which have been lately put down in the more northern waters of the Peninsula) are again becoming frequent, and as they are supported now by the sons of the Sultan and one Rajah Laut, it appears to have created a great deal of alarm, and are completely paralyzing the trade of Malacca. . . .

Your Excellency will consequently perceive that these attacks have at last reached a point when they are threatening the peaceful navigation of the Straits, the great highway between Europe and China.

I am therefore most anxious to take advantage of your Excellency's presence with an unusually large force, and endeavour by a vigorous effort to finally suppress these piratical expeditions from Salangore.

It is not entirely clear what a *bona fide* act of piracy may be taken to be, but the point of the contrast made between Perak and Selangor would seem to be that the Chinese piracies were exceptional and resulted from civil war whereas the Malays were revealing afresh their innate and normal character. Accepting the hearsay evidence against the Sultan's sons, Sir Andrew followed existing policy by planning a move designed primarily to strengthen the position of Tunku dia

[1] P.P., Encl. 3 in No. 53. Continuation of Report on the Proceedings of Government relating to the Native States in the Malay Peninsula, p. 187.

Oodin. His idea was to frighten the Sultan by a display of force, lending such naval assistance to the Viceroy as would enable him to destroy the stockades on the Jugra river and arrest the suspected chiefs—his brother-in-law (Raja Yacoob or Tunku Allang) included. The captured pirates would be handed over to Tunku dia Oodin for trial, partly to emphasize his authority and partly, perhaps, to secure their conviction upon evidence which a British court might have refused to accept. Apparently to gain the effect of surprise it was arranged that Shadwell should take his squadron up to Penang and then suddenly return, meeting the Governor, in the *Pluto*, on the evening of 6 February. The rendezvous was to be off the one-fathom bank on the North Sands. To the same rendezvous would proceed the *Rinaldo*, after fetching the pirates from Malacca, and the chartered vessel *Luzon*, after fetching Tunku dia Oodin from where Davidson knew he could be found (presumably at Klang). With Sir Andrew in the *Pluto*, ostensibly bound for Malacca, went Braddell, McNair, and the A.D.C., Brackenbury. With the *Pluto* went the colonial steam-launch *Mata Mata*, for use in the rivers. All took place as planned and, after a short conference, H.M. ships *Thalia*, *Rinaldo*, and *Avon* took up positions to blockade the Jugra river. H.M. ships *Salamis*, *Midge*, and *Frolic* went with the flagship *Iron Duke* to the Klang river. The Admiral then shifted his flag to the *Salamis* and, on the 7th, entered the river in the *Pluto*'s wake, with the *Midge* and *Frolic* astern. The *Salamis* presently grounded but the other two warships ascended the Langat river on the 8th to a point not far distant from the junction of the Langat and Jugra rivers.[1] There stood the stockaded town of Langat, where the Sultan lived. What followed is best told in the words of Sir Andrew himself:[2]

I dropped the men-of-war a little down the river and out of sight of the forts of Langat, and I then steamed up and laid the *Pluto* close along-side the principal fort, and went with all my party to breakfast on deck, where we could look up the muzzles of some big guns which were within a few feet of us. The fort itself, both inside and outside, was covered with some hundreds of very villainous-looking Malays armed to the teeth.

After breakfast I sent a letter to the Sultan telling him what I had come about, and asking him to come off and see me. Up to this, not a soul had come near us. I sent the letter by Major McNair, my Surveyor-General, and he was received respectfully by the chiefs but their followers looked alarmed and savage. He was taken to the palace and saw the Sultan, who

[1] There was about 4 fathoms for most of the way.
[2] In a letter to the Rt. Hon. H. C. E. Childers, 11 Feb. 1874.

said he had never left his country and could not break through etiquette and come on board to me. After some three hours' waiting, he said he would come down and look at me and the steamer from the shore. This he did, but someone telling him the day was unlucky, he quickly disappeared.

Braddell, my Attorney-General, then landed alone, smoking a cigar, as if for a stroll, lounged through the bazaar and town, passed the sentries, and stepped quietly into the Sultan's palace. Braddell speaks Malay better than a Malay, and knows their customs. It ended in his getting at the Sultan who at last consented to come on board, provided the steamer was attached to the shore by ropes, and that he might walk on board over a temporary jetty which was improvised on the spot, and on board he came with several hundred fellows. He is a jolly, good-natured opium-eater, but looked on piracy, as he said, as a young man's affair, and did not bother himself about it.

This went off well enough, and the Admiral and I then landed and went to the palace. After the complimentary interview in public I told him I wanted to see him alone with only a few of his great men. Of course to this there was much objection, but I stuck to the point, and at last he assented. I was taken with the Admiral, the Attorney-General, Surveyor-General and Aide-de-Camp into a small place where the Sultan was with his three sons and some eight or ten chiefs.

I opened on the subject of my mission, told him how much better for him, his family and country it would be if he would support his son-in-law, the Viceroy, against the pirates, and that I wanted to settle matters peacefully, without asking the Admiral to step in, who had the power to sweep him and all the pirates off the face of the country. After a couple of days, passed in negotiations, he assented to everything, swore to keep his treaty engagements, issued an order to try all offenders, and engaged to burn and destroy his strongholds. . . .

I fear that the Colonial Office will not easily be made to think that I have done well, but I know I have, and time will show it.[1]

Sir Andrew's difficulties with the Colonial Office would not have been lessened had anyone there known of the threats he had been using to the Sultan. In the light of the previous negotiations at Pangkor, the latter's reluctance to board the *Pluto* may have been more than a matter of etiquette. Abdul Samad had made a good impression, on the whole, and was thought quite capable of ruling Selangor if only he would take the trouble. Braddell described him afterwards as 'a rather careless heathen philosopher', too indolent to control his sons but mindful enough of his own interests to have saved up tin to the value (as was said) of $100,000.[2] Brackenbury, expecting to see

---

[1] Vetch, op. cit., p. 157.
[2] *Minutes of Proceedings* enclosed in dispatch 44 of 24 Feb. 1874, Clarke to the Secretary of State.

a confirmed opium addict, had to admit that the Sultan showed no sign of it.

On the contrary, he seems very sharp and intelligent enough, only showing a certain weakness of character by an indecisive manner of walking up and down when he is required to make up his mind and fidgetting with his head-dress which he constantly takes off and puts on again. In appearance he is a man of some fifty years, with a quantity of iron-grey hair and plaintive brown eyes, with which he gazes at one appealingly when any decisive action is required of him.[1]

What actually took place at this meeting on the 9th? Clarke spoke to the Sultan of the disorders and piracy prevalent in Selangor. During the more private interview, at which the Sultan's sons were present, Raja Yacoob said that Tunku dia Oodin was the cause of the disturbances. Clarke replied by asking whether the Tunku was not the Viceroy? This was at first denied but afterwards admitted, and the Governor then asked the Sultan whether Tunku dia Oodin had done anything to forfeit his confidence.

To this the Sultan said that the Tunku had not for two years past brought his wife, the Sultan's daughter, to see him; but that, excepting this, he had no complaint and was very well disposed to the Tunku. . . .[2]

Having gained his first point, Sir Andrew sent for Tunku dia Oodin (whom he had not so far seen) and was present at the latter's reconciliation with the Sultan. He held a discussion afterwards with the Tunku, during which he gained a clearer idea of the Viceroy's general position in Selangor. Clarke decided, as a result of these proceedings, to pursue the established policy of supporting the Viceroy. He was encouraged in this decision by the behaviour of Raja Yacoob, Tunku dia Oodin's chief opponent:

Yacoob left an unfavourable impression on everyone, as the type of a lawless cruel Chief, who would exercise power ruthlessly. He was vehemently suspected of being the leader of a gang of pirates established at his stockade at the mouth of the Jugra River. . . .

Rajah Moosa, the eldest son, and the only son by a mother of princely blood, left a better impression. He had just arrived from Perak; and although, at first, he had rather a wild appearance, he soon toned down, and was very earnest to be thought well of.[3]

As the initial hostility of the chief had been due to the belief that

---

[1] Ibid.   [2] Ibid.   [3] Ibid.

the Governor meant to make Tunku dia Oodin Sultan, the arrival of Raja Musa (and from Perak, where another succession problem had been so recently decided) was no coincidence. Nor is it strange that Musa was eager to make a good impression. He averted, in fact, any danger of his claim being set aside and sought to clinch matters by accepting an invitation to stay in Singapore.

Having thus decided to support the Viceroy, but without prejudice to Musa's right of succession, it remained only to demonstrate as publicly as possible that Tunku dia Oodin was to be regarded as the effective ruler of Selangor, supported both by the Sultan and the Governor in any action he might take against pirates or chiefs found to be in league with them. No better occasion could have been found than the trial of the pirates, the arrangements for which were made at a meeting which began at 1.0 p.m. on the 10th. 'It was necessary to fix such a late hour owing to the habits of the palace, where the inmates sit up very late at night and sleep all the morning.' The result of this interview was to fix the trial for the 12th. The Sultan had already decided (on the 9th) to appoint Tunku dia Oodin as one of the commissioners, so wording the decision as to make him appear a participant in a British trial. But Clarke insisted, on the 10th, that it should be a Malay court, upholding the Sultan's justice as Sovereign. Two British commissioners would attend but merely as observers. Enlightened on this point, the Sultan appointed Tunku dia Oodin as Wakil, with Dato Aru and Punghulu Dagang (two of his own advisers) and a Chinese called See Kang. These, with the witnesses for the prosecution, were to be at the stockade, at the mouth of the Jugra river, on 12 February. The Governor gave McNair and Davidson their commission to see justice done but to 'avoid taking an active part in the trial itself'.

On the 11th Sir Andrew completed his arrangements by sending the Sultan the following letter:

It is with much regret that I have to inform my friend that since my letter of this morning was sent to my friend, it has been brought to my notice that the friends of the persons murdered in the piracy case near the Jugra River have sent a letter complaining that my friend's son, Tunku Yacoob, was implicated in that piracy. I cannot myself believe that this can be true, but I inform our friend of it, and point out to him that the best proof he can afford as to his sincerity in this affair, and his desire to see justice done, will be for my friend to direct his son to appear before the Court with all the proofs he can bring forward in support of his innocence.

To this also the Sultan had to consent, and both Raja Yacoob and Raja Kahar were present at the trial. This was delayed for a day while the witnesses for the defence were collected and it was at 9.0 a.m. on the 13th that the formal proceedings began. The pirates' boat had been discovered and was now produced among the exhibits. The examination of the witnesses was undertaken, at the request of the court, by Mr. Davidson.

To understand the circumstances of the trial which followed it is essential to grasp, first of all, that it all took place in the shadow of the white ensign. The river junction was covered by a formidable concentration of naval artillery, the guns including those of H.M.S. *Rinaldo*, which many of the Malays had heard before. In the background lurked the even more formidable *Iron Duke*. The atmosphere was not one in which a harassed sultan would be likely to insist too much on his sovereign rights. It is equally essential to grasp that what might look like a criminal trial as seen from Whitehall, would seem to the Malays just one more phase in the Selangor Civil War. Such a phase in fact it was. Nor would any Malay seriously ponder the chances of an acquittal. For here was Tunku dia Oodin, leader of one faction, sitting in judgement on a handful of his enemies. One of the Tunku's chief opponents was a witness and almost one of the accused. Virtually prosecuting was the Tunku's own legal adviser, financial partner, and creditor, Davidson. The prisoners, by contrast, had no legal aid and no right of appeal. How the proceedings appeared to Clarke is apparent from his own letter of the 11th, written to his friend Childers before the trial even began:

As I am leaving the gunboat here to see that he [the Sultan] carries out his promises, including the hanging of some sixteen men caught in one of their boats with the plunder of a trading boat from Malacca, whose crew had been murdered, I have every hope of the success of my scheme, which is to compel the Native Government to punish crime, instead of leaving us to do so, as formerly.[1]

The details may be a little vague—sixteen prisoners instead of eight and a noose dangling where only a kris would be used—but the general intention is clear. In his mind (and probably in theirs) the accused were already as good as dead.

Reasons have already been given (see pp. 116–18) for querying the probability of the story elicited from the witnesses for the prosecution.

[1] Vetch, op. cit., pp. 157 et seq.

At the trial, nevertheless, the chief witness, Mat Syed, told his story with a wealth of convincing detail. He was supported, moreover, by other witnesses. That Haji Doraman had hired the scotchie was shown by the evidence of Tomby Ketchil. That goods and cash were on board was proved by the evidence of Mohamat Ahkim (a Chinese Muslim). That Mat Syed was aboard the scotchie appeared from the evidence of Mohamood, Mat's uncle. That the piracy took place was well established and that Mat Syed survived it was shown by the evidence both of Raja Yacoob (or Tunku Allang) and of the Datu Bandar. Much of Mat Syed's evidence was probably of a kind which no defending counsel (had there been such) would have sought to contest. That there were pirates operating from Langat was fairly manifest. That the men in the dock had taken Haji Doraman's boat was never, on the other hand, satisfactorily proved. Mat Syed's identification of them could almost certainly have been shaken by cross-examination. Had that been done the case for the prosecution would have rested almost entirely on the evidence of Daga; evidence which the court had finally to reject.

Daga, by his own account, was a man from Sumatra who came to Langat and sold fish there. He came to be among the prisoners because he was pressing Tunku Allang for payment of $10. He swore to having heard Tunku Allang give orders for the attack on Haji Doraman's vessel. He took part in that attack and was present when Tunku Allang divided the spoils, of which he himself obtained no more than what the Tunku owed him. Daga's boat was identified near that of the other prisoners at Malacca, but he himself was arrested at Kampong Kling. He promptly turned Queen's Evidence and it was his testimony that established the identity of the pirates and the men arrested. On the other hand, he was not with the prisoners when they were arrested and they all agreed in their assertion that they had never seen him before. This denial might have been concerted but Tunku Allang, without the opportunity of contact with the accused, was as emphatic as they in denying all knowledge of Daga. It was therefore incumbent on the prosecution to show that Daga had been seen in company with the other prisoners. It would even have been helpful to show that he had been seen at Langat before the date of the crime. But no evidence was produced to corroborate any part of his story except in so far as it agreed with Mat Syed's tale of woe. In its final verdict, the court found no evidence to show that Tunku Allang had instigated the outrage. In thus rejecting part of Daga's evidence, which was explicit in implicating Tunku Allang, the court was left with no reason for accepting the rest of it. More than that, a complete rejection of his evidence could not but imply that there had been a tampering with witnesses. Who had persuaded Daga to tell the story he did? One of the prisoners, by his own account, had been promised his release, by Mr. Hayward, if he would give evidence (that is, presumably, the right evidence) as a witness. What had Daga been promised, and by whom?

The rejection of Daga's testimony against Tunku Allang is the more striking in that Daga was never cross-examined. It should also be emphasized that all of the prisoners, with one exception, were Tunku Allang's men. One was the nacodah of his prahu, three were boatmen in his employ, another was his servant, a sixth lived in his house and was father to the last of the accused (apparently an imbecile). The one exception was a Chinese Muslim whose shop adjoined the Tunku's house. Called as a witness for the defence, Tunku Allang identified all these as his servants, except the Chinese, and described them as good men. If they were in fact guilty it is impossible to believe that they could engage in piracy without his knowledge. So that Daga's evidence, in so far as it indicated the Tunku's complicity, was at least plausible. If, on the other hand, these men were in fact guiltless of this particular crime, Daga's story must have been a complete fabrication, the work of Allang's enemies; and the work, presumably, of Tunku dia Oodin's friends. In that event, it must be conceded that no better choice of scapegoats could have been made. They were Tunku Allang's followers, claiming him as their protector and acknowledged by him as his men. Their guilt, if proved, was also his. It is hardly possible to establish the truth of this matter so long after the event. Among the facts, however, which should be remembered are, first, that further acts of piracy occurred after the arrest of these men[1] and, second, that local rumour (for what it might be worth) named Raja Mahdie, Raja Mahmood, and Raja Laut of Sungei Ujong as the instigators of piracy at Langat.

The doubts we may feel now about this case were not shared by the court which assembled on 13 February 1874. Its members dealt briskly with the evidence, concluding their labours on the 15th with a unanimous verdict of guilty against all the accused. Seven were

---

[1] A piracy at Kuala Labu was reported in July 1874. This place is only thirty-five miles from Langat and rumour attributed the crime to followers of Rajas Mahdie and Mahmood.

sentenced to death for piracy and murder, the eighth reprieved because of his youth. The executions, by the Malay method, took place on the 16th at the mouth of the Jugra river.[1] The British Commissioners then administered a serious caution to Rajas Yacoob and Kahar, at the same time demanding $5,000 as compensation from the Sultan. They next visited the Lukut and Linggi rivers, showing the flag and giving publicity to what had happened. Sir Andrew Clarke was no longer present, having indeed left on the evening of the 11th. He was back in Singapore on the 13th, the Admiral returning soon afterwards on his way back to China.

Sir Andrew soon discovered that his policy was generally approved in the Straits Settlements, where the terms of the Pangkor Engagement were already known.[2] A motion passed at a general meeting of the Chamber of Commerce on 18 February assured him of local support, and more especially if he pursued his policy to its logical conclusion. The Chamber expressed its trust

that H.E. will continue to pursue the just, firm and conciliatory policy thus inaugurated until the whole of the so-called independent States of the Malayan Peninsula be brought under similar control.

The Chamber is satisfied that it is by such measures only that a rich and fertile country, which has been too long neglected and allowed to lapse into Anarchy, can be brought under British influence and opened to civilization and Commerce, and that they constitute the course of action most worthy of a great nation.[3]

Sir Andrew could hardly accept this as a mandate for a career of unlimited conquest. He was bound, however, to recognize that it was difficult to intervene effectively in one State without also intervening in those most nearly adjacent. In Selangor he had done no more than prepare the way for the sort of action he had taken in Perak. He had said nothing as yet to the Sultan about a treaty or a Resident.[4] But if

---

[1] The deterrent effect of this example appears to have been good. Swettenham wrote afterwards: 'I had not been very long in Langat before I ascertained, without much doubt, that none of those executed had had any hand in the piracy, but the lesson was made thereby all the more forcible.

'We all know that with people who have no political institutions, there is nothing so impressive as the incontinent execution of a few innocent persons. It is a warning not only to the naughtily-inclined, but also to the quite, quite good; to the intriguer and the agitator, as well as to the thief. At any rate that was the effect produced in Bandar Termasa.' (*The Real Malay*, Sir Frank A. Swettenham, London, 1899, p. 70.)   [2] *Singapore Daily Times*, 9 Feb. 1874.

[3] Quoted in S.S. No. 43, 24 Feb. 1874, para. 12.

[4] For the Sultan's character, see the article by J. M. Gullick, 'A Careless, Heathen Philosopher?', *JMBRAS*, vol. xxvi, part 1, 1953, p. 86.

Selangor were to be pacified, even using Tunku dia Oodin as agent, some parallel action would have to be taken in Sungei Ujong. Characters like Raja Mahdie, Raja Laut, and Raja Mahmood confined their activities to no single State. They ranged happily between the Muar and the Krian, turning up now at Langat, now at Rassa. Tunku dia Oodin could maintain no order in Selangor if his opponents were free to withdraw at will and unpursued into the Negri Sembilan. The western Malay States were too closely related to present so many distinct problems. They presented, rather, different aspects of a problem which the Governor was beginning to see as one.

Whatever conclusions Sir Andrew Clarke may have reached, however, they were not, of necessity, shared by officials at the Colonial Office. He could do nothing more—and had been enterprising to have done as much—without written approval from London. To secure this, Sir Andrew wrote a lengthy dispatch to the Secretary of State, dated 24 February[1] and comprising a full narrative of the events which had led up to the Pangkor Engagement. By that agreement he had secured the right to provide Perak with a Resident and Assistant Resident. He was careful to emphasize, nevertheless, that his actions had 'in no way bound Her Majesty's Government to any particular course and that it is perfectly possible to withdraw from the position I have temporarily assumed'. There was a sense in which this was true, but the historical interest of this document would seem to lie in the contrast between its narrative (which relates solely to Perak) and its recommended policy (which extends, if vaguely, over the whole peninsula). Sir Andrew thus emphasized that occasional or even regular visits by an officer appointed for the purpose would be of little use. Only officers in permanent residence could have the necessary influence. But his 'Residents' and his 'States' are alike plural. Three paragraphs are especially significant:

17. The Malays, like every other rude Eastern nation, require to be treated like children and to be taught, and this especially in all matters of improvement, whether in the question of good government and organisation or of material improvement, by opening means of communication, extending cultivation and fostering immigration and trade. Such teaching can only be effected by an Officer living on the spot, whose time should be devoted to carefully studying the wants and capabilities of each State, the character of the Sultan and his Chiefs and to making himself personally

[1] S.S. No. 43, 24 Feb. 1874.

acquainted with every portion of the Country and thus fitting himself for the post of Counsellor when the time for opening up the Country arrives. . . .

23. One of the great difficulties which meets us at the outset in every one of the States of the Peninsula, even in Johore, is our absolute ignorance of the geographical or physical features of the Country, beyond the actual banks of the large rivers, and those only for a few miles from their mouths as high as our steam launches have been able to make their way. The extra-ordinary part of it is that this ignorance is not confined to ourselves, but extends equally to the Native Rulers. . . .

51. . . . Your Lordship will I feel sure allow me . . . to express my con-viction and that of all the members of my Councils that, looking to the long and intimate relations of Great Britain with the Malayan States, to the proximity of these Settlements and to the state of Anarchy and misrule which has for some years prevailed in Perak and Salangore, the time has arrived when as a Nation we shall be neglecting a great paramount duty if we any longer delay that intervention which the causes of civilization and good order now so loudly demand.

From this last and final paragraph of a long dispatch the Secretary of State might have concluded that Residents were needed in Perak and Selangor only. But a careful study of paragraph 17 would dis-cover a reference to 'each' State where a cautious official might have referred merely to 'both'. In paragraph 23, moreover, the Governor's eyes seem to be wandering over the whole peninsula, imperfectly mapped as it was. We might surmise that he was hoping to extract from Lord Kimberley a statement of policy going beyond what he himself dared propose. But Lord Kimberley, as we have seen (p. 141 above) was no longer in office, and his successor, Lord Carnarvon, was cautious about accepting a policy which he did not initiate. He wrote no official approval of the Perak intervention until 29 May; and he said nothing even then which could be construed as inciting Sir Andrew to establish British influence in Selangor. Any further enterprise must originate, or must at least seem to originate, in the expressed desire of the Malay rulers themselves.

To secure from the sultans and chiefs a free and unanimous request for British intervention was no easy task. There was one man, how-ever, who thought it possible and that was the Colonial Secretary, Mr. J. W. W. Birch. He had been excluded from all the recent negotiations, on the plea, no doubt, that he was needed in Singapore while the Governor was on his travels. To him it must have seemed, however, that the Governor was turning for advice to Braddell and McNair while ignoring the very man on whom he should principally have

relied. Birch had been brought in as an expert in colonial administration, a sage counsellor to other officials who might know the
Malay States (in so far as anyone did) but whose experience under
Indian rule was useless or misleading. It was the moment for him to
assert himself, gain first-hand and recent information, and demonstrate that he was no arm-chair administrator. He applied for the post
of Resident in Perak and hinted at his long experience of similar work
in Ceylon: 'I believe I can really be of use. My whole life has been
spent in opening up new country and in improving and enriching
a country, and in teaching the native chiefs good government.'[1]

To this application, made in February, Sir Andrew replied, no
doubt, that there was no vacancy until the Colonial Office agreed to
the creation of the post. Should his general policy be approved, there
would be several posts to be filled. In applying for one, Birch was not
seeking promotion—the new appointment might be thought junior
to the one he held—so much as a chance to make himself expert in
Malayan affairs. Eager to prove his competence as a traveller in the
wilds, he offered in the meanwhile to tour the western States and prepare the way for British intervention. He might even persuade the
sultans to ask for it. He had shown his powers of persuasion in the
past (see p. 55) under a Governor who knew how to appreciate his
services. There might be a little difficulty over language but that could
be overcome. Young Swettenham might come with him as interpreter, for one thing: and, in any case, that sort of difficulty is less
than some people suppose. While making no decision about the
appointment of a future Resident, Sir Andrew agreed that Birch
should make a 'semi-official visit' to the Native States, emphasizing
afterwards that it was a tour which Birch 'obtained my permission to
make'. These words are at least consistent with a faint feeling of distrust or even perhaps of dislike. As against that, Clarke lent Birch the
Pluto and borrowed H.M.S. *Avon* to act as escort. He also allowed
Birch to take Frank Swettenham with him, and it is, as it happens,
from Swettenham that we have the fullest account of all that occurred.[2]
As if to illustrate the story, Birch brought a photographer with him,
a few of whose prints have actually survived.

Frank Swettenham lived in Penang and was in charge, at this time,
of the Land Office for Province Wellesley. He was instructed to meet
Birch at Pulo Pangkor and hastened to do so, arriving there from

---

[1] Vetch, op. cit., p. 174.
[2] *Sir Frank Swettenham's Perak Journals, 1874–76.*

Penang in a hired steam-launch on 5 April. His prompt obedience was creditable but not justified in the event. 'I was compelled', he wrote, 'to refuse two invitations to stay on the Hill,[1] four dinner parties and two dances, probably more invitations than I shall get in the whole of the rest of the year.' The dates for these social occasions came and went while he waited at Pangkor police station. The *Avon* and *Pluto* did not appear until the 10th, the former bringing Birch, Tunku dia Oodin, and Davidson. Since leaving Singapore Birch had taken the opportunity of visiting various places on the coast including Langat. He had visited the Sultan, presenting him with gifts from the Governor, securing the release of some Chinese prisoners and bringing the Viceroy and his adviser on to Pangkor. By 11 April the *Avon* and *Pluto* were off the Perak river and the Sultan, Abdullah, was brought off by boat to dine on board ship. He was asked then to send up the river a letter addressed to Ismail from Birch, asking him to appear at Blanja on a given date. The messenger was a sergeant in the Malacca police, called Mohamed Syed. Birch preferred to reach the rendezvous via Larut and Kuala Kangsar, mainly no doubt in order to obtain information from Speedy. He asked that the Laxamana should accompany him and the Bandahara go to Blanja direct, and this was agreed. On the same occasion Birch revealed the object of his mission. His plan was to secure the Perak royal regalia, bring it down the river and arrange a proper coronation, with the Governor present, in May. After a further interview ashore at Batak Rabit, Abdullah's residence, Birch went on in the *Avon* to the Larut river, taking the Laxamana with him. The whole party then went up to the area of the mines where they were met by Speedy and the Mantri. As Sir Andrew reported afterwards:

The Colonial Secretary found the Assistant Resident busily engaged in laying out streets and building lots, and was surprised to find many respectable and substantial houses already constructed while materials for others were greatly in demand and being daily and hourly brought in. All around was an animated scene of industry and good fellowship, where only a few weeks before there was nothing but misery, ruin and bloodshed. . . .
  I feel sure that the results of our intervention are eminently satisfactory and that time alone is needed to render the district most prosperous and develop its great resources.[2]

------

[1] The Governor had a residence on Penang Hill, with the houses of some other officials adjacent. The Hill is the mountainous central feature of the island, some 2,000 feet above the town.   [2] S.S. No. 195, 16 June 1874.

Although the dividing-line was not marked on the ground, the See Kwans were at work at Kamunting, the Go Kwans at Klian Pau. All seemed well and Birch started for Kuala Kangsar on the 15th with Speedy, Swettenham, and the Laxamana. They and their baggage travelled on elephants, spent the night at Gunong Pondok, and reached Kuala Kangsar on the following day. Staying there as the guest of Che Mida (a notable lady of those parts), they heard complaints from her about the lawless folk of Kota Lama, including Panglima Prang Semaun.[1] They went there accordingly on 17 April, in some force, and were joined there by the Mantri. The robber chiefs were not there and the people were too frightened to say where they had gone. Birch returned, therefore, to Kuala Kangsar and prepared to descend the river by boat to Blanja. He decided, however, to send the Mantri on ahead as the man with most influence over Ismail.

We told the Mantri he should go at once, at least as soon as a boat could be procured, to Ismail wherever he was to be found, and explain to him that the Governor had sent Mr. Birch, his highest officer, to obtain from him either the Regalia or a positive refusal to give it up. That Mr. Birch, he might rest assured, would not return without one or the other.[2]

If the ex-Sultan would surrender the regalia to the Raja Bandahara and the Mantri, they would take it to Abdullah. If he preferred to surrender the regalia to Abdullah in person, Birch would bring the latter to him for the purpose. Failing either of these alternatives, the Mantri was to explain,

the Governor would to a certainty take it by force, and this would entail possibly the loss of many lives, of much property, and the certainty of great ultimate trouble and disgrace to Ismail himself. Everyone agrees that it is very necessary to explain this to Ismail because he has had no intercourse with Englishmen, and he knows nothing of England's power.[2]

British policy, as interpreted by Swettenham for Birch and vaguely approved by Sir Andrew Clarke, assumed a guise which would have been scarcely recognizable among those responsible for it in Whitehall.

Descending the river in the Mantri's wake, Birch arrived at Senggang on 21 April and there, for the first time, met Raja Yusof, in whose territory that village lay. He was, as Swettenham admitted, 'a man whose existence has been ignored in the most curious way'. His narrative continues:

I was considerably surprised to see a big, strong, good-looking man of

---

[1] This character appears in Swettenham, *Malay Sketches*.
[2] *Sir Frank Swettenham's Perak Journals*, p. 51.

45, a man who in appearance and manner is by far the most royal looking man I have seen in Perak. He said he was very pleased to see us, and asked what we were doing, and being told he said at once 'the Governor has made Abdullah Sultan, but it is not right. I am the man who by birth and the customs of Perak ought to be the Sultan of this country'.

Somewhat startled, Swettenham asked for details. From the explanation given, he quickly realized that Yusof had in fact the best claim by birth. That the chiefs were against him Yusof himself admitted.

I asked how this was, and he replied that it was because they know that if he were Sultan he would keep them in order, whilst they think they can do as they please with Abdullah, and more so with Ismail, and indeed I believed that he is not far wrong; but I explained to him that if they had supported Abdullah under this impression they would to a certainty be disappointed, as the Government would take care that Abdullah was Sultan in reality, and not in name only. 'Well,' he said, 'I am the right man. I was passed over in the reign of Sultan Jaffar, when most unjustly and contrary to all precedent Ismail, who is not of Perak blood, was made Bandahara, because Sultan Jaffar liked him and disliked me.' In this also he is right. There can be no doubt but that the election of Ismail as Bandahara was the original cause of all that has since occurred.

R. Yusof went on to say 'If the Governor will do what is right and elect the proper man as Sultan all will go well, but if not I will fight for my rights. But I think that by far the best way would be for the English Govt. to take over the whole of Perak for their own, and give the chiefs a certain amount per mensem each.' We asked if he would come to Singapore with us and see the Governor, and he said he would be very glad. . . .

In talking of the election of Abdullah he said that he was never asked to meet the Governor at P. Pangkor or he would have done so most willingly, and asked why the Governor had elected Abdullah . . . over his head. I explained to him that the Governor did not elect him, the chiefs elected him and the Governor acknowledged and confirmed the election.[1]

Birch, once this had been explained to him, was in a difficult position. He had been given good reason for believing that Abdullah was not the rightful Sultan. He also knew that the man with the better claim was abler, braver, and far more resolute than either Abdullah or Ismail. To make matters worse, Yusof was willing to go even farther than Abdullah in accepting British protection and advice, and would go to Singapore, moreover, to explain that willingness to the Governor. It was manifest that Sir Andrew was backing the wrong horse. Birch, on realizing this, could have abandoned his present mission and gone with Yusof to Singapore. That is evidently

[1] *Sir Frank Swettenham's Perak Journals*, pp. 54–55.

what Swettenham would have liked him to do. After that it would have been for the Governor to decide whether he really wanted Ismail to hand over the regalia to Abdullah. If he said 'yes' it would then be with a full knowledge of Yusof's claim, personality, and intentions. He would at least have had the chance to think again. Nor would such a course have been without its appeal for Birch. He could have returned to Singapore as the real expert in the affairs of Perak. He could shake his head sadly over the negligence of Irving and Skinner, in whose memoranda no mention of Yusof could be found. He could hint at the fallibility of Braddell and McNair. He could imply that a really good and experienced administrator would, not unnaturally, discover essential facts which might be overlooked by mere lawyers and engineers; good and useful men as they might be when kept in their proper place. He could make a mild civil service joke about the way McNair had abolished Yusof simply by mis-spelling his name in a report. He could, in a quiet way, have enjoyed himself for several days.

It must have been with some reluctance that Birch decided against an immediate return to Singapore. But it could not have taken him long to conclude that such a course would be unwise. He could not triumph over McNair without making the Governor look a fool. The Pangkor Engagement had been the Governor's own personal affair. Not a soul had known what he meant to do before he had almost done it. Worse still was his position in relation to Whitehall. Having decided to go beyond his brief, act first and report after-wards, he could not go on to remark casually that his action had been a mistake based upon misinformation; and directly resulting from that very haste on which he had rather prided himself. Birch realized that the Pangkor agreement must stand. He would have to secure the regalia for Abdullah if he possibly could. But he began now to emphasize that Abdullah had been the Malay choice, which the Governor had merely accepted. Swettenham apparently evolved this fiction during his first interview with Yusof, he and Birch there-after reiterating the theory with an insistence that the Malays must have found rather irritating. Birch realized, as Swettenham may not have done, the full significance of their discovery. But Swettenham, the translator at Pangkor of Mahomed Syed's genealogy, was himself the man whose mis-spelling had helped to conceal Yusof's existence. He was just as eager to show that it was not the Governor's decision that had placed Abdullah on the throne. Sir Andrew Clarke, by contrast, knew exactly what he had done. He wrote afterwards, in 1875: 'I believe in every way I was right in putting up Abdulla. Had I taken the other man, I could not have secured the peace of the coast. . . . Abdulla . . . was ten times better than old Ismail.'[1] His choice, of which he was unrepentant, had been between Abdullah and Ismail. Knowing now of the existence of this third candidate, superior to either, Birch wanted to make the Governor merely the passive witness of a Malay decision. His version of what happened at Pangkor was inaccurate and, as he had not been there, it was not even plausible.

Determined to proceed with his mission, Birch reached Blanja on 22 April, where Yusof followed him two days later. Ismail was not there when Birch arrived—he was visiting a tin-mine in the vicinity—but the Mantri returned with him on the 23rd. There was no formal meeting until the 25th, on which day Ismail told Birch that he would surrender the regalia but only to Abdullah himself. It should be explained that the Malays would hardly recognize as Sultan a ruler not possessed of the ceremonial swords, krises, drums, and elephants by which the dignity of kingship in Perak was normally upheld. Birch knew this and cannot have expected any very prompt response to his demands. For one thing, the regalia was not there. It was, as Birch knew, at Kinta. Apart from that, Yusof was as reluctant as Ismail to allow Abdullah's claim. Nevertheless, there was verbal agreement that Ismail should send for the regalia and that Birch should send for Abdullah, which he did. When Birch and Swettenham proposed to visit Kinta themselves, all the previously visible elephants were found to have vanished. When they wanted to buy rice there was none for sale. And rumour had it that Abdullah would never dare come into Ismail's country or would be shot on the way if he so much as attempted the journey. Birch resolved to leave, but made a final effort to extract from Ismail a written promise or refusal to hand over the regalia. He received neither, Ismail replying evasively on the point at issue but clearly refusing to recognize Abdullah 'whom our friend [the Governor] appointed as Sultan at Pulau Pangkor' and astutely referring to the old treaties, with the East India Company, which he considered perfectly adequate and which he saw no reason to modify.[2]

[1] See p. 139.
[2] The whole letter is given in translation in *Sir Frank Swettenham's Perak Journals*, appendix 3, p. 143.

Birch and Swettenham were furious at the 'calm insolence' of this reply, Swettenham adding (30 April):

The statement that the Governor chose the Sultan of Perak is simply absurd, and more than that it is insolent, because we have already several times explained to them that he did nothing of the sort, and in the whole letter he never says he is going to give up the Regalia at all.[1]

An attempt was made to persuade Yusof to intercede with Ismail but he replied simply: 'How can I advise him to give up the Regalia to Abdullah when he ought to give it up to me?' This was unanswerable and a maddening negotiation ended with Ismail's refusal to see Birch or Swettenham again. Some of the final asperities may have been due to the fact that the Englishmen were living, by this time, on claret. They left Blanja on the 30th, went down the river and on the afternoon of 1 May, met with Abdullah, ascending the river with fifty boats and 500 men. He went no farther after hearing their news but returned with them to Batak Rabit. From there Birch and Swettenham returned, via Pangkor, to Penang, arriving there on 4 May.

Clarke s reaction to Birch's report, when he received it, is reflected in his dispatch of 16 June. He describes without comment Birch's visit to Senggang, 'the residence of Rajah Yusuf', and goes on at once to state that Ismail, after discussion, professed 'perfect readiness to give over the Regalia to Sultan Abdullah if the latter would only go to receive them'. Rumour has it, he admits, that a meeting for that purpose is unlikely—'their newly established relations are not sufficiently cordial'—and he admits, further, that the atmosphere at Blanja was unfriendly. Lower down the river, by contrast, all was well. 'The whole country traversed was at peace and there is reason to anticipate that the appointment of British Residents will foster the feeling of security that now prevails.' Two motives underlay this misleading picture; the Governor's wish to justify his action at Pangkor and Birch's desire to become the first British Resident of Perak. It was Birch's first object to show that the country was at peace, for if it was not, no British Resident would be appointed at all. His second object was to demonstrate his success in handling Malays, failing which the Residency might be given to someone else. He failed, therefore, to emphasize sufficiently the fact of Ismail's hostility. He minimized also his failure to obtain the regalia for Abdullah. Clarke had his own motives for accepting Birch's report and

[1] *Sir Frank Swettenham's Perak Journals*, p. 67.

embodying it, still further softened, in his own optimistic dispatch, with its photographs enclosed of pretty scenery and picturesque chiefs. The Pangkor policy must be shown as successful.

But while Sir Andrew suppressed a part of what he had been told he did not altogether ignore it. He wanted to meet Ismail and Yusof, not in their native haunts but in the more civilized setting of Penang, and young Swettenham was the best man to fetch them. Sent back to Perak for this purpose, he was already at Senggang on 15 June. On the day, in fact, when Clarke dated his dispatch to the Secretary of State, Swettenham was telling Yusof 'in all kinds of flowery language'[1] that the Governor wanted to meet not only him but Ismail. This was the point on which negotiations almost foundered, for Yusof, eager to state his own case, showed no enthusiasm over allowing Ismail to state his. It was already clear, incidentally, that neither Ismail nor Yusof dared go down the river through Abdullah's country. As regards the general object of his interview, as proposed, with the Governor, he said: 'I shall be only too glad if the English will hoist their flag here in Perak and take over the whole country, but I won't agree to anyone except the real heir becoming Sultan.'[2] In the final upshot Yusof agreed to come, going via Blanja and Bruas. Ismail refused, partly perhaps because Yusof advised him against it. By 28 June Yusof, with Raja Mansor and Dato Nara, was at Penang.

No details seem to be known of this interview between Yusof and the Governor. It was too late to change British policy as affecting the choice between claimants to the throne of Perak, and Sir Andrew explained, no doubt, that he would continue to recognize Abdullah as the man freely elected by the rest. He must at the same time have made it clear that Yusof's rather wild talk about appealing to Siam or some European power could lead to no useful result. He evidently convinced Yusof, at least for the time being, that British intervention was an established fact and that active resistance would be fatal to his chance of succeeding to the Sultan's office at some future time. If Clarke recognized the error he had committed at Pangkor there is no trace of it. He was content, no doubt, to have quietened Perak for the time he would need to intervene elsewhere. From February onwards he had been increasingly concerned with Sungei Ujong. We need, at this point, to see how far his intervention had gone, and to what purpose.

---

[1] *Sir Frank Swettenham's Perak Journals*, p. 79.   [2] Ibid., p. 82.

CHAPTER VII

BRITISH officials of this period were apt to be impatient with the sultans and ministers of the Malay States. They were tempted to regard the Malays as stupid (which they were not) and unreliable (which they may well have been). It was only when they visited the Negri Sembilan, the hinterland of Malacca, that they realized how comparatively advanced and civilized the other Malays were. The folk of what we now call the Negri Sembilan, or Nine States, were not really Malays at all and their States added up to practically every number except nine. The people of this area were a mixture of Sumatran Minangkabaus with the local aborigines and it was from the former that they derived their tribal system, their matriarchy, their customs as regards land tenure and inheritance. The Nine States were, originally, Klang (now in Selangor), Naning (now part of Malacca), Jelai (in Pahang), Segamat and Pasir Besar (both in Johore), together with Johol, Sungei Ujong, Rembau, and Jelebu. These last four could be made up to nine, after a fashion, by adding Ulu Muar, Terachi, Jempol, Gunong Pasir, and Inas.[1] The internal organization of the local tribes was complex and peculiar to themselves, exemplifying 'a democracy that gave votes to women and protected the rights of the humblest'.[2] But Winstedt goes on to point out that 'this matriarchal democracy of Minangkabu colonists suffered from one flaw . . . it insisted that the election of all its representatives, from the Ruler down to the humblest tribal elder, must be unanimous'.

Originally the problem of electing a ruler had not arisen, for there was none. The Punghulus had once owed a vague allegiance to the Sultan of Malacca and this was transformed into an even vaguer allegiance to the Sultan of Johore, who was at most an absentee overlord. Their consequent lack of cohesion lessened their effective resistance to the Dutch between 1641 and 1795. The result was that Naning, Rembau, and Johol came under Dutch influence and Sungei Ujong (the principal source of tin in that area) was subject,

[1] *JSBRAS*, No. 46, Dec. 1906, and No. 56, Dec. 1910. See sketch-map opposite p. 96 in No. 56 illustrating 'Rembau, one of the Nine States', C. W. C. Parr and W. H. Mackray.
[2] Winstedt, *Malaya and its History*, p. 82.

especially after 1759, to a measure of economic control. Until 1773 the only officers with a federal as distinct from a State function were the four lawgivers (*undang yang ampat*), but in that year the chiefs and elders asked the Sultan of Johore to procure them a ruler for religious and social purposes. This he did, appointing a prince from Sumatra who was called Yam Tuan Besar, or Yang di per Tuan Besar, of Sri Mananti, where his Istana or palace was built. This ruler inherited only such powers as had not been resigned to the Dutch, and inherited them, moreover, in a community which lacked any tradition of kingship.

The office of Ruler or Yang di-pertuan, or, as it was abbreviated Yam-Tuan, was in fact a foreign and Hindu excrescence, which the Minangkabau tribal system never absorbed. . . . For though the Yam Tuan had, like other Malay rulers, the divine right of one whose ancestors had been the incarnation of Hindu gods, and who himself was the shadow of Allah upon earth, yet compared with the rulers of the patriarchal Malay States he had no authority. . . . He was supreme arbiter and judge, if the territorial chiefs chose to invite him to adjudicate, which they never did. He was Caliph or head of the Muslim theocracy in any territory where the local chief did not arrogate the title for himself—and he always did. The Yam-Tuan should have been first in a State Council as other rulers were, but no council ever met.[1]

To a society and polity none of the simplest was added an immigrant population of Chinese. There were, according to Newbold, 1,000 Chinese miners in Sungei Ujong in 1828. They were attacked that year by the Malays and numbered only 400 in 1830.[2] Trade continued to suffer such interruptions, more especially in 1848, in 1857, and 1860. As compared with that in Perak and Selangor, the Chinese population was still relatively small in 1874.

Such knowledge as the British had of this vicinity derived largely from the Naning War of 1831, which produced as a by-product the two books written by Captain Begbie of the Madras Artillery.[3] As its only other results were a heavy expenditure and a feeling of annoyance, the East India Company was cured, and permanently, of any interest in the interior of what is now Malaya. Its local officials could not avoid, however, being occasionally involved in its affairs. For one thing, the Malacca Government had inherited from

[1] Winstedt, *Malaya and its History*, p. 82.
[2] *The Chinese in Malaya*, Victor Purcell.
[3] *A Narrative of the Naning War*, P. J. Begbie, 1831, and *The Malayan Peninsula*, P. J. Begbie, Madras, 1834.

the Dutch a certain authority over the nearer States. For another thing, there was a close economic relationship between Malacca and the sources of its tin. This tin came mainly, though not entirely, from the vicinity of Rassa in Sungei Ujong. It would normally reach the sea by the Linggi river, the estuary of which forms part of the northern boundary of Malacca. The trader who entered this river would find, six miles from its mouth, the junction of its two branches at Simpang. By ascending the northern branch he would come first to the three villages forming the settlement of Linggi and then, thirty miles farther on, to the area of the tin-mines. By ascending the southern branch he would come to Bandar, the chief village of lower Rembau; but there was no point in that, for Rembau has no tin. What Rembau had, however, was a strategic position at which to levy a customs duty or blackmail (the term varies according to the point of view) upon such tin as came down the Linggi to Simpang. The only obvious means of evading this exaction was to take the tin out by a partly overland route to Lukut, near what is now called Port Dickson. In more settled and tranquil periods the duties payable were closely related, no doubt, to the cost of haulage on the other and less convenient route.

British concern was not with the Negri Sembilan as a whole but with Sungei Ujong, the chief mining district. Recognized by the British as ruler of Sungei Ujong was the Dato Klana. His claim to rule was disputed, however, by the Dato Bandar, who claimed coequal authority. It is probable that there was substance in this claim and that the Dato Klana's pretensions rested mainly on British recognition. The Klana had property in Malacca and often lived there, rather as the Mantri of Perak had lived in Penang and the Maharajah of Johore in Singapore. The Dato Bandar, 'a man of great wealth and considerable influence in Sungei Ujong',[1] had no comparable position in Malacca, but was none the less determined to uphold his rights.[2] The result was that there were conflicting claims over mining property in Sungei Ujong and further claims to collect dues on the Linggi river. If the Punghulo of Rembau was the chief blackmailer he was far from being the only one. No less than four chiefs were levying toll in 1855, when H.M.S. *Amethyst* intervened.

[1] S.S. No. 356, 29 Dec. 1874.
[2] Malacca merchants who petitioned the Straits Government in 1860 stated that order had previously been maintained in Sungei Ujong by the Dato Bandar, who had seen to it that none but the customary dues should be paid. The Dato Klana's authority seems then to have been the lesser.

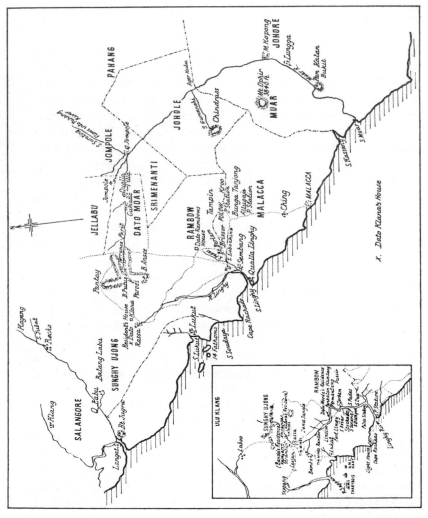

Map 4. Negri Sembilan

Between the 5,000 Chinese miners of Sungei Ujong and their agents in Malacca there lay, in 1860, a formidable area of Malay disturbance. Any vestige of federal authority in the Negri Sembilan disappeared with the death of Yamtuan Imam in 1869.[1] No agreement was reached as to who should succeed him, the two claimants being Yam Tuan Antah and Tengku Ahmad Tunggal, neither commanding any general support. The former was recognized in Johol, Ulu Muar, Terachi, and Gunong Pasir, the latter having his supporters in Rembau and Sungei Ujong.

Despite this political confusion, there was a growing interest in the tin-mines of Sungei Ujong. Proof of this came to hand when the Dato Klana on 14 May 1872 told the Governor, Sir Harry Ord, that he had given a mining concession to Mr. Henry N. Velge of Malacca. It was a grant, on favourable terms, of land in Setoh, Sempadan, and Rajang; a grant which Mr. Velge, a Dutch Eurasian, promptly made over to the Sungei Ujong Tin Mining Company.[2] Significant terms in this agreement were those by which the Klana undertook to make a cart road from Linggi to Setoh[3] and also to preserve order in the vicinity of the mines themselves. A sum of $30,000 changed hands and a useful arrangement came into being between the Klana, the Sungei Ujong Tin Mining Co., the Chinese merchants of Malacca, and the government of Malacca. It had the tacit approval of the government of the Straits Settlements and seemed likely to produce a good dividend for all concerned. Chinese miners flocked to the mines, many of them fleeing from the disturbed areas of Selangor and more especially from Klang. They were soon to number 10,000 or more, mostly members of the Triad. In point of fact, however, too many other people felt themselves entitled to a share of the royalties which the Klana proposed to keep to himself. The Yam Tuan Antah claimed to be his overlord. The Dato Bandar claimed to be his equal. The Rembau chiefs had always taken their percentage at Simpang and other individuals could see no reason why they should be excluded. To make matters worse, there was no certainty as to where the State boundaries lay. Tunku dia Oodin, on behalf of Selangor, claimed not only Lukut but the whole coast down to Cape Rachado and the

---

[1] *History of Negri Sembilan*, R. O. Winstedt, *JMBRAS*, vol. xii, part 3, Oct. 1934.

[2] *War in Negri Sembilan, 1874–1875*, academic exercise by T. Chelliah, University of Malaya, 1955, appendix D (1).

[3] This would have by-passed the minor blackmailers on the Linggi river, those above Bukit Tiga.

Linggi estuary.[1] To these varied threats the Klana had replied, as early as 1870, by ordering two brass field-guns and a hundred rifles from London. Procured by Velge in the name of Syed Ahman, the Klana's nephew, these somewhat unusual items of mining equipment had been detained in Singapore.

So matters stood when the Dato Klana and the Penghulu of Rembau both died. This was towards the end of 1872. By March 1873 Syed Ahman was able to inform Captain Shaw, Lieutenant-Governor of Malacca, that he had been unanimously elected as Dato Klana. No such unanimity was observed in Rembau, where the succession was hotly disputed by the Dato Perba and Haji Mustapha. Tunku dia Oodin supported the Dato Perba. The Klana supported Haji Mustapha. Fighting began, trade came to a standstill, and tin ceased to reach Malacca from Sungei Ujong. The result was the general petition of 28 March 1873, mention of which has already been made,[2] and the Malacca petition of 19 April 1873.[3] This last document, signed by sixty-five merchants, traders, and others is merely a complaint about illegal exactions. The petitioners state that the Rembau people have formed a customs barrier at Bukit Tiga and four more stockades higher up the Linggi river. It was at Bukit Tiga that the main exactions occurred (duties being levied upon tin, rice, and opium), the demands elsewhere amounting only to a couple of dollars here and there, sums strictly comparable with those we pay to car-park attendants. Sir Harry Ord, to whom this petition was referred, offered to arbitrate between the chiefs but had to report, on 10 July,[4] his failure to assemble them for the purpose. All that resulted from his mediation was a visit paid by the Klana to Singapore. Returning to Malacca that chief told Captain Shaw of the three interviews which had taken place.

On the first, Mr. Kim Cheng acted as interpreter; on the second, Mr. Swettenham; and on the third, Mr. Davidson, Tuanku Kudin's legal adviser; that the Governor consulted him about the disturbances in Rumbowe; that he had answered that Hajee Mustapha was the rightful successor; that this made the Governor very angry, who said he would not have it so; on which Syed Ahman went away much frightened. At the third interview he said the Governor desired him to recognise Datu Perba, on which he asked time to consult his chiefs.

There was a divergence in policy at this point between Malacca and

[1] Chelliah, op. cit., p. 9.   [2] See p. 109.
[3] Chelliah, op. cit., appendix B (4).   [4] S.S. No. 188, 10 July 1873.

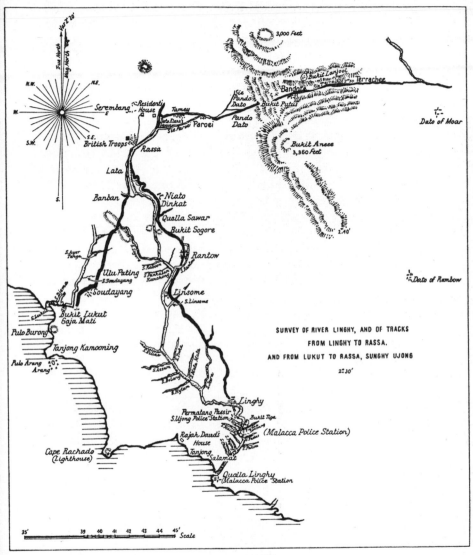

Map 5. Sungei Ujong

Singapore. Shaw's sympathies were with the Klana and against both the Dato Perba and Tunku dia Oodin. Ord, while supporting Tunku dia Oodin in Selangor, could not very well oppose him in Sungei Ujong. The commercial interests represented by Kim Cheng and Davidson were, in this context, a great deal more impartial. It is true that the Sungei Ujong Tin Mining Co. and the Chendras Gold Mining Co. had both been encouraged by Captain Shaw. These companies, however, were centred in Singapore and even the Malacca firms, L. Neubronner & Co. and H. N. Velge, were only branch offices dependent on headquarters in Singapore. Directors of the Sungei Ujong Tin Mining Co. included such people as Mr. Whampoa and Mr. R. C. Woods.[1] The interests, therefore, of those who had invested in the tin-mines (wherever situated) must have been broadly similar. As between Ord and Shaw, the difference was one of opinion on a subject of which Shaw had the more detailed knowledge. When the latter reported to Singapore on the crimes and outrages committed by the Dato Perba it was with a certain satisfaction. He was supported by the Malacca merchants in a further petition, dated 27 August, in which they asked the Governor to bring pressure to bear upon

the Malay Ruler of Rembow named Dattok Perboo, whose men have entered another Malay Chief's territory, viz. Bukit Tiga, which is in the Linghy District, under the rule of Datoh Mudah, and erected a large stockade there . . . and have also erected innumerable other stockades along the banks of the river up to Sunghie Ujong, where the Tin Mines are situated.[2]

This petition produced no immediate result, for Sir Andrew Clarke, to whom it was addressed, did not arrive until November. Nor had he, at first, any time to spare for Sungei Ujong. 'After Sir Andrew's arrival there was a sort of lull, as if all parties were waiting to see what the new Governor would do.' It was this lull which allowed Sir Andrew to concentrate at first on Perak and Selangor. He had trouble enough as it was, being at once overwhelmed with a mass of documents and mystified as to what Ord's policy had been. It was not until after his return from Selangor on 13 February 1874 that Sir Andrew could turn to the Sungei Ujong files. He tried to supplement this written information by sending for the chiefs themselves. Only the Klana came to Singapore in person but the others sent their

[1] Chelliah, op. cit., appendix A (11).
[2] Chelliah, op. cit., appendix B (5).

agents from whom he gained an idea of their views. The chief object of the Dato Perba was to obtain British recognition as the ruler of Rembau, but this Sir Andrew did not immediately concede. Such a recognition should be a part, he concluded, of a general settlement and one which would involve reopening the Linggi river. Knowing his views on this point, Captain Shaw arranged a meeting in Malacca between the Klana and the Dato Perba. There was a preliminary agreement on 28 March covering the removal of the stockades, but it soon became apparent that the Dato Perba lacked the power to interfere with them. The chiefs to whom he owed his accession were in effective control and were opposed in fact to any settlement being made. This fact was emphasized soon afterwards when a boat manned by Malacca police was actually fired upon and robbed of $600 in cash.[1]

The Klana, by contrast, came to Singapore and there, at Government House, signed an engagement on 21 April by which he and the Dato Muda of Linggi accepted British protection, assumed responsibility for protecting trade on the Linggi river, promised co-operation against wrongdoers and information concerning 'all events of political and mercantile importance', and finally agreed

that the Station, District or Settlement at Sempang, with all the river bank on both sides of the River Linggi, from Sempang as far as Permatang Pasir, shall be placed under the control, order and direction of the British Government.[2]

That the Klana had the power to make any such treaty as this was more than doubtful; that his authority to do so would be denied by the Dato Bandar was certain.

The Governor decided to repeat the tactics found effective in Perak and Selangor. He would call the chiefs together and force an agreement on them. His summons went forth, naming Kuala Linggi as the place and 2 May as the date. He and Braddell arrived with H.M. Ships *Charybdis* and *Avon* to find the Klana there with his followers and a message from the Dato Perba alleging that only a severe sickness prevented his appearance. Clarke disbelieved this excuse, concluding that the real obstacle was the opposition of the robber chiefs. He fixed another rendezvous, this time at Simpang on

---

[1] S.S. No. 142, 8 May 1874.
[2] Winstedt, 'History of Negri Sembilan', p. 69. The Klana also received the weapons he had ordered four years before.

the 5th. Again the Dato Perba expressed his inability to be present but adding this time that the stockades were not his. The Governor decided that, in that case, they must fall within the jurisdiction of the Dato Klana. Indeed, they were bound to do so if the engagement of 21 April was to have any validity at all. Did the Klana agree to their destruction? Did he need any assistance? The answer to both questions being 'Yes', Sir Andrew took the Klana on board the *Pluto* and they ascended the river together at the head of the warship's boats. As part of the same flotilla went three tongkangs laden with arms and ammunition for the Klana, from which the embargo had been removed. The stockades were found unoccupied, deserted by their garrison earlier that day, and were destroyed. The Dato Klana was left in possession and trade was already being resumed when Sir Andrew quitted the river on 7 May. He was back at Singapore on the following day.[1] He shortly afterwards recognized the Dato Perba as chief of Rembau, believing perhaps that peace was now assured. He was soon to be undeceived.

Immediately after the destruction of the stockades at Bukit Tiga the eighty-year-old Dato Bandar seems to have made some gesture which the Dato Klana accepted as the equivalent of submission. But this conciliatory mood ended with the arrival in Sungei Ujong of Raja Mahdie and Raja Mahmood. They had been driven from Selangor by Tunku dia Oodin and soon persuaded the Dato Bandar to adopt a more aggressive attitude. He already had a majority of the Malays on his side and could easily gain more adherents by pointing out that the Klana was selling his country to the British. The Dato Klana, whose main asset (apart from his rifles) was the British alliance, hastened to consolidate his position by asking for a British Resident, naming Mr. Isemonger (the Malacca magistrate) as a man highly suitable for the post.[2] The Governor was not yet ready for that step and the Dato Klana had to be content with protection of a less effective kind. His plan was to hoist the British flag in front of his house at Ampangan in the hope that the Dato Bandar's men would respect it, seeing him to be 'under the protection of the Great Governor'. At the first attempt to raise the staff the Dato Bandar appeared with his men and forbade it—this, after the Klana's men had killed and eaten buffalo in celebration. It was not perhaps a particularly tactful move, as the Klana himself began to realize. So

---

[1] S.S. No. 142, 8 May 1874.
[2] Winstedt, op. cit., p. 71.

much might be inferred from his letter of 24 September to Captain Shaw:

If we raise the flag, perhaps the Datu Bandar will attack our place; this we inform our friend. And further we would like very much to have our country populous, and a good straight road for traders to come and go on, so that the country may be populous, and doing good to all men. And further, we would like very much for an officer from the Great Governor, who can give good advice, so that we may do what is right under that protection. Now Datu Bandar wants to fight us; and of our men two-thirds wish to follow us, but the remainder will not as yet follow us in the fight. It will hurt our country: this is what we complain, and ask our friend's help, with which, together with the help of our men, we can destroy the Datu Bandar's district, because he it is who sets up the wicked people, and will not obey our orders.

To understand the full significance of this appeal it is necessary to hark back to certain events in the previous month. After a further piracy not far from Langat in July, the Governor had gone with the *Pluto* and *Avon* to Klang. There had followed a conference at Langat with Tunku dia Oodin and the Sultan, as a result of which there was a concerted movement against Labu, the *Hart* and *Avon* co-operating with Tunku dia Oodin's men and a request being sent to the Dato Klana to assist from the Sungei Ujong direction. This ambitious plan was not entirely without result. It left Frank Swettenham as the Sultan's unofficial adviser—he went in the *Hart* from Singapore on 12 August and remained at Langat (with twenty Malay policemen from Malacca) after the operation was over. It brought the Klana a visit from Mr. Isemonger, whom he would have liked to detain. It also had the effect of driving Rajas Mahdie and Mahmood into Sungei Ujong. This was not, strictly speaking, what the operation had been planned to ensure, but the Governor was to claim afterwards that the 'piratical band' had been 'so effectually dispersed that it has never been heard of since'.[1] Be that as it may, the more obvious result was the migration of Mahdie and Mahmood and the Bandar's decision to harbour them and indeed to make the latter his commander in the field. The situation may have improved in Selangor. In Sungei Ujong it had changed abruptly for the worse.

The Dato Klana's appeal reached Sir Andrew Clarke at about the end of the month. His reaction was to send for Mr. W. A. Pickering and instruct him on 3 October to proceed to Sungei Ujong with

[1] S.S. No. 356, 29 Dec. 1874.

advice for the Dato Klana, warnings for the Chinese and letters for the Dato Bandar and Dato Perba. He was chosen for this mission because of the paramount importance of preventing any Chinese intervention in a Malay dispute.[1] He left Singapore on 4 October and reached Sungei Ujong, via Malacca and Lukut, on 8 October. With Pickering went Mr. Hayward, Acting Superintendent of Police at Malacca, and a party of Malay policemen. Pickering had an interview with the Dato Bandar and finally returned to Singapore 'with a written assurance from the Datu Bandar that he had no intention of making any attack on the Datu Klana'.[2] It was apparently while Pickering was there that the Klana nerved himself to hoist British colours.

On Sunday 10 October, 1874, a flagstaff 'as large as a schooner's mainmast' was erected by the Klana's house at Ampangan and on the next day the British flag was hoisted to a salute of 21 guns: a pot of incense was burnt at the foot of the flagstaff and an old Haji knelt and recited prayers.[3]

On Pickering's return, after his visit to the Dato Bandar on the 14th, Sir Andrew began to have some doubts as to whether the Dato Klana was really superior to the Dato Bandar, and if so to what extent. Pickering may have had something to say on the subject. There was that petition of 1860 in which the Dato Bandar was named 'head of the trade', in whose absence the Dato Klana had been levying blackmail. He may also have recalled (without mentioning) the blunder made in Perak over Raja Yusof. Any doubts he may have had were reinforced by a letter from the Dato Bandar (or Shahbandar) himself, dated 13 October, and brought presumably by Pickering.[4] In it the Bandar claimed virtual equality with the Klana 'the first one is to rule the water and the second the land'. The two chiefs had to act together after consultation with their relatives and heirs. The Dato Klana had not done that. He had acted illegally in hoisting the British flag on his own authority. He had also (on 13 October) provoked the Dato Bandar still further by inciting some Chinese to steal two cannon from the Bandar's store-house at Rassa. It was this last misdeed and the erection of a menacing stockade which had driven the Dato Bandar into making his belated protest.[5]

---

[1] Sir Andrew thought Pickering 'the person of all others who would be most likely to influence the Chinese' and so avert a repetition of the Larut Wars but staged in Sungei Ujong. See S.S. No. 356.   [2] Ibid.
[3] Winstedt, op. cit., p. 71.   [4] Chelliah, op. cit., appendix H (I).
[5] Ibid. 'He has erected a stockade in the jungle in the middle of the path opposite to our own house.'

Sir Andrew Clarke felt that he was getting out of his depth. He wanted a Malay expert to find out the truth for him. Frank Swettenham was the man—he could consult his old Sultan at Langat and then go and investigate on the spot. Instructions to this effect were sent to Swettenham. Pickering was also sent back to Sungei Ujong, accompanied by a few police under a European sergeant—and bearing a letter to the Dato Bandar. In it the Bandar was urged to become a party to the engagement sealed by the Klana on 21 April. It is just possible that the Dato Bandar now learnt the details of this for the first time, for his response was anything but friendly. In an interview on 5 November he refused to agree to anything, asserted his equality with the Klana and denied the validity of a treaty made without his own concurrence. Frank Swettenham appeared shortly afterwards, coming from Selangor, and met the Dato Bandar unexpectedly. 'What!', said the old chief, '*another* European! You travel about my country as if it were your own.'[1] The result of Swettenham's travels and inquiries had been, in fact, to confirm the Dato Bandar's view of his constitutional position. The Klana was bound, at the very least, to consult him; and this he had clearly failed to do. Swettenham explained all this to Pickering, who realized at once the extent to which Captain Shaw's views on this matter had been coloured by his relationships (social and otherwise) with the Dato Klana. Something would have to be done about it.

Pickering decided that his best plan would be to draw up an agreement in which the relationship of the Klana and Bandar should be at once recognized and defined. With the help of the chiefs and elders a document was produced in which the Dato Klana referred explicitly to the 'hereditary powers' of the Shahbandar, 'based on the ancient rulings of the elders which may in no way be changed'.

Furthermore this is to confirm my agreement with the Shabandar that I shall, in every case and in every action, consult the Shabandar.

The Dato Shabandar also shall in every action consult me. Otherwise his action is invalid. This is the ruling of the elders on this point and this is how the Klana and Bandar shall rule the land.[2]

This document was sealed by all the chiefs (twelve of them, including the Klana and Bandar) on 10 November, and witnessed by Pickering.

[1] Vetch, op. cit., p. 167.
[2] Chelliah, op. cit., appendix I, p. 97. Admittedly, this leaves a doubt as to what would happen if the Bandar, when consulted, did not agree. The word 'consult' is slightly ambiguous, as we have discovered in another context. (See p. 137.)

For the moment it must have seemed that a clash had been averted. The trouble, however, about this agreement was that it applied logically to the past as well as the future. It invalidated the treaty of 21 April, which the Bandar had refused to seal. It also made nonsense of the Governor's contention, as afterwards expressed, that the Klana was the 'acknowledged Head' and 'Chief Ruler' and that the Dato Bandar had to be brought to a sense of his position.[1] There was doubt, and there may still be doubt, as to precedence between the Dato Klana and the Dato Bandar. That their authority was once more or less co-equal would seem to be beyond question.

Pickering had a difficult decision to make. He and Swettenham had a last interview with the Bandar on the 14th, in which they vainly exhorted him to come to terms with the Klana. They could do nothing more. The legal position was clear but the fact remained that the Klana was a man with whom the British could co-operate, the Bandar a man from whom they could expect nothing but a surly opposition. The Bandar denied all knowledge of Raja Mahmood, who was (as everyone knew) his Panglima Prang. Both sides were preparing for war. Pickering could have left them to it. He could have returned to Singapore and reported to the Governor that his information had been wrong and that the Bandar's claims were just. But that, he knew, was no way to gain official approval. Apart from that, he knew what the general policy was. The Malay States were to be brought under British protection, governed by approved native rulers and opened to peaceful commerce and development. What would be the use of leaving Sungei Ujong in a state of civil war? And yet war there would certainly be if the Klana were to pose as ruler and the Bandar were to refuse (as he did) to be one of those ruled. There was only one acceptable solution to the problem and that was for the Klana to gain a swift victory and so induce the Bandar to submit. Without leadership no such victory could be gained. The Klana was incapable of leadership, so Pickering himself would have to take command and direct such an offensive as the Dato Bandar would certainly not expect.

In the above paragraph there is admittedly a great deal of mere surmise. But what other conclusion is possible? In September we hear of the Dato Klana appealing pathetically for British protection. He wants to hoist a flag but the Bandar may attack him if he does.

[1] S.S. No. 356, 29 Dec. 1874.

A third of his men are cowardly or disloyal. In October he hoists his flag, still terrified of the consequences. On 10 November he freely acknowledges that the Bandar's authority is little less than his own. Then, on the 16th he is suddenly spoiling for a fight, kris in hand, barely to be held back. Who was there to urge him on, except Pickering? Who else was there to tell him that his best chance would be in a night attack? To this one obvious reply would be 'Swetten-ham'. But Pickering was evidently at pains to get rid of Swettenham before things began to happen. He was sent back to Selangor, pre-sumably on the 15th and probably without knowing what the Klana (or Pickering) had decided to do.

The Dato Bandar was himself at Kapayang with most of his men, but he had stockaded outposts at Rassa and Rahang, in the vicinity of the mines. It was decided to capture these on the night of 16 November, the Klana assembling 400 men for the enterprise. The attack succeeded, the stockades were taken and occupied, and the Klana followed up his success by advancing next day on Kapayang with his Arab bodyguard and some 200 Malays. 'I accompanied him', reported Pickering discreetly, 'to see that no cruelty was prac-tised, if victorious.' He need not have worried about that, as things turned out, for the Dato Klana was *not* victorious. As soon as the famous Raja Mahmood appeared with his men outside the Kapayang fort, all the Klana's Malays instantly fled in panic.

Finding himself helpless, he [the Klana] applied to me for assistance, and, with the help of Sergeant Kiernan and the Arabs, he was brought home safely. . . .[1]

Mahmood followed in pursuit and the remnant of the Klana's army prepared to defend the stockade at Ampangan. Pickering was back there on the 19th, by now frankly in command, and wrote on that day to Malacca for help. His army comprised, at that moment, besides himself and Kiernan, two policemen and twenty Arabs.

The Klana's men have given up every place, and have run away with their arms. Mahmood is within two miles of this, and by all accounts intends attacking to-night. The Tunku Klana is a cur, but we don't like to leave him. We will do our best and wait for your help. We are surrounded here, and only ourselves and the Arabs will do anything.[2]

This message reached Malacca on the 21st and Singapore on the 23rd. Captain Shaw acted promptly, sending off such troops as he

---

[1] S.S. No. 356, 29 Dec. 1874.   [2] Ibid. See also Vetch, op. cit., p. 168.

had. These comprised Lieutenant H. W. Palmer, Lieutenant G. B. Peyton, a sergeant, a bugler, and twenty-six men of the 10th Regiment, with a few policemen.[1] They went by sea to the Linggi river, landed there, and began an eighteen-mile march towards Ampangan. It would have been scarcely possible for them to arrive before the 24th and they did not actually arrive until the following day. Much could have happened in the meanwhile. Much actually did happen, for Pickering, unattacked on the night of the 19th, took the offensive and successfully recaptured Rahang and Rassa, the latter on the 23rd. In Pickering's words:

> After having been deserted by all the Malays, and being surrounded and threatened by Che Kari, the Bandar and Mahmood, thanks to Providence and the bravery of Sergeant Kiernan and the Arabs, we managed to turn the tables on them before assistance arrived, and to create in the minds of both Malays and Chinese a wholesome fear of the British Government.[2]

With a wealth of omissions, Pickering thus told a story which ceases to be exciting at the point when Palmer arrived with his platoon of the 10th Foot. From that moment the operations became merely punitive.

Sir Andrew, meanwhile, had not been idle. He collected what troops were available in Singapore and embarked with them on the 24th in H.M. ships *Charybdis* and *Hart*. With him went Captain Dunlop of the Singapore Police whom he appointed Civil Commissioner and ordered (on the 25th) to restore order, rescue Pickering, and garrison Sungei Ujong as necessary. Dunlop landed on the following evening at Lukut and marched inland on the 27th at the head of a mixed force numbering 187 combatants.[3] Sir Andrew Clarke went on in H.M.S. *Hart* to Langat with the object of seeing that the disturbances did not spread to Selangor. He was relieved to find that the Sultan was still on his side and ready to assure him that

---

[1] *Regimental History of the 10th Foot* (later the Royal Lincolnshire Regiment) quoted in Chelliah, op. cit., appendix P, p. 113. See also S.S. No. 356, para. 40.

[2] Vetch, op. cit., p. 170.

[3]

Officers	*Other ranks*
Inspector Cartwright	50 Native police
Captain Tatham	20 Royal Artillery
Lieuts. Huntley and Warton	50 10th Foot
Dr. McNamara	
Lieuts. Jones and Brooke, R.N.	40 seamen
Lieut. Montgomery, R.M.	20 marines
Dr. Gilson	
D'y, Commissary Boyes	

'the British and the Sultan of Selangor are one'. He was also relieved to find Swettenham still alive and at his post. Having asked the Sultan to send men to Kuala Labu to see that the Dato Bandar did not escape that way, Sir Andrew returned to Lukut and from there, on the 27th, wrote to his wife:

We got to Malacca on Wednesday at noon, and sailed the same afternoon for this place. After putting the troops and stores on shore, and arranging for their marching off this morning, I started to Langat in the *Hart* to visit the Sultan of Selangor, and see if Swettenham was safe; went up the Jugra River in the *Matta Matta* (steam launch), and got there by five in the afternoon, having captured on the river Mahmood's father. We saw the Sultan and Swettenham, had a very satisfactory interview with them, and arranged with them to send off people to watch certain places by which the enemy might escape.

Got back to *Charybdis* at three this morning, having had a hard but very satisfactory day of it. I thought we need not go on, and I think Brackenbury is much disappointed, but he is invaluable. Get Braddell [then Acting Colonial Secretary] to show you Pickering's letter. He is a rare good fellow and made of real stuff.[1]

Sir Andrew had meant to go with Dunlop's column, which set off that morning in the small hours, but there arrived Che Kari (the Bandar's son) with an offer of peace. It came too late to be of any use, although Clarke did give orders for a truce.

Dunlop and his men reached Rassa about midday on the 28th, finding it burnt and deserted, and pushed on to Ampangan, where he found both Pickering and Palmer. They told him that the Dato Bandar had withdrawn to Kapaying, so Dunlop made a reconnaissance of that position which ended in half an hour's firing before dusk. He deferred his attack until the following day, only to receive the Governor's message and a visit from Che Kari. The 29th was wasted in an abortive negotiation and, when the troops advanced on the following day it was to find the position deserted, with cannon and swivel-guns still mounted. In seeking to discover the Bandar's line of retreat, Dunlop questioned the Dato Klana but without much result. If ineffectual, however, the Klana was docile and promptly accepted Dunlop's advice—which was to imprison and frighten the two Chinese headmen or Capitans China, who had sided (not very actively) with the Dato Bandar. It was 'a splendid opportunity' as Dunlop observed 'of placing the whole of the Chinese in perfect

[1] Vetch, op. cit., p. 169. Clarke recommended Pickering for the Victoria Cross, but was told that he was not eligible, as a civilian, to receive it.

subjection to himself'. The next step was to locate the Bandar's tin reserve buried near Kapayang. This comprised 180 slabs and Dunlop made some of the Klana's cowardly and useless followers help in shifting the tin to Ampangan. 'What use these lazy fellows will be in the country I cannot see', sighed Dunlop. The value of the confiscated tin sufficed to meet the cost of the expedition.[1]

For some reason Dunlop concluded that the fugitive chiefs had fled southwards to Seppang. Mahdie and Mahmood had been seen there some time previously and might be supposed to have friends in the neighbourhood. Dunlop accordingly marched his troops to Seppang and, finding no trace there of the fugitives, marched back again to Rassa. This operation took place between 2 and 7 December and Dunlop felt that it had served its purpose.

This completed our jungle marching; and though we have done little, apparently, by our long and wearisome journeys, I believe they have produced an effect which will be felt throughout the whole peninsula. The Malays did not hesitate to say that we could not follow them into the jungle, and if we drove them out of their stockade, they had only to retire and remain in their jungles to be perfectly secure; now we have shown them that wherever Malays can go Europeans can go; and that after a whole week's marching in inclement weather, we were not half so much knocked up as the Malays who accompanied us.

This was perhaps an early demonstration of a truth which has been proved too often since and with a similar lack of any other useful result. In this instance it transpired that the Dato Bandar had not fled southwards at all. He had gone in exactly the opposite direction, to Battang Labu. Sir Andrew Clarke's first guess had been right—the fate of the defeated chiefs would rest with the Sultan of Selangor. He was right again in advising Dunlop not to start a full-scale hunt on the new trail. 'Do not venture too far into the jungle after the runaways, as it is not worth the risk of a torn pair of breeches.'[2] It also appeared that there had been a riot, during Dunlop's absence, between the Hwey Chews and the Kheys. Dunlop fined all three Capitans China impartially ($3,000 apiece) and received from Pickering some draft regulations which would tend to prevent further disputes among the miners; regulations framed to govern the mines, the opium and gambling farms, the pawnshops, the river traffic, and the possession of firearms. Then, on the 9th, leaving Captain Tatham as the Klana's adviser, with fifty soldiers (gunners

---

[1] Chelliah, op. cit., p. 36.   [2] Vetch, op. cit., p. 171.

and infantry) and thirty-two policemen, Dunlop sent off the rest of the troops. He and Pickering followed on 15 December, returning via Lukut to Singapore. The Governor himself had returned there some days before.

What, meanwhile, had happened to the fugitive chiefs? From the Labu neighbourhood the Dato Bandar and Raja Mahmood sent to inform the Sultan of Selangor of their whereabouts. The Sultan informed Swettenham, advising him that this was the moment to secure their submission. Sir Andrew, too, had seen his opportunity:

... and should it now be lost these men driven to desperation would betake themselves to the jungle from whence it would be almost impossible to dislodge them and where they would be able to renew the disturbances which had previous to our intervention last February distracted Salangore.

Their surrender, more especially that of Rajah Mahmood, would have a beneficial influence extending beyond the immediate scene of these late quarrels and throughout the Malay Peninsula, chiefly in the States on the western coast where his name has been a word of terror and his person regarded with superstitious dread for many years.

Mr. Swettenham, acting under instructions which I had given him at Lukut, sent word to the Datu Bandar and Rajah Mahmood that they would be received only on condition that they gave themselves up entirely and without reserve, and I am glad to be able to inform your Lordship that on the 21st instant they arrived in Singapore, and surrendered themselves unconditionally to the British Government.

I feel some difficulty as to their future disposal.[1]

There is a certain reticence about Clarke's dispatch. For one thing this insistence on Mahmood's warlike renown might serve to gloss over the fact that Mahdie had vanished. For another, this official verbiage about unconditional surrender squares ill with what we know about Swettenham's diplomatic skill. The Dato Bandar knew from Sheikh Mat Ali what the Governor's terms would be and there can be little doubt that it was Swettenham who talked Mahmood into surrender:[2]

[1] S.S. No. 356, 29 Dec. 1874.
[2] Swettenham told afterwards that the Dato Bandar's son-in-law Tuan Sheikh Mat Ali (aged nearly 100) lived at the time in his stockade, with the police. When the Dato Bandar and Raja Mahmood arrived in Langat they stayed with a Sumatran Malay called Dato Dagang. Dagang, on the Dato Bandar's behalf, offered Swettenham $1,000 (as first instalment of $20,000) if he would gain permission for the Bandar to return to Langat. The Bandar confirmed the offer in the presence of Sheikh Mat Ali as witness. Swettenham refused it, but nevertheless persuaded the Bandar and Mahmood to come with him to Singapore. See *The Real Malay*, F. A. Swettenham, London, 1899, pp. 63-85.

I have good reason to remember Raja Mahmud as he walked into my dilapidated stockade at the head of a dozen men who, like their master, feared God, but had no sort of fear of man. I suppose he was under thirty years of age, of average height for a Malay, very well built, and extraordinarily alive. He had a fine open face, looked you straight and fearlessly in the eyes, and you realised that he always spoke the truth, because the consequences of doing so were beneath consideration. He was very smartly dressed, with silk trousers and a silk sarong, a fighting-jacket, a kerchief deftly and becomingly tied on his head, and in his belt the famous kris *Kapak China*—the Chinese hatchet. . . . It was only a visit of ceremony, but Raja Mahmud's strong personality, his straight-forward manner, and his fearless courage attracted me immensely. We made fast friends . . . and in all the years which followed he never failed me, or any one else who understood him. Only he was not an everyday man: he was a type of the best quality of old Malaya, with all the Malay prejudices and hatred of innovation. One had to realise all this, to remember it, and to consider his view of life if you wished to see the best of him and earn his regard.[1]

Swettenham's impression of the Dato Bandar has also survived. From that, too, we might infer that he knew how to handle Malays.[2]

So much for Swettenham, at least for the time being; but what of Raja Mahdie? He seems to have reached Johore in safety, where he was induced to stay. As for the Dato Bandar and Raja Mahmood, they were sentenced to a strange punishment—a year's residence in Singapore—and the Bandar was replaced in office by Haji Ahmad bin Mohammed Ali, a friend and ally of the Dato Klana and one destined to live until 1928.[3] To these troubles there is a hint of a happy ending in the account of a ball at Government House, Singapore, reported in the *Straits Observer* of 11 February 1875. It was essentially a naval affair, designed to welcome Shadwell's successor, Admiral Ryder, who had arrived on 1 February in H.M.S. *Audacious*. We read, however, that the 250 guests included, besides the Maharajah of Johore, the Dato Shahbandar of Sungei Ujong, Raja Mahmood of Selangor, Raja Musa of Selangor, and Raja Mahdie of Klang. There is more than a touch of the picturesque in such a scene as this. Not two months before, Mahmood had been a fugitive in the rain-soaked jungle, trapped with the old Shahbandar between Dunlop's forces to the southward and Swettenham's old Sultan to the north. Seawards had been the slim masts of the

---

[1] Swettenham, *British Malaya*, p. 191.
[2] Swettenham, *The Real Malay*.
[3] The old Bandar was given a house and pension in Singapore, where he lived until his death.

warships and in his nostrils the acrid smell of powder from the recent rifle fire. Now his name was being announced above the music and chatter of the ballroom. We should give much to see Lady Clarke moving that night among her guests: 'Rajah Mahmood, how good of you to come! Allow me to introduce Captain Smith of the *Charybdis*, and Mr. Huntley of the 10th Regiment. Have you met Captain Dunlop? Mr. Pickering, I am sure, you already know. . . .' We are not to guess how impressed or puzzled was Mahmood by such a scene as this. All we know is that he next appears in history as a British ally, convinced that civilization is best or convinced at least that civilization was bound to come.

If Mahmood came to any such conclusion he was not alone in doing so. During this Sungei Ujong affair, from August 1874, Frank Swettenham was with the Sultan of Selangor at Langat, or to be exact at Banda Termasa. He did not waste his time and few weeks had passed before the Sultan was writing to thank the Governor in words which have been quoted more often perhaps than they have been understood.

We are very much obliged to our Friend for the officer whom our Friend has chosen. He is very clever; he is also very clever in the customs of Malay Government, and he is very clever in gaining the hearts of Rajahs and sons of Rajahs with soft words, delicate and sweet, so that all men rejoice in him as in the perfume of an opened flower.[1]

We may agree that Swettenham was clever, but we should also observe that the Sultan was no fool. With his sense of irony, how-ever, went a sense of reality. By 3 October he was offering to place Selangor under British protection.

As regards our friend's intention of having us enter into an engagement so that our friend will collect the revenue of our country, we feel very glad of it, provided our friend will put to right our country and collect the revenue. This letter, with our seal attached thereto, will be a sign that we trust to the assistance that will be afforded to us by our friend, and we leave everything regarding the opening of our country and the collecting its revenue in the hands of our friend, because from this day we have become good friends, and we trust our friend will render us every assistance in this matter. From this day our country is free from disturbances, and to our friend only we look that our country may be in perfect peace. . . .

Moreover, with regard to Mr. Swettenham, the officer of our friend, we have already reported in our last to our friend. At present we are building

---

[1] It was probably in this letter that the Sultan offered to pay Swettenham's salary.

a house for the residence of that gentleman so that he may live comfortably with us.

It will be realized that by December 1874 Sir Andrew Clarke had acting or unofficial advisers alongside the native rulers of Larut, Selangor, and Sungei Ujong. Of the Malay rulers, moreover, three (Abdullah, Tunku dia Oodin, and the Dato Klana) were virtually the men of his choice and supported by his authority. More than that he had not dared to do. It was only on 4 September that Lord Carnarvon wrote to confirm Speedy's appointment and authorize the Governor to appoint Residents to Perak and Selangor (the former at £1,800–£2,000 a year, the latter at £1,000–£1,500). This authorization led to the issue of a proclamation on 2 November, confirming the Pangkor Engagement and expressing the hope that the chiefs and peoples of the Malay Peninsula would realize how much they would benefit from the 'natural and unrestricted growth of commerce, which will surely follow upon the maintenance of peace and order'. This was followed by the announcement on 18 November that Sultan Abdul Samad had agreed to the opening up of Selangor. It was not until 14 December, immediately after the Governor's return from Sungei Ujong, that the following appointments were announced:

J. W. W. Birch	Resident at Perak.[1]
Captain Speedy	Assistant Resident at Perak.
F. A. Swettenham	Resident at Salangore.
Captain W. T. Tatham	Assistant Resident, Sungei Ujong.

The announcement was signed by the Hon. T. Braddell, Acting Colonial Secretary and 'Secretary for the affairs of the Native States'.

Exactly what protests were made locally about the appointment of Swettenham (aged twenty-four, of four year's seniority) to a post equivalent in rank if not in salary to that occupied by Birch (aged forty-eight of over twenty years' seniority) we are not to know. The result, however, of the internal conflict was that a further and hasty dispatch was sent to Lord Carnarvon on 30 December, submitting a different nomination for Selangor, as follows:

Mr. J. G. Davidson to be Her Majesty's Resident at Salangore, with the Viceroy of that State, Tunku Dia Oodin, at a salary of 1,500 l. a year.

---

[1] His salary was to be £2,000 in this post as compared with £1,740 as Colonial Secretary. The latter's salary was soon afterwards, however, raised to the same figure.

Mr. F. A. Swettenham of the Straits Civil Service, to be Her Majesty's Assistant Resident with the Sultan of Salangore, with a salary of 750 l. a year.

The reasons for this change were outlined privately. Swettenham, to whom they were no doubt explained, may not have found them convincing. To Birch they must have seemed unanswerable.

CHAPTER VIII

THERE is an authorized, official version of how the British came to intervene in what we now call Malaya. It is necessary at this point to emphasize that this accepted view is quite untenable. Swettenham states the orthodox view in his principal work and others have repeated it since. He described the chaos of Sir Harry Ord's day and alleges that:

between his departure in October, 1873, and the arrival of his successor, the plot so thickened that it might truly be said the western States of the Peninsula, from Perak to the borders of Johore, were given up to native warfare, with all the evils and miseries that follow in its train. At the same time, the Straits of Malacca were the scene of daily piracies, and all trade by means of native craft was paralyzed.[1]

At an earlier date he put the same idea into different words:

the hand of the Government was forced, not by our too-enterprising countrymen, not by the more modern mission of adventure and exploration, but by the inability of the Malay rulers to administer their own States, or control the Chinese, who had been attracted to them by the richness of their mineral deposits.[2]

He admits that 'British expansion, in the East at all events, is a record of the doings of courageous, capable, and masterful men'[3] but allows the general impression to remain that the change of policy was brought about by the unprecedented disorders of 1872–3. While we might agree that these internal disorders provided the occasion for British intervention, they were certainly not the cause. Had they, in fact, been the cause, we should be at a loss to explain why the British had not intervened before, why their intervention in Malaya was as extensive as it proved to be, and why they simultaneously intervened in places as remote as Fiji. To take these points in order, it is surely manifest that disorders in the Malay States had been endemic for years. The troubles in Sungei Ujong, for example, went back to 1845 or earlier and were probably at their worst in 1860. The troubles in Larut, even, went back to 1862. As for piracy,

---

[1] Swettenham, *British Malaya*, p. 132.
[2] Swettenham, *The Real Malay*, p. 7.
[3] Ibid., p. 9.

the authors of *The Malay Peninsula* say briefly 'The practice was inbred.'[1]

Regarding the scope of the policy of intervention, it is hard to believe that the disorders in Perak, Selangor, and Sungei Ujong reached a simultaneous crisis in 1874, suddenly compelling a reversal of British ideas about Malay independence. And one who was prepared to accept this coincidence might well be startled to hear of comparable troubles in Pahang, calling for interference at exactly the same time. That being so, it is relevant at this stage to record that Sir Andrew Clarke was told on 28 August of the murder of Inche Jawa, a Johore headman, on the Indau River. According to his informant—the Maharajah of Johore—the murderers were from Pahang and were instigated by the Bandahara of that State. On 17 September, therefore, before the affair in Sungei Ujong, Sir Andrew in the *Pluto* sailed for the Pahang river with H.M. Ships *Charybdis*, *Hart*, and *Avon*—and the Johore gunboat *Pulai*. This was two days after the meeting of the Legislative Council at which Mr. W. R. Scott said: 'You have met with a considerable amount of success on the western coast; you are now going to the eastern coast, and I wish you equal success there also.' The Governor saw the Bandahara on 21 September, offering his services as friend and arbitrator. It soon appeared that the Bandahara knew nothing of the murder, which investigation showed to have been the result of a purely private vendetta.[2] An inquiry was conducted by Mr. W. H. M. Read, who concluded his report by expressing a general opinion of the affair:

I must say that I never heard of such serious accusations, supported by such flimsy evidence. There is not an iota of proof to show that the Pahang Government was in any way concerned in the disturbances. The evidence produced was most defective. Important witnesses were not on the spot, although residing at no great distance in Johore territory. The exaggeration of the statements, and the carelessness with which they were drawn up, are highly reprehensible.

I have further to state, that I have not been able to obtain any evidence as to the truth of the report of the blood-thirsty nature of the Bandahara; on the contrary, all spoke of him as a remarkably mild ruler—one man stating, that in the whole of the countries ruled by Malays, there did not exist a Rajah so beneficent.[3]

This report formed but an indifferent basis for an active policy

---

[1] *The Malay Peninsula*, Arnold Wright and T. H. Reid, London, 1912, p. 124.
[2] S.S. No. 292, 16 Oct. 1874.
[3] *Play and Politics, Recollections of Malaya*, London, 1901, p. 37.

designed to restore order in Pahang and Sir Andrew may have regretted his decision to invite Read's co-operation. He did so, by his own account, because Read's sympathies were well known to be in favour of the old Johore dynasty 'so that although privately on excellent terms with His Highness the Maharajah, he does not wholly uphold the past policy of the Government of India with regard to that Chief, a fact which would commend him to the confidence of the Bandahara'. The Bandahara's first reception of Read was not, in fact, particularly cordial, but Read certainly served to counterbalance the Governor's other adviser, Braddell, who was the Maharajah's legal adviser. One might add, however, that the presence of the *Pulai* did little, in itself, to convey a sense of impartiality. Read evidently went out of his way to exonerate the Bandahara, even to quoting an unsolicited testimonial to his character. Read's misjudgement of Ahmad's character was not entirely due, however, to his bias against the Maharajah. Hugh Clifford (who was to know Ahmad better) thought him 'the mildest mannered man that ever scuttled ship or cut a throat'.[1]

This episode is briefly described outside its chronological sequence not because of its importance (it was, after all, abortive) but as illustrating the trend of policy. In concluding his report[2] Sir Andrew Clarke made his own intention clear.

I have just learnt that the Bandahara has, in writing to his principal Chinese agent here alluded to my recent visit and saying that, acting on the advice I had offered to him, he was desirous of opening up his country to immigration and giving foreigners very favourable terms for settlement, assuring them of every protection for their lives and property. He also asked to have engaged for him at good wages 200 Chinese Miners.

Whatever else this action of Ahmad's may have meant, it certainly did not foreshadow a request for a British Agent or Resident. That Sir Andrew should have seized upon it may serve, however, to indicate that Pahang would have been placed under British control at this time had there been any possible pretext for intervention. Sir Peter Benson Maxwell was surely justified in regarding this Pahang affair as the prelude to a further action for which no excuse could be found.[3] The sole immediate result was that Ahmad gave the Governor, as a curiosity, a myna bird that could talk. It was perhaps significant that it could talk only Malay.

[1] *Bush Whacking*, Hugh Clifford, London, 1929, p. 202.   [2] S.S. 292, 16 Oct. 1874.
[3] *Our Malay Conquests*, Sir P. Benson Maxwell, London, 1878, p. 46.

That the general trend of policy resulted only in a minor degree from these local disorders, which Pahang lacked, is shown not only from the fact that Disraeli's policy in 1874–80 was generally active, but from the fact that a forward movement in the East was not even confined to Britain. As Professor Harrison points out, France 'from 1874 . . . used a combination of armed force and diplomatic pressure on the government of Annam in order to gain control in Northern Indo-China'.[1] The Dutch drive towards control of northern Sumatra had begun the year before and continued in 1874 with fairly heavy casualties. Nor were these examples unnoticed. As Mr. W. R. Scott remarked in the Legislative Council on 15 September: 'We see Holland gaining ground through this Archipelago. . . . We have France in Cochin China. . . .' There are, altogether, many reasons why we should conclude that Sir Andrew Clarke, if showing initiative and going at times beyond his brief, was fairly interpreting what he knew the general policy to be. It remains to see how his dispatches were received and how his actions came to be approved.

There was no doubt, of course, that the Governor would have the unanimous support of his Legislative Council, which was given him on 15 September. In the local press he was criticized for not doing more and criticized again for being so often absent from the colony. The *Penang Gazette* came out as early as 8 January 1874 with a demand for the annexation of the whole peninsula from Krian to Johore. In an editorial of 30 November 1874 the *Straits Observer* demanded a more vigorous policy in the peninsula but one which would allow the Governor to remain at his post on the island.

For a great length of time we have been acknowledged as holding a Protectorate over these States, and in addition to the power of interference we possess under existing treaties, we have the greater right—the moral duty which appertains to our position, to put a stop to a condition of things entailing so great a destruction of human life, hindering the progress of civilization, and impeding the honest effort of peaceful industry to bring forth the neglected wealth of the Peninsula for the use of the world. To the Government of the Straits has been appointed, or has been assumed by it, the carrying out of this duty, and it is more than pitiable to see a great opportunity so wasted by the timidity of those who apparently are unable to grasp the importance of the results dependent upon their policy. It is unbecoming in a high official of the British Government (as the Governor of the Straits' Settlements is) to be running backwards and forwards between one petty Malay chieftain and another, entreating them to be peaceful,

---

[1] *South-East Asia; A Short History*, B. Harrison, London, 1954, p. 200.

neglecting the local interests of the colony he is appointed to rule over to patch up hollow treaties and agreements with sham sultans and puppet princes; worthless treaties concluded with potentates without power, when by boldly seizing the reins of Government the contending factions now fighting but for plunder would be cowed and a permanent peace would ensue. It was thus that Brooke maintained himself in Borneo, and, stronger proof of the policy too, it is that followed by orders of the Home Government towards Fiji. The trimming tactics of Sir Harry Ord, and we presume from the tenor of his lengthy minute, of his Attorney General, have notoriously failed in everything excepting in increasing the disorder. . . . It is high time that Government should drop playing at Machiavel and try the effect of a little Bismarck. This is neither claptrap nor bombast. It is a straightforward exposition of what should be done, and which we have as perfect a right to do as we have any right at all to interfere as we are at present doing. No law of nations, no law of justice, nothing can be urged against our administering the Government of the country ourselves with so great an effect as can be against our selecting one claimant over another and installing him on a disputed throne. If we do the latter, it is ten chances to one that we pick out the wrong man, and, whether or no, we are bound to keep him in his seat after we have put him there. . . . We say that the chances are that we should select the wrong man to favour—and if rumour be correct, we have done so already as far as the wishes of the people of Perak and Larut are concerned. . . .

In the meantime, the affairs of the Colony itself are neglected. As everything requires His Excellency's initiation as well as sanction, things much wanted are seldom begun, and when begun are allowed to take far too long time to finish. . . .

The rest of this significant article is about the quarantine establishment, the roads, the drainage, education, and defence.

Even the popular Sir Andrew Clarke was thus subject to local criticism. He was not criticized, however, for going too far but for not going far enough. In England, by contrast, there was some real opposition to his whole policy. This centred, in the first place, upon Sir Peter Benson Maxwell, but was taken up by Lord Stanley of Alderley. This peer, the third Baron, had travelled extensively in 1859–69, visiting the Malay Peninsula among other places and returning with a reputation as an orientalist and as a friend of Sir Richard Burton, the explorer. In a supplement to the *Dictionary of National Biography* there are some clues to his position and character, notably in the statement that 'Though he was a Mussalman, he was an ardent supporter of the Church of England, especially in Wales.' He was a constant writer of letters to the *Morning Post*.

In the House of Lords, although a frequent questioner and speaker, he was handicapped by deafness, a weak voice, and hurried articulation. Despite conservative predilections he sat on the cross benches, declining to identify himself with either political party.

Much of what he had to say might have been entertaining had it been audible. However handicapped he may have been, none the less it was he who first compelled Lord Carnarvon to come forward publicly and avow his responsibility for Sir Andrew Clarke's policy.

The main point of Lord Stanley's speech lay in his assertion that the policy of the Straits Government 'must inevitably lead to the invasion and conquest of the whole of the Malay Peninsula'. He also pointed out, however, that the policy to be pursued in the Malay Peninsula was exactly that of the Dutch in Sumatra—where all Straits sentiment was on the side of the Achinese. He deplored the proposal to call the British officials 'Residents'—'a title which in Java was equivalent to that of Governor, and which in British India was associated with annexation'—and he begged that the Government would appoint to these posts 'respectable persons, responsible to the Home Government and independent of Singapore local interests and influences'. Then he went on to assert that Sir Harry Ord and other officials had received presents from 'Native Chiefs and others'.

The noble Earl [the Earl of Carnarvon] had the ill luck to appoint this Governor, who disorganized the public service, squandered the revenues of the colony on building a house for himself—and for that purpose seized the bricks which the municipality had provided for water-works and drainage, and on their remonstrating threatened to suppress them—a Governor who had left behind him a reputation which could only be compared to that of a Roman Proconsul of the time of Cicero. . . . Under the auspices of the noble Earl, an Attorney General was appointed who had no knowledge of law, and who had been specially passed through Gray's Inn within one year, as he was only to practise in a colony.[1]

The rest of a rather rambling speech, which was very imperfectly heard, dealt with the Straits judges' lack of independence, with Selangor piracy, with H.M.S. *Rinaldo*, and with other kindred matters. He moved that copies should be presented of the Straits Government's correspondence relating to the Malay States.

Coming from a cross-bench critic these accusations and complaints found favour with neither party. It so happened that Sir

[1] Hansard, vol. ccxix, 1874, cols. 467–73. Mr. R. C. Woods, Acting Puisne Judge when he died in 1875 (aged fifty-nine), had been admitted to Gray's Inn in 1873. The former Attorney-General was now Acting Colonial Secretary.

Harry Ord had been appointed by Lord Carnarvon but had been later responsible to Lord Kimberley, while Sir Andrew Clarke, appointed by Lord Kimberley, had been responsible to Lord Carnarvon. It was thought neither fair nor convenient to make a scapegoat of either governor. No doubt by previous arrangement, the present and the former Secretary of State for the Colonies spoke with one voice. Lord Carnarvon mentioned the complexity of the situation in the Malay States—'no Governor ought to be judged severely if he made some mistakes'. He saw no objection to the proposed appointment of Residents 'at the distinct request and entreaty of the Rajahs to whose courts they had been sent'.

In regard to the question whether the Home Government would approve the proceedings which had been taken, he might state that they were awaiting a further and, as he believed, final report from Sir Andrew Clarke. Till that report came to hand it would, of course, be improper to express any final opinion on the subject, but he felt no hesitation in saying that, in so far as he had become acquainted with the proceedings, the conduct of Sir Andrew Clarke seemed to him to deserve approval.

The Earl of Kimberley then rose to defend the Colonial Office in his turn. He knew nothing of the recent treaty engagements beyond what he learnt from the Press.

He was inclined, however, to think it would be found that Sir Andrew Clarke, in whom he had great confidence, had exercised a wise discretion in the proceedings he had taken.

The motion was rejected and nothing more would have been said on the subject had not Lord Stanley's speech contained its critical reference to Sir Harry Ord. No reply was made to this at the time for the good reason that Lord Carnarvon had 'failed to catch the noble Lord's words'. Ord, however, saw the report of the speech and protested. The result was a further speech by Lord Carnarvon on 21 May in which he denied all that had been alleged against Ord and his Attorney-General. He was again supported by Lord Kimberley, who mentioned how difficult the situation had been at the time of the Colony's transfer. Ord may not have pleased everyone but he had done good service. 'As to the Attorney-General, I must say that I never before heard a syllable disparaging to him.' Lord Stanley refused to withdraw anything that he had said and there the matter ended.

Little support as he was likely to obtain, Lord Stanley was right in at least two respects. The colonial policy he criticized would certainly lead to the conquest (by whatever means) of the whole or nearly the whole Malay Peninsula. And the first Residents were not to be the 'respectable persons' Lord Stanley would have approved, but the very men, subject to local interests, whose appointment he obviously expected. Sir Andrew was at pains to justify each appointment, but his explanations did not entirely convince the public then; nor do they satisfy the historian now.[1] Speedy was not so much appointed as bought out, the first plan being to pay him £2,000 a year in lieu of the far larger salary he had expected to receive from the Mantri. Apart from the special circumstances, his was a very odd appointment indeed. So far from being independent of local influences, he had actually been in the Mantri's pay. Davidson's appointment was still more difficult to justify, as Clarke realized.

Although Mr. Davidson has, as I have assured myself, a very considerable and profitable practice at the bar here, that practice would be still larger had he devoted, or would devote, himself entirely to the exercise of his profession; but his attention having been diverted to native subjects, he first began by taking an interest in them, and then eventually dedicated himself to a very great extent to the task of advising Tunku dia Oodin during the last three years, and has been so far successful in restoring tranquillity to that portion of Salangore over which the Tunku's Viceroyalty extends, not only by frequently being present with him in the field but also by assisting him very freely with funds.

Under ordinary circumstances the latter fact would indeed have made me hesitate in suggesting Mr. Davidson for the office of Resident, but the confidence which he possesses amongst the entire European community of these Settlements, as well as amongst the Chiefs and people of this Malay State, combined with qualities of training which specially fit him for the labours he has undertaken, has influenced me to consider these qualifications as neutralizing the objections which doubtless would otherwise exist.[2]

With this dispatch Clarke enclosed a letter from Davidson, dated 15 December, stating that:

My private relations with His Highness the Viceroy of Salangore are now nearly closed and they will all be closed in a few days. I have arranged to transfer my claim against the Salangore Government for money advanced and services rendered as soon as it is finally adjusted, to Messrs.

---

[1] Sir Andrew Clarke told the Legislative Council on 15 Sept. about the appointment of Residents and Assistant Residents, adding: 'No doubt such officers will be difficult to select, but I hope among Englishmen they will be easy to find.' The meaning is not entirely clear but the difficulty of selection seems to have been more apparent, in practice, than the ease of discovery.

[2] P.P., 30 Dec. 1874.

Guthrie & Co., merchants here, to hold for me and to receive the interest and dividends in their own names.[1]

Does that really end Davidson's financial interest in the Viceroy's rule? Does it sever him completely from the Selangor Tin Mining Company? And, granted that we accept Clarke's motives for offering him the post, do we know exactly why Davidson accepted it?

Bitterest critic of British policy in the Straits was Sir Peter Benson Maxwell, the former Chief Justice. While regarding the appointment as highly improper, he thought that Davidson's personal character well fitted him for the post.

Of course a ruler in Tunku Kudin's position saw a saviour of society in an English Resident; and he gladly welcomed the officers whom Sir A. Clarke sent to reassure and support the Sultan of Salangore by their constant presence. The principal of them was Mr. Davidson, a lawyer of considerable reputation and practice at Singapore, and who was in many respects highly qualified for the post; for he had good sense, calm temper, and intimate knowledge of the Malays, as well as sympathy and consideration for them. But he was a large creditor of Tunku Kudin; his personal interests were much involved in the fortunes of the Viceroy, and for this reason his appointment was open to question.

It is but just to Mr. Davidson, however, to say that all accounts concur in describing him as having been an efficient officer and as having won the most friendly feelings of the Salangore people.[2]

Swettenham had a strong claim in some ways. He was purely a civil servant, with no commercial interests to serve, and he knew the Malay language and customs. But he was junior in the service and new to the responsibilities of office. That he had a brilliant future must have been generally realized. His earlier reports, however, from Selangor were destined to cause a certain annoyance, being worded in too pontifical a style for his age. Tatham's appointment to Sungei Ujong was, and was probably known to be, a temporary expedient. He fell sick early in 1875 and returned to England, his place being taken (but as Resident, not Assistant) by Commander P. J. Murray, R.N. (retired), appointed by Clarke in April of that year. Of Sir Andrew's appointments, that of Murray was the most successful. His choice of Mr. J. W. W. Birch as Resident of Perak was, by contrast, a serious blunder.

It is easy for us now to look back with our knowledge of what followed and say that Sir Andrew Clarke should have picked his men

---

[1] P.P., 15 Dec. 1874.
[2] Maxwell, op. cit.

more carefully. At the time it cannot have been an easy task. On the face of it, Birch was too senior for the post but his mere seniority made it the more difficult to reject his application. His experience had been mostly gained in Ceylon, his knowledge of Malay was slight and he was probably too old (at forty-eight) to learn the hundred ways in which Malay etiquette may be infringed through a stranger's ignorance. To set against all this, his personal qualities were admirable and he had worked hard to fit himself for his difficult task. It could not be said that his diplomacy in April–May 1874 had gained any startling results, but it was not apparent that anyone else could have done more. And since then Birch had scored a small success. He had been sent by Clarke to deal with a band of pirates headed by Raja Mat Samaun, 'a notoriously lawless character'. These criminals or customs officials (fine distinctions are not to the present purpose) were collecting duty on the tin from the Salama mines up a tributary of the Krian river in Perak, and collecting it, moreover, in the name of the wrong Sultan. Birch arrived on the scene on 9 October, sent by the Governor to investigate, and his police finally arrested sixty of the offenders, with Speedy's help, and sent them 'to the Sultan of Perak for punishment'.[1] On his return, however, to Penang, on 22 October, he found himself appointed Boundary Commissioner under Clause XII of the Pangkor Engagement. He returned to Perak, therefore, in this capacity and was still there when his appointment as Resident was announced. Sir Andrew Clarke wrote to him encouragingly:

Singapore, 16 November 1874.

My dear Birch

I must now content myself with saying that so far you seem to have done right well. I hope before you have got to Ismail you will have seen Yaha. Keep him with you and make much of him, but be sure of him.

Do not bother about the regalia, or any ceremony of making Abdulla sultan, and above all things I hope you will not forget to show every gentleness and deference to Ismail. Do not hurry him to any settlement of his own affairs, or to giving up anything. Interest him in inducing him to live where Abdulla will live, with all the honours of a sultan. Interest him in planting sugar, tobacco, etc. Swettenham has in this direction managed his old Sultan very well. . . .

[1] S.S. No. 349, 23 Dec. 1874. See also Vetch, op. cit., p. 175, for a quotation from Birch's letter in which he writes: 'Everything is quiet, and we have shown them this time that we do not mean to be played with. . . . We have no casualties and no sickness. . . .' The offenders were not punished, but merely sent back to their kampongs or villages.

You will have to watch the Mantri with all your eyes, and urge Speedy to do the same. Speedy will still believe in him. . . . [ref. to Abdullah] I should make him, I mean *induce* him, to go with you everywhere. Tell him the Sultan of Selangor is doing it with Swettenham; that his doing so will make him stronger in his country, etc. In short, organise a regular 'progress' with him, you, of course, taking care to be A1 and the prominent figure.

Yours
A. C.

P.S. Why not make Abdulla his own Commissioner to settle boundaries with you?[1]

From this it is clear that Birch was acting as Resident from 4 November 1874 and that only a serious blunder could have made him lose the appointment. He virtually assumed office when he joined Abdullah at Passir Panjang. The Sultan was living there in his boats, driven from Batak Rabit by fear of cholera. He showed no particular haste about appointing his commissioner to act with Birch under Clause XII of the Pangkor Engagement. He seems instead to have indicated that all the chiefs would have to be consulted before such an appointment could be made. Birch welcomed this idea because it presented an opportunity of bringing the two sultans together, as Sir Andrew wanted him to do and as he had tried to do in April. He went up the river accordingly and visited Ismail, whom he found this time in a more receptive mood, ready now to seal the Pangkor Engagement provided that Abdullah would meet him first. Such a meeting was accordingly arranged, with fourteen of the chiefs to be present and everything to be 'as imposing as possible'. Birch reported to the Governor that all arrangements were complete and that the meeting would take place in a few days' time. It was at this juncture that Sir Andrew Clarke made public his choice of Residents (14 December), convinced at last that Birch was the right man for Perak. He told Lord Carnarvon about Birch's success in a dispatch dated 24 December.[2] He followed this up with another letter on the 30th[3] in which he announced and explained the appointments he had recently made:

To the Sultan of Perak I have nominated as Resident Mr. J. W. Birch, the Colonial Secretary. I have not done this until after long and anxious consideration, nor until Mr. Birch had, by the success which has attended one or more missions with which he has lately been entrusted, given evidence

[1] Vetch, op. cit., pp. 176–7.
[2] S.S. No. 351, 24 Dec. 1874.   [3] P.P., 30 Dec. 1874.

of his ability, and still more of his tact and judgment in dealing with natives.

He goes on to mention Birch's long experience in the East, as also his untiring physical energy.

Sir Andrew Clarke's testimonial to Birch's ability is oddly defensive in tone, taking all the circumstances into account. Birch was his Colonial Secretary, his chief adviser, his right-hand man. One would have expected him to explain, in the first instance, how serious his personal loss would be and how so valuable an officer might be replaced. One would have expected him to dilate on the importance of the Perak Residency, in view of which even a Colonial Secretary might be spared to become the first Resident. But he says nothing of the Executive Council's loss, nothing of the bereaved Secretariat, and as little (in this dispatch) of any possible successor. He tries to explain, not how Birch can be spared, but how he has come to think him good enough for the post. Nor has he reached this conclusion without 'long and anxious consideration', even after Birch's recent success. This curious language about Birch having 'given evidence of his ability' (used with reference to a very senior official) contrasts oddly with his remarks about Swettenham, 'a young officer of very high promise' who has shown 'consummate judgment and ability'.

Granted that Sir Andrew was dubious about Birch, we might reasonably wonder why he appointed him. It would have been easy to say: 'No, you are too valuable here—you can't be spared.' Three possible explanations suggest themselves. In the first place he may have wanted to replace Birch as Colonial Secretary, putting Braddell into the vacancy. In the second place, he may have failed to find anyone better. His officers were, after all, relatively few. For such a post as this some were unsuitable (like Irving, to judge from subsequent events), some were indispensable (like Braddell and McNair), some were too junior (like Skinner), and others (like Willans) were probably too old. And of those theoretically available, both military and civil, some would certainly have refused to leave the Tanglin Club.[1] In the third place, Birch had apparently succeeded where the Governor himself had failed. The effort to bring Abdullah and Ismail together had begun at Pangkor and continued since, but now it was Birch, not Sir Andrew, who had managed to bring it about. If all went well at the meeting, Birch would certainly score a considerable success. As he himself said: 'Whenever Ismail joins the Treaty and

[1] Of which Birch was President.

receives his money, all difficulties in the government of the country will disappear.' This may have been fairly near the truth and no one (whatever his previous doubts) could have questioned the tact and judgement of the officer who had somehow persuaded Ismail to retire gracefully in favour of Abdullah. On 24 December the Governor believed that this feat had been performed. On the 30th a doubt had crossed his mind—he speaks of Birch's success in 'one *or more* missions'. With the new year must have come the realization of his mistake.

The sad fact was that Birch had not succeeded at all. Birch was still struggling to bring the chiefs together in January but his failure (about which he was reticent) was complete.

I made an attempt early in the year to bring the Sultan and ex-Sultan together and to effect a reconciliation. But to do so I was obliged to assemble all the Chiefs, and it was owing solely to the jealousies of all these Chiefs amongst themselves. . . that a perfect reconciliation was not then brought about. . . .[1]

We learn more from his diary than we do from this guarded statement. Abdullah was persuaded to meet Ismail at Blanja on 5 January. He did so in the presence of Yusof, the Bandahara, Birch, and a number of the chiefs. The Mantri, the Temenggong, and the Maharaja Lela were present in Blanja but kept away from the actual place of meeting. They thus spared themselves an embarrassing scene.

I went in front of 'Abdu'llah and took him up to Isma'il. The old man came forward with both hands out but 'Abdu'llah never took them; and he then in a most polite and kind manner pointed to him a chair and begged him to sit down. . . . Isma'il said a few nice kind words to 'Abdu'llah and he looked at him and just bent his head but nothing more. . . . Then there was an awful pause, 'Abdu'llah looked very sulky. Isma'il made several attempts at conversation with him but to no effect. I then said that speaking in the Governor's name. . . .

Birch tried desperately to say the right thing, through his interpreter, expressing the hope that, now the two sultans had met, there would be peace in Perak. To this Ismail replied 'Yes' and Abdullah said nothing. There followed prayers, conversation about the crops, cigars, syrup, and water ('improved a little'), oranges, biscuits, and painful silence:

but Yusuf who must have noticed my signs to 'Abdu'llah to speak to

[1] P.P., Birch to Clarke, 2 Apr. 1875, forwarded to Secretary of State on 26 Apr., as enclosure to the dispatch of that date received 7 June.

him, at last told me he was going to leave as he was hot and tired, and went out. . . . After making every effort on my part, Bacon's and Munshi's and Isma'il's—who gladly and in a very nice manner helped, I saw nothing could be done and as we had been there three hours I took my leave with civil speeches and hoped the friendly intercourse now begun would get stronger every day by interchange of visits.[1]

Birch groaned over this travesty of a reconciliation but hardly grasped its significance. On his theory of the situation Abdullah (wanting the regalia) should have been polite, eager to make friends and influence people; and Ismail (resolved to keep the regalia) should have been stern and forbidding. But the parts had been somehow reversed. Abdullah did not want the regalia and was terrified in case the good-natured Ismail should offer to surrender it. He had sent Ismail a private message, saying

I am now ascending the river, not by my own desire but by that of Mr. Birch. If he asks for the regalia or desires to instal me, do not consent. Should you consent to my installation as Sultan, Perak will be given over to the English; for my words have caused me to be much indebted to them. . . . Should I myself ask for the regalia in the presence of Mr. Birch, do not consent to give them up![2]

Doubtful as to whether this message had been received and understood, uncertain whether Ismail would act upon it, Abdullah had resolved to take no chances. He would wreck the meeting by a boorish refusal to say anything; and that was exactly what he did. Birch's failure to reconcile the two sultans was not as complete as he supposed at the time. They were agreed in one thing and that was in their dislike of him. In the meanwhile, Birch was being given the credit for a feat of negotiation which neither he nor anyone else had performed.

Sir Andrew Clarke would obviously have deferred placing a British Resident in a country as apparently divided as Perak now proved to be. He must have realized, at this point, that Birch's earlier reports had been too optimistic. To save the situation and avert possible bloodshed, his best policy would be to meet Ismail at Penang, allowing him to see the warships there and making him realize that his cause was hopeless but his pension certain. Failing that, it would be of some use to bring Abdullah to Penang with the other chiefs and convince them, at least, to follow a Resident's advice. There can be

---

[1] Winstedt and Wilkinson, *A History of Perak*, pp. 105–6.
[2] Ibid., p. 105.

no doubt that Sir Andrew was planning some move of this kind when he first received, by telegram, the offer of a high office in India and one for which he was well qualified. He seems to have accepted the offer at once, further telegrams relating mainly to the date by which he would be available for the new post. It was eventually settled that he should remain in the Straits Settlements until his successor should arrive in May 1875. Notice of his new appointment was released in Singapore on 13 February:

The appointment of Sir Andrew Clarke to the high Indian office we made known in our *Observer Extra* on Saturday last has taken the Colony by surprise. The post of member of the Council of the Viceroy of India and Minister of Public Works, to which Sir Andrew has been called is one that has just been formed, and is a result of the great scandals which have of late years occurred in the management of public works in India. The emoluments of the office are £8000 per annum, and the duties to be performed will be about as onerous and unthankful as can be imagined. . . .

There is but one feeling manifested upon the matter, that of regretful disappointment. We have heard His Excellency's removal spoken of as an irremedial loss to the Colony. Without going as far as that, it can be said with truth that it will have the effect of throwing public matters in this part of the world back to an extent impossible to overrate and unpleasant to think about.[1]

Sir Andrew Clarke had become identified with the new policy in the Native States and it was obviously feared locally that his removal might signify a changed outlook at the Colonial Office. The plan might be to replace him by one less inclined to act first and report afterwards. Even were there nothing deliberate about his transfer to India, his successor might prove more timid. Only a few days before, on 4 February, the same newspaper carried an editorial on England's imperial mission. It included the words 'To halt is to go back. We must go forward . . .'. It praised Sir Andrew's policy more than his genius:

That policy may in some parts be ill-digested. His Excellency may not possess, and we do not suppose he is vain enough to think he does, the attributes or prescience of a great statesman, but that policy on the whole shows that Sir Andrew Clarke can appreciate circumstances at their full value and know how to take advantage of them . . . which it would be well if more public men of greater pretensions could do.[2]

[1] *Straits Observer*, 15 Feb. 1875.
[2] Ibid., 4 Feb. 1875. Clarke would not have resented this. He was primarily not a statesman but an engineer.

In point of fact these local fears were groundless. Sir Andrew Clarke had not been disowned by the Colonial Office. He had received a spontaneous offer from Lord Salisbury, the Secretary of State for India, possibly at the instigation of Mr. Montagu Corry, and saw in it a path towards his real object of ambition. For Sir Andrew, politician as he was, owed his first loyalty to the Royal Engineers. His colonial interests were real enough but when his own party returned to office in 1880, with Childers in the Cabinet, it was not another governorship he wanted. All he wanted was to become the recognized head of his own Corps. With his appointment as Inspector-General of Fortifications in 1882, his main ambition was satisfied.[1] Towards that ambition the post in India was another step, and he took it all the more willingly in that he had not been given the military command in the Straits. He had accepted the governorship in the belief that this command would be his—'restoring me', as he said, 'to the active duties of my profession'[2]—only to find his name relegated to the reserve list. An appointment which placed him at the head of his Corps in India was a useful preparation for that final appointment in England which carried with it the rank of Major-General. He retired with the honorary rank of Lieutenant-General and cannot have regretted for a moment the decision which ended his governorship in the Straits.

What he must have regretted, however, was his removal before the Perak problem had been solved. There might have been time to solve it between February and May but fate intervened on 6 February, drawing his attention to a different problem of equal or perhaps greater importance. He had known in January of the growing tension at Bangkok between the First and Second Kings of Siam—tension which had resulted in the *Charybdis* being sent there to protect British interests. When it appeared that the Second King had sought refuge in the British Consulate, Sir Andrew pointed out to the Colonial Office that if Britain did not interfere, France certainly would. The result was that Clarke was instructed to mediate between the two kings. He sailed for Bangkok on 13 February in H.M.S. *Vigilant* with Admiral Ryder and crossed the bar of the Menam river on the 19th. The story of the negotiations which followed, and which were entirely successful, is not to the present purpose. Clarke played an important part in restoring supreme power to the

---

[1] Apart from becoming Colonel-Commandant of the Royal Engineers, which he did in 1902, just before he died.   [2] Vetch, op. cit., p. 120.

progressive King Chulalonkorn but the effect was to keep him fully occupied for weeks. He did not reach Singapore again until 4 March, upon which day he cabled home the news of his diplomatic success. He was unable, even then, however, to turn his attention to Perak. In his absence (and indeed on the day he had left) a riot at the criminal prison, Singapore, had resulted in the death of the superintendent of prisons. An inquiry would have to follow into the system, or lack of it, which allowed of such an outbreak.[1] Reports arrived from Aden concerning the overloading of ships in the pilgrim trade.[2] There were the Colony's annual estimates to prepare for the current year; estimates which included sums set aside for the establishment of a Museum and Library, as also Zoological Gardens.[3] A committee had been appointed to discover whether government departments were working efficiently and economically. Its report would probably recommend increased expenditure. A reconciliation was to be arranged between Sultan Ali of Johore and Abubakar, the Maharajah of Johore.[4] To make matters worse, the Acting Colonial Secretary, Mr. Braddell, had 'succumbed to the extra labour and anxiety' involved in 'Native Affairs' and gone to England on sick leave. For these and other reasons it was not until about the middle of April that the Governor was able to turn his attention to Perak.

Sir Andrew Clarke's last tour brought him in the *Pluto* to Penang on 15 April. He was accompanied by McNair and Dunlop and his hope was that the Sultan and his chiefs would meet him there. He received, instead, a lot of excuses. Birch, by contrast, appeared to make his report in person; essentially a report of his failure to influence Abdullah, with whom by this time he was hardly on speaking terms. At Penang the Governor's next concern was in attempting to settle the Mantri's debts. He then went on with Birch to visit Larut on the 18th. After inspecting Taiping, he called at Malacca on the 23rd and was back in Singapore on the 25th.[5] He had reason by then to be deeply concerned about the whole situation. We know, moreover, that he *was* concerned. He expressed his anxiety to Anson as early as 25 March, when he wrote:

I am very much annoyed with Birch, and the head-over-heels way in which he does things; he and I will come to sorrow yet, if he does not mind.

---

[1] S.S. No. 62, 9 Mar. 1875.
[2] S.S. No. 68, 12 Mar. 1875.
[3] S.S. No. 92, 5 Apr. 1875.   [4] S.S. No. 95, 6 Apr. 1875.
[5] The tour is described in the *Straits Observer*, 26 Apr. 1875.

He has made a regular mull of the farms, and does not seem to have impressed either the Sultan or the ex-Sultan very favourably.[1]

Having seen Birch again he was more worried still. On 22 April he wrote to Abdullah a letter of remonstrance, warning him not to collect taxes, not to delay fixing the new boundaries, not to overlook crimes such as murder (even when committed by a Raja), and not to ignore the Resident's advice. All this admonition resulted from Birch's complaints about the Sultan. But the Sultan, in the meanwhile, was preparing to complain about Birch. He did so (very guardedly) in writing and entrusted the letter, which was dated 26 April, to Raja Dris, the Laxamana, and Mahomed Arshad. These went as a deputation to Singapore. The letter with which they were armed asked only vaguely for help and especially for the Sultan's position to be confirmed, but his chiefs were to explain that what he wanted was to ensure that 'if anything is to be done the Resident must consult the Sultan'. They were also to make it clear that there was a general refusal by the Ulu chiefs to recognize Abdullah as Sultan at all.

Sir Andrew was back in Singapore, as we have seen, on 25 April, with only a fortnight to go before his successor should arrive; a fortnight devoted to farewell speeches and dinners. He had lacked the time for a visit to Selangor or Sungei Ujong, believing anyway that all was quiet in those parts. The reports received in April were reassuring and the commander of H.M.S. *Lapwing* had found the west coast a scene of perfect tranquillity.[2] As against that, his own popularity, to judge from the press, had recently declined. One journalist described the men he had appointed to the Malay States as 'unsteady and incompetent colonial officials' together with the same officials' 'impecunious and unsteady friends'.[3] Swettenham's cheerful report of 18 December 1874 had been printed and apparently gave offence:

we would guard the public against putting any great amount of confidence in the report we published last week by the Government Agent at Langat. Yet it is hardly necessary to do so; the egotism of Mr. Swettenham is so apparent, that it will place any sensible person on his guard against implicitly believing either his facts or his theories. Mr. Swettenham seems

---

[1] Anson, op. cit., p. 323.
[2] S.S. No. 64, 10 Mar., S.S. Nos. 12 and 123, 27 Apr. 1875.
[3] *Straits Observer*, 29 Mar. 1875.

to have but appeared upon the scene, and discord vanished. He showed his face and all was peace. No apparition of an irate beadle disturbed from his forty winks repose by the noise of a workhouse play-yard ever had such an effect as that of the amiable countenance of the four-year Colonial Cadet upon the dispute between the Sultan of Selangor and his naughty son-in-law Tunku Oodin. Governor Ord may have stormed, Lieutenant-Governor Anson have 'my friended' them, and Governor Clarke may have wheedled, it was reserved for Mr. Swettenham to gain the victory that was refused to the courage, the courtly epistles, and the lollipops of the others. Read the report and (if you believe it) you will not be long in deciding who had the most right to use the *veni, vidi, vici* style of address, JULIUS CAESAR or FRANK SWETTENHAM.[1]

Davidson's report of 16 March had also been published and attracted criticism for a different reason. His first difficulty at Klang had been to persuade the Sultan that Tunku dia Oodin was not plotting to succeed him and that Raja Musa's succession was agreed. But Raja Musa had his friends in Singapore (more of them, possibly, since he had been detained there) and one of these wrote to describe Tunku dia Oodin as 'a needy adventurer with his wits about him' and the main cause of the Selangor disorders; a man who had used the British to strengthen his hold on the Selangor coast, introduce the Chinese, and weaken the position of the Sultan's proper heir. The letter continues:

This is the whole history of Salangore politics in a nutshell. Tunku Di-Oodin . . . has played his cards very cleverly. He managed to raise the necessary funds to carry out his scheme and is now repaying his debts by a rebate of one-third of the Klang customs—that is, from his father-in-law's pocket—and has the Colonial Government pledged to support him . . . it may be that Sir Andrew Clarke has cleverly availed himself of the necessities of the man's position to the benefit of colonial and imperial interests.[2]

Nor were these criticisms confined to Selangor:

Weeks ago we said that Mr. Birch was not doing as he was expected to do, and had neither made friends with the Sultan nor the Chiefs, and had disgusted capitalists who wished to make ventures in the new territory. . . . We are told that a bungle has been made in the matter of the Opium and Spirit Farms in Perak. . . . It is well for Sir Andrew Clarke's popularity that he is soon to leave the colony, for His Excellency appears to be fast drifting

---

[1] *Straits Observer*, 29 Mar. 1875.
[2] Ibid., 26 Apr. 1875. One man who could not have written this was John Simons Atchinson. He had died on 23 Dec. 1874.

into the same stream that swamped his predecessor. By placing too implicit confidence in the shallow advisers around him and appointing to offices in the new territory men who are unworthy or unfit, he thus endangers the success of his otherwise well considered policy.[1]

Sir Andrew was consoled for this criticism by the praise of his adherents. At the dinner and ball given in the Town Hall on 5 May 1875 the Hon. Thomas Scott paid eloquent tribute, saying:

Sir, before you left England in 1873, you were entertained at a banquet by the Merchants of the Straits Settlements. . . . At that banquet, there would seem to have been shadowed forth what has been the distinguishing feature of your Governorship, your policy towards the Native States of the Malay Peninsula.

The Chinese spoke kindly of him and even more so of Lady Clarke (who had been charming to everybody). Almost Clarke's last public act, incidentally, was to recommend Hoo Ah Kay (Mr. Whampoa) for the award of the C.M.G.[2]

From the farewell addresses Sir Andrew turned to receive the deputation from Perak, perhaps fully realizing then for the first time how far he had been from settling the problems of that State. He was still preparing a written reply when Sir William Jervois, his successor, arrived in the French mail steamship on 8 May, two days before he had been expected. Sir Andrew had ceased to be Governor. He accompanied Jervois to the Town Hall on 10 May and heard him take the oath. It had been arranged that Sir Andrew should remain for a few days after vacating the governorship and he may well have welcomed the opportunity to discuss things with his successor. He might reasonably have told Sir William what he himself would have done, if still in office, to save the situation in Perak. This is probably what he did, but not, as Anson thought, with much effect.

It was arranged that Sir Andrew should remain at Singapore for a short time after Sir William's arrival, to give him any information he might require. This was a great mistake, for Sir Andrew wanted to dictate to Sir William the policy he should adopt, and Sir William declined to be dictated to. There was jealousy between the two and I received the confidences of both. Sir William was the senior officer in the Royal Engineers, to Sir Andrew.[3]

Before he left on 26 May[1] Clarke thanked Anson in a personal letter for his loyal support 'often when I fear you did not agree with my views'. He added ominously: 'Jervois has plunged into native states head-over-heels. He seems determined to get along. I hope he may not go too far.'

[1] In the S.S. *China*. Unlike Jervois, Clarke travelled in orthodox fashion by P. & O.

CHAPTER IX

THE choice of Sir William Francis Drummond Jervois to succeed Sir Andrew Clarke might have seemed to arise from a desire to console the Straits Settlements with a Governor as nearly as possible similar to the one they had lost. Jervois was three years older than Clarke and had been commissioned five years sooner. Their careers were otherwise much alike. Both came of military families. Both graduated from Woolwich into the Royal Engineers. Both served overseas, the one in South Africa the other in Australia. They were both experts on fortification and each was destined to end as Colonel-Commandant of the Corps to which they both belonged. They looked sufficiently alike, in uniform and side-whiskers, to create a doubt as to which of them a photograph is supposed to represent. They differed, nevertheless, in character and it is important to realize, at this stage, wherein that difference lay. First and foremost, Clarke was more of a politician than Jervois and less of a professional soldier. His interests were more diffused. He thought as a statesman, creatively and imaginatively, having had early experience of political office. Even as an engineer, his mind ran to railways, dirigible balloons, and torpedoes, far beyond the scope of the ordinary soldier. And as an imperial administrator he could think of a House of Lords for India and a museum for Singapore. He had a certain Irish plausibility to go with his Irish or partly Irish vision.

Sir William Jervois was more narrowly professional, more concentrated and more thorough. Fortifications played a bigger part in his life and he probably knew more about them. It was he, not Clarke, who studied the defences of Singapore—and then, later, did the same thing in New Zealand. He published many papers on purely engineering matters and even his drawings as a Woolwich cadet came to be framed on the lecture-room walls. It was he, not Clarke, who ended as a Fellow of the Royal Society. It was Clarke, not he, who thought of employing E. Onslow Ford, R.A., to design his wife's tomb. Jervois had for his first friend and patron the Prince Consort, an enthusiast for fortification. Clarke belonged to a select dining-club called 'The Owls', the other members of which—apart from

Childers and the inevitable Mr. Corry—included Evelyn Ashley, Laurence Oliphant, Lord Brabourne, Sir Henry Bulwer, and Lady Tankerville.[1] Significant, finally, is the difference between the ways in which they severally spent the leisure of retirement. Jervois wrote and talked about coastal and naval-base fortification, served on defence committees, and belonged to several scientific societies like the Institute of Civil Engineers. Clarke stood for Parliament (unsuccessfully) as a Liberal and became a director of Palmers Shipbuilding Co., the Colonial Life Assurance Society, the Delhi–Umbala Railway Co., and the British North Borneo Company. Jervois left as his monument a sheaf of technical papers. Clarke is commemorated by a bronze bust placed originally in the Singapore Chamber of Commerce.

In making such a comparison as this, it is important to remember that we are assessing or attempting to assess the merits of two extremely able men, each at the very top of his profession. Few of us today could claim to have the energy or brains of either of them. The fact remains, however, that the history of Malaya was influenced by their failings as well as by their abilities. In his handling of the Malay States Clarke foresaw 'a federation which will secure to the whole of the Malay Peninsula what it has so long wanted, and that is peace . . .'.[2] He lacked nothing in imagination. Where he had failed was in thorough investigation of the immediate problem. He spent only eighteen months in Malaya, all told, so his time was necessarily short; but it must be emphasized that he settled the problem of the Perak succession without having visited Perak at all. It is in that sense that his judgement was superficial. He left that State in the unstable situation which resulted from his first wrong decision; a situation prolonged by his refusal to see (and his officers' refusal to tell him) that it had been wrong. Had he remained in Malaya for another year he might have resolved the problem by the diplomatic skill he displayed at Bangkok and the powers of persuasion he used in Council at Singapore. He left instead, handing over the tangled reins to a man of a very different type; to a man of a more brusque, logical, and military character; to a soldier who had actually seen service in the Kaffir War; to an intellectual in whose eyes most of the Malay chiefs would be little better than imbecile. He handed them

---

[1] *The Life and Correspondence of the Rt. Hon. Hugh C. E. Childers, 1827–1896*, E. S. Childers, 2 vols., London, 1901, pp. 145-6.
[2] From his brilliantly astute speech to the Legislative Council of 15 Sept. 1874.

over, moreover, to a fellow officer, of similar status but slightly his senior, whose first instinct was to show, by a change of policy, that he was not merely following his predecessor's lead.

From 10 May to 12 July Sir William Jervois remained at his post and mastered the details of the Colony's administration and Sir Andrew's policy. He dealt in June with a demand sent to Tunku dia Oodin from the Bandahara of Pahang for compensation in respect of military aid afforded him in 1872-3. With help from Irving and Swettenham, Jervois arranged for the debt to be settled by instalments. He dealt in July with the question of the Krian boundary and Salama mines (which will be mentioned again in another context). He discussed plans for making a first, even approximate, map of the Malay Peninsula. Then, on 12 July, he embarked in the *Pluto* and went, escorted by H.M.S. *Thistle*, to visit Pahang, Trengganu, Kelantan, Patani, and Singora. He was accompanied by Swettenham and by his A.D.C., Lieutenant McCallum, R.E. The only immediate result of this tour (apart from a certain extension of knowledge) was a return visit to Singapore paid by the Sultan of Trengganu. The *Pluto* was sent to fetch him, returning on 29 August with His Highness and a retinue of 110 men and 40 women.

His Highness the Sultan of Tringanu arrived here in the Colonial Steamer *Pluto* on Sunday last and landed under a salute of 15 guns from Fort Canning yesterday morning at 7 o'clock. . . . His Highness is living in the house at the corner of Albert Road and Rochore Road, and was accompanied by eight carriage loads of ladies and a large number of retainers. The Sultan expressed himself much gratified with his reception and it is very probable he is so, especially when His Highness calls to mind how he was treated by Governor Cavenagh, and how his capital was bombarded a few years ago by H.M.'s ships *Scout* and *Coquette*, because he gave an asylum to His Highness's relation, the Sultan of Lingiu.[1]

Jervois reported afterwards that Trengganu, although potentially rich, needed developing, and that he hoped his visit had done something to improve the trade between Trengganu and the Colony. A local newspaper was more outspoken beforehand on that subject, and referred not merely to Trengganu but to all the States subject to Siam:

That all these States are rich in resources of every description there can be no doubt from the fact that the population, which may be pronounced the laziest in the world . . . are able to live with the smallest amount of work and even export gold, tin, gutta etc., procured in the rudest and most

[1] *Straits Observer*, 31 Aug. 1875.

wasteful manner. It only requires safety to life and property to be once assured, and capital will at once flow in with Chinese labour, roads will be made, the jungle cleared and planted . . . and a general era of prosperity and enterprise take the place of one of sleepy stagnation and idleness.[1]

Be that as it may (and the wealth of Trengganu has still to be revealed), the Sultan evidently enjoyed his visit and was still in Singapore when the Governor left for Perak on 31 August. His Highness had therefore to express his thanks in writing, which he did, wishing Jervois long life and prosperity and adding: '. . . may he become Governor permanently at the three Settlements until the last day'. His hope was that '. . . our friend and ourselves may continue to love one another and assist one another for ever, and may it never end during the revolution of the sun and moon, night and day'. Sir William was not, in fact, destined to enjoy the permanence of office to which the Sultan thought him entitled. Nor, we might conclude in retrospect, would such a tenure have been a fortunate arrangement.

While dealing with other and simpler problems, Jervois was receiving reports from Birch, including his dispatch of 13 May in which he alleged that Abdullah was failing to observe the terms of the Pangkor Engagement. He had farmed the Perak taxes to a Singapore Chinese for the absurdly low figure of $26,000 per annum, accepting and pocketing $15,000 in advance. He had imposed other taxes without the Resident's consent, failing to agree to the fiscal scheme which the Resident had proposed. Abdullah was also, according to Birch, unfit to rule. Jervois, in forwarding a copy of the Resident's letter to Lord Carnarvon, added the comment: 'Your Lordship will observe that it draws an unfavourable picture of the man who had been placed upon the throne through our instrumentality.' It did indeed. But Jervois was not content to form his opinions solely from written reports. He decided, and rightly, that he must see Perak for himself. He left Singapore in the *Pluto* on 31 August, taking with him Major McNair, Dr. Anderson (Colonial Surgeon), and Lieutenant McCallum, R.E., as private secretary. With the *Pluto* went H.M.S. *Thistle*. By the time these two ships had reached the Dindings, the party had been joined by Mr. Birch, Mr. Davidson, Mr. Swettenham, Captain Innes, R.E. (Assistant Surveyor-General), Commander Stirling, and Lieutenant Abbott, R.N. There was an escort comprising fifteen sepoys and eleven

[1] *Straits Times*, 31 July 1875.

ratings from the *Thistle*. Thus accompanied, Sir William Jervois went to Larut and inspected that district over a period of three days. He reported afterwards:

The Tin districts are peopled almost exclusively by Chinese, who regard the British Government as virtually the ruling power, and the British Officer residing there has been able to act their improvement without interference or opposition from the Chiefs of Perak. The Mantri, who had engaged in large speculations there, was saved from bankruptcy by our intervention and ever since that occasion the business of Government has been in the hands of our Officers.[1]

Under Speedy's rule, Larut was quiet and prosperous. Speedy himself was to be criticized for being weak and unmethodical (as he may well have been), but Larut had progressed since the time in January 1874 when Dunlop, Pickering, and Swettenham had gone about destroying stockades, releasing prisoners, and allotting the mining area between the two contending parties.[2] Taiping, scarcely heard of in 1874, was now a thriving town, known by its Chinese name, which means 'everlasting peace'. Speedy had already made his first report from which we derive our first detailed information about the district. He was governing Larut without much reference to the Mantri, as Jervois observed, but this was fairly easy to do, as 'The district of Laroot is unlike any other part of Perak'. Realizing this, Jervois spent only three days there, proceeding on 8 September, to Kuala Kangsar by elephant over an eighteen-mile track of which only five miles had been made up as a road.

At Qualla Kangsa I met the Raja Bandahara Usman, the second in succession to the throne of Perak. He is a great opium smoker and very weak in intellect. I also met here the Sri Maharajah Lela, a minor chief and an imbecile old man. I also had an interview with the Lacsamana (apparently a man with some sense and cunning) who had accompanied me since my first arrival, and with the Mantri who joined me at Laroot. I did not discuss any serious business with these Chiefs on this occasion.[3]

Jervois went by boat down the river to Senggang, where on the 10th he met Yusof.

Both in bearing and intelligence Yusuf is superior to the other Perak Chiefs. Instead of the listless apathetic disposition, which is the normal characteristic of the Malay, he appears to possess energy and activity. It is

---

[1] S.S. No. 291, 16 Oct. 1875.
[2] Swettenham, *Footprints in Malaya*, pp. 34–38. The Mantri's debts amounted to £75,000.
[3] S.S. No. 291, 16 Oct. 1875.

probably due to these qualities, so peculiar in a Malay, that he has incurred an ill-feeling which exists against him amongst some of the Chiefs.

I had a long interview with Yusuf, and I found that representations previously made to me, that he wished the British Government to undertake the Government of the Country, were quite correct. He told me distinctly that he thought this was the only way to put an end to the present unsettled state of affairs in Perak.[1]

The Governor went on down the river to Blanja, followed by the chiefs he had already met, and there on the 11th found Ismail, Raja Dris, Raja Ngah, the Maharaja Lela, the Panglima Kinta, and some minor chiefs.

I had three interviews with Ismail, and found that he had not an idea of his own. Without any claim to the throne, he was made Sultan of Perak at the instigation of the Mantri, with a view to pave the way for the Mantri's own eventual succession. Ismail is completely in the hands of the Mantri and other minor chiefs about him.

He is no doubt still regarded as Sultan by the majority of the Chiefs of the Ulu, or Upper districts. He acknowledged to me that the Country was in a very unsettled and disturbed state.[2]

Jervois proposed that Perak should be governed by British officers, to which Ismail returned a written reply expressing his willingness to accept British help if he (not Abdullah) were Sultan. 'This letter', wrote Jervois, 'I have good reason to believe was written by the Mantri; and as Ismail can neither read nor write, I think it probable that he was not alive to its contents.'[3] In this belief, and on the supposition that Ismail must be more isolated than hitherto—through Yusof and Dris taking a line of their own—Jervois concluded that Ismail's opposition would soon weaken.

Sir William now proceeded to meet Sultan Abdullah, who had collected a large body of his adherents at Pasir Panjang. Their first meeting on the 14th was merely ceremonial—in the Governor's boat at Kampong Gaja—but they met the next day at the Residency, Bandar Bahru. Jervois spoke at some length, with Swettenham as interpreter, repeating much of what he had already said to Ismail and his party.

I then told him that he as well as other Chiefs of Perak had violated the engagement entered into with the British Government at Pangkore. Instead of following the Resident's advice he had thwarted him in his endeavour to improve the condition of Perak, that there was no real Govern-

[1] S.S. No. 291, 16 Oct. 1875.   [2] Ibid.   [3] Ibid.

ment in the State, that the system of debt-slavery in practice in the country was oppressive, and at variance with Mohammedan Law, that the present state of affairs in Perak was detrimental to the interests of his country and his people and calculated to lead to disturbances, and that, interested as the British Government is, both by Treaty obligations and by the near neighbourhood of Perak to its own settlements, in obtaining good and settled government in that State, in the development of its resources, in the wellbeing of its inhabitants and in the prevention of oppression, we could not allow the affairs of Perak to remain in their present condition. . . .

I now found that the representations that had been made to me as to Abdullah's unfitness and inability to govern were correct. On every occasion he appealed to someone near to him, especially to the Shabandar, who has been his evil adviser from the commencement of his rule. His other advisers are three Malays of the worst character, who have gained his consideration by their readiness to carry out any business which honest men would refuse, and who, in the advice they offer, seek merely to make a tool of Abdullah for their own profit.

Abdullah, in replying to me, promised to do right and carry out his engagements in future, but asked to consult the Ulu Chiefs at Blanja before giving me a written reply to my suggestion that British Officers should undertake the Government of the Country and that the Sultan, Ex-Sultan, and other Chiefs entitled to payment by the State, should receive allowances from the revenues of Perak.[1]

As this proposal made by Jervois can be regarded as a turningpoint in the history of Malaya, its significance needs to be emphasized. Jervois had understood the position up to a point, reaching certain important conclusions. He had decided that Ismail would be hopeless as a ruler, illiterate, wavering, weak, and easily misled by others. He had decided that Abdullah was utterly unfit to rule, being unreliable, feeble, and surrounded by bad advisers. He had decided that the best Malay ruler would be Yusof but that Yusof was unacceptable to the other chiefs. Faced with this situation, all Jervois's instincts urged him to annex Perak there and then. He explains in his dispatch why he resisted this impulse. Annexation would be more expensive, for one thing, and it would be inconvenient 'if the inhabitants of Perak all at once became entitled to the rights and privileges of British subjects'. How could one deal with rebellious chiefs if hampered by the laws of evidence and trial by jury? The reasoning is cogent enough, but he omits to observe a far greater obstacle to annexation, and that was the absence of any authorization from England. In going beyond his instructions, Clarke had set an example which Jervois was

[1] Ibid.

prepared to better—and Clarke, remember, had been *promoted*. But while fully prepared, apparently, to embark on unauthorized conquest, he decided against it in the present instance and at the present time.

What, then, was he to do? Continue the system of 'advice' by Residents? But this, in Perak, was unworkable, as he saw.

The position of a Resident at the Court of a Malay State is in many respects a peculiar one. If his advice be followed he is in a position to be of great benefit to the State, for the prosperity of which he is in a great measure held to be responsible. When, however, as has been the case in Perak, his advice is for the most part not followed, his powers of usefulness must obviously be very restricted.[1]

The only alternative, as Jervois saw it, was to regularize the situation as it actually existed in Selangor and Larut. British officers should not advise but rule. They should control (in Abdullah's name) the revenue, all official appointments, the police, and the development of roads. They should assume a position from which it would be possible, later, to withdraw or advance. There should be a Malay Council to assist them, with Yusof and Dris as the 'working members', but Abdullah and Ismail allowed to be present if they chose.

My proposal, therefore, is to govern the country in the name of the Sultan by means of officers to be styled Queen's Commissioners. I consider it very desirable that the change of policy from one of mere advice to one of control should be marked by a change in the titles of the British Officers.[2]

His plan was to make Davidson coequal Commissioner in Perak with Birch, with Swettenham to take the former's place, temporarily, in Selangor. Then Birch was to become Resident in Selangor, with a new Assistant Commissioner to replace him—the latter to be at Kuala Kangsar, and Speedy to remain as Assistant Commissioner at Taiping. The object of this reorganization was obviously to remove Birch without acceding to Abdullah's request that Birch should be removed. It could not, however, take place immediately because the Residents' appointments had been confirmed by the Secretary of State and it was not within the Governor's powers to replace them at will.

If Jervois contemplated the idea of removing Abdullah from the throne, he quickly decided against it. One reason for so deciding was presumably that the validity of the Pangkor Engagement—which alone justified his intervention—depended upon Abdullah being

[1] S.S. No. 291, 16 Oct. 1875.   [2] Ibid.

Sultan. With any other ruler installed, Jervois would be in the position of having deposed the ruler whom Clarke had only recently recognized. On the other hand, the appointment of Queen's Commissioners would be impossible without a new agreement. When Sir William left Perak in the *Pluto* on 16 September, Abdullah had still made no formal reply to the Governor's proposals. His answer was promised in ten days, allowing him time to consult Ismail (which of course he never did). In the meanwhile, Yusof and Dris had written a letter, drafted for them by Swettenham, inviting the Governor to rule Perak. Receiving this, Jervois wrote to Abdullah, suggesting that he should follow suit. Birch received from the Governor, simultaneously (on 30 September), a letter in which the Sultanate was offered to Yusof. This letter Birch might deliver or not and its purpose was evidently to bring pressure upon Abdullah. This proved needless, for Abdullah yielded to Birch's verbal threats and sealed a duplicate of the letter drafted by Swettenham for Yusof and Dris. This reached Jervois on 5 October. Thereupon he issued, on 5 October, a proclamation—Birch wrote it and Swettenham brought it to Singapore with Abdullah's seal upon it—in which the people of Perak were told that they were henceforth to be ruled by British officers in the Sultan's name.

Concluding the dispatch in which these events are described, Jervois mentioned the possibility of a Malay rising but only to dismiss it as extremely unlikely.

It might possibly be suggested that the Malays might make some forcible resistance to the Government of Perak being undertaken by British Officers. I beg to assure your Lordship that I have made most particular enquiry on this point, and am convinced that there is not the least probability of such an event.

As I have already explained, the Chiefs are divided amongst themselves. Abdullah is against Ismail, and Yusuf, who was Ismail's great support, is now detached from him. Moreover, the new policy has been to a very great extent brought about owing to the representations and requests of Perak Rajahs themselves, and it is to be remarked that nearly all the Chiefs in any way renowned for their fighting propensities such as Rajah Yusof, Rajah Ngah, Haji Ali, and the Bughis warriors have declared themselves bound to the British Government without reserve. I should add that I believe the desire is general amongst the great body of the population that the British should take into their hands the government of the country, for they know that they would then be protected, be paid for their labour, and receive justice, which they neither get nor expect under the Sultan's rule. We may perhaps occasionally have to deal with a refractory Chief who may find it hard to surrender his privilege of squeezing the people but the armed Sikh Police we already have as a guard in Perak and Laroot (consisting altogether of more than 200 men) will suffice for this object. . . .

I considered well whether it might be desirable as a matter of precaution to place a small body of our troops in Perak, but feeling confident that there is no necessity for such a step, I determined not to do so. . . .

I have, in this despatch, touched on the main points connected with the affairs of Perak which rendered action necessary on the part of the British Government. I have also informed your Lordship of the action I have consequently taken. Your Lordship will see that it was impossible for me, under the circumstances which I have stated, to adopt a passive attitude, and allow engagements with the British Government to be violated and your Lordship's injunctions to be disregarded.

I am sensible that, in acting without instructions, I have incurred a grave responsibility, but I felt that it was impossible to carry on negotiations with Abdullah and the other Chiefs unless I spoke as if charged with full authority. I accordingly took upon myself to do what, under the circumstances, I considered your Lordship would wish to have done, and in the course which I pursued, I endeavoured to avoid any step which could in any way embarrass Her Majesty's Government. Should the policy I have adopted not be approved, it will be possible without difficulty either to recede or to advance, according to your Lordship's desire.

I trust that when your Lordship weighs the reasons which I have given for action and for that action which I have taken, your Lordship will not fail to appreciate the advantages which may fairly be expected to result from establishing a more direct control over a semi-barbarous State in which the interests of these settlements are so intimately associated, and in which so much may be done, with the power that we shall now possess, to further the cause of humanity and freedom.[1]

In the Legislative Council, on 7 October, Jervois explained his policy at some length, commenting upon the Resident's lack of authority:

In Perak especially . . . the relations between the adviser and the advised have been unsatisfactory from the very commencement. . . . The Resident's advice is disregarded, and he must consequently either passively look on, whilst acts are committed which he disapproves but cannot control, or he must assume a power which is inconsistent with his position as adviser, thus practically taking upon himself the Government of the State, so far as the opposition of Rajahs and Chiefs will permit him to do so. The result is eminently unsatisfactory to all concerned.

With regard to the course which should be adopted with respect to these affairs, I am glad to say that I have just been able to introduce in Perak a policy which I have every reason to believe will be satisfactory both to

[1] S.S. No. 291, 16 Oct. 1875.

ourselves and to the native Chiefs and people, and which will place that State on such a footing as will foster the growth of commercial enterprise, and lead to the importation of the labour and capital necessary for the due development of its rich resources.

Jervois was generally supported in Council, and, to judge from the local Press, he was doing only what old residents of Singapore had urged all along. This attitude changed later, his policy turning out to be the very one they had always opposed. In one editorial it was pointed out that Sir Andrew's half-measures had failed, placing the Government 'in a position which will test the abilities of the present or any Governor to extricate it from'.[1] Sir Andrew heard a rumour in October that Jervois meant to annex Perak. He disapproved, writing to Childers that annexation would mean wasting money and losing lives.[2]

Use has been made of extensive quotations to show the situation as it appeared to Sir William Jervois. His is not, however, the only point of view, and certain comments on his policy are inevitable. We must note, to begin with, that he was going far beyond the letter of the Pangkor Engagement. He might be morally and theologically justified in telling Abdullah that debt-slavery was an oppressive custom and contrary to Islamic law, but it was clearly a matter of Malay custom in which Abdullah was not bound to follow the Resident's advice. There is reason, as we have seen (see p. 137), for doubting whether the Pangkor Engagement was as explicit in the Malay as in the English version. Quite apart from that, however, there was nothing in it to justify interference with debt-slavery. In thus seeking to interfere, Jervois was clearly influenced by Birch, who had been preaching against debt-slavery ever since he came to Perak. He was again influenced by Birch in believing that Malay resistance was wildly improbable. It was a question upon which he would have done better to seek advice from someone else.

One man who scented trouble all along was Frank Swettenham, whom Jervois left with Birch as his temporary assistant. Agreeing whole-heartedly with Birch about debt-slavery, Swettenham did not make the mistake of thinking that it could be abolished without protest. 'My visits, the general gossip of the countryside, and the information gained from friendly Malays made it clear that trouble was brewing. . . .'[3] The danger was greater even than Swettenham realized at the time. He records that he noticed a well-known Selangor

---

[1] *Straits Observer*, 24 Sept. 1875.   [2] Vetch, op. cit., p. 182.
[3] Swettenham, *Footprints in Malaya*, p. 54.

fighting man among Abdullah's followers at his first meeting with the Governor. This was the famous Syed Mashor, a man he came to know better in later years.

> He was one of the three leading fighters in a State where fighting was regarded as the only reputable sport for men. . . .
> Discussing the only subject which interested him, the adventurous lives of himself and his friends, I was led into reminding him of his presence at that meeting which, I was told, he had attended on the understanding that, if Abdullah gave the signal, the famous Seyyid and his followers were to meng-amok—destroy—the Governor and his party. I asked if that was true. Rather hurt, and deprecating the question, he said: 'Yes, but the signal was not given.'[1]

In the light of this subsequent admission there is something incongruous in Jervois's trying to decide whether to depose Abdullah or not. His escort numbered little over thirty and he was surrounded by hundreds of armed Malays, but he was sternly rebuking the Sultan for treaty-violation and other sins, little realizing that a decision to depose Abdullah might have been the signal for massacre. He was not, one imagines, a particularly sensitive man.

If Sir William Jervois lacked a keen sense of 'atmosphere' he may still have been superior in this respect to Mr. Birch. For he realized (with or without the help of the local Press) that Birch had failed to make allies of any single group, and that Davidson was far more likely to gain adherents, if only from his knowledge of the language. In point of fact, Davidson was as reluctant to serve outside Selangor as Speedy would have been to serve outside Larut. Nevertheless, Jervois's proposed reorganization revealed his sense of Birch's failure. What he did not realize was how complete that failure had been. In his assessment of the likelihood of resistance (see p. 215, above) the Governor had naturally emphasized the hostility between Abdullah and Ismail. He had not reckoned upon a diplomacy which could actually turn them into allies, agreed if only in their common dislike of Birch. In this dangerous situation there were three factors which deserve comment at this juncture: Birch's character, Birch's policy, and the adjustment of the Perak boundary.

It would be difficult now to improve upon the sketch of Birch and Abdullah written by Sir Richard Winstedt.[2] Admitting that Birch

---

[1] Swettenham, *Footprints in Malaya*, p. 54. Syed Mashor of Selangor was Raja Mahdie's ally against Tunku dia Oodin and fled to Perak in 1873.

[2] Winstedt and Wilkinson, op. cit., pp. 102 et seq.

had very real virtues, Winstedt comments upon his nervous irrita-
bility, his haste, his public-school loyalty, his narrow and rigid ideas,
his lack of psychological insight, and his lack of humour.

... Four days after arrival, he wrote in that full and frank diary, which is at
once his own condemnation and excuse, the motto destined to wreck his
hopes and his life: 'I see that nothing but decision is necessary with these
people'. Some fifteen days later he added: 'Firmness will, I trust, do it all;
and with Abdu-llah one must be firm and even peremptory. God help a
country left to a man like that, unadvised by sound counsellors! I very
often despair when I think of him; but he will only be a puppet and, I believe,
do all that one advises'. Peremptory with a Sultan, with whom even his
own father had never been peremptory! Firm with a clever timid youth, who
saw in firmness only rudeness and longed to get rid of his tormentor; a
polite weak youth whose words, as he said himself 'caused him to be much
indebted to the English.'[1]

It may be that the simile of the eager form-master in Perak reporting to the headmaster at Singapore—together with any ideas associated with the word 'birch'—may involve an over-simplification of
Birch's character. He was something more than a school prefect, as
is shown by his helpfulness to the passing traveller, his interest in
photography, and his fondness for children. One group photograph
was allegedly spoilt because Abdullah's son, aged four, 'who was
sitting on Mr. Birch's knee', kicked about all the time.[2] He seems at
least once to have aroused the worst suspicions by patting a little
girl on the head.[3] He was unfailingly kind to the poor, the sick, the
oppressed.[4] He was clearly quite approachable. He was popular too
in the Colony and

... did a great deal during his term of office in the Straits to remove the
general feeling of distrust and want of harmony which existed between
officialdom and the general community.[5]

As against all these real virtues we have the evidence of his diary
in which his impatience and ignorance are apparent. Abdullah
exasperated him by staying in bed until 1.0 or 2.0 p.m. 'He is, moreover, I see every day, an evident coward. . . . He is eminently silly and
foolish. Opium, too, has become his bane again, and he is good for
very little.' He complained that Abdullah was surrounded by 'lots of

---

[1] Winstedt and Wilkinson, op. cit., p. 103.
[2] *Swettenham's Perak Journals*, p. 43.
[3] Maxwell, op. cit., p. 57.
[4] *Twentieth Century Impressions of British Malaya*, Wright and others, London,
1908, p. 103.   [5] *Singapore Daily Times*, 3 Dec. 1874.

women . . . all of whom are slaves, and most of them prostitutes. . . .
God help a country left to a man like that. . . . I very often despair
when I think of him.' Most revealing of all is the passage:

My patience is tried to the utmost with this man. I have often been told
that I was a good-tempered man, but never was able to accept the compli-
ment, for I knew I was not, but I begin now to believe that I must be to put
up with the vagaries of this man. However, I am determined, if I can, to
carry through what Sir Andrew Clarke has begun, and if patience can do it,
patience shall. . . . I wish, for my own sake and for the peace of the country,
that Abdullah was not such a vain little idiot. I cannot help calling him
this, for he really is one. . . . Every day Abdullah is doing some foolish
thing or saying some foolish thing, and people begin to distrust him.

These are not words we should associate with a good-natured
tolerance. And his attitude about debt-slavery was coloured by a
Victorian disapproval of its immoral (as opposed to its merely
oppressive) aspect. It was the slave *girls* he wanted to emancipate,
allowing the Malays to draw the sort of conclusion that a modern
psychologist might partly endorse.

But the brutal haste with which Birch tried to put things right was
not wholly due to his missionary zeal. It originated, surely, in part,
from a craving for personal success and a dread of humiliating and
imminent failure. He had greatly admired Sir Andrew Clarke and
had expressed an almost schoolboy grief when the Governor resigned. But this admiration was not returned. Clarke had turned for
advice to Braddell and McNair, to Read and Davidson, to Dunlop
and Pickering. Birch had striven to gain attention, studying the
Malay problems[1] and finally asking to be made Resident of Perak.
Sir Andrew had finally agreed to this but with manifest doubt and
reluctance and after a probation as humiliating to recall as it had been
embarrassing to undergo. It had become vital to Birch that he should
succeed. His self-respect demanded proof that Sir Andrew's hesitation had been unjustified. Perak must be pacified and he alone must
be the man to do it. Clarke should be made to realize that his unwilling choice had been the right one. But what if he should fail and
be known to have failed? Could he return as Colonial Secretary to
Singapore—to overhear or imagine the remarks which would pass at
the Tanglin Club ('Poor old Birch—Perak a bit too much for him—

[1] It has been too often assumed that Birch knew nothing of Malay character.
There were, in fact, many Malays in eastern Ceylon, where he had previously
worked. He evidently needed an interpreter but he was almost certainly a better
Malay scholar than Swettenham would admit.

H.E. wants McNair to take it on')? This, it may be objected, is mere conjecture. What is a fact, however, is that Birch's future was under discussion in the local Press. In the words of one editor:

> The policy we must adopt in future must be more decided, with less talk and more action, and assuredly such a policy cannot be carried out with the instruments Sir Andrew Clarke chose to use. If these are relegated to their former positions they cannot blame either the present governor or the Colonial Office, they must rather impute it to their patron's rashness and their own incompetency.[1]

Birch's return as a failure, to be greeted by further articles from the same pen, would not be a pleasant experience. It may not have been an experience that Birch was prepared to face. A man sufficiently proud might think that an heroic death was preferable. He might find that failure was unthinkable, and that he had somehow to succeed.

Clarke had been replaced by Jervois, much to Birch's dismay. Then came the Governor's tour of Perak. Sir William's cold stare had summed up one chief after another 'weak in intellect', 'imbecile', 'led by others', and then come to rest on Birch. What had the verdict been? 'No good for this job, although he *might* do for Selangor. Davidson is the man for Perak.' Jervois obviously said this in all but words. Birch then knew what his fate was to be and cared little, from that moment, whether the chiefs were plotting against him or not. If there was a revolt, moreover—if he himself were killed, for that matter—there would be a punitive expedition. Perak would be conquered by force of arms and probably annexed.

And he would be the true founder of British Malaya; not a man who had failed but a man who had died in the hour of victory. The Rajah of Sarawak said of Birch that

> All who knew him and the Malay character foresaw his sad fate when he left Singapore to take up his duties.[2]

Such wisdom after the event is easy. We need not believe that so many foresaw so much. But if anyone predicted what would happen, it was Birch himself. He made light of the obvious dangers, saying in reply to one warning: 'If one Mr. Birch is killed, ten Mr. Birches will take his place.' In a letter to his sister, moreover, he seems again

---

[1] *Straits Observer*, 24 Sept. 1875.
[2] *Queries, Past, Present and Future*, Rajah of Sarawak, p. 7.

to have foreseen how it would all end. There was to be an element of suicide in Birch's death.[1]

If we come now to consider Birch's policy as Resident, we must be struck at the outset by the way in which he ignored Sir Andrew Clarke's instructions. These had been explicit on three points: 'Limit all your efforts to the sea-coast and navigable waters, never mind the regalia. . . . Debt-slavery is a bad thing, but . . . let it for the present alone. . . .'. (See p. 195 above.) Birch would let nothing alone. Why? Because, presumably, he wanted the regalia as a tangible proof of success, because it lay with the up-river chiefs to produce it, and because Jervois had been persuaded to take his own line on the debt-slavery question. But while Birch's divergence from Clarke's policy is striking, it was not the central theme of his administration. Finding that the Perak chiefs all lived on the dues they collected from the river traffic, as also to some extent on the work of their slaves, Birch resolved to abolish all such irregular dues and substitute for them a proper system of revenue. There would be official custom-houses, a fixed and known scale of duties, all collected by tax-farmers in the Sultan's name, and the chiefs would eventually be consoled with allowances on a scale to be decided in due course. And while debt-slavery was not as yet made illegal, Birch made it clear that he disapproved of it. In thus striking at the chiefs' means of livelihood, Birch managed to create a common resistance among men who agreed, perhaps, in nothing else. He made it clear on 5 November 1874, soon after his arrival, that the private collection of dues was to end almost at once and that the scale of allowances was to be fixed later on. Opposition would have diminished if the allowances had been paid beforehand but Birch had initially no funds from which to pay them. A principal merit, in fact, of the farming system was that it would give him some money in hand for this purpose. The chiefs would have been somewhat mollified by a prior announcement of what their incomes were to be, but Birch delayed over this, perhaps through inability to discover what the future totals of revenue and expenditure were likely to reach; and perhaps to emphasize that the chiefs' scale of compensation would depend on their present behaviour.

Birch's revenue system was constructed between January and July 1875. Tenders were invited for the Perak farms with 15 January

[1] See *J. W. W. Birch: Causes of his Assassination*, M. A. Mallal, Singapore, 1952. M.A. dissertation in the Library of the University of Malaya.

as the closing date,[1] and they were eventually let to a syndicate which offered $6,000 a month, and eventually $84,000 a year. Birch then drew up six notices, all dated 1 May, imposing taxes on boats, introducing port-dues, announcing a poll-tax, and forbidding the private collection of dues, more especially by the Sultan, Shahbandar, Laxamana, Mata Mata, and the Orang Kaya Mat Arshad. Had the Sultan sealed these proclamations they would have had effect from 1 June. In fact they were not given royal approval until 2 October, by which date they had been extended and elaborated, and made to become effective by 1 November. Arguments over this fiscal system began with Birch's arrival, led to quarrels with Abdullah in February 1875, with the Kinta chiefs in March, with the Shahbandar in June. By 8 June Birch was threatening Abdullah with removal from his throne. By 23–25 July the Resident had been empowered by decree to impose and abolish taxes and also to act as Judge.

Friction with the chiefs of the Ilir (the lower part of the river) was inevitable in any case where customs dues were concerned, but Birch was careful to annoy the Ulu (or upper river) chiefs to an equal degree. He first scolded them on 17–23 November 1874. He ordered the arrest of two of Ismail's men on 18 December, one of them his prospective son-in-law. On 13 December he committed perhaps the worst blunder of all. Believing that Raja Ngah was a bad character and the collector at Bidor of blackmail which even Malay custom would not authorize, he ordered the Punghulus to drive him out and burn his house down as an example to other evildoers. Raja Ngah had in fact as good a right to these taxes as other chiefs had to theirs. He was, moreover, a relative of Ismail's and one whom Ismail had quite recently appointed as Tunku Panglima Besar. This act created a deep and unfavourable impression. To complete the effect, Birch publicly castigated the Mantri (Ismail's chief supporter) on 17 April, and went on to quarrel openly with Ismail and his immediate adherents between 25 April and 3 May. As he was already on bad terms with Speedy, there were few others left for him to alienate.

The reaction against Birch began at a meeting of the Ilir chiefs on 10 November, a few days after his fiscal schemes were first announced. By 6 February resentment was reaching such a height that, following another meeting of the chiefs, their own clerk, Yusuf, was killed as a possible spy in Birch's employ. There was a further meeting on 19 March which resulted in a deputation being sent to Singapore with

[1] The *Penang Gazette*, 11 Jan. 1875, quoted in *Straits Times*, 20 Mar. 1875.

a memorandum of complaint as from Abdullah against Birch. This, as we have seen (see p. 203 above) arrived at the moment when Clarke was ending his tenure of office. It produced only a fatherly admonition dated 22 April, urging Abdullah to follow the Resident's advice. The chiefs met again on 26 April, by which time rumours of war had become rife, based partly on the fact that the Mantri had removed his family to Larut and partly on the fact that the Maharaja Lela was known to be fortifying his house at Passir Salak. With the failure of this appeal to the Governor the situation deteriorated rapidly. By May 1875 Birch's reforms and his methods of urging them had created an opposition which extended to all the Perak chiefs, almost without exception.

A third factor in the situation, apart from Birch's character and policy, was the Perak boundary. Were this issue excluded we might have some reason to deplore the selfishness of the Perak chiefs in opposing reforms which were for the general benefit. There can be no doubt that Birch's policy was governed, in the main, by the most enlightened motives. There can be no doubt that poorer folk would welcome (when they understood) the changes he had in mind. Nor need we question that the British motives were as genuinely philanthropic as human motives ever are. But there was an element of sharp practice in the Pangkor Engagement which gave the Malays some excuse for reaching a very different conclusion. Articles XI and XII redefine the boundaries, respectively, of the Dindings and of Province Wellesley. There was confusion about both these definitions, the chiefs believing that they had been swindled and that these small annexations were but the prelude to the annexation of Perak itself. The Dindings boundary was not perhaps important in itself, a British commentator merely remarking that 'Our title to it would be questionable if it were worth questioning',[1] but the interpretation placed upon Article XII involved the transfer of some 200 square miles of territory; a tract including the recently opened Salama mines. Jervois repudiated this extreme interpretation in one of his earliest dispatches[2] but found it difficult to make an arrangement more consistent with British good faith. No proper map existed on which the boundary could be shown. The administration of a part of the disputed territory had begun, with Mr. W. E. Maxwell (the former Chief Justice's son) as Assistant Government Agent, and the opium

[1] *The Times*, 11 Mar. 1874, quoted in Mallal, op. cit., p. 54.
[2] S.S. No. 196 of 8 July 1875.

and spirit farms already let. Jervois proposed a compromise solution, pending further investigation.

By this course, I believe that we shall avoid, on the one hand, what appears to me a breach of faith towards the State of Perak, and on the other, a sudden surrender of our present position, an action which would expose us to the charge of weakness, and which would probably produce a bad effect upon the Native population, and indeed upon the whole community in these parts.

Mr. Birch assures me that he will have no difficulty in obtaining the signature of the Laksamana and the chop of the Sultan to this course, and if, in dealing with the case, there were no other considerations to be borne in mind than those to which I have referred in this despatch, I believe, My Lord, that our course would be clear, and that we might ultimately surrender to the State of Perak the territory and the revenue which, to my mind, we have unjustly appropriated to ourselves.[1]

Such a surrender eventually took place, but the situation in 1875 remained vague, Birch being associated (see p. 195) with the extreme interpretation of the Pangkor Engagement and Jervois reluctant to make any concession which would look like weakness. Mingled with their more selfish motives, the Malay chiefs could boast a certain measure of patriotic fervour.

This, then, was the situation at the time of Jervois's visit to Perak between 31 August and 15 September 1875. We have seen what his decision was. He could have eased the situation considerably by removing Birch but that too would have been interpreted as weakness. He therefore decided upon a change but postponed actually making it. What is so striking about the Governor's tour is his failure to realize how dangerous the position had become. His visit was the Malays' last opportunity for a redress of their grievances, and its main result was a decision to make Birch's powers more absolute. Another result, however, was to encourage Birch in his policy of protecting runaway slaves. After Jervois had spoken against debt-slavery (to Abdullah, on 14 September) Birch doubtless felt more at liberty to follow his conscience in the matter. He was protecting some five fugitives on 18 September and, soon afterwards, on 9 October, connived at their escape to British territory at Pangkor. After he had been empowered as Judge, on 1 October, he immediately warned Abdullah that 'the condition of the slaves in Perak must in time form the subject of investigation'.[2] On 8 October two of Abdullah's

---

[1] S.S. No. 196, 8 July 1875.   [2] Mallal, op cit., p. 107.

slave-women and one belonging to the Shahbandar ran away and hid near the Residency. When the pursuit began Birch told the Shahbandar that:

If they could find them they could take them, if the girls would go, but if they came before me and complained of ill-treatment, now that Abdullah had given all power to me, I should interfere.[1]

As these three fugitives apparently left with Birch on the 12th, disguised as boatmen, and so reached Pangkor, the chiefs concerned were furious.

The crucial date in the conspiracy against Birch was 21 July when, for the first time, the Ulu chiefs were present under Abdullah's chairmanship and with Ismail's tacit approval. The decision to kill Birch was unanimously agreed in the light of the Governor's refusal to replace him. Methods were discussed, with mention of poison, of magic, and of assassination at the hands (and with the kris) of the Maharaja Lela. A letter was sent to Ismail asking him to authorize an attack on Bandar Bahru 'with the object of driving the British out of Perak'. All this had happened before the Governor's visit, action being taken to procure firearms and ammunition from Penang. An extraordinary 'seance' was held on 24 August at which Abdullah tried supernatural (although ineffectual) methods of attack.[2] Ismail was given a progress report on the 28th but the agenda of the conspirators seems to have been pretty generally known.

What must seem odd about this story is that all this should have been going on before and during the Governor's visit—with the Governor's own assassination as one item for discussion under 'other business'—without Jervois discovering what was afoot. The only possible explanation is that Birch prevented him from finding out. Obsessed with the need to demonstrate his own success, Birch must have concealed from the Governor a great deal of what he knew. He had been told of the poison plot on 12 August.[3] He probably knew of the purchase of arms in Penang.[4] He knew of Syed Mashor's presence among Abdullah's adherents. He knew of the

[1] Mallal, op. cit., p. 109.

[2] A witness at this ceremony told Sergeant Mohd. Syed about it on the 27th but the sergeant made no report because white people would not believe ghost stories.

[3] Mallal, op. cit., p. 150.

[4] Jervois suspected that arms were being imported and wrote to Anson about it on 27 Sept. Mallal, op. cit., p. 174.

rumours which had been current since May. He could, nevertheless, assure the Governor on 13 October[1] that:

Nothing can exceed the general good feeling, and this Yusuf and Dris do all they can to foster. Everything is perfectly quiet. Yusuf is most confident that he can bring in Ismail. Your Excellency's visit has done an immense amount of good, and the people are only waiting for your Proclamation.

The Governor had the more reason for accepting this assurance in that it was confirmed by a letter dated 16 October from Commander F. Stirling of H.M.S. *Thistle*, who had stayed at Bandar Bahru for some days and who told the Governor how impressed he was by the friendliness of the chiefs and the people at large—'I do not anticipate the smallest probability of a disturbance.' Sub-Lieutenant Abbott remained at Bandar Bahru, at Birch's request, after his Commander had gone.

If Birch really believed that all was well on 13 October, he had changed his mind since 16 September when he recorded in his diary the reports of Abdullah's exasperation.

I was told Abdullah was very angry with me. . . . I was met by reports, on all sides, that they [Abdullah's people] wanted to kill me, and that they said if I was killed, as I knew the country now so well, a new man coming would be at their mercy; and, moreover, if I was killed, they might do something before another officer came. I got back, however, all right, without anyone attempting anything, and I do not believe they ever will.[2]

A distinction must surely be drawn between a state of baffled hostility, as here described, and 'the general good feeling' about which the Governor was told. Nor can there be any doubt that Birch realized something of his peril. On the 18th he wrote in his diary:

A great many rumours were afloat to-day, and the alarm exhibited by some as the reports came in, and the grave faces of others as in portentous whispers they communicated some absurd story that my latter day had arrived, were really amusing. However, I created some alarm on the other side, by doubling the sentries, and having the men out firing blank cartridges in the afternoon, and big gun firing now and then, with patrol parties up and down the river.[3]

He affects here to laugh at the danger but takes action enough to show its reality. It was, incidentally, a peculiarity of his position that there was no officer to command such forces as he had. He was himself responsible for their discipline, equipment, and training; as also

[1] S.S. 291, 16 Oct. 1875.
[2] Mallal, op. cit., p. 104.   [3] Mallal, op. cit., p. 105.

for their deployment. It was he who decided at this point, for example, to bring thirty of Speedy's sepoys to Kuala Kangsar and ten to Gunong Pondok. It may have been Swettenham, however, who suggested the idea of this demonstration. He remarks in his diary on 16 September:

There seems to be only one opinion amongst the Malays of any sense, and that is that a very little would lead to a quarrel now, and the only way to prevent a disturbance in Perak is to let them see we are in earnest.[1]

The blank-firing exercise took place next day but one, and Swettenham comments: 'It did good, I think.' It would have done more good if the men had been mostly there and not dispersed between Gunong Pondok and Kota Stia.

During the period which elapsed between the Governor's return to Singapore (15 September) and Abdullah's reluctant signing of the proclamation on 2 October,[2] there was continual intrigue going on, with Yusof much in evidence as Abdullah's possible supplanter. Swettenham heard numerous reports—that Abdullah was plotting with Syed Mashor, that the Mantri talked of dismissing Speedy whenever he chose—but felt at that moment no particular forebodings. Birch sent him up to Kuala Kangsar to arrange accommodation for the sepoys, who arrived there (twenty-two of them, with a field gun) on 23 September. He then returned, rejoining Birch at Passir Panjang on 29 September. After the final negotiations which ended with Abdullah's signing the proclamation, Swettenham was sent to Singapore to have the proclamation printed for distribution throughout Perak. He boarded the *Pluto* during the night of 3–4 October and called at Langat on the 5th. He had been told of an impending attack by Raja Mahdie on Klang but could do nothing about it. So he went on to Singapore and reported to the Governor on the 6th.

If there was to be serious trouble, whether in Perak or Selangor or both, it was unlikely to begin before November, for October was the fasting month, Ramlan; a good period for excited talk and intrigue but not for the commencement of a civil war. As against that, the beginning of November, when the fast ended, would be very much the time of year when trouble might be expected. October was devoted to plotting. It was on 5 October that Abdullah authorized the Maharaja Lela to kill Birch. Information about this was sent to Ismail on

---

[1] *Swettenham's Perak Journals*, p. 96.
[2] Giving full powers to Birch as Judge and as the Sultan's representative. See p. 215 above.

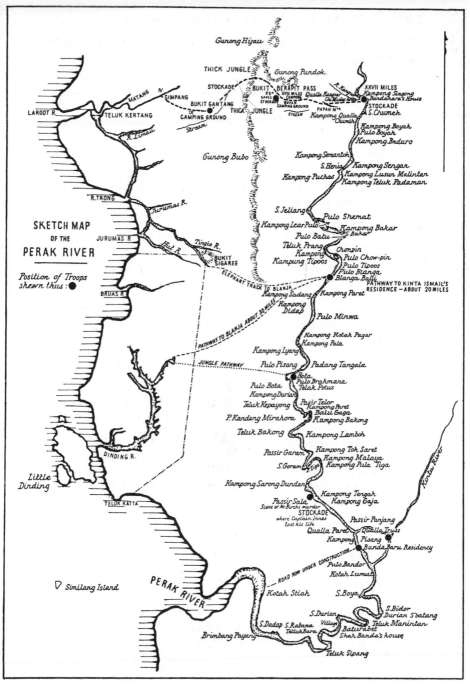

Map 6. The Perak River

the 12th. A meeting of the Ulu chiefs was held on the 15th, at which the whole plan was discussed in Ismail's presence. The Ilir chiefs met on the 27th and decided that Passir Salak should be the place for the deed and that Birch's next visit there, in November, should be the occasion. On the 31st Abdullah himself visited Passir Panjang and told the Maharaja Dindah the date when Birch was to be expected. By the end, in fact, of the fasting month, the place, the means, the method, and the date of the murder had been arranged. It only remained for the victim to walk into the trap.

While the plot was hatched in Perak, Sir William Jervois was confident, as assured by Birch, that he had prescribed the remedy for all Perak ills. At a meeting of the Legislative Council on 29 October he made his intentions and ideas abundantly clear.

Firmness has now to be called into play. . . . One more subject for your consideration, gentlemen, is that of debt-slavery. . . . It is in Perak that this cruel practice . . . is most prevalent, and if we could but deal with it in this State, a blow would be given to the system as practised in other States. . . . I found that the representations made with respect to Abdullah's character, so far as I was capable of judging, had not been exaggerated. His imbecility and want of character were manifest at every turn.

He then went on to speak of his policy on the mainland as affecting the whole future of the Straits Settlements:

a future which, I venture to say, the Straits Settlements have to look forward to with some anxiety. Several things combine to cause such anxiety on the part of many who have long had at heart the interest of this Colony, and who have watched its progress in trade, commerce, and general enterprise. . . . Commercial transactions here were once confined to English merchants, and large fortunes were speedily amassed by them. But how did these riches accumulate? I need not tell you, gentlemen, that then, as now, the prosperity of the Colony was gauged by the amount of passing traffic—but with this difference—that the prizes which are now distributed to the many then fell to the few. European enterprise now competes with English capital; while the Chinese merchant, contented as he is with very small profits, also promises to be a formidable competitor in the commercial arena. The consequence is, that (and I speak of a fact which is now very generally recognised all over the East) the rapid making of princely fortunes has given place to hard work and moderate returns; and, in the ordinary course of things, the spirit of competition will render the one more laborious, the other still more moderate.

Another consideration which should be reviewed is, that the very trade which is now the standard of the Colony's prosperity may, perhaps at no distant day, wane and ebb. Already, as you know, gentlemen, a proposition for cutting a ship canal to the northward of our Settlements, through the Isthmus of Kraw, at the neck of the Malay Peninsula, and another for tapping the Empire of China through the Kingdom of Burmah, furnish the disturbing elements calculated to lead to such a result.

Forewarned is forearmed; and it is our duty to adopt such measures as will secure the permanent prosperity of the Straits Settlements and, if possible, afford a vent for the great competition which is now so heavily weighing upon our countrymen who are engaged here in mercantile pursuits.

Now, gentlemen, it seems to me that one remedy for the sources of anxiety to which I have alluded lies at our very doors. Behind us runs the Malay Peninsula, stretching to our Indian possessions on the Eastern Coast of the Bay of Bengal, and it is to this peninsula that we must look for the field where British commercial enterprise can find a scope in these waters for its undertakings and speculations. The establishment of close relations with the states of the peninsula,—I allude more especially to those on the western coast with which we are now connected—will render these Settlements far less dependent on passing traffic, for such establishment will increase the traffic and business of the Colony.

The resources of these states have been recently shown to be even richer than the most sanguine had anticipated. The planter and the agriculturist have here a magnificent scene for their labours. Thick alluvial deposits are to be found on sites especially adapted for the cultivation of tea, coffee and tobacco; and I have been informed that there is no reason why the crops grown on these sites should not be equal, if not superior to those grown in Delhi, Assam, and Ceylon respectively.

Why should not this Malay Peninsula be as prosperous as our last-named possession, which has become so important of late years, although it does not possess the extraordinary mineral resources and good water communications which are to be found in the peninsula? Why should not a large labouring population of immigrants be imported into or voluntarily enter the states? Why should not English capital be invested as readily in these rich states as it is in the other parts of the world, to feed the labour so imported and to aid the general development? The answer can be given in two words:—Malay rule.

To the reason given in these two words may be traced all the difficulties which are or may be encountered in our relations with the Malay States or in opening up the peninsula.

Capitalists will not invest funds in them, when they can have little or no security for their investments; immigrants will not enter when there is no sure protection to life and property; development cannot take place without capital and labour.

In order, therefore, to secure the remedy sought, it may be assumed that these States must not be administered exclusively by the Malays, but that the British should establish such relations with them, and have such a voice in the general administration, that the requisite security can be guaranteed, and immigration consequently encouraged.[1]

There is much that is of interest in this frank explanation of policy, but the important thing to realize is the extent to which it derives from Birch. Jervois had just spent ten days in Birch's company and, while dubious about Birch's fitness for the post he held, he had to rely upon him for information. Birch had evidently been enthusiastic about the development of Perak, and he was always talking about Ceylon. It was from him that the comparison derived—Jervois, after all, had hardly been there—and the analogy (on the political side) may have been misleading. Jervois's picture of the situation in Perak derived (and could only derive) from Birch; and it was more a picture of future economic possibilities than of present political danger. To conceal the extent of his own failure Birch had withheld from the Governor a part of what he knew. It would have been easy, of course, for Jervois to seek further information from Frank Swettenham, who was in Singapore from 6 to 23 October. But Swettenham was aged only twenty-five, with only five years seniority. He was in a position to answer specific questions. He was not in a position to offer advice, least of all in opposition to the advice of the Resident. He may have been thought conceited but he was far too able (and ambitious) to offer his opinion before it was asked. His present task was to have the proclamations printed in translation, correct the proofs, and return with them to Perak. And this was exactly what he did. The proclamations were three in number. Two of them were those signed by Abdullah on 2 October, in one of which the British Resident and his assistants were made Abdullah's representatives 'to carry out in Our name all the affairs of Our country'.[2] The third was the proclamation issued by the Governor on 15 October[3] announcing, among other things, that 'Her Britannic Majesty's Government have determined to administer the Government of Perak in the name of the Sultan'. Bearing copies of these proclamations, as printed for distribution, Swettenham embarked in the *Pluto* on 23 October.

One paragraph of the Governor's proclamation is worthy of emphasis at this point. It is among the explanations given for the policy involved:

And whereas the Rajas and Chiefs of Perak are divided into factions,

---

[1] Legislative Council Minutes.
[2] *Perak Journals*, appendix 3, serial 12, p. 147.
[3] Mallal, op. cit., appendix ix, p. 267.

parties, and individual interests, fostering and encouraging jealousies and enmities which they confess themselves unable to reconcile. . . .

When written and printed this paragraph proclaimed a fatal misconception. The chiefs of Perak were not, at that moment, divided into factions. They were united, as never before, in a single purpose. They had agreed, almost unanimously, on murder.

CHAPTER X

WITH Frank Swettenham in the *Pluto* there sailed half a dozen Malay chiefs who had been visiting Singapore. Among these were Raja Dris and Raja Mahmood of Selangor. Mahmood had been detained (see p. 182 above), but was now given permission to leave. His object was to fetch his wife and family and settle again, eventually, in Selangor. In the meanwhile, he remained with Swettenham, perhaps in the expectation of a fight. Swettenham was to say of him that 'he fought for no political reason, but for friendship's sake, and because he liked it'.[1] They called together at Langat, where the Sultan of Selangor received Mahmood as a reformed character.

... He said he knew Mahmud had been the tool of others and not the originator of disturbances; Mahdi was the responsible man. Mahmud replied that the Sultan's own sons had ordered him to make war. That rather hit the old man, but he said 'Yes, you were all bad'. He told Mahmud he would give him a place to live at if he would be respectable in future, and he also promised to look after his wife and family and see they wanted for nothing.[2]

The *Pluto* went on to the Perak river, anchoring at Durian Sabatang on 26 October 1875. Swettenham and Mahmood went on by boat that evening to Bandar Bahru. Birch was there, crippled with a sprained ankle, together with Lieutenant Abbott, R.N., and five seamen from H.M.S. *Thistle*. Swettenham read and explained the Governor's proclamation to the Laxamana and the Dato Bandar. Next day Birch, Abbott, and Swettenham went to Kunala Kinta in the afternoon, where 'an iniquitous toll' was being collected; 'so we went and saw them off the premises'. Birch had a guard of about fifty Sikhs and Pathans, indifferently disciplined and trained, and their sergeant-major was put in irons on the 29th for being drunk and mutinous. It was then arranged that Swettenham should go up the river with two boats, distributing copies of the proclamations, as far as Kota Lama. On his return he was to join Birch at Passir Salak on 3 November. Birch and Swettenham separated on the 28th, Birch going in the opposite direction to Kota Stia and to visit Abdullah at Batak Rabit. It was on the 29th that Indoot, a boatman, living with one of Abdullah's escaped slave-women and a witness of the 'seance' (see footnote, p. 226 above),

---

[1] *Swettenham's Perak Journals*, p. 113, footnote.   [2] Ibid., p. 114.

came to Birch and reported that Raja Ngah was plotting against him, as well he might (see p. 223 above and p. 238 below). Birch apparently sent for Raja Ngah and ended a verbal castigation with the words: 'This time I forgive you, [but] don't imagine that you can fight with me.' Abdullah, the Laxamana and Shahbandar were alleged to be involved in the plot, but there is no record of Birch upbraiding them for it. A merchant called Dyang Ismail gave Birch a similar warning at Kota Stia. Birch replied: 'Don't bother yourself about me, take care of Kota Stia; I am an old man, if I am killed the country will become the Queen's.' He had said something to the same effect towards the end of September when given a warning by Tunku Syed Mashor. 'I am an old man. If I die, what does it matter?' Birch was only forty-nine and these are significant words.

Swettenham failed to obtain an interview with Ismail at Blanja on the 30th, learning from Haji Ali and Krani Ismail that the ex-Sultan was asleep. So he left copies of the proclamation and went on to Senggang, where he saw Yusof, and so to Kuala Kangsar. He finally reached Kota Lama on 3 November and from there began his return to Blanja on the following day. It was obvious to Swettenham throughout this journey, that there might be an outbreak at any moment. He remarked at Blanja that 'To have heard their talk and behaviour one would have thought a disturbance imminent, conversation was most warlike'.[1] He was told at Kuala Kangsar that the men of Sayang and Kota Lama planned to drive the sepoys out as soon as the Fast was over, on 1 November. At Kota Lama Swettenham 'felt that but for the fact that I had with me Raja Mahmud, most feared of Selangor fighting Chiefs, there might have been serious trouble'.[2] Yusof, at Senggang, fully expected a conflict—'he had heard that Ismail intended to collect all the chiefs with the intention of asking them whether they would combine to resist the Govt.' but was uncertain as to whether it was true. Whether this particular rumour was true or not, the atmosphere was evidently explosive.

Birch, who simultaneously visited the villages below Bandar Bahru, would appear from his immediate reactions to have reached exactly the opposite conclusion. During the Governor's visit there had been some talk of sending him fifty soldiers, but Birch, after his posting of the proclamations in the down-river kampongs, gave Welner, the master of the *Pluto*, the text of a telegram (dated 1 November) which

[1] *Swettenham's Perak Journals*, p. 117.
[2] Swettenham, *Footprints in Malaya*, p. 57.

read: 'Laxamana and Shahbandar have written to you and accept offices. Troops not required. Sailors return in *Pluto*.'[1] This reached Jervois on 3 November, sent from Penang. Having sent this telegram, Birch prepared to go up the river to Passir Salak. This was on the evening of 1 November, the day on which the Muslim fast was ended and a day sooner than his arrangement with Swettenham had implied.

We have already seen that the plan for killing Birch at Passir Salak had been agreed on 27 October and that his coming there was expected. Several historians have been content to assume that he knew nothing about this conspiracy, but such ignorance is difficult to understand. Could such a plot have been elaborated entirely without his knowledge? It would hardly seem possible. And granted that the impending disturbance was almost as obvious to him as it was to Swettenham, he could have no doubt that Passir Salak was likely to be one storm-centre and Kota Lama presumably the other. He had been told as much, for one thing, by Syed Mashor. Passir Salak belonged to the Maharaja Lela, first of the eight major chiefs, the Shahbandar's nephew and normally of Abdullah's party. He had not been at Pangkor, however, and had never agreed to the Engagement, which made it easier for him to be a friend of Ismail. Birch threatened him in January and then heard, in September, of the stockade he was building round his house.[2] Swettenham had heard of his offer to kill Birch.[3] Rumours of his expected resistance had been current, and were known to Birch, in October. Finally, on 28 October, Birch wrote to the Maharaja Lela and warned him to desist from his stockade-building. The Maharaja Lela is reported to have replied verbally: 'You can go back and tell Mr. Birch to get all the troops he can from England and India and I will fight.'[4]

With the Maharaja Lela's attitude known, Birch might have been expected to approach Passir Salak in some strength. His sepoys were not particularly reliable but there were about fifty of them available. He had five British seamen in addition, and these he deliberately sent away. Of the sepoys he took only ten. With Abbott, the remainder of his party comprised Mat Arshad, his interpreter, and a dozen Malay boatmen. His boats were three, his 'Dragon' houseboat mounting

---

[1] S.S. No. 327 16 Nov., 1875. The sailors mentioned were Sub-Lieut. Abbott and four ratings from H.M.S. *Thistle*, lent to Birch in order to train his police in the handling of the gun with which Jervois had equipped the Residency. The *Pluto*'s sailing was postponed until the 3rd, by which date there was good reason for Abbott and his seamen to remain, which they did.

[2] Mallal, op. cit., p. 111.   [3] Ibid., p. 157.   [4] Ibid., p. 111.

a 3-pounder gun, a 'sampan panjang' for the sepoys, carrying a small mortar, and another 'sampan panjang' used by the servants as a floating kitchen. By going a day earlier than planned he had ensured that Swettenham and Mahmood could not be there; and he discarded Abbott, in effect, before the moment of greatest danger. When leaving Bandar Bahru, Birch is reported to have said: 'If the Maharaja Lela wants to fight, I will fire into him.' But he made nonsense of this by telling his sepoys not to use their firearms even 'if the Passir Salak people tried to make a disturbance'.[1] The effect of his plan was to combine the maximum provocation with the minimum strength. Birch's last journey could be plausibly described as something between a desperate gamble and deliberate suicide. Had he been able to establish effective control of Perak, announcing the success which his own reports seemed to foreshadow, Jervois might have relented and agreed to keep him in office. Failing that, Birch may not have wanted to live. But human motives are not easy to analyse and we may never know with certainty—and he may not have known himself—what exactly he was trying to do. If his mission was to ensure the military conquest of Perak, he could hardly have gone about it in any more effective way. If he wanted to turn a personal failure into a legend of heroic martyrdom, he took every step which would make this almost certain. Of his physical courage there can be no doubt at all.

Birch's party reached Passir Salak at 11.0 p.m. on the night of 1 November. His 'Dragon' boat was moored with the other two in mid-stream opposite the kampong. At 5.0 next morning, 2 November, the boats were moved close into the bank near a Chinese goldsmith's shop. Sub-Lieutenant Abbott then went off shooting on the Kampong Gaja side of the river. Birch sent his interpreter, Mat Arshad, to tell the Maharaja Lela that he wanted to see him. His sepoys and boatmen went ashore, meanwhile, to cook their rice and clean their unloaded rifles. Mr. Birch was visited, apparently, by the Dato Sagor (the chief from the opposite side of the river)[2] but the Maharaja Lela remained in his house. 'Why should we go down and see him?' he asked Mat Arshad. 'This is not his Country or village. It is ours.' Knowing Birch's errand, he sent Mat Arshad back with a warning that he would allow no one to post the proclamations at Passir Salak. A large crowd of armed Malays began to assemble near the Chinese shop. Birch thereupon ordered Mat Arshad to put up the proclamations on the shop walls ten yards from the 'Dragon' boat. Then,

[1] Mallal, op. cit., p. 176.　　[2] Winstedt and Wilkinson, op. cit., p. 114.

ignoring the abuse of the restive crowd, he entered an adjacent bath-house with no other precaution than posting a single sentry armed only with a revolver.

The proclamations were torn down almost as soon as they were posted. Told of this, Birch ordered his interpreter, from the bath-house, to put them up again. Mat Arshad is said to have protested to the bystanders, pointing out that the pieces of paper did not matter in themselves. 'Let them remain,' he pleaded, 'you can do what you like when we go away!' He then tried to post the notices again, push-ing aside Pandak Indut, one of those who were trying to prevent him. Pandak Indut instantly stabbed him. This was the signal for a rush at the bath-house, Birch being speared by Pandak Indut through the palm-leaf walls. A Malay called Seputum hacked him with a sword and his body fell into the river. The sentry merely saved himself by swimming. The other sepoys mostly escaped in one of the smaller boats to Bandar Bahru.[1] So did Mr. Abbott, apparently against the advice of the Dato Sagor, whom he met while shooting and who warned him not to cross the river. Abbott escaped in a dugout canoe, under fire from both banks, and accompanied by a single boatman.[2] Perhaps on hearing the uproar, the Maharaja Lela is said to have shouted from the steps of his house:

This is not the will of the Rajah or his order. It is our will because we cannot stand it any longer; others' houses have been burnt and where are we to go if our houses are burnt too? It is better that we should die at once.[3]

Afterwards the Maharaja Lela came down to the river and divided the Resident's property between the murderers. He himself kept the two boats, the 3-pounder gun, the British flags (a union flag and two blue ensigns), three boxes of documents, a few private belongings, and less than $100 in cash. Seputum was given, not the $25 he had been promised, but a kris—'he went home with a head-ache and slept'[4] but not before he had said to his wife (correctly) 'I shall die for this.' There was feasting for two days and a general feeling that an awkward problem had been rather neatly solved. It only remained to kill Swet-tenham on his way down the river. Then all could live happily thereafter.

---

[1] The casualties, apart from Birch and the interpreter, comprised one sepoy and one boatman killed, three sepoys wounded, two seriously, and three boatmen wounded, one seriously.
[2] McNair, op. cit., London, 1878, p. 372.
[3] Mallal, op. cit., p. 181.   [4] Winstedt and Wilkinson, op. cit., p. 115.

Swettenham returned to Blanja on the afternoon of 4 November.

I reached that place at 4.00 p.m. and found the shallow side of the river, in front of the village, crowded with boats. There must have been at least fifty, while between 200 and 300 armed men were on the sands behind them. As we pushed our boats through the shallow water a man named Haji Ali, a noted fighter, waded through the water and came aboard. I knew him pretty well as a plausible rascal not to be trusted; but we were outwardly on friendly terms. Without wasting words, he said: 'Mr. Birch has been murdered at Pasir Salak. His house and island have been taken by the Maharaja Lela, and his guard of Indians killed or dispersed. The river at Pasir Salak has been staked from bank to bank so that no boat can pass. They are waiting for you, and the only thing you can do is to come ashore and stay here.' I did not believe this very unpleasant news, and said 'How am I to know that what you say is true?' He answered, 'Because the Maharaja Lela has written to Raja Ismail to tell him, and sent his letter by Mr. Birch's boat to prove his statement. Raja Ismail refused to have the boat here, and told the messengers to take it back to Pasir Salak. They left two hours ago.' He concluded by saying that he brought a message from Raja Ismail inviting me to see him.[1]

Swettenham was in a difficult and dangerous position. His first move was to get rid of Haji Ali, telling him to inform Ismail that the Assistant Resident would come and see him.

As soon as he had gone, Raja Mahmud said that to land would be suicide, and we agreed that our only chance was to continue our journey down-stream and take our chance.[2]

Some of the boatmen preferred to stay; so Swettenham manned one of his boats and left the other. There went with him Raja Mahmood and two of his followers, three foreign Malays, the coxswain from Manila, and a Chinese servant; nine men in all with a shotgun and two rifles between them. Swettenham wrote up his journal (scribbling in pencil) and brought it up to date with the following paragraph:

We have just reached Blanja and Haji Ali has come to say Mr. Birch and 16 others . . . have been killed at Passir Salak by the Maharaja Lela's people. They brought Mr. Birch's boat here an hour ago to Ismail, but he refused to take it saying the Maharaja Lela had killed Birch and might keep the boat. They are waiting now at Passir Salak for me, for they say I am 10 times worse than Mr. Birch. They came to try and keep me here, but Raja Mahmud and I are of one mind, to go down. . . . Mahmud is a real plucky fellow and I'm fortunate to have him.
     I will leave this book with a man of the boat who'd rather not go, in case

[1] Swettenham, Footprints in Malaya, pp. 57–58.
[2] Ibid., p. 58.

I should not get through to Singapore. But D. V., we will go for them yet; anyway I can't turn back.

Frank A. Swettenham.
4.30. p.m.   4. 11. 75.[1]

Swettenham was just pushing off when Haji Ali returned and was told what was intended. 'It is impossible,' he said, 'the whole country down-stream is in arms and watching for you. It is certain death.' They left him, knee-deep and shouting after them 'No doubt you think yourselves very fine fellows, but you will be killed all the same!'[2] An hour or so later they saw Birch's 'Dragon' boat moored by an island and knew that the report of his death must be true.

Aided by the river being in flood, Swettenham's party reached Passir Salak soon after 1.30 a.m. on the 5th. There were bonfires at intervals along the left bank with groups of armed men round each. But their boat slipped past in the mist, the barrier across the river turning out to be a myth. Opposite the last watch fire the boat ran aground and was challenged, 'Whose boat is that?' Someone replied, 'Haji Mat Yasin's.' 'Where are you from?' 'From Blanja.' 'Where are you going?' By that time the boat was moving again and vanishing into the mist, so that the answers to the last questions were misleading and derisive.

Five miles farther down the river we passed Birch's house, with a sentry walking backwards and forwards under a lamp, apparently inviting anyone to shoot him. He did not seem to see us, and we went on for another ten miles. Then we were challenged in English from a Selangor steam launch, and we knew we were safe.[3]

Swettenham returned next day upstream to the Residency, where Mr. Abbott was in command, supported by Mr. Bacon, Mr. Keyt, and Inspector Warne, who had come from Pangkor. Swettenham then took charge, his first care being to recover Birch's body through a Bugis intermediary and see to its burial, later, on the island. He and Abbott began at once to plan an attack on Passir Salak and would have done it with the men they had but for news coming that Innes was on the way. They decided to await his arrival 'which we were afterwards glad of'.

News of Birch's death, sent by Abbott in the *Pluto*, had reached Penang on the evening of 3 November. Mr. Welner, the commander of the *Pluto*, called first on the Superintendent of Police, the Hon.

[1] *Swettenham's Perak Journals*, p. 122.
[2] Swettenham, *Footprints in Malaya*, p. 58.   [3] Ibid., p. 60.

H. Plunket. They went on together to see the Lieutenant-Governor, Colonel Anson, whom they found just returned from his evening drive. What followed is best told in Anson's words:

while the superintendent engaged my wife in conversation, the captain took me aside behind one of the pillars at the entrance of my house, and said: 'Mr. Birch has been murdered, sir. I have just arrived from Perak.' After some further conversation, he said 'Well, I must get back to my ship. I want 40 tons of coal on board, and I know I shan't get that on board before to-morrow evening.' He then left me, when I at once telegraphed to the town, three miles away, and ordered the 40 tons of coal to be put on board immediately, and when he arrived at the wharf he found his vessel being coaled. I hurriedly had my dinner, and then went to the infantry barracks to see the officer commanding the troops, but he was not at home. I therefore left word for him to meet me at the central police office in the town. I went on to a house near, occupied by the Judge and Captain Innes, R.E. (the Colonial Engineer, seconded for that office). They were both in bed and asleep. But the front door was not locked, so I went upstairs, and looked into a room on one side of the passage, in which I saw a judicial-looking four-post bed. I then looked into the room on the other side, and saw a military officer's bed. In a low voice I called out 'Captain Innes'; receiving no answer, I repeated this in increasingly loud tones. At the third time, Captain Innes sprang up, and asked what was the matter. I said 'Mr. Birch has been murdered, and I want you, as Commissioner, to accompany the force I am going to send to Perak to protect the Government officials there.' I added, 'I am going to the central police office, meet me there.' He jumped out of bed and said, 'If you will wait a minute, sir, I will accompany you.' He did so. Poor fellow; on the 6th he was shot through the heart. Such a nice fellow and good officer.[1]

The house from which Innes was fetched by Anson is still in existence. Innes had formerly shared it with Frank Swettenham when the latter was Collector of Land Revenue for Penang and Province Wellesley (1872–3). They named the house 'The Baronial Hall' from its pretentious appearance, but at a later date it was again allocated, apparently, to the judge.

At the central police office Colonel Anson completed his arrangements. He wrote out instructions for Innes, appointing him Assistant British Commissioner and defining his first tasks; one being to inquire into the circumstances of the murder, another being to call upon the chiefs to hand over all those implicated. The *Pluto* would leave Penang at 6.0 a.m. on the following morning with two officers and sixty men of the 10th Regiment, thirty policemen led by the Hon. H.

---

[1] Anson, op. cit., p. 330.

Plunket, Superintendent of Police, an apothecary, Captain Innes as temporary Acting Assistant Resident, and Mr. S. Kynnersley as interpreter. Simultaneously, Anson telegraphed the news to Jervois at Singapore, adding details of the action he proposed to take. This telegram reached the Governor at the same time as Birch's telegram of 1 November (see p. 235) in which all was said to be well. This telegram had come in the *Pluto* and Welner had not thought to prevent its transmission in the ordinary way. The result was that Jervois, receiving a telegram from Birch (which he thought must be misdated) and another announcing Birch's death, considered that the latter must be a mistake. He wired asking Anson, 'When and how did you receive information?' Anson replied that he had the news from Welner. Jervois quoted Birch's telegram, expressed incredulity, but authorized Anson to take the action he proposed. It was not until the following day, the 4th, that Anson was able to clear up the mystery, explaining to the Governor that Birch's telegram had been written *before* he went up the river.

Anson's action requires some comment. Why, to begin with, did he not lead the expedition in person? The answer is that he had no information of any disturbance other than the actual murder; which might be the work of only a small group. Why did he send Innes as Acting Assistant Resident? Why should he, for that matter, be at pains to supersede Swettenham? The answer to that is that he had written Swettenham off as dead. Nothing had been heard of Swettenham since the 28th and it was assumed that he would go to Kuala Kangsar on hearing of Birch's death. He had himself posted the sepoys there and planned their accommodation. A rumour was current that he, too, had been murdered. All that Anson could do was to instruct Speedy to send every available armed man from Larut to Kuala Kangsar. Speedy did so, sending Malay and Chinese detectives to learn what they could of the Resident's and the Assistant Resident's fate, 'and to obtain, if possible, the remains of these unfortunate officers'.[1] It was some days before it was known that Swettenham was still alive, and his successor had meanwhile been found. It is important, however, to realize that Innes was not in command of the expedition. Although an army officer, he was serving in a civilian capacity. He was the political officer who was to summon and authorize military action in aid of the civil power. As Anson put it 'He was not sent as a combatant'[2] and Anson it was who had sent him. To a limited

[1] Swettenham, *Footprints in Malaya*, p. 60.   [2] Anson, op. cit., p. 330.

extent, Plunket and his men came under Innes's control. So perhaps did the Sikhs of the Resident's guard. But the soldiers of the 10th Regiment were under the orders of Captain Booth and the four sailors would remain under the orders of Sub-Lieutenant Abbott. Not for the last time in Malayan history, an expedition was going forth with no single leader. Perfect co-operation would be needed between the miscellaneous elements of a force hastily assembled for the first time. Such co-operation is not easy to ensure, least of all when there is no language in common. Lacking their sergeant-major, the Sikhs could be addressed only through an interpreter. Abbott and his four seamen 'were endeavouring, without much success, to get [them] into something like discipline'.[1]

Innes went no farther than the island of Pangkor on the 4th, trying to ascertain the situation by a reconnaissance; the time devoted to which, we are told, is seldom wasted. He expected to find H.M.S. *Thistle* there, but in this was disappointed. There he seems to have received instead an encouraging message from Sub-Lieutenant Abbott and as a result of this he reached Bandar Bahru on the 6th. The chief development since the day of the murder had been the appearance of Abdullah, with the Laxamana, the Shahbandar, and a fleet of armed boats, uttering condolences and offering help. At Swettenham's request he withdrew these forces farther down the river and remained inactive during the next phase of the story. There would seem to have been some movement of the Maharaja Lela's men towards Bandar Bahru, but nothing came of it.[2] Innes found the Residency still resolutely held by Swettenham and Abbott and was there just in time for Mr. Birch's funeral. What information there was about Passir Salak came, in fact, from Dein Patundo and the other Bugis, who had recovered Birch's body. They said that a stockade there was being held by the Maharaja Lela and the Dato Sagor and that a further stockade had been constructed 400 or 500 yards farther inland and in the rear.

At a conference held on the evening of the 6th Swettenham proposed attacking Passir Salak next day, a party to go up either bank of the river, supported by one gun and one howitzer and by rockets, mounted and fired from boats.[3] This plan was generally agreed and Swettenham recruited a Sumatran Malay called Nacodah Orlong

[1] MS. Journal kept by Lieutenant Bayly, R.N., and inherited by his family.
[2] Swettenham, *British Malaya*, p. 207.
[3] Swettenham's report dated 18 Nov. The 9-pdr. field-gun and the 12-pdr. howitzer were actually lashed in position in boats and tested by firing. See also McNair, op. cit., p. 376.

with fourteen followers. These, with Swettenham, Raja Mahmood, his two followers, and the coxswain from Manila made a Malay scouting party of twenty.

We all agreed that it was necessary to act at once, to avoid the appearance of indecision, and to give the enemy no time to strengthen his position. It was decided, therefore, to get up at 4.30 a.m. next morning, put everyone into boats, pole upstream two miles, land, and walk the other three miles to Pasir Salak. It was arranged that the bluejackets should take the howitzers in boats, and keeping in line with the advance of the shore party, deal from the river with any stockade that might be met with.

The required number of boats and boatmen were only secured with great difficulty, and it was 7.30 before we got under way. Only when in the boat was I told that, after I had gone to bed, the others had decided to leave the guns behind.[1]

The guns under discussion, important in this narrative, were the 'few small pieces of Ordnance' to which Jervois referred in his dispatch of 16 October (No. 291). He found them in store at Singapore and sent them to Birch 'to be used in boats by the Police'. It did not occur to him at the time to provide Birch with anyone trained to handle these guns, but Birch sought naval advice and mounted a 3-pounder brass gun in his 'Dragon' houseboat. It is not clear that his men knew how to aim this (or any other) weapon; and it fell, of course, into the hands of the Maharaja Lela. So did the small mortar carried in the 'sampan panjang'. There remained at Bandar Bahru a 9-pounder Vavasour field-gun, a brass 12-pounder howitzer, and a small Coëhorn mortar, with ammunition apparently for all of them. The mere variety of this equipment might have confused the sub-lieutenant's efforts at instruction, even if he knew anything about this miscellaneous and probably antiquated artillery. 'The rockets', wrote Abbott 'were of an obsolete pattern (9-pounder, tail, shell) and used in wooden troughs, with paper primers stuck in one of the holes in the base, and ignited by a common match, this being the only means I could devise of using them.' He had probably never seen the things before; and certainly never wanted to see them again.

The seamen were to be equipped with rockets, to be used ashore, and it may have been discovered that the handling of the howitzer was still beyond the capacity of the Resident's Sikhs. It was better,

---

[1] Swettenham, *Footprints in Malaya*, p. 61. There was a brief argument between Innes and Swettenham, the former saying that it would be difficult with only four sailors to manage both guns and rockets. Although mustering forces at 4.30 a.m. they were unable to leave until 7.0. It was 10.30 before their actual advance began.

perhaps, to leave this weapon behind than have its shells dropping short. And, lacking the howitzer, it was arguably wiser to keep the whole force on the Passir Salak or right bank of the river. As against that, the lack of artillery would make it impossible to assault the prepared positions that the Malays were known to have constructed, or not at least without suffering heavy casualties. As Swettenham pointed out (afterwards), 'hardly any consideration will justify an attack without at least one gun'.[1] Without guns, nevertheless, the troops went forward, after landing at Passir Panjang (at 8.0 a.m.) in the following order: Malay scouts, Booth's platoon of the 10th; Innes, Abbott, and the sailors; the Sikhs; the Penang police under Plunket; and the other platoon of the 10th under Elliott. This was a marching formation, for no resistance was expected until they came near Passir Salak. They were still in single file therefore, when suddenly fired upon from a stockade which stopped their advance some two miles short of the village. Emerging from cover the scouts were faced by

a wide and deep ditch backed by a strong stockade of trees and logs built on to a bank of earth. The timbered top of the stockade was full of loopholes, and as we appeared from the corn stalks we were greeted by a volley from pivot guns and muskets.[2]

Nacodah Orlong was killed instantly, the remaining scouts (who carried no firearms) went to cover and Captain Innes came up to reconnoitre the enemy. He found himself faced by a stockade which rested its one flank on the river, the other in dense jungle. Swettenham by his own account suggested a flanking movement which he offered to lead. Innes agreed to this and Swettenham moved to the left with twelve men of the 10th Regiment and two Malays. As they moved in the required direction, however, they were fired on by the Sikhs (almost untrained recruits from Lahore) who had advanced with the same idea but who soon afterwards retired in confusion. Plunket's policemen had fled at the outset, 'saying they had not been engaged for a job of this kind'.[3] The naval party fired their rockets at the stockade but with no obvious result, most of their projectiles falling far beyond it.

After a space of desultory shooting which achieved nothing, Innes, who was now on the extreme right, gave the order to rush the stockade.

---

[1] Swettenham, *Malay Sketches*, p. 273.
[2] Swettenham, *Footprints in Malaya*, p. 62.
[3] Ibid. See also the story entitled 'Nakodah Orlong' in *Malay Sketches*.

That was done, with the result that Innes was killed, the two officers of the 10th Regiment were seriously wounded, and there were other casualties. We got to the edge of the ditch, but it was impossible to cross it and climb the fence above the bank in full view of an unseen enemy a few yards distant and completely protected. We had to retire, and if the defenders of the stockade had known how to use their weapons no one should have got away. I did not know that Innes had been killed, for I was in the centre and delayed by helping to carry a severely wounded sergeant of the 10th, so when we reached the path, and joined Abbott and Plunket, who were waiting for us, the other casualties had already been removed. We had no surgeon and no stretchers, and the journey back was far from pleasant. We expected our enemies to follow us; but later we learned that they had retired when we did, as they did not appreciate being rushed.[1]

The story of the enemies' retreat was brought by Allang, Nacodah Orlong's boy, who had stayed to bring in his master's body. This he did, swimming with it down the river, but not before he had seen the Malays withdraw. The party of Nacodah Orlong's men who went back for their leader's body and found Allang with it, actually entered the stockade and found it deserted.

Swettenham's later narrative makes Innes the commander of the expedition. Anson, by contrast, puts the blame on Swettenham and Abbott,[2] and Jervois, in writing to Anson, praised his selection of Innes, adding that 'Entre nous, I believe if *he* had been the military officer in command, the business would have been a success'.[3] According to Jervois it was Booth who gave the order to withdraw, admittedly after Innes's death, and Swettenham's contemporary report, written on the 18th, explicitly names Booth as 'in command'. An intercepted Malay letter afterwards described a battle in which 'Tuan Man' (Swettenham?) lost a hundred of his men, all killed. The real trouble was that there was nobody in command until Innes's death gave some added authority to Booth; and all he did was to order the withdrawal of all who had not already retired. He can scarcely be blamed, however, for his decision, however unfortunate the sequel. The skirmish had shown that a force with a nominal strength of 147 officers and men amounted, for all practical purposes, to about sixty-three effectives. The remainder included Malays who were virtually unarmed, Sikhs who were virtually leaderless, and policemen who were virtually useless. There had been seventeen casualties in less than two

---

[1] Swettenham, *Footprints in Malaya*. The attack was presumably made by the rear platoon of the 10th, the only troops by then uncommitted.
[2] Anson, op. cit., p. 331.   [3] Ibid.

hours' firing and of these four were killed. It was not, however, the number of the casualties that brought the attack to an end so much as the fact that there were practically no officers left. Innes had been killed, sword in hand, Booth wounded in the foot, Elliott severely wounded in the arm and side, and Nacodah Orlong killed by a shot from a 'lela'. The Sikhs lacked an officer in the first place and had recently lost their senior N.C.O., removed by Birch for drunkenness and insubordination. Only Plunket remained , whose efforts to rally his policemen had completely failed. It was, therefore, a disconsolate party that re-embarked at 2.45 and landed back at the Residency at 3.15 p.m.—only to learn soon afterwards that the enemy had fled before the retirement had even begun.

The day after the Maharaja Lela's victory, supposed to have taken place 'on the left side of Bandar Tua, towards Kampong Pisang' and a mile beyond Raja Cheh Muda's house, Frank Swettenham sat down to write his report to the Colonial Secretary.

Bandar Bahru. November 8. 1875.

Sir,

Captain Innes, the Acting Assistant Commissioner, having been killed yesterday in action, it devolves upon me to inform you of the last two days' occurrences.

In continuation, then, of my report of the 6th instant, I have the honour to inform you that on the arrival of Captain Innes and party our preparations were hurried on, and I informed Captain Innes of the plan Lieutenant Abbott and I had proposed, namely to send a force up each bank of the river, supported by two guns.

Swettenham never underrated the significance of his own part in any historic event—a part which had usually become still more vital when the time came to write his autobiography—and he was careful to point out that the lack of artillery on this occasion was in no way attributable to him. He concluded his story as follows:

When we returned yesterday I found a telegram from Penang, stating that the *Pluto* was to meet his Excellency the Governor at the mouth of the river this morning, and Mr. Kynnersley had already sent her down.

I wrote letters to his Excellency the Governor and the Honourable the Lieutenant-Governor of Penang, and directed Mr. Kynnersley to take them to the *Pluto* this morning and meet his Excellency, as I did not like to leave the Residency without a relief being sent.

At 6.30 p.m. Dr. Orton arrived and saw the wounded, whom he found

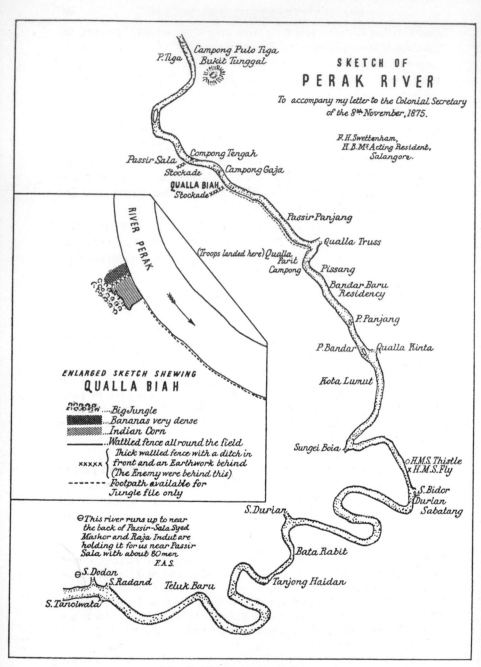

Map 7. The Lower Perak River

doing well, and Major Dunlop, R.A., arrived with Dr. Randall in the course of the night, and took charge as Special Commissioner.

I have etc.

Frank A. Swettenham.

H.B.M.'s Acting Resident. Selangor.

It is something to be an Acting Resident, if only between the death of one superior and the arrival within two days of the next. Bandar Bahru had, at the moment, little other comfort to offer.

If Swettenham's moment of authority ended with the arrival of Dunlop, Anson's period of prominence ended with the arrival of Sir William Jervois. It was on 4 November that the Governor was finally convinced that Birch was dead. He telegraphed this conclusion to the Secretary of State and added 'I think this affair is one of an isolated character' before describing the action he proposed to take. In his telegraphed reply Lord Carnarvon demanded full information and expressed the hope that the murder was 'an individual outrage', not leading to military operations 'which would endanger British policy in native States'. In this respect Lord Carnarvon's views contrasted sharply with those expressed in the Straits Settlements Legislative Council on the 5th. Nor was he aware of the reasons Jervois had for fearing that Birch's death was the result of a widespread movement.

To say that Birch's murder was welcome to the Members of the Legislative Council would be, of course, a gross exaggeration. But they all mingled with their grief a realization of how useful the event might prove to be. Mr. Shelford said that 'our flag has been insulted', and that the Governor might rely on the support of the community. Dr. Little was prepared to endorse a more stringent policy than had so far been pursued.

Looking to the future happiness of the Malay people, he thought the sooner the Chiefs were disposed of, the better,—amicably, if possible, but certainly in some way—and there he went the whole way with his Excellency, and only, for the present, stopped short of advocating annexation.

Mr. Read wanted to extend British protection to the other Native States. The Chief Justice said that the news, if true, gave a better reason for carrying out H.E.'s policy 'boldly, fearlessly and promptly'. The Acting Colonial Secretary (Mr. Irving) justified the recent change in policy by describing the deadlock reached in Perak and the need to break it by advance or withdrawal. But to retreat was hardly practicable: 'We had gone too far, and excited too many hopes, and given too many implied pledges. The only course was to advance.' Irving thought that it would soon be apparent whether 'the disaster we are deploring was an isolated outbreak' or the symptom of a 'serious movement'. He felt that, in either event, the British Government would have to finish the task that it had begun.

With these assurances of support ringing in his ears, Sir William Jervois embarked that same afternoon in the chartered steamship *Staat Rochussen*, accompanied by Major Dunlop, Captain Peyton (his A.D.C.), Captain Whitla of the 10th Regiment, and twenty artillerymen. H.M. Gunboat *Fly* had sailed earlier in the day, carrying eighty other ranks of the 10th Regiment. No one could say of the Governor that he was lacking in energy or decision. At the same time he can have felt none too happy. He was caught once more between his Council crying 'Forward!' and the Colonial Office crying 'Back!' It was all very well for Little to talk about annexation—it was not he who would have to explain to Lord Carnarvon what the colonists would like to do. Nor would Read or Shelford have to explain, for that matter, what they had already done. Introducing the 'Queen's Commissioner' system into Perak had been something of a risk, justifiable only by success. But this affair at Passir Salak could not be described as a success. And he, the Governor, would be held to blame for everything! And what was 'everything' going to mean? Davidson had written an alarming letter from Selangor on 27 October and one still more alarming on 1 November. There was talk, too, of impending trouble in Sungei Ujong. To listen to Irving one would think that a general rising was to be expected. But what if it really took place—and if he were thought to have caused it!

Jervois rightly concluded that his first task was to discover the extent of the trouble. He did not, therefore, proceed directly to the Perak river. He decided to call on the way at Malacca and Klang. His call at Malacca was brief but he learnt there of recent and disturbing events; the election of a Yam Tuan Besar and the action of the other chiefs in meeting to depose the Dato Klana (the British protégé) of Sungei Ujong. All Jervois could do at the moment was to promise reinforcements. He went straight on to Klang, meeting H.M.S. *Thistle* in the vicinity and proceeding afterwards with this warship in company.

In his letter of 1 November Davidson had stated that 'things are now sufficiently alarming to ask for a small party of the 10th Regiment'. He had feared that 'We are on the eve of great disturbances in this Residency. . . . The enemy seems to be coming in from all sides. . . .'

What was disconcerting about this (quite apart from any wider implications) was that Selangor had seemed completely quiet and Jervois had come to rely on its remaining so. He had taken Swettenham off to Perak, leaving Sultan Abdul Samad to his own devices. Swettenham, for one, had doubted the wisdom of this (see p. 228). Then he had planned to take Davidson as well, to assist (and then replace) Birch in Perak. Now it was becoming apparent that Selangor could not be safely neglected like that. With Raja Mahdie again in the field anything might happen. Davidson would have to stay and someone else would have to go to Langat—Hayward from Malacca, perhaps.

Jervois was at Klang on 7 November and saw Tunku dia Oodin. From there he wrote a stern letter of reproof to the Sultan. As Davidson was not there, the Governor could do no more than send him the news by letter:

I believe the act to be one of an isolated character, and that it has no significance as regards the general feeling of the Perak people. Irving considers that, taken in connection with the disturbed state of Salangore, there is a general rising to be apprehended throughout the Malay Peninsula. I cannot say that there appears to me any sufficient grounds for such belief.

Finding things at least momentarily quiet in Selangor, with Davidson actively in the field, Jervois went on to the Perak river, the *Thistle* going there ahead of him and the *Pluto* coming down the river, as instructed by telegram, to meet him on the 8th. With the *Pluto* came news of the defeat at Passir Salak on the previous day. It came as the most unpleasant shock at the worst possible moment. If anything could encourage the dissidents in Selangor and Sungei Ujong it would be the news of an actual British reverse. It was bad enough in itself, but the Malays could be relied upon to enlarge the story to epic proportions. Trust them for that! What Irving feared might have been absurd before—it was no longer so improbable in the light of this disaster. If prestige was at stake, something would have to be done.

Upon receipt of this intelligence, I immediately took such measures as seemed to be urgently required. I telegraphed to the Acting Colonial Secretary at Singapore to ask for 300 men of the 80th Regiment from Hongkong, and to summon H.M.S. *Modeste* from Labuan, and issued general directions for holding Bandar Bahru and maintaining our communications with Durian Sabatang, the highest navigable point for Gun Boats on the Perak River. I proceeded myself to a point on the river between Batarabit and Durian Sabatang where Sultan Abdullah, the Laxamana and the Shahbandar came to see me. The Sultan promised me to give assistance in men and boats for operations on the river.

Before leaving the Perak River, I appointed Major Dunlop, R.A. (who had accompanied me from Singapore), Commissioner, and Mr. Swettenham Deputy Commissioner, with the force which will proceed up the river from the Residency.

I have also appointed Major McNair, Commissioner, and Mr. Maxwell Deputy Commissioner, for the force which I have proposed to move through Laroot to Qualla Kangsa.

I left Batarabit on the evening of the 9th instant and arrived at Singapore on the 11th.[1]

The Governor's telegram to Irving, conveying the news of the failure at Passir Salak and asking help from Hong Kong, arrived via Penang early on the morning of the 9th, the gist of it being passed on at once to the Colonial Office. Lord Carnarvon authorized help from Hong Kong that day and wired Singapore to that effect, adding 'I have requested 250 more from India. Immediately telegraph whether Governor considers this enough'.[2] The Governor was not there, so Irving took his tale of woe to the military Commandant. Following that consultation, Irving wired as follows to the Secretary of State:

Commandant recommends thousand men from Calcutta with artillery and mountain guns. Have telegraphed accordingly. General Colborne offers three Companies. Have telegraphed to accept. *Ringdove* and *Modeste* on way from Hongkong. *Egeria* will follow.

The telegraph wires were now buzzing between London and the Viceroy of India, between the Viceroy and Calcutta, between Singapore and Calcutta, between London and Hong Kong. The feeling of crisis, originated perhaps by Irving, spread elsewhere, infecting the Governor himself as soon as he returned. His own account reads as follows:

On my return to Singapore on the 11th, I was cheered by the telegram which I received from your Lordship in which your Lordship authorised me to call for troops from India, and having reference to the state of things which were reported to me from the other native States, more especially from Mr. Davidson in Salangore, looking moreover at the possibility of attack being made on our own possessions in the Malay Peninsula, viz: Province Wellesley, and even our old settlement of Malacca, I not only fully endorsed the telegram which was sent by the Acting Colonial Secretary, after consulting the Chief Justice and the Members of the Executive Council, but I added to it by asking that a larger force might be sent.[3]

[1] S.S. No. 327, 16 Nov. 1875.
[2] Quoted in S.S. No. 309, 9 Nov. 1875.
[3] S.S. No. 94, 2 Dec. 1875.

A telegram to this effect went off immediately and produced from Lord Carnarvon his plaintive message of 12 November:

Secretary of State[1] tells me you now ask for two regiments of European infantry, or 1,500 bayonets, with artillery, 50 miles telegraphic apparatus, and a million cartridges.[2] I am extremely disappointed at getting no reply to all my requests for full explanation and details. I cannot judge for what purpose you want a military force apparently so much larger than what would be required to punish what you originally called an isolated outrage.

Before India is told to send soldiers, explain what policy you have in view; what is now the state of things; whether disturbance is spreading; what cause to apprehend danger in future; and why natives may not form part of the force.

Please send quick and full answer.

Lord Carnarvon had indeed been demanding news in vain. His first reaction had been to send help at once, promising reinforcements and instructing Jervois 'Do not attempt to attack without sufficient force'. But this initial mood soon gave way to a fresh anxiety on a different score. Was Jervois going to make this murder the excuse for the conquest and annexation of the entire Malay Peninsula? This, as we have seen, is exactly what the Executive Council at Singapore would have liked Jervois to do. Well aware of that, Carnarvon began to look more critically at these requests for troops. Jervois sent off on the 12th at 6.30 p.m. and Carnarvon received on the following day an account of what the Governor had learnt and done but little of what he meant to do. Carnarvon complained about this on the 14th, saying that he had rather reluctantly authorized the dispatch of troops from Calcutta:

I am sorry to be obliged to act without knowing many essential details or the special object which you have in view. I cannot assume the responsibility of further delay in the despatch of the troops in face of your urgent demands, but responsibility of asking for them from Calcutta will rest with you, and you must clearly understand that these troops are allowed only for punishment of outrage, and that in no case will Her Majesty's Government sanction their use for annexation or any other large political aims. All such questions must be referred home by telegraph or despatch.

I wish you immediately to explain why I have received no reply to my several questions, and transmit complete answers to them.

One reason, of course, for the Governor's failure to correspond at length had been his absence from the 5th to the 11th. Another reason

---

[1] i.e. the Secretary of State for India, at this period the Marquess of Salisbury.
[2] The demand was excessive. See p. 255 below.

lay in the amount of work which the crisis entailed. Jervois had issued his first orders on the Perak river but he had now to implement his own plans with all possible speed. He asked the Commandant to send eighty more men of the 10th Regiment to Perak. He ordered the construction of forty flat-bottomed boats for use on that river, with six more to use as gunboats. He ordered supplies to be collected at Durian Sabatang and Larut. He took up a merchant ship called the *Argonaut* and ordered 800 tons of coal to be loaded, with 1,200 planks for hut-building, the ship to form a coaling depot at the Dindings. With fuel supply thus assured, the Navy could be asked (and was asked) to blockade the Perak coast. An ordinance was issued on the 11th to prohibit the sale of arms and ammunition—Jervois, on landing, went straight to the Legislative Council, then in session, to see this done. He sent Lord Carnarvon a telegram on the 12th as we have seen, containing a mysterious and disquieting reference to a proclamation which Birch had been making public at the time of his death. For more detailed explanations he lacked the time (or the inclination). At this period he could be fairly described as busy.

No colonial governor, however distracted, would ordinarily fail to respond to such a telegram from the Secretary of State as Lord Carnarvon dispatched on 14 November 1875. There was, however, no reply from Jervois of any kind and it was only after a period of stunned amazement that his silence was explained. It is common knowledge that a shoe-lace will never break except when its wearer is hurriedly dressing for an important party. In this instance it was the telegraphic cable that had snapped at a point off the Nicobar Islands, somewhere between Penang and Madras. Lord Carnarvon delivered further exhortation into the void and then realized, on the 15th, that he was completely out of touch. That night he was reduced to telegraphing the Cable Co. superintendents at Rangoon and Galle, asking them to forward an urgent message by the first passing steamship. In it Jervois was urged again to explain his policy:

> As soon as possible send complete replies to all questions. Do not permit Davidson to act except on defensive under strict orders from you. Inform me of substance of Proclamations posted in Perak. Troops ordered yesterday to leave Calcutta with the least possible delay.

The Secretary of State was using a rather unpromising line of communication and it was not before 22 November that he heard again from Singapore. In a telegram beginning 'Communication open via Siberia' Irving explained that the Governor had left again for Perak:

Full telegrams sent Ceylon Wednesday by mail, stating danger of national rising as reason for demand for troops; subsequent information strengthens belief in such danger. Satisfactory news from Davidson, Salangore, to 8th instant.

The parting of the electric cable had not only cut off Singapore from London—which Jervois probably welcomed as a respite—it also cut off the Straits Settlements from India. The original demand for a million cartridges had been a clerical error, some trembling clerk adding a nought while agog to be in touch with great events. It could not be corrected while the line was dead. Nor did Irving know whether the troops from India were actually on the way—which in fact they were. Other troops available included a body of irregulars raised by Jervois in Singapore for service in Selangor. These were described by the *Straits Observer* as:

120 picked men, chiefly Arabs and Seedie boys, who are expected to proceed across country, with Mr. Davidson, to the 'seat of war'. If this little force only carries out one half of what is promised we may expect grand results. At present we say nothing. . . .

This auxiliary force, commanded by Mr. de Fontaine (Tunku dia Oodin's officer in the last Selangor campaign), did not leave until the 19th, the day on which Captain Morison took the flotilla of boats up to Perak. In the meanwhile, on the 16th, the P. & O. steamship *Kashgar* arrived from Hong Kong with 300 men of the 80th Regiment, embarked on the 11th. With these men came Major-General the Hon. F. Colborne.

In noting the extremely prompt arrival of these and other troops, one must bear in mind the whole Victorian attitude to war. To those who have experienced, in any degree, the warfare of the twentieth century, it may seem mildly surprising to read of the eagerness with which the soldiers of 1875 went in search of armed conflict. At that time, however, there had been no real war since that in the Crimea. Of that war Anson might claim to be a veteran. But other and quite senior officers of the day—Clarke, Jervois, McNair, and their contemporaries—had seen little or no active service. Fortunate were they who could boast of their deeds during the Indian Mutiny. At the least hint of a campaign the less fortunate would rush to the scene from all points of the compass, sword in hand and eager for decorations.

In the present instance Jervois's demand for two regiments from India has evoked from Calcutta no protest but only a suggestion that the Commander-in-Chief (India) should appoint a commander 'who will probably be senior to officer commanding in the Straits'. With the selection of Brigadier-General J. Ross this probability was translated into fact. But the planners at Calcutta had reckoned without Major-General Colborne. That he should have rushed into the fray—bringing only 300 men of his own—was an unexpected and unwelcome development. He was, beyond question, senior to everybody, Jervois included.

Sir William Jervois discussed the situation fully with General Colborne on the 16th and 17th, and then wrote to Commander Singleton (Senior Naval Officer) on the 17th, requesting him to embark troops for Perak on the following day in H.M. Ships *Ringdove* and *Egeria*. Then, on the 18th, Jervois handed General Colborne a letter in which the political objects of the ensuing campaign were for the first time defined:

The first object is to bring to justice the perpetrators of the murder of the British Resident, and the suspicions that point to the Maharaja Lela as the instigator of the crime are so strong that the occupation of his village, to be followed by an uncompromising demand for his surrender, is the first object to be aimed at. The occupation of Passir Sala will probably present no difficulty, but the demand for the surrender of the Maharaja Lela is not to be expected [to succeed] until an imposing display of force has been exhibited.

This display (Jervois suggested and Colborne agreed) should take the form of an advance up the Perak river to Passir Salak, an advance through Larut to Kuala Kangsar and, possibly, an advance from Bruas on Blanja.

. . . With the establishment of the force at Passir Sala, Qualla Kangsar and Blanja, and the holding of the river, the definite views at which I have arrived come to an end.

To this rather lame conclusion Jervois added one further suggestion, that a road should be made from Kota Stia to Bandar Bahru. Thus advised, General Colborne embarked with his troops on the 18th and proceeded towards the potential battlefields of Perak.[1]

---

[1] On this passage a problem of etiquette was solved with typically naval ingenuity, and recorded in Lieut. W. V. Bayly's Journal. 'Having no military flag on board to hoist for the General, we manufactured one out of a Union Jack and the sitting-down part of a pair of white trousers, on which latter was painted the proper device.'

When thus briefing the General from Hong Kong, Jervois was unable to tell him whether the troops from Calcutta were actually on their way. With the breakdown of telegraphic contact, he could only say that his commissariat department was working on the optimistic assumption that the troops had left Calcutta on or about the 12th. They had not done that, but they made up for it by the excellence of their organization. Anything lacking in speed was more than made up in staff work. The force which finally embarked, the first ship sailing on 20 November, the last with the Brigadier-General on the 26th, comprised:

Brigadier-General J. Ross	In command.
Major Mark Heathcote	A.Q.M.G.
Major H. L. Hawkins	Brigade Major.
Lieutenant J. J. Preston	A.D.C.
Captain A. R. Badcock	D.A. Commissary-General.
Major Twigge	Royal Engineers.

Headquarters and 600 men of the 3rd Regiment (the Buffs).
Headquarters and 400 men of the 1st Ghoorkhas.

3/5th Royal Artillery with $\begin{cases} \text{four 7-pdr. mountain guns,} \\ \text{two } 5\frac{1}{2}\text{-in. mortars,} \\ \text{500 rounds per piece,} \\ \text{200 rockets.} \end{cases}$

Signal detachment, 11 men with 100 miles of wire.
One Company Madras Sappers and Miners.
Medical officers, orderlies, stretcher-bearers.
Camp equipment, tents, &c.
Sea provisions for six weeks.
Shore provisions for ten days.
A *Times* War Correspondent (Mr. Man).

Of this expeditionary force Major J. F. A. McNair wrote with almost aesthetic appreciation.

It was so admirably adapted for the service in hand, so complete in itself in every detail of its composition, and showed throughout how all had been contrived by a prevailing master-mind, that it may be well here to give an account in full of this miniature army designed for jungle fighting. . . .

This force was capable of division into three parts, and was composed with this view in officers, men, equipment, guns and ammunition. Each ship had a complete equipment for the number of troops aboard, so as to make them independent of the movement of the other vessels.[1]

[1] McNair, op. cit., pp. 382–3.

All things considered, and allowing for the confusion which resulted from the broken cable, to have embarked that number of men in those few days was more than creditable, and to have the ships tactically loaded in that time was something of a triumph. First definite orders were issued on the 14th and the first elements of the force were ashore in Penang on the 27th, and in Perak on the 30th. By that date the campaign was supposed to be launched.

On 18 November, after Jervois had handed General Colborne his brief, it was known that there were three distinct forces in the field. There was Major Dunlop at Bandar Bahru, reinforced by eighty men of the 10th Regiment and some artillerymen, and left to hold the Residency. There was Major-General Colborne with 200 of the 80th Regiment, bound for the scene of hostilities in the *Ringdove* with a hundred more to follow in the *Fly*. There was, finally, a whole brigade on its way from Calcutta, loaded with ammunition and thirsting for glory. Suddenly, on the very eve of Colborne's departure, there arrived a telegram which transformed the whole situation. It was from Major Dunlop, dated 16 November, and it read as follows:

Yesterday morning we made a combined land and water attack on the enemy. After a long day's fighting, the enemy making an obstinate and prolonged resistance, we took and destroyed four stockades, including the Maharajah Lela's house and campong, the Datu Sagor's house and campong, in fact all Passir Sala and Campong Gaja. We captured five guns, recovered Birch's two boats, brass gun and papers and much of his property, in the Maharaja Lela's house. Only Ladgis wounded. The campaign is by no means finished yet but I do not propose to act again immediately; particulars follow by post.

The only crumb of comfort in this shattering message was the assurance at the end that the campaign was not yet finished and that Dunlop did not as yet intend to finish it. The campaign not yet finished! It was not supposed to have *begun*! Dunlop had spoilt everything and would now expect to be thanked for it. It was the sort of situation in which one's natural annoyance could not even find expression. There was little he could do about it but Sir William Jervois stood now in grave danger. He could be made to look very foolish indeed.

The story behind Dunlop's telegram begins with Jervois's departure from Batak Rabit on 9 November. In the aftermath of the reverse in which Innes was killed, the Governor had made Dunlop Commissioner and told him to defend Bandar Bahru and keep his communications open with Durian Sabatang. For the latter purpose he was provided with four steam-launches and two gun-vessels. His task was to hold the position from which a later advance would be made. Passir Salak was now deemed a proper objective for a full-scale offensive. For perhaps two days this theory was allowed to hold.

With the enemy apparently quiescent, some patrol activity would have seemed desirable if only to locate the areas of expected resistance. Nothing of that kind was attempted, but information began, nevertheless, to arrive from up the river. Among four Chinese in a boat was found the goldsmith of Passir Salak, a witness of the murder, who said that the Maharaja Lela had about 300 men but practically no food for them. This was confirmed by other reports and Dunlop told Jervois, on the 13th, in a private letter, that the blockade was having its effect:

One thing is very certain, rice is becoming scarce, and this in my opinion will do more towards weakening our enemies than anything else. Indeed our last report is that one-third of the force in Passir Sala has cleared out already. . . [should this be confirmed] we may find it advisable to attack the stockades before we receive reinforcements.

In Commander Stirling's report the same idea is expressed as forcibly:

Sir—In continuation of my letter of the 12th instant I beg to inform you that on the following day, a report having been received that the stockade at Passir Sala was likely to be abandoned, and it being considered extremely advisable that a blow should be struck at them before this took place, an immediate attack on their position was determined on.

This decision was evidently reached on the 12th or 13th in the knowledge that the enemy were few and likely to become fewer still. The idea was to attack them while they were still to be found. Major Dunlop accordingly wrote to Abdullah on the 13th asking him for the loan of river craft and boatmen. Commander Stirling, R.N., took this request to the Sultan and was promised sixteen boats. Boatmen were less easily obtainable (most of the populace had fled) and Stirling summoned help from his ship, H.M.S. *Thistle*. There arrived thence, early on the 14th, ten officers, sixty ratings, and fifteen marines —a total which, exceeding the *Thistle*'s entire crew, included men from the *Fly* as well and practically all officers from both ships. On the same day there appeared one of Raja Yusof's advisers called Lamsah with a letter from Yusof to Swettenham. It was from this man that further detailed information was obtained about the enemy strength and position; information which suggested that success might result from a carefully planned attack.

A man whose influence at this stage may well have been important was Frank Swettenham. He believed that the failure of the previous attack had been due to lack of artillery—or, more properly, to the Governor's mistake in providing guns but no gunners. Such a theory would be supremely acceptable to Dunlop, an artilleryman himself and one now provided with an officer and twenty men of his own corps. Swettenham was eager for action—'But D.V. we will go for them yet' he had written after hearing about the murder. Commander Stirling and his seamen were obviously spoiling for a fight, and the men of the 10th Regiment had both a reputation to retrieve and casualties to avenge. It only remained to work out the details, and this was done on the afternoon of the 14th when Major Dunlop, Commander Stirling, and Frank Swettenham walked up the river to find a suitable landing-place. They decided upon Passir Panjang, practically repeating the plan of the previous operation but with the needed artillery support and the needed unity of command. And this time it was decided to leave behind most of the Sikhs and all the policemen.

Everything being in readiness, we roused up the force at 3 a.m. on the 15th, and began getting the troops into the boats at 5 a.m.

It was 6.30 a.m. before the whole force was embarked, the Naval Brigade, under Captain Stirling, being in charge of the gun-boats.

The larger portion of the force had already started with Mr. Swettenham to show them the place of disembarkation, and I followed in the steam gig 'Perak' with Captain Stirling.[2]

The manifest advantage of this plan was that it provided one man to direct the whole operation, a second to direct the covering fire, and a third to lead the actual assault. Dunlop and Stirling were together and afloat, the entire land force being commanded by Captain Whitla. The total strength was as follows:

(a) *Naval detachment*: Commander Stirling and H.Q. in steam-gig. Six boats led by Commander Bruce mounting one 7-pounder M.L.R. gun, two 12-pounder howitzers, one small Coëhorn mortar, and two rocket tubes. Officers, 10. Seamen, 60.[1]

---

[1] The flotilla was organized as follows:
Steam-gig: Commander Stirling. Mr. Harrison, Assistant Paymaster.

1st native boat:	Sub-Lieut. Abbott	7-pdr.	9 men
2nd ,,	Lieut. Lowe	12-pdr.	8 ,,
3rd ,,	Mr. Tyler, Boatswain	24-pdr. rocket	8 ,,
4th ,,	Chief Gunner's Mate	12-pdr.	8 ,,
5th ,,	Sub-Lieut. Ross	Coëhorn mortar	8 ,,
6th ,,	Lieut. Forsythe	24-pdr. rocket	8 ,,

Boats for troops and wounded under Dr. Lloyd and Mr. Vosper, Boatswain.
[2] Major Dunlop's Report.

(b) *Landing party*. Captain Whitla commanding.

(i) *Advance guard*: Hon. H. Plunket and Mr. Swettenham with 15 Marines, 2 of Swettenham's men, 5 Sikhs, Raja Mahmood and 2 of his followers.

(ii) *Main guard*: Three officers and 131 men of the 1/10th Regiment. One officer and 20 gunners of the 9th Battery, 2nd Bde. R.A., with one brass 12-pounder mountain howitzer.

Total, officers and men: 255.

'The advance was sounded about 9.30 a.m.' following a disembarkation at about 8.0, and the flotilla moved off ahead of the column on land. When the stockade was sighted at Kampong Pisang the gun and rocket boats opened fire, initially at 1,100 yards, and then steadily closed the range.

The advance guard entered the Indian cornfield immediately in front of the stockade and had half crossed it when a fire was opened on them from the stockade, to which they at once replied.

The Artillery brought up the gun without delay, and after four or five rounds of case had been fired into the stockade, and the enemy's fire being silenced, the advance guard moved on again and entered the stockade which they found deserted.[1]

Another stockade, a mile farther on, built a hundred yards below the place where Birch was murdered, was dealt with in turn, using the same recipe, 'and here the navy drove out the enemy before the troops came up'.

Our whole attention was now directed towards Passir Sala stockade, which was keeping up an ineffectual fire against the boats, whilst the Naval Brigade were making excellent practice with rockets and guns. The moment we came in sight of Passir Sala, we had recognised Mr. Birch's barge moored to the bath where he was murdered, and this sight gave us an additional desire to push on. No time was lost then in getting over the ground and the Passir Salah stockade was entered with a rush, the advanced guard of the land force and Captain Bruce, R.N., from the river getting in almost at the same moment.

This stockade was also deserted, and in it we found the 3-pr brass gun taken from Mr. Birch's boat, a small brass lela, an iron lela, and the fragments of a 6-pr iron gun which had evidently just burst and been hit by one of our shells.

'Passir Salah was now our own. . . .'[2] The evident rivalry between navy and army, tempting the seamen to go beyond their role as

---

[1] Major Dunlop's Report.   [2] Ibid.

originally planned, led in this instance to no satisfaction for either, for 'Mr. Swettenham and Mr. Plunket with the advanced guard were always first to get into the stockades'.[1]

The Maharaja Lela's house, 'an exceptionally good one' and well fortified, was found deserted and also found to contain Mr. Birch's boxes of documents, Mr. Abbott's gun-case, and Swettenham's own dispatch box; as also documents belonging more rightly to the owner of the house. It was while following up this journalistic opportunity that Mr. Cope, Reuter's correspondent, was shot and slightly wounded by an undetected but obviously British marksman,[2] thus becoming almost the only casualty on the British side. After this search for evidence the whole of Passir Salak, beginning with the Maharaja Lela's house, was burnt. Later that day at about 5.0 p.m. Kampong Gaja was also burnt, that village being equally deserted. After these acts of vengeance the whole force was re-embarked at 6.30 and reached the Residency again at 8.0 p.m. No further operations took place immediately but the famous Syed Mashor (now on the British side) went with Raja Indut and eighty Selangor Malays in pursuit of the Maharaja Lela, who was believed to have fled towards the Dedop river. At Bandar Bahru Swettenham and other experts now had the leisure to study a captured document of some interest, an unaddressed letter drafted for the Maharaja Lela's signature and seal. It read as follows:

The submissive allegiance of Toh Orang Kaya Maharaja Lela, of Passir Sala, begs your Highness to assist him with men and money for expenses. The money which your Highness directed me to raise from each district, unless I hold a written authority from your Highness to that effect, no one will regard me.

As regards the white men, in four days they will attack me, and therefore I beg for Your Highness' assistance and also for money for expenses. I trust in your Highness' help.

There were some to whom this document seemed very interesting indeed.

Sir William Jervois received news of this action by telegram, as we have seen, on 18 November and decided to leave for Perak on the following day. He embarked in the *Pluto* with the Hon. G. Phillippo (Attorney-General), Captain Paton, A.D.C., and Lieutenant

---

[1] Swettenham was the author, however, of the dispatch in which this is stated. (See below, p. 263.)

[2] There is no record of the alibi of *The Times* Special Correspondent being tested.

McCallum, R.E. (acting private secretary), and arrived in the Perak river on the 22nd. There he found General Colborne in H.M.S. *Ringdove*, at Durian Sabatang, and asked him to suspend hostilities for the time being. On the same day he issued a proclamation calling on the inhabitants of Perak to support the cause of law and order, and followed this up by notices in which rewards were offered for the apprehension of the murderers.

If the Governor's situation was made uncomfortable by the murder of Mr. Birch, it deteriorated sharply again with the news of Major Dunlop's bloodless victory. For while it would be said that Jervois had, by his policy, provoked the rising in which Birch died, it might now be said that he had over-estimated Malay resistance, sending for troops from Hong Kong and India instead of using the troops already there to overcome what had proved a negligible resistance. It was while thinking these gloomy thoughts that he was handed Dunlop's report dated 16 November in which the previous day's action was described in detail. He instantly sent for Swettenham, who tells us the sequel in his autobiography:

I started early, long before breakfast, and on reaching the yacht was ushered into the presence, when Sir William Jervois said: 'I have received your report of the successful expedition against Pasir Salak, but you have omitted to say that it was made by my instructions.' I said: 'Yes, sir, but I was not aware that you had given such instructions.' Whereon he replied: 'You don't suppose that I am going to allow the report of a successful operation like this to be made without saying that it was done under my instructions.'

I found it difficult to reply to that, so I said: 'But it is not my report; it is signed by the Commissioner, Colonel Dunlop.'

'Yes, but here it is, and you wrote it. You must add words at the beginning to say that acting on my instructions the expedition was arranged.' I replied: 'I am sorry that I cannot alter a report signed by the Commissioner.'

'Very well,' said the Governor, 'then I shall send for Dunlop.'

I was dismissed and shepherded into a remote spot on the deck, from which I saw Dunlop arrive two or three hours later, during which no one offered me breakfast.

Dunlop's interview did not last long, and when he joined me I asked: 'Did you alter the letter?' And he answered: 'Yes.' 'But you know it isn't true. Why did you do it?' 'Because I was told that you agreed, but said I must make the alteration because I had signed the letter.'

Then we went home, and I to breakfast.[1]

---

[1] Swettenham, *Footprints in Malaya*, p. 63.

The report, as thus improved, reads:

In accordance with instructions from his Excellency, dated the 9th inst., I at once communicated with Captain Stirling, R.N., the Senior Naval Officer, and with Captain Whitla of the 1/10th Regiment, commanding the troops, with respect to the arrangements to be made for a combined attack by land and river upon Passir Sala as soon as possible.

Support was given to the italicized insertion by the concoction, for the record, of letters from Jervois to Stirling, Dunlop, and Whitla, dated from the Perak river above Batak Rabit on 9 November and calling upon them to attack Passir Salak 'so soon as the necessary preparations can be made'. That these letters are a subsequent forgery, and that Frank Swettenham's story is substantially true may be inferred from Commander Stirling's report to Vice-Admiral Ryder dated 16 November. No command from a Governor could alter that, and *he* says no word of any instructions received. He says plainly[1] that, after due consultation, it was agreed (for reasons which he explains) to attack Passir Salak. There can be little doubt that this is exactly what happened.

There is about this episode a certain pettiness and a certain lack of scruple which places Jervois in an unfavourable light. Dunlop, on the other hand, in agreeing to alter his report, was showing a soldierly loyalty to his superior. He may, incidentally, have felt some remorse about the operation itself. He had put the Governor in an awkward position. That Jervois was so placed was obvious to critics much farther afield. Chief of these was old Sir Peter Benson Maxwell, who described the situation unfeelingly:

And now up came the Buffs and the Blue-jackets; the Goorkhas and the artillery; and the Hong Kong troops and the Madras sappers and miners, all fresh from Rangoon. The electric wire, let us hope, was to the fore and the engineers were surely not left behind. Everything seemed complete; and yet there was a want—an uncommon want. Where was the enemy?[2]

Where indeed? It was rightly assumed from the start that the murder at Passir Salak must have been done by order of the Maharaja Lela and with the cognizance of the Dato Sagor. They and their adherents could be regarded as enemies. But what did they amount to? They had been routed by Dunlop's advance guard at the cost of scarcely a casualty. Innes could have routed them as easily had he brought a gun capable of firing an explosive shell. The complicity of other chiefs

[1] See p. 259 above.
[2] Maxwell, op. cit., p. 61.

and of both sultans might be suspected and could possibly be proved. But no proof of this could allow them to be classed as open opponents, for they had not gone to war. The murder of Birch and (still more) the reverse at Passir Salak should have been the signal for Abdullah and Ismail to announce a holy war against all infidel intruders. They should have gone whooping to the fray with frenzied appeals to Malay patriotism. But they had done nothing of the kind. Abdullah probably sniggered when he heard of Birch's death. He is said to have cheered almost openly when he heard of Innes being defeated and killed. In the meanwhile, however, he had been uttering words of sympathy mingled with promises of a half-hearted assistance. He had done nothing to take advantage of a seemingly hopeful opportunity. The Maharaja Lela had evidently expected help from Ismail, but the appeal he had been about to send was itself the proof that no help had so far been afforded him. Apart from that, Ismail had done nothing one way or the other. And while Swettenham's death at Blanja may have been intended, the fact remained that Swettenham had twice passed unscathed through Ismail's country. The ex-Sultan's hostility was evidently of a most inactive kind. Nothing, therefore, that had so far happened in Perak could possibly justify the deployment of a brigade of infantry. Such a force was, nevertheless, and inexorably, on its way.

After an interview with Abdullah, attended also by the Laxamana, Shahbandar, and Raja Mahkota, in which all professed their friendship, Sir William Jervois left the Perak river on the 22nd and went on to Penang, which he reached on the afternoon of the 23rd. He at once began energetic preparations for an invasion of Perak via Larut. Speedy was already organizing a supply base at Matang and preparing camp sites at nine-mile intervals between there and Kuala Kangsar. Major McNair was now sent off, on the 25th, to assume his duties as Commissioner. In his instructions, dated the 24th, he was told to visit the Perak river first, consult with Dunlop, then collect Mr. William Maxwell (his Assistant Commissioner), from Penang and so proceed to Larut to contact Speedy, detain the Mantri and Temenggong—unless there should be cogent reasons for not doing so—and hasten the completion of the road. Major Dunlop was similarly but perhaps less expertly engaged in overseeing the road-making between Kota Stia and Bandar Bahru. There was much to organize before the troops from India arrived. It was on 27 November that the S.S. *Arabia* dropped anchor in Penang harbour with 200 of the Buffs on board.

She had sailed on the 20th and it was known that the *Abyssinia, Malda, Caesarwitch,* and *Ethiopia* would be following within the next few days. H.M.S. *Modeste* also arrived on the 27th from Labuan, Captain Buller becoming Senior Naval Officer. General Colborne had also come to Penang on the 27th, leaving Major Amiel to command at Bandar Bahru,[1] and it was he who ordered the first detachment of the Buffs to leave for Larut on the evening of the 29th. By the end of the month the march of the northern column had fairly begun.

While all these troop movements were taking place, Sir William Jervois was trying to discover whether or not Ismail was to be regarded as an enemy. Towards discovering this, his first step was to write to Ismail on 22 November expressing surprise at his silence. 'We wish to hear from our friend. Unless we do hear . . . we can only conclude that he is our enemy and the enemy of Perak.' In point of fact Ismail had already written the day before, his letter reading as follows:

We write this letter to inform our friend that at the time we write this letter we are in very great distress; and we do not know why all the things which come from the sea cannot be taken into Perak.

All the people are very afraid; some of them have fled to the far jungles, for a great many white soldiers have come into the districts of Perak. In our opinion, we have never done anything wrong.

Regarding the death of Mr. Birch, we took no part, nor did we allow the people who did it, and we do not know why they committed the murder.

Ismail wrote again to the same effect on 24 November, but this time addressing Speedy and asking him to allow supplies to reach Upper Perak through Larut. On the 30th he wrote to the Governor, acknowledging receipt of his letters and protesting innocence:

In our heart, we may say that we don't wish to disobey our friend or deny his requests whenever those requests will lead to our good, and that of the country of Perak.

Jervois was dissatisfied with this sort of a reply. He wrote again, therefore, on 29 November, defining exactly what he expected Ismail to do. He should come to meet the British troops in Lower Perak, showing a white flag and making early contact with Major Dunlop. If any of his people had built stockades with a view to resistance, he was to have them destroyed. He was to do all he could to provide accommodation for the British troops. He should supply them with

---

[1] Amiel proceeded to raid Passir Salak again on the 27th 'and committed the whole town to the Flames' as described and illustrated in Lieut. Bayly's Journal.

all the information he could. He must, finally, do everything possible to discover and arrest the murderers.

If our friend will listen to us and be guided by us, we feel quite sure that even now we can make such arrangements as will lead to the happiness and prosperity of the Chiefs and people of Perak.

Ismail had already written on 3 December to explain that he never sanctioned the murder and had no idea where the murderers were. Now he replied to this further letter of the 29th saying (on 6 December) that he knew nothing of any stockades. He said nothing of any action he proposed to take and left his impatient correspondent to assume that the murderers, in Ismail's country, might roam where they pleased; which was, of course, substantially correct.

The Governor's abrupt 'Friend or Foe?' interrogation might have produced something better than this inane dithering had his pistol been kept out of sight. But this exchange of notes was accompanied by significant troop movements and the reception of Ismail's letter of the 6th was the signal for a general advance which formed the background to all further correspondence. General Colborne's southern column began its movement northward on 8 December with 50 boats, 240 soldiers, and 70 seamen. The northern column, under Brigadier-General Ross, was already approaching Kuala Kangsar, with headquarters just nine miles short of it. On that day, from Kampong Boyah, McNair wrote directly to Ismail but received only a verbal reply and that merely a complaint about the rice shortage. McNair insisted (and Ross agreed) that a written answer should be sent. Ismail replied accordingly on 10 December, expressing his willingness, in principle, to visit Kuala Kangsar, but saying that his boatmen would do nothing without rice and salt. McNair sent him four bags of rice, telling him that Mr. Swettenham was at Bhota but would advance no farther, provided that Ismail would come to Kuala Kangsar. But the southern column was already at Pulo Pisang on the 10th and only three miles from Blanja on the 11th. The pincers were closing swiftly, as is apparent from Dunlop's letter to the Governor dated the 14th:

Finding that Ex-Sultan Ismail was still in Blanja, I wrote to him, stating I wished to see him. To this I received an answer from Rajah Mahmood, a relative of his, that Ex-Sultan Ismail had gone to Kinta. This we afterwards ascertained to be false, as he only left yesterday morning. I laid before the General all the information I had obtained, and he considered it advisable early yesterday morning to continue our journey to Blanjah.

It was this approach from the south which clinched matters for Ismail. He had some vague notion of negotiating with McNair while his line of retreat was still open—the track from Blanja to Kinta. He realized now that if he went north to see McNair, Blanja would be occupied before he could return. He would be trapped beyond all possibility of escape. He decided on the 12th to use the back door while it was still open. On the 13th he fled towards Kinta. On the 14th Colborne's forces were in Blanja, which they found deserted. On the same day the General sent his forward elements some six miles up the track towards Kinta. They were fired upon and, finding the path blocked by trees, called a temporary halt:

From all the information we can obtain [wrote Dunlop] the Maharaja Lela is at present at Kinta, and from the opposition offered to our advance, it is clear that Ex-Sultan Ismail is determined to shelter him. He is a determined liar, and no faith can be placed in him.

If this information were correct, the next move must be to occupy Kinta, or so Colborne and Dunlop agreed. They were admittedly going beyond their instructions (see p. 256 above). But who was Jervois to complain of that? They decided to press on.

Colborne had expected Brigadier-General Ross to reach Blanja almost as soon as he did. There was no sign of the Brigadier, however (he had been unable to collect enough boats, apparently), and Colborne decided to push on with the forces he had. Swettenham and Raja Mahmood did the scouting and soon reported the way clear. General Colborne, with Commander Stirling, R.N., reached Kinta on 17 December, against trifling opposition. They found Kinta deserted, including houses recently occupied by Ismail and Panglima Kinta. They were told that the Maharaja Lela had been there for days and had then fled northwards with Ismail. With them had gone, on elephants, the Panglima Kinta, Raja Ngah (the Tunku Panglima Besar), Panglima Prang Semaun, two lesser chiefs, and a party of followers. The direction of their retreat might lead them into the southern provinces of Siam and all that remained to do at the moment was to ask the Siamese to deny them refuge. This Jervois did, through the Foreign Office, on 30 December. If the troubles in Perak were not entirely ended they had at least reached a point at which the enemy had been more or less dispersed and, better still, identified. By his panic flight Ismail had apparently made himself the leader of a band of assassins. It only now remained to hunt them down.

Before the hunt was fairly organized, the Governor's attention was distracted by two other and more serious conflicts. He had to face, simultaneously, two other crises. One attack came from Downing Street, the other from the Negri Sembilan. The first and more disquieting of these offensives was caused by the reception at the Colonial Office of Sir William's long and detailed dispatch (No. 291) of 16 October in which he explained what his Perak policy had been. To this Lord Carnarvon replied by telegram on 25 November:

Your telegram of 18th received, and despatch dated the 16th of October, describing your policy in Perak matters, which, on referring to my telegram of the 14th, you will see that I altogether disapprove. I then telegraphed troops must not be employed for annexation or other political objects. I have only to repeat this instruction in strongest terms. They are sent to inflict punishment for outrage, and should be withdrawn as soon as it can be done with safety.

Her Majesty's Government cannot adopt principle of the permanent retention of troops in Peninsula to maintain Residents or other officers, and unless natives are willing to receive them on footing originally sanctioned, of simply advising the ruling authorities, I doubt whether their continuance in country can be sanctioned.

If, in the present circumstances, it is necessary to retain any Resident at Perak, it is a question whether he should not be stationed on sea-coast.

Neither annexation nor government of country by British officials in name of Sultan can be allowed.

Reading this unpleasant message, Jervois knew that his explanation would require some care. He would have to prove that there had been a rising sufficient to justify the summoning of aid from Hong Kong and India. He would also, however, have to show that the rising, although widespread and dangerous, was not due to any mistake made by him. This was no easy task but he had at hand, in Penang (which was still his headquarters), one adviser to whom he could turn for counsel. Colonel Anson had never concealed his disapproval of Sir Andrew Clarke's choice of Abdullah and he pointed out at an early stage in the Perak crisis that this was the cause of the trouble. On 9 November Sir William replied guardedly that 'as you say, there is a great deal to be said upon the question', adding 'I had to take the matter up in the position in which I found it'.[1] Anson records that, by 14 November, Jervois was admitting that 'There is a great deal of truth in what you say about the Abdullah case'.[2] By 26 November

[1] Anson, op. cit., p. 331.
[2] Ibid.

suspicion had turned into belief and Jervois wrote to Sir Andrew Clarke and gave fair warning of what his own defence was going to be:

I am deluged with work now, and it would take me too long to go into the causes of the state of things in Perak, but I hope to be able to tell you what I think on this on a future occasion.

I can, however, now say that I believe one cause was the putting of Abdullah on the throne, another, poor Birch's impetuosity.[1]

Sir Andrew was unrepentant about Abdullah, and wrote thus of Birch in a letter to his friend the Hon. A. E. M. Ashley:

Poor Birch, it is said, was impetuous and hot-headed, and that I was to blame for selecting him. He was energetic, zealous, and loyal, and as long as I kept him to a policy of patience and conciliation, all went well.[2]

In any public controversy with Clarke, Jervois would have been in a strong position. As against Lord Carnarvon, however, his position was feeble, and the latter's telegram was a sure indication of the sort of dispatch which would soon be on the way. It was on the very day that Jervois found time for his letter to Clarke that the Secretary of State was acknowledging Jervois's dispatch of 16 October. The paragraphs of his official reply—written presumably by his cousin—had already perhaps reached draft form before the end of the month or early December to be signed finally on 10 December. They would refer to Jervois's missive in these terms:

This despatch, conveying to me the first intimation of any kind that a serious departure from the policy which had been, after much consideration, sanctioned by Her Majesty's Government, and which it must be remembered was an experiment to be very cautiously proceeded with, was being commenced or even contemplated reached me on the 22nd of November last, nearly three weeks after your first telegram announcing the disastrous consequences which had ensued upon this change of policy. . . . I am still without any more detailed information than your telegrams have been able to supply.

While, therefore, it is my duty to allow no further time to elapse without expressing the strong opinions which I feel compelled to form on some points connected with this subject, I desire that you should understand that I am not now pronouncing a final decision upon your proceedings, and if I state freely and unreservedly what I conceive to have been grave errors of policy and of action, my present object is to elicit those full explanations which it is on every ground desirable that I should receive.[3]

[1] Vetch, op. cit., pp. 182 et seq.   [2] Ibid.
[3] No. 218, 10 Dec. 1876.

They would refer at length to the instructions and warnings previously sent from the Colonial Office, concluding that:

These despatches you must unquestionably have received, and the instructions contained in them, expressed in no uncertain or ambiguous language, though certainly not framed to guard against an entire reversal of existing policy as sudden as it was unexpected, were before you. But I am at a loss to understand how a careful and experienced observer should fail to recognise in them from first to last a clear and consistent series of directions calculated to keep before both your predecessor and yourself the nature and extent of the relations which the British Residents had been permitted by Her Majesty's Government to hold with the native authorities. I can, therefore, hardly express the surprise with which I received the first intimation that those relations had been violently interrupted, and the still greater surprise with which I learnt from your despatch of the 16th October that the official course of proceedings in Perak which was the signal for resistance and attack was in opposition to the whole tenor of my directions.[1]

Jervois did not wait for this to arrive. He had already, in his dispatch of 16 November (No. 327), tried to forestall this conclusion that the murder was the sequel to his change of policy. He asserted instead that 'from the day when we deposed the late Sultan Ismail and set up Abdullah upon the throne, it was merely a question of time' when trouble should begin. He now followed this up with a long dispatch dated 2 December (No. 335) in which he puts some of the blame on the interpreter Arshad, but for whose striking the Malay 'the murder of Mr. Birch would not have taken place'. Feelings of suppressed resentment (which he admits his failure to detect) were not produced by the proclamation but existed beforehand among the chiefs so that there was 'more concert between the parties than they are now willing to admit'. Anticipating criticism on another score, Jervois admitted that 'having obtained a sufficient force may destroy the apparent necessity for having asked for it', but pointed out that 'as a question of Imperial Policy we cannot afford a reverse of any importance in this focus of Eastern communication':

I can scarcely hope in the multitude of arrangements that I have felt myself compelled to make with reference to these affairs to secure your Lordship's concurrence in every particular, but I trust that my conduct throughout this matter may meet generally with your Lordship's approval.[2]

This last hope was not justified in the event. But Jervois, in having two additional campaigns on his hands, was more fortunate perhaps than if he had merely had the one. For the alarming reports from the

[1] No. 218, 10 Dec. 1876.   [2] S.S. No. 335, 2 Dec. 1876.

Negri Sembilan, while presenting a fresh problem, provided the best possible answer to any criticism about the size of his army. His reasoning in the dispatch of 2 December was all very well, but the forces already in Perak (with the rest still to come) were probably as large as could be maintained there with the existing means of supply. To a limited extent the threats from Whitehall and the Negri Sembilan could be said to cancel out.

It was apparently while writing this carefully worded dispatch on 2 December that the first telegram came from Irving with news of this fresh outbreak. Jervois was therefore able to add this postscript:

P.S. Since writing the foregoing despatch I have received a telegram from Singapore of to-day's date, stating that the Resident at Sungei Ujong apprehends a general rising of Malays in the States in his neighbourhood. The telegram also mentioned that the tone of Malays in Malacca is unfriendly, if not hostile. I have requested the General Commanding to send reinforcements in a vessel of war forthwith.[1]

There was his answer to this talk of sending for too many troops. It might yet appear that he had barely enough. But if there was to be a new theatre of war in the Malacca area, another senior officer would be required. He would have liked, in the normal course of events, to go there in person and decide on the spot what force and what commander would be needed. But that was impossible. He had at the moment his own campaign to conduct, a defensive battle fought with dispatches and telegrams against a formidable antagonist. Yet a further complication (as if there were not enough already) was provided by the reports, which persisted, of Raja Mahdie being about to stage a revolt in Selangor. Placed in the care of the Maharajah of Johore, he suddenly disappeared from Johore Bahru. The alarm ended, however, when he was found to be living at, of all places, Rochore, in the outskirts of Singapore itself. He was promptly imprisoned at the earnest request of Tunku dia Oodin and Mr. Davidson, although otherwise 'treated with every consideration'. With less likelihood, therefore, of serious trouble in Selangor, it now became the more possible to deal with the Negri Sembilan as a single problem. How that problem was initially tackled is best told in the words of Colonel Anson.

On the 4th December, just after the Perak war had commenced, on a Saturday afternoon, Sir William Jervois, who was still at Penang on account of that war, came into my office and, standing at the back of my office table, said: 'Look here, Anson, there is this affair now in Sungei

[1] S.S. No. 335, 2 Dec. 1876.

Ujong; I ought to go there'. To this I said only, 'Yes'. Then he added, 'But I don't think I ought to go out of telegraphic communication with the Secretary of State'. I said 'I quite understand that'. Then he said, 'Will you go?' I answered 'When would you like me to go?' He replied, 'When would you be ready to go?' I said 'Now'.[1]

[1] Anson, op. cit., p. 332.

CHAPTER XI

THE telegrams from Singapore which thus brought Colonel Anson into the field read as follows:

December 2, 1875.
Murray reports general rising; fears attack and asks reinforcements; will communicate with Tanglin and telegraph further. Irving.

December 2, 1875.
Murray reports general rising; States round Sunghei Ujong; 500 men at Terrachee. . . . Plunket says Desboro' reports tone of Malacca Malays unfriendly if not hostile. Irving.

December 3, 1875.
Murray, Hinxman, Daly, Vaughton, Plunket all write in tone of serious apprehension. Myself believe 500 men at least required at Malacca and Sungei Ujong. Have misgivings about Klang. Commandant considers garrison here should be strengthened. Daly reports narrow escape at Terrachee, rescued by armed force, 50 men. Fought their way back. Hinxman reports whole country up in arms; threatened attack, 1000 men. Linghie road and river stopped. Relative of Datu Klana reports Rumbow, Johole, Sri Menanti and Moar all combined; 1000 men at Terrachee; many thousands coming from Johole. Irving.

How much of this drivel did Jervois believe? Momentarily, he thought it possible that there was a widespread movement, perhaps involving Selangor as well as the Negri Sembilan, but he had changed his mind within the week, reporting correctly by the 9th that there were 'no foundations for apprehension of national rising'.[1] In the same telegram he described the action he had taken:

Three hundred and fifty Goorkhas and thirty Artillery gone to Malacca and Sungei Ujong. I think accounts thence much exaggerated. Have sent Colonel Anson there instructed to enquire and report and to prevent hasty movement.

What he hoped to avoid was 'another hostile expedition to provide for whilst the Perak matters remain unsettled'.[2] His action in this respect shows a certain distrust of Murray's ability, a fear of hasty decisions.

[1] S.S. No. 346, 9 Dec. 1875. [2] Anson, op. cit., p. 333.

Patrick James Murray, Commander, R.N. (retired), had been appointed Acting Assistant Resident of Sungei Ujong in April 1875. It was not clear whom he was to assist, for he was the only officer appointed, but he inherited, initially, the lower salary fixed for Captain W. T. Tatham, R.A., his predecessor. Murray's appointment (agreed by the Admiralty and approved by Lord Carnarvon on 16 June 1875) was the best of those made by Sir Andrew Clarke. He was praised on appointment for his energy, tact, and discrimination, his service record, and his experience as an explorer in Africa. It was through his service on the Malay coast that he became known to the Governor, who thought him perhaps more of a Malay expert than he really was. He enjoyed, however, a long and fairly successful period of office and the troubles of 1875–6 were not of his making. The essential difficulty of his position arose from the fact that he was accredited to the Dato Klana, one of the two rival chiefs in a State which was not in fact entirely independent. The Klana owed his position in Sungei Ujong to British support, which had given him recognition as the chief or sovereign ruler. But while his authority in Sungei Ujong could be thus artificially maintained, he was still a chief of the Negri Sembilan, a larger if vaguer federation in the hierarchy of which his position was subordinate. That had not seemed to matter in 1874 for there had been no Yam Tuan Besar since 1869. But the jealousy felt by the other chiefs for the prosperity of Sungei Ujong under British protection took the form of a movement to restore the central authority of the federation to which Sungei Ujong properly belonged.

For the vacant office of Yam Tuan Besar there were two possible candidates, Tunku Antah of Sri Menanti, son of Yam Tuan Radin, and Tunku Ahmad Tunggal, son of Yam Tuan Imam. Support was divided and the Dato Klana was one of those who favoured Tunku Ahmad. Tunku Antah retaliated by favouring the cause of the Dato Bandar, the Klana's rival in Sungei Ujong. The chiefs led by those of the Sri Menanti States, Terrachi, Gunong Pasir, Ulu Muar, and Jempol, came together in 1875 to elect Antah to the office of Yam Tuan; for which purpose unanimity was essential. It was not achieved, for the Dato Klana—well knowing the object of the proceedings—refused to be present. The remedy for this was to depose the Dato Klana and recognize in his stead 'a worthless character, the Laxamana of Sungei Ujong'. This done, and with some show of unanimity, Tunku Antah was elected Yam Tuan Besar. He was not recognize as such by the Dato Klana, and the latter was not recognized by Yam Tuan Antah as the ruler of Sungei Ujong.[1]

Of these events Sir William Jervois wrote as follows:

If the election of the Yam Tuan Besar was invalid, the deposition of the Klana was still more so, and considering that the Klana was supported by us and that we had a Resident assigned to him, it was a distinct act of hostility towards the British Government.

I therefore caused Raja Antar to be informed that we could not recognise him as the head of the Nine States, and that we were surprised at the action taken as regards the Klana. The supporters of Raja Antar were doubtless discontented at his not being recognised but no open hostility was apprehended, so much so that up to the 25th November, Captain Murray, the Assistant Resident in Sungei Ujong, reported that everything was perfectly quiet and peaceful in that state and those adjacent to it, the only trouble experienced being from Datu Moar the chief of which state gave protection to robbers and other bad characters who took refuge therein.

There were rumours, however, that the Chiefs of some of the States were caballing against us, and I was consequently induced to strengthen the detachment in Sungei Ujong in spite of the seeming quiet in that state.[2]

From the information which I have been able to obtain it would appear that the feeling of dislike manifested by some of the Chiefs to the Klana and the English has been fed by designing persons in Malacca itself, and it is probably due to their representations that the smouldering feeling of hostility has burst into an open flame. The four main causes appear to be a hatred of the Klana and a desire to put another in his stead, a dislike to the English by whose instrumentality the Klana's importance had been augmented to the diminution of their own, the intention of establishing the position of Rajah Antar and the fear that they would be called to account for the insult which they had offered to the British Government. I have also been informed that the Malays had designs on our settlement of Malacca itself, hoping that an attack on Sungei Ujong would lead to a withdrawal of the troops from Malacca, and that a successful surprise might then be effected.[3]

Hostilities broke out over the district of Terrachi, which lies on the eastward side of the range of hills separating Sungei Ujong from the Sri Menanti States. Terrachi was claimed both by the Dato Klana and by Tunku Antah, the latter's claim being the more effective in that the territory lay on his side of the Bukit Putus pass. The Klana appointed

---

[1] A special study has been made of these events in Chelliah, op. cit.
[2] Lieut. Hinxman was reinforced on 7 Nov. with twenty-one men of his own regiment.
[3] S.S. No. 334, 17 Dec. 1875.

his own Punghulu to Terrachi in 1875. Tunku Antah deposed him or, to be more exact (as was later discovered), made the same man his own nominee. Hearing of imminent disturbance, Captain Murray paid a visit to Terrachi on 26 November 1875 escorted by Lieutenant Hinxman and twenty men of the 10th Regiment together with thirty police. With him also went Dr. Hoysted and Mr. Daly the Australian surveyor. They crossed the Bukit Putus pass and encamped at Terrachi, about sixteen miles from Seremban where the Resident and the Dato Klana normally lived. Murray and Hinxman slept at the Punghulu's house, supposing that he was still on the Dato Klana's side. On the morning of the 27th, finding all quiet, Murray decided to return, leaving Daly, with six policemen, to begin a survey of the area, for which purpose he pushed on towards Kuala Pilah. He had gone no farther than half a mile when he was threatened by armed Malays numbering (as he thought) about 200, with their host among them. He sent a message and Captain Murray came to his rescue. Some shots were exchanged and then a regular engagement began, Hinxman trying to drive the Malays from their position and the Malays tending to work round his flanks and so threaten his line of withdrawal. Hinxman's men expended most of their ammunition in twenty minutes, whereupon he ordered a withdrawal. Murray and his escort reached Rassa that evening at 6.0 p.m., leaving their opponents in triumphant possession of the Bukit Putus pass. There were no casualties.

Murray's total strength in Sungei Ujong amounted to forty-five men of the 10th Regiment and sixty-eight police, of whom only fifty had rifles. With these he prepared to defend Ampangan and Rassa, receiving a warning from Tunku Antah to keep out of Terrachi in future.

What is passed, let it be passed, but do not let it be happened again. We should be a little polite, because a good man is always polite, and a bad man without manners. We are the children of good people and the Captain also the same. Politeness should be our garment.

Murray seems to have been insufficiently contrite about his breach of etiquette. He sent word to the Hon. C. B. Plunket, Acting Lieutenant-Governor of Malacca, who promptly came to his rescue on 3 December with Lieutenant Peyton and another twenty-three men of the 10th Regiment. During the previous night Tunku Antah had moved his forces to Paroe, only six miles from Seremban, and Plunket sent off his first message to Singapore, asking for reinforcements.

Hinxman, meanwhile, decided to reconnoitre Paroe on the 5th. He
did so with the result that the Malays who drove him off established
themselves near Ampangan. Hinxman reported on the 5th that his
detachment had to be divided between the barracks and the Residency
(which Murray refused to quit); that the enemy were three miles
away and likely to attack that night; that the Lukut road, his only
line of retreat, was unsafe; and that he was short of ammunition and
food. Plunket reported to the same effect, adding: 'We are, as you
will see, in a very serious predicament, and nothing but the presence
of a considerable force here will get us out of it.' The Malays were
dislodged, however, by the Dato Klana's brass cannon and retired
once more to Paroe. By then, moreover, Plunket's appeals for help
began to produce results. On the Governor's instructions the eighty-
five Arab irregulars recruited in Singapore by Mr. de Fontaine and
Mr. Robinson were embarked at once in S.S. *Rainbow* and landed at
Lukut on the 5th, reaching Seremban on the following day. The
Rainbow was already an historic vessel, originally presented to Rajah
Brooke by Miss Burdett-Coutts and now ending her career as a
colonial steamship. The arrival of this force, originally destined for
Selangor but now hastily sent to Sungei Ujong, encouraged Hinxman to attack Paroe before further help (and more senior officers)
should arrive. His force available for this operation, after a group had
been detached to hold Seremban, comprised:

	Officers	Other ranks	
10th Regiment . .	2	46	
Arabs . . .	2	85	
Police . . .	2	46	
	6	177	Total = 183

The 9-pounder brass gun was brought along by a possibly amateur
gunner, Mr. Skinner, but could be moved only slowly, thus failing to
keep up with the infantry.

Parading at daylight on 7 December, this force marched to within
a mile of Paroe where paths diverged to the left and right. Hinxman
then detailed Mr. Robinson to take twenty Arabs to the right, an
Arab sergeant to take as many to the left, both parties to take the
enemy in flank or rear. Hinxman then advanced with the remainder
and halted under cover of a bank, 170 yards from the enemy stockade.
When he heard his flanking parties (as he thought) engaged he opened
fire to his front and began at once to suffer casualties.

Hinxman seems to have realized at this point that his left flanking party was lost and that a frontal attack on the main stockade would come under enfilade fire from the detached stockade on the left. That on the right was being attacked by Mr. Robinson. He decided that his best plan would be to move across to the left and attack the outwork himself—thereby coming under enfilade fire from the main stockade to his front. A majority of his men failed to follow him and the result was that he took the outwork with a relatively small party (Lieutenant Peyton and ten soldiers, Mr. de Fontaine and six Arabs), bayoneting the resolute defenders of it. Any further advance towards the main enemy position was checked by heavy fire from his front. On the right, Mr. Robinson captured his objective but was unable to hold it. A somewhat critical situation was relieved by the timely arrival of Mr. Skinner and his cannon, in the position whence Hinxman's attack had been launched. Skinner and Captain Murray, with a few police, brought this into action against the main stockade. After six rounds the gun capsized but it had served its purpose. Peyton meanwhile went back, collected all the men he could, stragglers from the left flanking party included, and brought them forward to Hinxman's position. With these Hinxman charged the corner of the main stockade, from which the Malays fled, and then burnt the stockades and village. He marched back to Rassa that afternoon, the Malays withdrawing to the Bukit Putus pass.

This skirmish at Paroe was more remarkable for courageous leadership than for tactical skill. Colonel Anson (veteran of the Crimean War) thought the casualties too heavy. There were, in fact, 42 killed and wounded on the British side[1] the enemy losses being more or less unknown but variously estimated at 80 killed and 200 wounded,[2] 'three Rajahs and over 100 men killed',[3] '35 Malays killed . . . great numbers wounded' (Plunket's estimate), '60–80 seen dead by Chinese (Murray's report), and 'only two Malays were wounded' (rumour repeated by Vaughton). Wrote Anson:

This affair seemed to have been badly managed, for had the officer in command waited for the gun to be brought up, very few casualties, if any,

10th Regiment	2 killed	12 wounded	
Arabs	5 ,,	12 ,,	(incl. both officers)
Police	4 ,,	5 ,,	
Total 11		31	Grand total 42

[2] *Singapore Daily Times*, 7 Jan. 1876.

[3] *Regimental History of the 10th Foot* (later the Royal Lincolnshire Regiment), supplied from Regimental Depot.

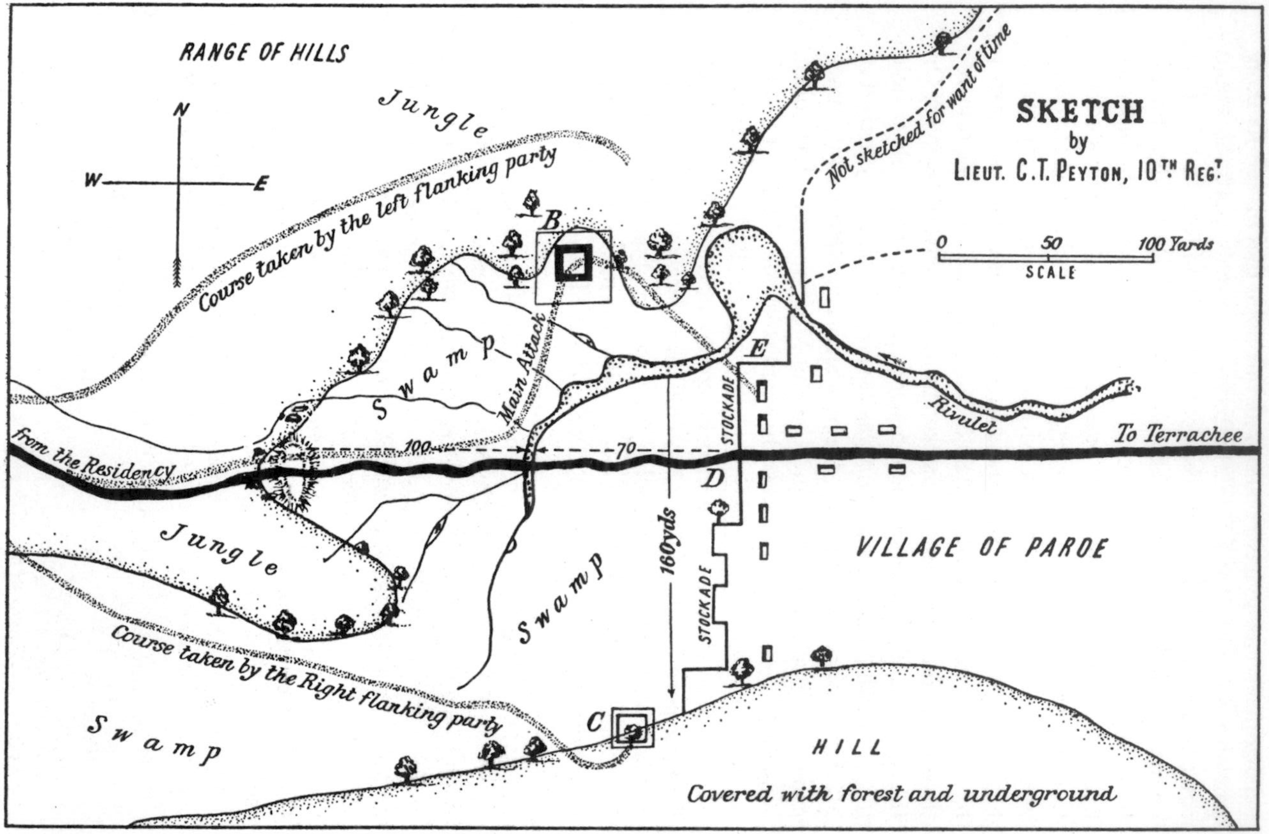

Map 8. Stockades at Paroe

would probably have occurred. The gun was brought up later and did good execution. The affair was one of those foolhardy ones that British officers have too often undertaken when undervaluing the natives.[1]

Local newspapers were inclined to 'give every credit to the gallant Peyton of the 10th for his dash, with his baker's dozen of the 10th, at the stockade at Paroe',[2] reserving their criticism for Murray and Plunket. Granted, however, that heavy casualties had been needlessly incurred, Mr. Chelliah is certainly right in maintaining that 'after Paroi, the Malays were thoroughly demoralised'.[3]

The Governor's decision to reinforce the troops in Sungei Ujong was taken before the capture of Paroe and in the light of previous and exaggerated reports. Willing as Anson was to start on the instant for this new theatre of war, he was unable to embark until 6 December. The delay was caused by discussion as to which troops should go. General Colborne could spare none from Perak but ordered a hundred men from Singapore. When, however, the Singapore Commandant questioned the wisdom of weakening his garrison, Jervois decided to draw instead upon the Indian troops which would otherwise go to reinforce Brigadier-General Ross. So Anson finally boarded the S.S. *Malda* (British India S.S. Co.) on the evening of 6 December, finding 358 officers and men of the 1st Ghoorkhas already embarked under Lieutenant-Colonel Clay, with Mr. Kynnersley and Mr. Neubronner as interpreters and Mr. Daly as topographical expert. A half-battery of artillery (two guns, a Coëhorn mortar, and fifty rockets) were to follow in S.S. *Abyssinia*. There was also to follow a reserve, 200 of the Buffs, which it was hoped there would be no occasion to use. There were, after all, 200 infantry and twenty gunners already in Malacca and Sungei Ujong. Jervois thought that it would probably prove feasible to send the Buffs back to Perak.

The *Malda* passed the North Sands Light on the 7th and anchored off Malacca early on the following day. The Lieutenant-Governor's boat came off containing not Plunket, but Captain Vaughton of the 10th Regiment, acting in his place and having to explain, first of all, that Plunket had joined Murray in Sungei Ujong. The substance of Vaughton's information is known because he also put it in writing. He said that Sungei Ujong might be attacked at any moment; that the Chendras mines were in danger; that there was great excitement in the whole country; that wells were being poisoned; that the Malays were

[1] Anson, op. cit., p. 334.
[2] *Straits Observer*, 17 Dec. 1875.   [3] Chelliah, op. cit., p. 51.

encouraged in aggression by the news from Perak—and indeed expected help from Turkey; that the Malacca people were very nervous, and that Malacca itself might need defending. While Anson listened to all this, Kynnersley was listening to Assistant Superintendant Hayward, who had also come on board and who was sceptical about Vaughton's imagined perils. Anson learnt at the same time of de Fontaine's Arabs having been landed at Lukut with ninety Snider rifles, ten more for Captain Murray, and 9,500 rounds of ammunition; of Mr. Trevenen having gone on to Selangor with forty-nine rifles (one lost already) and 21,000 rounds for Tunku dia Oodin; and he may just possibly have discovered that two mountain howitzers, which should have gone with de Fontaine, had been kept at Malacca. These and other reports received, Colonel Anson went ashore at midday with Lieutenant-Colonel Clay, Mr. Kynnersley, and other officers. A hundred Gurkhas were landed at the same time. They went to the Stadthaus where Mr. Neubronner was taking down the statements of two Malays, and there they discovered the source of the local panic.

Mr. de Wind, a large landowner in Malacca, came into the office and I had a conversation with him as to state of feeling in Malacca. He appeared much excited and was evidently under apprehension that the Malays on the frontier were about to pour into the place in thousands, while the Government provided no adequate protection and left the Settlement at the mercy of the Malays, whilst interfering where they had no right to. The Datu Klana, whom we supported, he described as a weak man who was not recognised by half his people. He told me he had called a meeting of justices to consider the state of affairs and that at the present alarming crisis a large force was required to protect Malacca. He is evidently a great alarmist, and, having considerable influence in Malacca, has probably done a good deal to produce the state of panic which exists among a portion of the community. The wildest rumours are spread and believed, and if anything would induce the Malays on the frontier to make a descent for the sake of plunder it would be attributable to this state of panic. I should not apprehend any attack on our territory, especially now that 100 men of the Goorkhas have been stationed there. . . . I could not hear of any disaffection on the part of the Malays in our territory, nor do I believe that any such feeling exists. The Malays know when they are well off. . . .

There was evidently no certain information to be obtained in Malacca as to the state of feeling among the Malays supposed to be hostile. That the people are being armed, are well supplied with arms and ammunition, and are making every preparation for resistance in case of being attacked, appears tolerably certain. Their numbers are probably much exaggerated.

Malays never move in large bodies, but each small Chief with his following of from 50 to 100 men is prepared to dispute the passage of troops through his territory, and it is possible that in the neighbourhood of Sunghei Ujong there may be a considerable number of men.

This was Kynnersley's conclusion and Anson probably shared it. The main feature of the situation, however, as it must have seemed to Anson, was Plunket's desertion of his post. The Acting Lieutenant-Governor had gone off with a platoon of infantry (subaltern complete) to join a somewhat larger force (already provided with a political as well as an infantry officer) in an adjacent territory to which he had not been appointed. He had detailed to take his place an inexperienced soldier, petrified by the novelty of his office, believing every ridiculous rumour and wildly telegraphing for help. The Acting Lieutenant-Governor should have stayed at his post and sent Vaughton with the troops—or let Peyton take them on his own. So Anson's first or almost first reaction was to send Plunket a letter with instructions to return to Lukut at once. Then, on the next day, Anson went there himself in the *Malda* and was joined on the same day (the 9th) by the S.S. *Abyssinia*. The artillery from that ship was landed but Anson decided to send the Buffs back to Penang, and did so. He was joined that evening by H.M.S. *Thistle* (Commander Stirling) and received, at 11.0 p.m. that night, an account of the engagement at Paroe. The process of unloading was slow, owing to a lack of coolies, and the troops went forward to Rassa in groups, the first on the 9th and the last on the 11th. In the meanwhile, after dark on the 10th, Plunket arrived on board the *Malda*, gave all his news, and was then told to go back to Malacca and stay there. Arriving on the 12th he was assailed by Captain Vaughton with a new crop of hearsay. But the interview with Anson had changed Plunket's attitude. He mentioned these reports only to add 'but I attach very little weight to these rumours, which I believe are kept up by interested parties to forward their own plans'. And this was probably very near the truth.

Theoretically, Colonel Anson was the Governor's representative, present only in a civil capacity. In practice he simply took command of the operation and issued orders in the framing of which, he said afterwards, 'I had consulted no one'.[1] He reached Rassa on the 12th with the rearguard, thirty seamen led by Commander Stirling, R.N., of the *Thistle*. Then, in his own words:

After arriving at Rassa, and having got all the force, guns, ammunition,

[1] Anson, op. cit., p. 338.

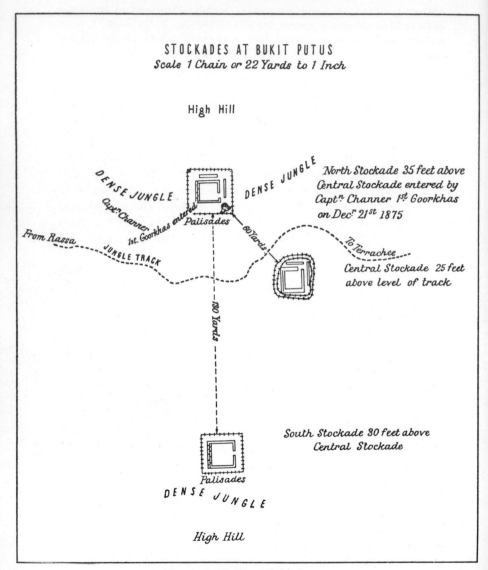

STOCKADES AT BUKIT PUTUS
Scale 1 Chain or 22 Yards to 1 Inch

High Hill

DENSE JUNGLE

DENSE JUNGLE

Capt.ⁿ Channer
1st. Goorkhas entered
Palisades

North Stockade 35 feet above
Central Stockade entered by
Captⁿ. Channer 1ˢᵗ Goorkhas
on Decʳ 21ˢᵗ 1875

From Rassa

JUNGLE TRACK

80 Yards

To Terrachee

Central Stockade 25 feet
above level of track

180 Yards

South Stockade 30 feet above
Central Stockade

Palisades

DENSE JUNGLE

High Hill

Map 9. Stockades at Bukit Putus

stores etc., complete, and in good order, I gave instructions to divide the force into two divisions,—one to start in advance of the other, and to proceed by an old, unused jungle path, and work round to the rear of the stockades; and the other to advance by the direct path; the object being to attack these stockades in front and rear at the same time.[1]

The stockades in question were those which the Malays were known to have built in the Bukit Putus pass. Anson had a substantial force (about 540 men) and his two columns were organized as follows:

1st Division
Lieutenant-Colonel Hill
Captain Murray
Commander Stirling

Gurkhas	3 officers	120 men
Seamen	2 officers	30 men
Artillery	1 officer	10 men
Total	9 officers	160 men

Guns, one 24-pdr.; rockets, 83

2nd Division
Lieutenant-Colonel E. B. Clay
Lieutenant North, R.E.

10th Regt.	2 officers	41 men
Gurkhas	2 officers	232 men
Arabs	1 officer	70 men
Artillery	1 officer	22 men
Total	8 officers	365 men

Guns, one mortar, one 9-pdr.; rockets, 36

Lieutenant-Colonel Hill began his outflanking movement on 19 December, marching to the Dato Klana's house, halting there for the night, and marching on next day towards Pantai. From there he crossed the Langkap pass, entering the Terrachi valley on the 21st after an exhausting march through almost unknown territory, pushing through dense jungle and swamps and incidentally having to cross the Muar river on seventeen different occasions. This manœuvre proved needless and achieved no obvious result beyond the destruction of the Dato Muar's house. The enemy he was to outflank had already gone.

Lieutenant-Colonel Clay made a frontal approach to the Bukit Putus pass on the 20th, preceded by a vanguard of fifty men commanded by Captain Channer and accompanied by Lieutenant North. Channer followed the bed of a torrent until he reached a point at

[1] Anson, op. cit., p. 335.

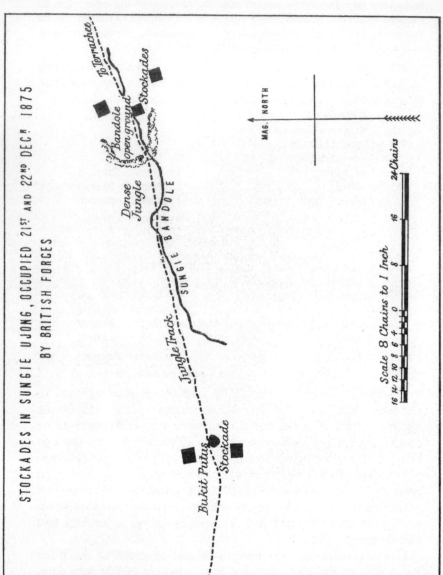

STOCKADES IN SUNGIE UJONG, OCCUPIED 21ST AND 22ND DECR. 1875 BY BRITISH FORCES

To Terrachee

Bandole open ground

Stockades

Dense Jungle

SUNGIE BANDOLE

Jungle Track

Bukit Putus Stockade

MAG. NORTH

Scale 8 Chains to 1 Inch

16 14 12 10 8 6 4 0 8 16 24 Chains

Map 10. The Bukit Putus Pass.

which it was completely blocked by felled trees. Leaving North with a party detailed to remove these obstructions, Channer sent out flanking patrols in either direction, he himself leading the twenty-five men who were to work round on the left. Seeing smoke rising and hearing voices ahead, he presently sighted a strongly built and loop-holed stockade, strengthened by the Malay equivalent of barbed wire (stakes of sharpened bamboo). It was one of a group of three, the other two being respectively 80 and 160 yards distant from the first. In the words of the Commanding Officer's report,

He proceeded cautiously with a party of 25 Goorkhas as if he were on a sporting expedition. He advanced, himself, to within a few yards of the stockade—the enemy had kept no look-out, they were cooking at the time. Captain Channer seized the opportunity, and, followed immediately by two men named in the margin,[1] was the first to jump into the stockade. He found it occupied by 25 or 30 men. The first man, Captain Channer shot dead with his revolver, and the two Goorkhas each shot his man. They were soon followed by the rest of Captain Channer's party. Having expelled the Malays, Captain Channer opened a smart fire on the other two stockades and soon emptied them. In this affair six were killed in the stockade, and doubtless some were wounded in that and the other stockades; but the Malays always carry off their dead (if they have time) and wounded, but they must have suffered, as proved by the track of blood they left behind. . . . [Of the Gurkhas, one was killed, one seriously and two slightly wounded.]

Of Captain Channer's gallantry, coolness, and intrepidity I cannot sufficiently express my approval.[2]

This concluded the actual fighting and Clay pushed on to Bandole on the 21st, burning a couple of stockades on the way, and so made a junction with Hill's force at Terrachi on the 22nd. Colonel Anson, who had been dealing with the supply problem at Rassa, now moved his headquarters forward to Terrachi, accompanied by the Dato Klana. He then ordered Clay to advance on Sri Menanti, again by two differ-ent routes. From there Captain Rankin was sent with two officers and ninety-two men to occupy the Dato of Jumpole's kampong, which they did unopposed, afterwards burning the place. Most of the force was then withdrawn to the neighbourhood of Rassa or Malacca. 'At the same time Qualla Jumpole, Parit and Terrachi were occupied by bodies of police and a road was ordered to be made through the Bukit Putus Pass.'[3] This last task was carried out by coolies from

[1] Marginal note: 'Sepoy Bulbeer Ghurtie, Sepoy Geltman Thappa, B. Company 1st. Goorkhas.'   [2] S.S. No. 18, 14 Jan. 1876.   [3] Ibid.

Singapore. Colonel Anson, meanwhile, had relieved the fears of the kampong folk, written to the chiefs, and received unusually polite replies. He had also decided that, in the absence of both candidates for the office of Yam Tuan Besar (Rajahs Antah and Ahmat had fled) the office should devolve on Dato Sultan, son of a previous Dato Klana of Sungei Ujong. To this plan he received the ready assent of the few and unimportant people he could find, concluding optimistically that his scheme had received unanimous support. All being quiet, he went down the Linggi river by boat and joined Commander Stirling in the *Thistle*. They returned together to Penang, believing that they had taught the Malays 'such a lesson as will effectually satisfy other native States of our supremacy'.

Left in control again, Captain Murray had now to expect a visit from Jervois, whose responsibility it was to decide upon a policy. Jervois, however, had come to no decision before the end of December, apparently from want of information.

> When I have been able to obtain reliable information as to what extent there has been a general movement in the Nine States, and what Datus and Chiefs have been really friendly or hostile, I shall be able to arrive at a conclusion.[1]

Towards making any decision the first step was to inquire into things on the spot. Jervois accordingly left Penang on 15 January, taking Braddell and Phillippo with him, and reached Malacca on the 18th. There he held a discussion with Plunket, Davidson, and Murray and had interviews with the Dato Klana and the Dato of Rembau. His tentative conclusion was that the revival of the office of Yam Tuan Besar would be undesirable and that Tunku Antah (the man with the best title to it) had forfeited British support by his invasion of Sungei Ujong, if not indeed by his insolent letter to the Resident. He considered that the best policy would be to remove the Dato Sultan from his temporary office and install Tunku Ahmat as 'Malay Captain' of Sri Menanti, Ulu Moar, and Jumpole. Plunket had wanted to make Ahmat the Yam Tuan Besar but the Governor preferred the lower title. He had consulted the Maharajah of Johore on this point and whereas Mr. Hole (His Highness's Secretary) had approved Plunket's suggestion, the Johore Secretary of State had thought otherwise. Had Jervois been tempted to decide about this without consulting the Colonial Office, that temptation was lessened by the failure of Ahmat to appear

[1] S.S. No. 373, 30 Dec. 1875.

at Malacca when summoned. Jervois left again, therefore, without deciding upon anything; leaving Murray to suppose, however, that Tunku Ahmat was the coming man.

Captain Murray went to Terrachi on 29 January 1876 with Captain Channer, Mr. Skinner, 30 Gurkhas, and 10 police. His first task was to finish disarming the people. He thus collected 36 iron guns and lelas and 198 muskets in Sri Menanti and Muar; 9 guns and 150 muskets in Jumpole. He promulgated the decree, already law in Sungei Ujong, that no one should carry arms without a written permit. He held discussions with Dato Sultan and Tunku Ahmat, discovering incidentally that most of the local Malays had come from Sumatra to escape Dutch rule. He reported that all was quiet and reported again to the same effect in March. In point of fact there was to be fresh disorder in April but apparently of little political significance.[1] Of earlier date, contemporary with Anson's campaign, were the Chinese Riots in Malacca; and these, too, were unconnected with political events. Malacca had three main secret societies, the Ghee Hin, the Ghee Boo, and the Hoh Beng. The original quarrel, between the last two of these, began on 7 December 1875 and the riots were still serious on the 18th, not so much in Malacca town as in the vicinity. Disturbances were reported again on the 25th with the general effect of detaining in Malacca some troops which might otherwise have been sent to Sungei Ujong. It was well into 1876 before the Malacca Settlement and the adjacent Malay States had regained such tranquillity as they had previously had.

From Malacca Sir William Jervois returned to Singapore, arriving there on 20 January 1876 after an absence of over ten weeks. He returned to find a formidable accumulation of work, piled up not merely through his own absence but through the absence of his senior officers. Lacking any staff specifically recruited for service in the Malay States, he had drawn heavily upon the resources of the Straits Settlements. He had called at various times for the help of Anson, Plunket, Birch, Braddell, McNair, Dunlop, Phillippo, Irving, Speedy, Swettenham, Maxwell, Kynnersley, Neubronner, and McCallum. He had left the Colony without a Lieutenant-Governor, without a Colonial

---

[1] The *Ringdove* was involved in this and W. V. Bayly records in his Journal how: '[7 April] . . . News arrived to-day of the storming and destruction of several British police stations in the State of Sri Menanti near Malacca, and we were ordered up there at once with the troops. We had one watch on general leave at the time, and had to send all over the town for them. They all came off in time somehow though many were in a condition generally attributed to fiddlers.'

Secretary, without an Attorney-General, without its Engineer. He returned to find the Treasury empty—its balances literally exhausted on 24 January, four days after his return. Matters awaiting his attention included the plans for the new hospital at Singapore, the provision of a quarantine station at Penang, the alleged robbery on board the steamship *Medina*, the payment of Straits Lights dues by the Netherlands India Steam Navigation Company, the bridge over the Prye river in Province Wellesley, the appointment of a Protector of Indian Immigrants, and the strange case of Mr. W. O'Connor, a convict from New South Wales.

The Governor's next task was to meet the Legislative Council on 29 January and gain support for all he had done.

As regards political considerations, the question of the policy to be adopted, whether in Perak or in the states about Malacca, is one upon which, I regret to say, I am not at present in a position to afford definite information. I have been, and still am, in communication with the Secretary of State on the subject. You have seen the reply given by His Lordship to the deputation from the Straits Settlements Association in London, and can judge that I am not at present in a position to afford you information which the Secretary of State himself declines yet to make public. I may, however, say that Her Majesty's Government are decidedly opposed to a policy of annexation.[1]

He was certainly on safe ground in this last assertion but it gave the Legislative Council little to discuss. A rather lame debate followed in which Mr. Shelford took the initiative by maintaining that the two chief mistakes had been in choosing Abdullah as Sultan and Birch as Resident.

. . . the Resident attempted single-handed, when a single hand was an impossibility, to effect vigorous reforms—to accomplish in one year that which he could not with cordial recognition have accomplished in five; law among the lawless, just taxation with the extortionate, and a sharp correction of abuses.

. . . Ignorant of their language and unobservant of the signs of dis-satisfaction round him, or at least but little regardful of them, the Resident was deceived, and what is worse, looking to the subsequent action, he deceived others.[2]

Shelford ended by declaring himself in favour of the Governor's policy—that is, to retain the Residents but with more than advisory duties. 'For Residents in the same sense as before I consider the time has passed.' Mr. Brown, making a maiden speech, could express no opinion without further information. Mr. Read supported, by

[1] Minutes of Legislative Council.   [2] Ibid.

implication, Shelford's view of Birch's unsuitability. With the right men, the Governor's policy could be made to work.

I am of opinion that the system of Residents is the best possible. If only a fit man is chosen and made Resident of Perak, I have very little doubt that as long as he is supported by troops, as he must be at the commencement, everything will go on quite correctly. If such a fit person cannot be found amongst the Colonial Officers, the only way is to seek him beyond that circle. It is proved by experience that our best Resident is a non-official.[1]

After the Governor had thanked Members (perhaps a little coldly) for their views, the Council adjourned.

Turning from the Council Chamber to the public Press, and scanning back numbers which he had hitherto perhaps lacked the time to read, Sir William Jervois would find that the Malay War was regarded in London as a religious revolt. Supporting this theory, *The Times* had drawn comparisons with the war in Achin. This had begun in 1873 with what was virtually a Dutch reverse, leading, however, to the theoretical annexation of Achin on 31 January 1874. As the Achinese continued to resist, the Dutch blockaded the Sumatran coast, mainly to prevent the importation of rifles from the Straits Settlements. Eight fairly prominent Achinese had settled in Penang 'for the double purpose of rousing feeling in all the Archipelago against the Dutch and organizing the export of military stores to Atjeh'.[2] The period 1873–8 was therefore a period of Dutch aggression and yet of Dutch ill success; a period also in which there was a close connexion between the Malay Peninsula and Sumatra. What would be more natural to assume than that the Perak War and the war in the Negri Sembilan were aspects of a general movement among the Malays, exemplified also in Sumatra?

The Singapore newspapers would not accept this theory. They denied that there was any religious revolt and they attrihuted the Dutch failures to cowardice. They saw no problem that could not be settled by force. Their hope was that the Perak War would lead to annexation, and their annoyance was the greater as they came to realize that it would lead to nothing of the sort. It was generally believed that Sir William, left to himself, would conquer the whole peninsula, but that he was restrained by his officers, men imbued with the caution they had been taught by Sir Harry Ord. Few of the local men realized that Jervois, like Ord, was restrained, first and foremost,

[1] Ibid.
[2] *History of the Netherlands East Indies*, De Klerck, Rotterdam, 1938, vol. ii, p. 353.

by the Colonial Office. So when they heard of the cease-fire in December which preceded the Governor's attempt to discover whether Ismail was actively hostile, they hastened to point out that the Dutch had failed through just such a display of weakness.

Had they done what Sir William Jervois, as a gallant soldier and a clever man, intended to have done with these Malays until his head was turned and his hands were tied by the counsels of the Attorney-General and Puisne Judge and his never-smelt-powder-except-in-peace Colonial Engineer—had they done what the Governor, we believe, really intended to have done, the Dutch would not have been the laughing stock as they now are to the rest of the world, and which we promise to become also from Sir William Jervois' conduct of affairs in the Peninsula. It will not do to blow hot and cold with the same breath; nor will it do to allow Government subordinates to act in the way the Lieutenant Governor (Acting) of Malacca has done. No one doubted Mr. Plunkett's courage; very few has confidence in his discretion. In the same way as we accuse Captain Murray of folly in sending away his troops from Sunghei Ujong ... we must accuse the Government of doing wrong at Penang, and wonder at what is being done at Perak. There is no real government at all in the country. Lives are being sold of Englishmen who in obedience to orders do and dare all that Englishmen dare do, and the Governor is at Penang, the Colonial Secretary is at Singapore, the Colonial Engineer at Perak, the Puisne Judge of the Colony is enjoying himself somewhere else. Our treasury is exhausted. No money is to be had from Mr. Willans; all is absorbed for war expenses. Our trade is stopped; our commerce is strangled —and for what? That Sir William Jervois might be enabled to enter into agreements and stipulations with Sultan Ismail! So lame and impotent a conclusion to a good beginning, such a wilful wanton throwing overboard of all the experience of an honourable life as our Governor can be proud of, would surprise any one unacquainted with the dismal results that have always resulted from the Governor of this Colony placing a too implicit reliance upon the advice of Singhalese counsellors. What the Government is driving at puzzles us to tell. Its policy is apparent to no one but from its failures. Two thousand British troops engaged in a disreputable contest with half-clothed ill-armed savages, and then our Queen's representative asking for peace? ...

It is a pitiful tale. Here we have a good man, a clever man, and above all, an honest man, throwing his hardly-earned reputation to the winds. . . . Had His Excellency but consulted the much vituperated, but really hard-working honest officer, Colonel Anson, he would have been saved the awful mess his Colonial Secretary, his Puisne Judge, and his Colonial Engineer have landed him in . . . [all will be well when] Sir William Jervois has become himself again, has sent the second Judge of the Appeal Court back to his duty, has called upon the Colonial Engineer to look after

Singapore Waterworks and Drainage . . . and has relegated the Irvingite Adelphi to their proper element of testing totals and noting records of Councils.[1]

If Sir William Jervois read this advice he must have laid the paper down with a certain feeling of despair. Did they think he was the deity, to annex territories at will, provide funds that had not been voted, employ officers who did not exist to fill vacancies that had not been established, and direct campaigns against people not even known to be hostile? Above all, did they think that he and his officers could be in two places at once? But the Governor may well have been hardened to journalistic criticism. Against newspaper attacks the simplest defence is the most effective. There is no need, after all, to read them.

[1] *Straits Observer*, 17 Dec. 1875.

CHAPTER XII

By the end of 1875 all effective resistance had crumbled. The key points in the western States were garrisoned and it only remained to set up such an administration as would prevent further disorder. Towards this reorganization the first step was to arrest and punish those thought responsible for past troubles and likely to inspire future disturbance. To make any sort of 'residential' system feasible it had to be shown that each British officer would be supported, in the last resort, by the whole strength of the British Empire. This had been done.[1] It had also to be shown, however, that vengeance when it came would also prove thorough, patient, painstaking, and relentless. This was the chief task of 1876, the first step being to offer, on 13 January, rewards for the capture of the Maharaja Lela ($6,000), the Dato Sagor ($3,000), and Pandak Indut ($3,000). But the actual process of hunting down the culprits depended neither upon British troops nor paid informers but upon existing Malay feuds, jealousies, and racial difference. The pursuit of the fugitives might have seemed as hopeless then as similar hunting has proved since, but the Malays of different immigrant tribes had divergent interests and a general tendency to turn against the defeated side.

Most important of the wanted men was ex-Sultan Ismail; the man incidentally to whom the others might have turned, or might yet turn, for help. His flight northward from Kinta might take him into Siamese territory but might also bring him back to the Perak river north of Kuala Kangsar. The people of Kota Lama were known to be

[1] The nominal strength of the forces in the Malay Peninsula in 1876 was as follows:

3rd Regiment	950
10th ,, ...	700
80th ,, ...	300
1st Gurkhas	600
One battery, R.A.	120
One company Bengal Sappers . . .	80
Total approx.	2,750

Behind these land forces were H.M. Ships *Thistle, Fly, Modeste, Egeria, Ringdove,* and *Philomel*. Behind these was the remainder of the China Squadron, with H.M.S. *Audacious*, flying Vice-Admiral Ryder's flag, at Shanghai. Behind that flag again was the whole of the Indian Army.

disaffected and it was always in Ulu Perak that Ismail's supporters had been found. He went there, it seems, about a fortnight after his flight from Blanja. Early in January 1876 Jervois received the information that Ismail and his followers (200 in number)[1] were at Jarnai in Perak, as seemed not improbable, and that the Maharaja Lela was at Bada, two days farther up country, and living under the assumed name of Che Ali. This information reached the Governor at Penang together with an offer of help from Inche Karim of Salama, who had (so he said) 300 followers ready to assist him in making the capture. Jervois accepted the offer and instructed John E. Hewick, Assistant Superintendent of Police, Province Wellesley, to go with Karim. Towards the capture of Ismail, Hewick had already taken one important step. He had sent a man called Tuam Chee to join Ismail's party two and a half months previously. This agent found no means of easy contact with Hewick, but planned, instead, to lure Ismail into Kedah, where his capture would be easy. Judging, however, from the information received, it seemed that there might be a shorter way. Hewick acted swiftly, leaving Butterworth for Salama on 5 January with 29 police and 21 Malays. Inche Karim's followers turned out to number, not 300, but 28. With these and 20 Rawahs, Hewick made a rapid march via Biah, Hijow, and the Thirty-three Hills to a kampong called Batu Badinding. Karim meanwhile had, at Hewick's suggestion, sent Ismail a letter dated from Salama 'to the effect that he was desirous of assisting Ismail if he would allow him to have an interview'. This stratagem might have worked if Ismail's son, Raja Lat, had not been at Batu Badinding when Hewick's party arrived. While 'Seedeekah Rajah', in charge there, was shot dead, Raja Lat contrived to warn Ismail, who was living not far distant, on the other side of the Perak river. Ismail fled in the direction of Pulai, in Kedah, leaving seventeen of his elephants, some of which were caught. A small party reached his encampment, killed four or five of his men, captured three more, and burnt the houses in which they had been living. Che Karim was instructed to send one party in pursuit of Ismail while Hewick sent another after the Maharaja Lela. Hewick then returned to Province Wellesley, reporting progress on 19 January.

It was immediately after this affair that Ismail first wrote to the Sultan of Kedah, asking for protection (on 14 January). At a loss what to do about it, the Sultan went to ask Anson's advice. Wrote Anson: 'I advised him to recommend the Sultan to go into the State of Kedah,

[1] S.S. No. 17, 14 Jan. 1876.

and then to allow himself to be handed over to me. He said, "That is not a thing one Sultan should do towards another", but after a moment's thought, he said, "But I will do it for you." [1] Anson at that telegraphed the Governor, suggesting that he call the hunt off. He feared that the Sultan's party might be massacred.

Essentially Hewick's raid was a failure. With 400 men it would, according to him, have been a complete success. As it was, Hewick had killed 'Seedeekah Rajah' (Sri Adika Raja), who was, as he said, one of the Eight Chiefs, 'and held the highest rank as a fighting chief equal to Panglima Prang Samaon'. That, however, had not been the object of the exercise. All he had done otherwise was to drive Ismail farther northward, depriving him of some (not all) of his elephants. Southward he could not have gone because Brigadier-General Ross's northern column was operating from Kuala Kangsar. It was a detachment of this column that suffered some casualties at Kota Lama on 4 January. The kampong had been disarmed without opposition and Ross had landed with his staff and a small escort when a body of fifty or sixty Malays suddenly attacked him, rushing out of the jungle. The Brigade Major, Hawkins, was among those killed with the spear, and it was only by the steadiness of the seamen that the attack was beaten off. McNair wrote afterwards that Hawkins

received a frightful spear wound, the blade passing through his chest. A sailor named Sloper ran to his help, and shot two Malays who were running up to continue the attack, when Major Hawkins is reported to have exclaimed: 'Save yourself, you can do me no good now.' The officers who had gone on towards the river now returned, and tried to move him, but they were compelled in turn to fall back towards the river, Surgeon Townsend being the first to be assailed by three Malays with spears. One he shot with his revolver, but the man struck him down in falling, and his two companions dashed in to spear him, when they were bayoneted by a couple of the seamen. [2]

'I myself attach no political meaning to these disturbances', [3] wrote Jervois, but he authorized the punitive expedition which followed on 20 January and in which the place was completely destroyed by Ross, whose column was accompanied by Captain Garforth, R.N., Captain Speedy, and Mr. W. E. Maxwell. Of the Kota Lama Malays, few, according to Maxwell, were 'really anxious to carry on a hopeless

[1] Anson, op. cit., p. 348.
[2] McNair, op. cit., p. 387.
[3] S.S. No. 17, 14 Jan. 1876.

contest'. They nevertheless followed Toh Sri Lela in an attack upon the Raja Muda Yusof's followers, the sequel to which was a further expedition in which the Kota Lama people were driven successively from Enggar and Prek. One way and another, Ismail had little temptation to join the Kota Lama Malays, even if sure of their support.

By the end of February Jervois had prepared a more elaborate plan for Ismail's capture. After receiving promises from Kedah, Trengganu, Patani, and Kelantan that Ismail would not be received in any of those States; and after receiving information that Ismail was near the river Muda, almost on the boundary between Perak and Kedah, he ordered a threefold movement: Yusof and Maxwell to move up the Perak river, Che Karim and Hewick to move inland again from Salama, and the Sultan of Kedah to move a body of Malays southward.

Before this expedition was organised, however, Mr. Hewick, who had been sent to watch the movements of the ex-Sultan, reported that Ismail was going to cross into Quedah. I therefore ordered preparations to be suspended.[1]

Hewick had not waited for orders but had arranged a different plan with the Sultan of Kedah on 4 February. Two Kedah chiefs, Tunku Ibrahim and Haji Aboo, were to go up the Muda river to Baling with orders to go on from there and locate Ismail. Tunku Ibrahim was father-in-law to Tuan Chee (or Tunku Syed Hussain) whom Hewick had already 'planted' in Ismail's camp. Hewick himself with Wan Mat and his followers would follow up but go no farther than Baling. There was no direct road between Perak and Kedah and it was not even known whether they adjoined or whether Patani interposed. This plan was carried out, Hewick waiting at Padang Geeas (to allow Tunku Ibrahim to go ahead) and then moving to Kuala Koopang.

On the 9th [March] Hadjee Aboo came to me, saying that Ismail was on the frontier waiting. I directed him to return, and get him into Keda territory, as far as Cheeah, about 10 miles from Koopang, so as to be away from any chance of molestation on the part of the Patanis, who had sent parties out. This was done, and on the 9th instant I proceeded to Cheeah to see Ismail. On arriving I found him encamped in the jungle with his men, and with him a number of women and children, in all about 174. I had an interview, and he promised to proceed quietly to Kedah, and then go on to see the Lieut-Governor at Penang.[2]

A conversation followed in which Ismail 'strenuously denied all knowledge of the conspiracy to murder the late Mr. Birch'. Hewick

---

[1] S.S. No. 129, 21 Mar. 1876.   [2] Ibid.

saw that Ismail was destitute, his people emaciated and sick, numbers having indeed died in the jungle.

With regard to his not going in to see Major McNair, he said he was starting when Rajah Mahmood was reported as close at hand with a force, and that, as he had no intention of fighting, and did not wish to expose his wife and children to the horrors of war, he fled into the jungle, and had continued to do so ever since. From what I saw personally, Ismail had no power over his Chiefs, nor had he any respect paid to him; he built his own huts and caught his own elephants.

After leaving I consulted with Wan Mat and had men placed in the rear of Ismail to prevent any attempt to escape. On reaching Koopang I met Che Drahman, who had returned from Kedah, with the news that the Rajah of Kedah was on his way up.

Ismail came to Kuala Ketee on 13 March, where the Sultan of Kedah had a thousand men 'disposed in Ismail's rear' but tactfully out of sight. Ismail was brought by river to Tisa Jantai, to Koobang Hong, to Pantai Pry, and so on the 17th to Kuala Muda. Hewick learnt that the Maharaja Lela had been somewhere near Ismail but not in contact. As he explained in his report, 'I did not go for him then for fear of losing Ismail'.

The Rajah of Kedah went to see Colonel Anson on the 18th and completed the arrangement by which Ismail and eighteen of his followers were brought over on 20 March in the steam-launch *Mata Mata* and lodged in the Rajah's Penang house. His followers included Toh Narah, Panglima Prang Samaon, and Rajah Loh. His women and children remained, with his twenty-seven elephants, in Kedah. Wrote Anson of this occasion:

On the 23rd, Sultan Ismail was brought to my office, in Penang, and handed over to me the Regalia (except of course the elephants that had formed part of it) of Perak. I found him a very gentlemanly and pleasant old man, and I felt much sympathy with him. His possession of the Regalia showed that he had been the actually recognised Sultan. . . . The great mistake was appointing the good-for-nothing Abdullah.[1]

The regalia of Perak comprised a sword which once belonged (so it was said) to Alexander the Great, a chain of office, armlets, a gold-sheathed kris, and the seal of Sultan Muhammad Shah. Other heirlooms not strictly needed at a Perak coronation included the kris of that legendary hero the Laxamana Hang Tuah.[2] All these were afterwards exhibited at the Colonial Exhibition in London.

[1] Anson, op. cit., p. 348.
[2] Winstedt and Wilkinson, op. cit., appendix G.

Colonel Anson sent both Ismail and the regalia on board H.M.S. *Ringdove*, which left at once for Singapore. One of the *Ringdove*'s officers was Wentworth Vernon Bayly, who wrote in his journal of Ismail: 'He is a fine intelligent looking old man, and in every respect a great contrast to Abdullah.'[1] The *Ringdove* reached Singapore on the 26th and Ismail, after handing over the regalia to the Governor, returned on board and was taken to Johore, being there placed temporarily in the Maharajah's custody.

While Hewick was securing Ismail, the men actually implicated in the murder were hunted down. First of these to be caught was the Dato Sagor, who was tracked down by Syed Mashor on 9–10 March and took refuge with the Dato Bandar, who promptly handed him over to Swettenham. Unlike the Maharaja Lela, the Dato Sagor had been present when the murder took place. His trial was deferred, nevertheless, perhaps until after the Maharaja Lela should have been taken. Birch's actual assailants offered a simpler problem. These were Seputum, Che Gondah, and Ngah Ahmat, the first having been arrested by Udu Pulao and Mah Amin, the last being taken by Syed Mashor. They were tried before Raja Dris (appointed by Sultan Abdullah), with J. G. Davidson and Frank Swettenham present as assessors, the trial taking place at Bandar Bahru on 3 and 4 March 1876. All three of the accused pleaded 'Not Guilty', and each made a voluntary statement without calling witnesses. Witnesses for the prosecution included Hamid, coxswain of Birch's boat, Kok Ah Yong, the Chinese goldsmith, Mat Tahir, a boatman, and Hoo Ah Choey (Ah Yong's cook). All four identified Seputum as present when Birch and the others were murdered. Kok Ah Yong and Hoo Ah Choey saw him hit Birch with a sword. Three of them identified Che Gondah as present and as many would swear to the presence there of Ngah Ahmat. Another witness, Haji Fatimah, identified Che Gondah as one of those who had set off to attack the Residency on the night after the murders. Seputum's plea was as follows:

If I had not gone the Maharaja Lela would have burnt my house and taken my property. I am nobody. I am a cooly. If I did not do it Maharaja Lela would have killed me. He wanted me to give him dollars afterwards and so I had to run away. If I have done wrong, it is in doing the Maharaja Lela's business.

Seputum admitted striking Birch, but stated that the Resident was first speared by Ngah Jabbor, the Maharaja Lela's brother. Che

---

[1] MS. Journal in descendant's possession.

Gondah made a rather similar defence, pleading compulsion and stating that the foremost in the attack were Pandak Indut, Ngah Jabbor, Che Alli, Tuah, and Seputum. By his account it was Ngah Jabbor who went to ask Ismail's help and was given two barrels of gunpowder, but no money. Ngah Ahmat was the Maharaja Lela's clerk and wrote the letter to Ismail. He denied, however, that he had been there at the time of the attack, claiming to have arrived when it was over. After hearing the evidence, Raja Dris pronounced all three guilty and sentenced them to death by hanging, subject to the Sultan's confirmation. On being informed of this, and after studying the evidence in Council, Jervois advised the Sultan, through the Deputy Commissioner, to commute the sentences on Che Gondah and Ngah Ahmat to penal servitude for life. Seputum was hanged at Bandar Bahru on 20 May in the presence of Abdullah and the chiefs.

The next object was to capture the Maharaja Lela, last heard of in the area where Ismail was found. A first effort to catch him was made by Mr. W. E. Maxwell, who afterwards wrote and published an account of the operation.

Early in March, information reached me which described Maharaja Lela as living with a few followers at a place called Kwala Piah in the North of the State. . . . I received orders to attempt the capture of the fugitive.[1]

Concluding, and very reasonably, that a move through the hostile territory round Kota Lama would at once be reported to the wanted man, Maxwell went a different way. Starting from Butterworth on 24 March, with forty Malays, he followed Hewick's path to Salama and Batu Berdinding and then struck at Kendrong, the Maharaja Lela escaping in the nick of time. Maxwell assumed that his prey had fled into Patani, so he tried to persuade the local chiefs to co-operate in the search. Having no success with them, Maxwell wired the Governor, who wrote in turn to the British Consul-General at Bangkok. In point of fact, however, the Maharaja Lela had not entered Patani at all. He had gone in the other direction, seeking refuge in the vicinity of Kota Lama and already perhaps despairing of any final escape.

Jervois was staying with the Maharajah of Johore when first told that the Maharaja Lela was at a kampong between Sala and Kapayang and would probably surrender if promised a fair trial. He had said as much to someone from Johore in May and the Governor at once gave

---

[1] *A Journey on foot to the Patani Frontier in 1876*, H. E. Maxwell, p. 4.

the required guarantee. The Orang Kaya Abdulrahman of Johore was sent to find the Maharaja Lela and did so between 16 and 25 June. A telegram from Davidson, sent on the latter date, told Jervois that the Maharaja Lela would consent to go to Johore in the Maharajah of Johore's steamship, *Pantai*. This vessel was accordingly sent to Penang with a party of officers from Johore, and then on to Larut. After some negotiation, the Maharaja Lela embarked in the *Pantai* on 13 July, accompanied by Pandak Indut (his brother-in-law) and Ngah Jabbor (both wanted men) and was taken to Johore on the 20th.

Two or three days after the arrival of the prisoners, I had an interview with the Maharajah of Johore, when I requested him to cause Lela, Nga Jabbor and Pandak Indut and two other Malays named Panjang Buh and Kulup Alli, against whom there is evidence, to be informed that they must surrender themselves to the British Government, that I guaranteed them a fair and impartial trial, and that, if found innocent of the crime with which they are charged, they will be set at liberty. They in consequence have surrendered themselves to-day and they are now lodged in the Civil Prison in Singapore.[1]

The Maharaja Lela's decision to surrender is explained by the fact that Abdullah was in danger now of being revealed as his accomplice. Jervois pointed this out to Lord Carnarvon in a private letter dated 22 July, remarking that Abdullah was terrified. As he watched Seputum's execution, Abdullah knew that he had given the Maharaja Lela a written authority for committing the crime which had brought Seputum to the gallows. That may have been one reason why Davidson and Swettenham saw to it that he was present. As Jervois said in his letter,

understand that one of the reasons—perhaps the main one—which induced Lela to surrender, was a fear that he would be krissed or poisoned at the instigation of the chiefs interested in getting rid of him, on the principle that ' dead men tell no tales '.

As yet I have not considered the evidence against Abdullah sufficiently clear to have him arrested, but I believe that it will be found that he and the Chiefs about him are mainly responsible for the murder of Birch.

This last prediction fell short of the uncanny, for an inquiry into Abdullah's and Ismail's complicity had been ordered in March and had been proceeding relentlessly ever since. Mr. Plunket and a new officer (from Sarawak), Mr. Paul, were to collect the evidence, which was to be reviewed afresh by the Puisne Judge, Mr. Justice Phillippo, and finally submitted to the Governor. Evidence apart, Paul was

[1] S.S. No. 272 of 30 July 1876.

interested from the start in 'the general demeanour' of Abdullah and his people and 'the state of abject terror to which they have been reduced'. Reasons for this dismay emerged with the evidence. Mr. Edward Bacon, who had been employed by Birch, showed that Birch and Abdullah had been on bad terms. He also described the scene when Birch reprimanded the Dato Sagor for bringing a spear into his presence, and indeed had the spear taken from him. Dyang Ismail had overheard Abdullah plotting Birch's death. Indoot, a boatman, gave evidence about the 'seance'. Seekye, wife of the executed Seputum, told how the Maharaja Lela had built a fort on Abdullah's orders and promised Seputum $25 to kill the Resident. Some of this was hearsay and some of it inconclusive even if true but a document handed in by the Maharaja Lela was rather more difficult to explain. It was dated 1 October 1875 and ran as follows:

Let them all know [i.e. Be it known to every one] that we order this Seputum to do Mr. Birch to death. Seputum must do this work without fail. When Mr. Birch is dead, if any complaint is made by anyone [lit. comes from any direction] we will bear it [i.e. accept the responsibility] and let not Seputum hesitate to carry out the above-mentioned work.

Moreover, when Mr. Birch is dead, Seputum must return this document to us, and we will pay Seputum a reward of $1000. That is why this is authentic and true, and we have put our chop and signature at the head of this paper.

The policy outlined in this document seems sufficiently clear and Abdullah's signature and seal were found to be genuine. But the historian who accepts it as 'authentic and true' must explain why Abdullah was willing to pay $1,000 for a murder, when $25 would obviously have been ample. He must also explain why this uncashed cheque should have been in the wrong man's possession. The Maharaja Lela had it, but the document was only of value to Seputum. The Governor's conclusion, which seems sufficiently astute, was that the original document had been addressed (almost in the same words) from Abdullah to the Maharaja Lela, offering the superscale fee which that chief would expect; that Abdullah had given the Maharaja Lela, in addition, a blank paper, signed and sealed, with which to summon such further aid as he chose; and that the Maharaja Lela had wisely destroyed the first document after transferring the text (with Seputum's name replacing his own) to the second. It is known that the Maharaja Lela was very excited before the murder and regarded himself as exceptionally empowered; as with such a blank cheque from Abdullah he would have been. So the Governor's theory may well afford the right explanation. By producing this trump card on 21 July the Maharaja Lela may well have thought that he had weakened the case against himself. For if Seputum was directly obeying the Sultan it might seem more difficult to implicate Seputum's immediate chief—who was not even present at the scene of the crime. But the Maharaja Lela was implicated, in fact, by other evidence, including that given by Seputum himself.

The Inquiry dragged on through June and July, the result being that the Colonial Secretary (the Hon. J. Douglas, C.M.G.) was able finally to draw up an indictment. Abdullah, the Laxamana, the Shahbandar, Raja Mahkota, and Orang Kaya Mat Arshad were summoned to Singapore on 10 August. Davidson was told to fetch them, by force if need be, and they finally arrived in the *Pluto* on 4 September, Raja Dris also attending voluntarily and the Mantri not being among those summoned. Abdullah was informed on 16 September of charges which, if proved, would make him a party to the murder and an accessory after the fact. He was accused of conspiracy, of inciting the Maharaja Lela to murder, of supplying that chief with food and ammunition, and of assisting the Dato Sagor to escape. He replied on 6 October, denying the charges but in terms which the Governor thought 'entirely unsatisfactory'. The problem, meanwhile, was one of procedure. Jervois had decided as early as 1 September that Abdullah could not be tried in a court of law. Lord Carnarvon had agreed on 23 October, instructing Jervois to hear the evidence in Executive Council and then report to him and await instructions. All that could be done, in any case, would be to deport Abdullah— say, to Labuan or the Seychelles. During Abdullah's absence in Singapore, Jervois proposed that Raja Yusof should act as Regent, but Abdullah preferred that the Bandahara should act for him, and this was agreed. But the Bandahara died almost immediately, so that Yusof became Regent after all.

Plunket's Summary of Evidence (of 1 December) was considered by the Executive Council at a meeting held in Government House, Singapore, on 9 December 1876. Those present were the Governor, the Officer Commanding the Troops (Colonel McLeod), the Acting Judge of Penang (Mr. Justice Ford), the Colonial Secretary (J. Douglas), Braddell the Attorney-General, Willans the Treasurer, and C. J. Irving the Auditor-General. From the evidence it was fairly clear that all the chiefs except Raja Yusof had been more or less cognizant

of the plan to kill Birch and that the Maharaja Lela had received
ammunition from Abdullah and money, at one juncture, from Ismail. All this was as easy to understand as it was to establish. What
was far more difficult to explain was the course of events after Birch's
death. This was evidently to have been the signal for revolt, for a
massacre of all foreign intruders. The murder was an untidy job but
it duly took place—and then came the anticlimax. Instead of attacking
Bandar Bahru that night, the Maharaja Lela's men merely wandered
in that direction and then wandered back again. Why? Wan Hoosein
had an accident and turned back half-way. It was raining. The Dato
Sagor should have joined the party but did not. There was a rumour
that Bandar Bahru was strongly held. The whole idea of the attack
proved unattractive when further examined. So everyone went home.
But why was there no mass movement after the British reverse at
Passir Salak? Plunket's explanation was as follows:

That the scheme for a combined movement by ex-Sultan Ismail and
Sultan Abdullah, with the view of driving the British out of Perak, collapsed from the following causes:—1st, that the Mantri, Tumonggong and
Bandahara failed to join Ismail at Blanja after the murder of Mr. Birch;
2nd, that Punghulu Mat Alli was afraid to attack Kota Stia by sea on
account of the presence of men-of-war on the coast; 3rd, that there was no
general ill-feeling . . . ; and lastly, that the prompt action of the Government took the Chiefs by surprise.

In fact, the only major chief who took any action was the Mantri,
who ordered Mat Alli (the Punghulu of Kurow) to attack Kota Stia
in co-operation with Haji Mat Yassim and Haji Alli. This order
served only to implicate the man who issued it. If the armed boats
ever assembled, they certainly never came near their objective.

Faced with fifty-three paragraphs of summarized evidence, the
Executive Council reached the following conclusion:

Notwithstanding the fact that Abdullah owed his elevation to the Sultanship to the Government of the Straits Settlements; that the appointment of
Mr. Birch as Resident was made at his personal request; it appears impossible to doubt that not only was Sultan Abdullah aware beforehand
that Mr. Birch's murder was in contemplation, without taking any steps
to prevent it, but there is no reason to doubt that it was committed with
his approval and consent, and that for a considerable time before it took
place he and his chiefs had been plotting Mr. Birch's destruction. There is
also evidence, apparently reliable, that after the murder was committed
he assisted and protected some of the perpetrators thereof.

It must be admitted that provocation was given to the Sultan and his chiefs. The late Mr. Birch was a most zealous and conscientious officer. He was, however, much thwarted from the outset, and there is reason to believe that his manner may at times have been overbearing. It must also be admitted that, in some instances, he showed a want of respect for Malay custom. It was also injudicious to interfere with local taxes before the general scale of allowances had been fixed in lieu of them. These are circumstances which may tend to palliate the criminality of the acts, but they cannot, in the opinion of the Council, be held to justify them.[1]

The Executive Council had to tread warily. It would not suit the Governor to find that the Maharaja Lela had acted entirely on his own; for he would then have to explain why he had put nearly 3,000 troops in the field. It would not do to discover that the trouble had been connected in any way with Sir William's innovations in policy. Nor would it be of any use to incriminate Abdullah merely for the benefit of Ismail and the Mantri. The safe line was to put some of the blame on Birch, whose appointment was due to the previous Governor, whose career could not be affected, and who could not, in any case, answer back. Apart, however, from these reflections on what had taken place, the Council had to decide on a policy; or at any rate announce the policy already agreed between Jervois and the Secretary of State. This the Council did, as follows:

The Council do not consider it possible that Sultan Abdullah should be allowed to return to Perak.

Agreed so far, the members of Council differed over the next step, three considering that Abdullah might remain in Singapore, four (the Governor included) wanting to send him and the Shahbandar to Labuan, the Mantri and Laxamana to the Seychelles. It was generally recognized, however, that Ismail's case was entirely different. As he had never agreed to the Pangkor Engagement, there was no element of treachery in his resistance to its fulfilment. As for Raja Dris, he had 'taken a less active part than the others in the plot against Mr. Birch', although doubtless present at meetings where it was discussed. After some further correspondence, it was arranged that Abdullah, the Laxamana, the Shahbandar, and the Mantri should all be deported to the Seychelles. They were sent to those islands in 1877 but Sir Andrew Clarke interceded for Abdullah and gained permission for him to return to Singapore in 1894. He afterwards visited England and learnt the language. The Mantri also came to Singapore and eventually died there. This wholesale removal left the Regent Yusof in a peculiarly strong position.

[1] Minutes of the Executive Council.

It remained to deal with the Maharaja Lela, Pandak Indut, Ngah Jabbor, Panjang Bur, Che Alli alias Kulup Alli, Dato Sagor, and Che Tuah. The first difficulty was to find any Malay judges not themselves under suspicion. Seputum had been condemned to death by Raja Dris, the judge appointed by Sultan Abdullah. By 9 December when the *Pluto* took the accused men up to Perak for trial, Abdullah's case was actually coming before the Executive Council, together with that of Dris, and neither was to emerge with an unblemished character. In the end it was the Bandahara (as Regent) who nominated as judges the Raja Muda Yusof and Raja Allang Hoosein, Dris's name being crossed off in the nick of time. The assessors were Mr. Davidson, now Resident of Perak, and Mr. W. E. Maxwell, now Acting Assistant Resident at Larut. Major Dunlop and Mr. Swettenham were to prosecute and Mr. J. D. Vaughan defended the accused. The trial took place in the Mantri's house at Martang, which was guarded by a company of the 10th Regiment. The hearing began on 14 December and lasted until the 22nd, on which day all the accused were sentenced to death. Defending counsel based his plea on the Court's insufficiency and upon the Maharaja Lela's claim that he had been promised not merely a fair trial but his life. Neither plea was allowed and the prosecution had no difficulty in establishing the guilt of the accused. Quite apart from other evidence, it was obvious that Birch could never have been murdered at Passir Salak except by the Maharaja Lela's orders. The Dato Sagor was present when the 'amoq' took place. Pandak Indut was certainly one of the murderers and foremost in killing both Birch and Mat Arshad. On these three sentence was confirmed. They were hanged near Larut jail on 20 January 1877. Sentence on the other four was commuted by the Raja Muda and they were imprisoned for life; one of them, however (Che Tuah), turning out to be imbecile.

The trials and investigations of 1876 removed from the Perak chess-board nearly all the pieces (other than pawns) on the Malay side. They also served to remove many of the pieces on the British side, including (beside the soldiers) Mr. Davidson and Mr. Speedy. Neither Lord Carnarvon nor Sir William Jervois had been very happy about Davidson's position in Selangor and the latter had welcomed the chance to transfer him temporarily to Perak.[1] When, however, he

---

[1] Lord Stanley of Alderley had reminded Lord Carnarvon that the Selangor Tin Mining Co. with a nominal capital of £200,000 had paid £100,000 of this to Davidson and his partner as vendors of the concession, or so it was stated in *The*

wished to make this transfer permanent Lord Carnarvon asked why Speedy was thus to be passed over. Jervois, in reply, hinted that Speedy, as the Mantri's adviser, had been rather opposed to British intervention (by which his salary was reduced to a tenth of what the Mantri had agreed to pay him) and would have greatly preferred to retain his former free-lance role.

But irrespective of the considerations to which I have just referred, I think that Captain Speedy is wanting in many of the qualifications which are required as a Resident or Assistant Resident in Native States. Doubtless he is acquainted with both the Hindustani and Malay languages, and he possesses much physical power. It is also stated that he has considerable influence amongst the Chinese and Malays. If, however, the latter be the case, this influence has existed to very little purpose in obtaining means of transport for the troops passing through Larut at the end of last year. Brigadier-General Ross, who commanded that force, informed me that the so-called influence of Captain Speedy did not exist and that he was powerless to induce the Headmen to obey his orders or requisitions. At that time, I had great difficulty in raising elsewhere supplies of coolies, who, if Captain Speedy had the influence attributed to him, should have been very easily obtained by him, in any number required, from amongst the Chinese in Larut.

I do not think that the facility with which Captain Speedy can acquire languages is any guarantee for the possession of other qualifications essential for the position of a Resident.

From personal observation I must say that he does not appear to be a man of business habits; he is decidedly lazy; and submits very unwillingly to the necessary discipline of the public service. He is, moreover, extravagant in the expenditure of money. . . .

The salary which Captain Speedy has drawn, viz. £1500 per Annum (in addition to a large and very comfortable house) is a very high one for the duties performed. . . .

Taking all these points into consideration I strongly recommend that, if possible, employment may be found for Captain Speedy elsewhere.[1]

Reading between the lines, one can realize that Speedy had founded a kingdom for himself at Larut and rather resented its invasion by a foreign power. Fifty years earlier and left to himself, he would have been issuing coins in his own effigy. As things were, he had to be removed and Jervois got rid of him by the simple means of reducing

London and China Telegraph of 6 July 1874. See Hansard, vol. ccxxx, 3 July 1876 col. 826.

[1] Confidential letter, Jervois to Lord Carnarvon, 18 Oct. 1876. His slightly fantastic house still exists and provides accommodation for the District Officer, Taiping.

his salary to £750 and announcing that the Assistant Resident would be posted in future at Bandar Bahru. Speedy went quietly, but the refusal to promote him led to Davidson's resignation. For although Lord Carnarvon agreed reluctantly to Davidson's appointment to the Residency which Speedy had wanted, and had even agreed to his salary being fixed at £2,000, he had done so in a grudging sort of way.

But it must be understood, and this you will make clear to Mr. Davidson, that this appointment is of a provisional nature and liable to be terminated at any time without notice, and without further compensation than the payment of three months' salary, and further that the rate of salary must be considered as subject to revision at the end of a year from this date [8 September 1876].

So Davidson, whose interests were only in Selangor, promptly resigned too. Swettenham was near the truth, no doubt, when he said that Davidson, 'although he liked his post in Selangor, where he was well known,   . did not care for a similar but far more difficult task in Perak'.[1] The post of Resident (at £1,500 per annum) was now offered to Mr. Hugh Low, magistrate of Labuan, on 12 February 1877, with the further and unreasonable request that he would embark at Marseilles on 25 February. Mr. W. E. Maxwell was appointed Assistant Resident. To train the proposed Perak Police, the War Office was persuaded to release Lieutenant Paul Swinburne of the 80th Regiment, and did so at last on 29 January 1877. Mr. Leach was recommended to the post of Assistant Superintendent of Police. Although a colour-sergeant in the 10th Regiment, he turned out to be a gentleman by birth and a graduate of Trinity College, Dublin.

Captain Murray would remain, it was decided, in Sungei Ujong. Captain Bloomfield Douglas, R.N.R., had been already appointed to Selangor as Resident, and now Mr. Paul (an Etonian) was made his Assistant. The tendency in these appointments was to bring from Sarawak or Labuan people who already knew Malay. Hugh Low and Paul came from there and Douglas had been master of Rajah Brooke's schooner *Royalist*. Other and later appointments were to follow the same pattern. Mr. Frank Swettenham, cheated for the second time of the Selangor Residency, was made Assistant Secretary for the Native States, thus definitely gaining a lead over his obvious rival, Mr. W. E. Maxwell. Residents would in future, as before, address their letters

---

[1] Swettenham, *Footprints in Malaya*, p. 69.

to the Colonial Secretary, but now it was Frank Swettenham who would draft the replies.

Apart from thus providing for the future administration of the western Malay States, the time had come to reward all those who had performed faithful service. Captain Buller, R.N., was made C.B., Colonel Anson (like Mr. Hoo Ah Kay) was made C.M.G., and Captain Channer received the V.C. Commander Stirling was promoted Captain, Sub-Lieutenant Abbott was promoted Lieutenant. The *Thalia* and *Ringdove* were sent back to Portsmouth and paid off there. Major McNair went home on sick leave. Major Dunlop was granted a year's leave of absence. Mr. A. M. de Fontaine was made 'Guardian to Government House'. Presentation swords were given, as from the Queen, to Raja Mahmood, Syed Mashor, Raja Indut, and Raja Asul. These were honoured at Swettenham's suggestion because 'they have fought entirely for friendship's sake, and have received no pecuniary reward. . .'. The Queen's condolences were sent to Birch's father, the Rev. J. W. Birch, Vicar of All Saints', Hertford. For Mr. Birch's eldest son a place was found in the Colonial Service. To each of his other children the Queen, advised by Disraeli, granted an allowance of £75 per annum. The troops received a medal for the Perak Campaign and two of the Gurkha soldiers were gazetted. General Colborne had counted on obtaining the K.C.B. but was awarded nothing; probably because he quitted his proper post at Hong Kong. Brigadier-General Ross narrowly escaped a court martial on account of a war-crime, probably the only one committed. This was the hanging of a Malay called Panjang Meroo at a kampong near Kuala Kangsar. This summary execution was carried out by seamen under Captain Garforth's command but acting on Ross's orders. McNair and Maxwell disclaimed responsibility, but Jervois blamed them for not preventing it. This incident robbed the Brigadier-General of any award and apparently made him reluctant to recommend the decoration of those junior to him. The Navy received more generous recognition. Sir William Jervois received none.

It will be apparent from the narrative of the Perak and Sungei Ujong campaigns that the Governor had acted efficiently and swiftly if not economically.[1] It was largely due to him that the country was so

---

[1] Jervois reported on 6 April 1876 that the campaign had so far cost $334,467, which, with the dollar at 4s. 3d., came to £71,074. The total had risen to $349,531 by 30 June, only in part expended from Native State Treasuries. The Straits Settlement Government was £65,000 in debt by Oct. 1876. Instructions from the Colonial Office (31 Oct.) were to issue debentures on the London market to the

quickly pacified and with so little bloodshed. But this would not save him from the reproof due to him for going so far beyond his instructions. Lord Carnarvon had already (25 November 1875, see p. 269 above) expressed his disapproval of Sir William's policy and the correspondence had continued thereafter, mingling with reports of operations and implying incidentally what the future policy should be. For the present it will make for lucidity to treat these topics separately, dealing first with Lord Carnarvon's censure. One important document in the series was, as we have seen (p. 271 above) the Secretary of State's letter of 10 December 1875 referring to 'grave errors of policy and of action' and expressing pained astonishment at Jervois's temerity. This eventually elicited from the Governor his long dispatch of 10 February 1876. This is quoted in full (see Appendix C) and need not be summarized here, but the paragraph which produced the most electric effect was No. 58, beginning: 'But I was anxious if possible not to reverse the policy as approved by Her Majesty's Government. . . .' What followed from this unpromising start is not to the present purpose but we know something of the immediate impression made.

A furious controversy arose in 1876 between the Governor and Lord Carnarvon. . . . The office was extremely annoyed, and Meade asserted that they had never seen the instruction to the Residents, and consequently could not know what they were doing. Lord Carnarvon was so annoyed that, after beginning: 'I am afraid that I must characterise this despatch as one of the least satisfactory that I have read since I have been connected with this office. It unquestionably has the merit of cleverness: but it is unscrupulous in argument, unbecoming in tone and very disingenuous in character.' He went on to answer the despatch, paragraph by paragraph. What hurt most was paragraph 58, where the Governor wrote that he was anxious 'if possible, not to reverse the policy as approved by Her Majesty's Government.' That was too much for the Secretary of State. 'He was anxious not to reverse Her Majesty's Government's policy *if possible*!!' However, the Governor apologised and was forgiven.[1]

Or was he? Lord Carnarvon's reply of 20 May is given in full at Appendix D, but it must be recalled that there was private as well as official correspondence. And while the apology was thus made privately there is some reason to suppose, from the sequel, that its

value of £150,000 so as to cover future Native State expenditure as well. Some of the strictly military expense was met by the British Treasury. Immediate needs up to £25,000 were met by the Crown Agents borrowing from the Bank of England.

[1] *The Colonial Office, a History*, H. L. Hall, London, 1937, p. 238. See also Appendix E.

acceptance was accompanied by a hint that Jervois's resignation from the governorship of the Straits Settlements would be appropriate and timely. As regards the public dispatch, the reproof is softened somewhat by paragraph 39, which reads:

It is not my object to convey censure, and indeed, I have already highly approved the conspicuous ability and determination with which you acted subsequently to the outbreak of these disorders. . . .[1]

That such ability and resolution had been shown was in fact beyond question.

As regards future policy, Lord Carnarvon was in no great hurry to commit himself. He merely emphasized from time to time that no further rash decisions were to be taken. Jervois, on his part, pressed repeatedly for a directive from home, implying that if he might not decide upon a policy, Carnarvon must. On 2 February 1876 he sent a telegram in these words:

Unofficial members and public here generally press me for information concerning future policy in native States. I have told them I cannot afford information which Secretary of State declines yet to make public. Does your Lordship approve this answer?

This was followed by a further telegram on 7 April:

Want of information as to future policy to be adopted by H.M. Government towards Native States is disadvantageous.

The same theme recurred in a telegram of the 19th, which elicited the following response:

. . . instructions as to future policy in Native States will shortly be sent, and pending the consideration by H.M. Government of your proposal you should take no action whatever.

This warning was repeated on 28 April in more general terms:

Use utmost care not to take any action without authority.

One way and another it was made clear to Jervois that major decisions would be made, in future, in Downing Street and not in Singapore.[2]

---

[1] Carnarvon had praised Jervois's judgement and calmness, energy, and humanity in his dispatch of 1 Feb.

[2] 'An annexation policy may or may not hereafter become necessary—but one thing I lay down in the clearest language, that I will not sanction a great measure of State policy being adopted by a Colonial Government without the sanction and in opposition to the instructions of the Home Government. When annexation has become expedient Her Majesty's Government must have the exclusive responsibility of the measure.' See *Life of Lord Carnarvon*, Hardinge, vol. ii, p. 140.

Towards making the decisions that now lay with him, Lord Carnarvon's first step, taken probably in December, was to consult Sir Harry Ord, who replied with a memorandum dated 3 January 1876. He began by remarking that events had landed Perak on our hands and that British policy towards that and the other States would need attention. We could, of course, withdraw 'But something more than this seems to be expected by the public'. We could, on the other hand, annex most of the peninsula. What had occurred might be held to justify the annexation of Perak and the recently hostile States of Sungei Ujong and Rembau. 'For the annexation of the independent kingdom of Salangore no legal warranty can be found; our necessities must be our justification, if any be required.' But annexation would be a costly business and would mean pensioning off the rulers, chiefs, and their followers. Where was the money to come from? There was little agriculture or planting and the extent of the mineral wealth was uncertain. There might be no appreciable revenue for years.

If the Straits Colony were called upon to furnish this assistance, fresh taxation would be required, which could not with any justice be added to the burden already borne by the native population, and would not certainly be willingly assumed by the mercantile community, anxious as they are to see fresh commercial fields opened out to them.

It may be thought that too much stress has been laid upon the question of cost, and that if the result of the annexation of this native territory would be to substitute in a short time civilised rule and respect for life and property, with an increase in its material wealth, for the barbarism, anarchy, recklessness, and poverty which are now its prominent features, no question of expense should be suffered to stand in the way of such a measure. But all our knowledge of Malay character and habits assures us that this is not to be expected. It would be long before they would learn to accept quietly the restraints imposed on them by our rule, and there would be a bitter and constantly recurring struggle with the dominant power seeking to bring them under the yoke of its civilisation. Moslem fanaticism would also without doubt be invoked against the infidel, and would probably still further increase our difficulty.

Still, such an annexation as has been contemplated would ultimately prove most beneficial to the country—the question is, is it worth the cost?

If it be not, the next question is, would it not be possible to obtain by some other and simpler means all that we are really bound to seek for?

Ord finally advised retaining the Resident system but instructing the Residents to restrict their formal advice to such matters as would ensure the safety of lives and property of persons other than the natives. Their advice on other topics should be informal, without enforced acceptance, and they should be paid out of the Colony's revenue. As regards the question of the throne of Perak, Abdullah was useless (as *some* people had realized as long ago as 1872) but the Raja Muda 'would be a good person to put forward' or, failing him, there was Tunku dia Oodin.

Lord Carnarvon did not follow Sir Harry Ord's advice in every detail, but he probably found that Ord was speaking for the public (the public that mattered, the readers of *The Times*) when he rejected both withdrawal and annexation. What was wanted was a middle course, uniting the economic advantages of annexation with the financial consequences of withdrawal. Lord Carnarvon was not without a sense of mission when it came to diffusing civilization and abolishing slavery but he was working within the financial bounds set by Parliament and public. He knew that, beyond a certain limit of expense (and the Malay States had cost something already), he would rapidly lose support. More than that, it would be thought that the expenditure was merely for the benefit of a few investors in the Straits, and a few missionary cranks at home. Typically British in his approach, Lord Carnarvon wasted no time on philosophic principles. All he wanted was a workable solution to an immediate problem. Nor did he think such a solution difficult to find. Reading the dispatches from the Straits, he had evidently realized that the military situation was favourable to his plans. Jervois's demonstration of force would be remembered for years. But, apart from that, the Malays had been found to be essentially unwarlike and the Chinese given only to fighting each other. There never was, there never had been, a local disturbance which could not be quelled by 200 men and a field-gun. Any large assembly of either race could be broken up by a simple blockade. All that was needed in Perak was a well-disciplined guard. All this he said or implied in his letter of 1 June 1876, which ran as follows:

Carnarvon to Jervois.

Downing Street,
June 1, 1876.

Sir,

In my Despatch of 20th ultimo, I stated that I would address you separately on some points connected with the future policy of Her Majesty's Government in relation to Perak, and I will now proceed to touch briefly on those considerations which seem to me at this moment of most pressing importance.

As you will have remarked, I did not in that Despatch make any special comments on the suggestions made in some of your earlier communications to annex the State of Perak to Her Majesty's dominions, but the telegraphic and other communications which I have during the last few months addressed you have I think made my opinion on this point sufficiently clear, and it will now be enough if I say that after full consideration of the grounds on which you based the proposal, the circumstances of the case do not, in the opinion of Her Majesty's Government, warrant the adoption of that policy, nor are they prepared to depart in any considerable degree from the instructions that have already been given you.

In my telegram of the 25th November I informed you that neither annexation nor the government of the country by British officers in the name of the Sultan (a measure very little removed from annexation) could be allowed, and that Her Majesty's Government were not prepared to adopt the principle of permanently retaining troops in the Peninsula in order to impose Residents or other Officers upon the Natives against their will. It is, I think, clear that to press such officers upon a resisting population would, under the present circumstances of the country, be productive of at least as much risk and inconvenience as of political or commercial advantage.

Subsequently (on the 29th December) I informed you that you might retain for the present whatever force you considered indispensable, but that the troops so retained were not to be employed for purposes of annexation, and that Her Majesty's Government were disposed in favour of maintaining the established system of Residents, but that they required further information from you on various points, such as the stations proposed to be occupied, the force to be employed, and any other modifications desirable for the security or improvement of the system.

To this latter telegram I received an immediate and necessarily brief reply from you by telegraph, but I have not received as yet any Despatch giving full explanations and information on the specific points which I then raised. I need not, however, delay longer to say that on a general review of the correspondence which has come before me, I fail to perceive any proof that the system under which Residents were appointed to the native States has had such a trial as to justify me in pronouncing that it has failed, or that any other course which has been indicated is not open to graver risk, larger expenditure, and more doubtful results. The obstacles which have interfered with its success are apparently such as can be removed. The system has been in existence for little more than two years, and independently of the fact that during a great part of that time it has been subject to some exceptionally adverse conditions, it is clear, from the official reports which you and your predecessor have forwarded to me, that if it has broken down in one part of the Malay Peninsula it has enjoyed a fair amount of success in other parts. I see, therefore, no ground for an entire and abrupt reversal of existing arrangements, followed, as such reversal must be, by a further period of uncertainty and transition.

It is indeed clear that the Residents have exceeded the function of

Counsellors which they were intended to discharge, but I do not think that on that account it is necessary either to withdraw them from Perak and the other States, or to revolutionise the conditions of their political and administrative functions. A modification of the previous arrangements will probably be enough for the present, if combined with watchfulness and great caution on the part of the Government; and under such conditions officers may, in my opinion, continue to be stationed in Perak, who may render active and valuable assistance in the administration of the country. They will, however, need for the present at all events, to be supported by an armed force which can be relied upon to preclude the probability of any treachery or open resistance.

In a recent Despatch, when describing the temporary appointments, which you have made, you adhere to the designation of 'Commissioner'. I doubt whether any adequate advantage will be gained by the change of name from Residents (a designation well understood in the East as indicating that amount of influential advice to the native ruler, and that amount of responsibility on the part of the adviser, which Her Majesty's Government have contemplated) to Queen's Commissioners, and I am averse to the change as implying either a greater responsibility or an undefined and doubtful alteration in the relations of the two parties.

I am of opinion, therefore, that the English officers to be stationed in the Malay States should continue to be styled 'Residents'.

I am, however, disposed to approve your proposal of establishing a Council of mixed Malay Chiefs and British officers. Such a Council would, as you observe, give an opportunity to some of the principal Chiefs to take a useful part in the administration of the Country, and thereby uphold their influence with the body of the people. It would, moreover, give the Resident and any other officers nominated by you to such a Council an opportunity of gauging the strength of native feeling on questions of proposed reform; and the knowledge so gained would tend to the exercise of greater discrimination in the nature of the advice given by the Resident to the chief native authority.

It will, of course, be desirable to settle by regulation at as early a date as possible the nature of the questions that must be brought before this Council, and the position they are to hold in relation to the acts of the Executive Government.

I understand that in your proposal for the establishment of such a Council you had in view the circumstances of Perak only; but, assuming the principle to be good in the case of Perak, it would probably be desirable to adopt it in each of the native States, or in each group of contiguous States that can be conveniently treated in combination.

Whatever may be the ultimate policy which it may be necessary to adopt in the Malay Peninsula it is clearly our object to make the best use of existing materials, and with this view it should be our present policy to find and train up some Chief or Chiefs of sufficient capacity and enlightenment to appreciate the advantages of a civilized government and to render some effectual assistance in the government of the country.

It is, in my opinion, undesirable that the British officers should interfere more frequently or to a greater extent than is necessary in the minor details of government. Their special objects should be the maintenance of peace and law, the institution of a sound system of taxation, with the consequent development of the general resources of the country, and the supervision of the collection of the revenue so as to ensure the receipt of funds necessary to carry out the principal engagements of the Government, and to pay for the cost of the British officers and whatever establishments may be found necessary to support them.

At the time of the engagement of Pangkore it was contemplated that the Sultan should have a Civil List, that Ismail should be pensioned, and that other Chiefs should have fixed incomes. As far as I can gather from the papers before me, though this subject has been considered further, no definite settlement of allowances has ever yet been made. Although there may not at present be money available for the payment of the whole of such allowances, I consider it desirable that the amounts to be assigned should be fixed as soon as possible, so that the Chiefs should understand their interest in supporting the system of revenue devised by Mr. Birch, and that should they continue to attempt to exact revenue not legitimately due to them, they will forfeit their right to their fixed allowances.

With regard to the retention of Abdullah as Sultan, I am obliged to infer, both from late events and from your recent communication, that his selection was not fortunate, and that he has not the proper capacities for a ruler. . . .

[The following discussion about Abdullah's position soon became out of date as a result of inquiries into his complicity in the murder of Birch.]

It will, as I have already indicated, be necessary to secure by far more effectual precautions than those hitherto observed, the protection of the Resident, and to provide against such sudden outbreaks as that which recently occurred in Perak. This can only be done by the maintenance of an adequate force on the spot. What the precise strength of this force should be, I cannot now undertake to define, but I am informed that probably a guard of not more than 150 or 200 men would be fully sufficient. I have to request that you will take an early opportunity of considering the strength and organisation of a police force such as would enable Her Majesty's Government to provide for these objects and to remove all troops from Perak as soon as possible.

The Residents will naturally render assistance in the organising of this police force, which will be under their orders and responsible to them, and they will periodically transmit to the Governor of the Straits Settlements a Report detailing the numbers, employment and character of the body, which the Governor will in turn forward to the Secretary of State with careful comments from himself. The force will be paid, as far as is practicable, out of the funds of the Province, and the appointments to it will be made by the Secretary of State. It is a question deserving careful consideration how far in the composition of this body the Foreign element should be allowed to have any large proportions. On the one hand it may be desirable that it should not appear to the Malays to be that of a dominant power imposed on them from without; on the other a force drawn from beyond the Peninsula may be found more reliable. You will at once carefully consider and report on this subject.

Looking to the necessarily tentative character of this body it should be clearly understood that such British officers as may be employed in it have no claim for pension. . . .

Although this letter was to afford general guidance, it related more particularly to Perak; and indeed the situation in the Negri Sembilan was then too obscure for any final decision to be made. It was not until 12 June that Lord Carnarvon received news of Rajah Antah's surrender with Jervois's comment: 'I have seen him and he engages to remain quiet.' Antah actually gave himself up to the Sultan of Selangor on 9 May 1876, thus preparing the way for a settlement involving his recognition as one in fact of the 'chiefs of sufficient capacity and enlightenment' upon whom Carnarvon relied for maintaining the future peace. Antah and his immediate followers were sent to Johore, news of their arrival there reaching the Governor on 5 June, who reported as follows on Antah's visit (on the following day) to Singapore:

On the 6th instant, Tunku Antar came to see me accompanied by two nephews. The information which I had received that he had been wounded turns out to be incorrect. Tunku Antar is a proud truculent looking character, and apparently possesses much determination. My interview with him, however, was very satisfactory.

He promised that he would settle down peacefully in Johore, and, at my request, the Maharajah, who was present at the interview, consented to give him and his people every facility for living comfortably in that state. Tunku Antar assured me that it was now desired to be friendly with the British Government and that he had done his best to induce the Datu of Muar, the Dato Jumpole, the Datu of Terrachee, the Datu of Gunong Passir, the Datu of Eenas, and Baginda Tan Mas (whom he named as now being the leader of the disaffected) to come in, but that he had not been successful in persuading them to do so. . . .[1]

No final solution of the Negri Sembilan problem was yet in sight and it was some time before Jervois realized that Ahmat had nothing like the support enjoyed by Antah. In the meanwhile, Lord Carnarvon

[1] S.S. No. 216, 7 June 1876.

called a halt to any more ambitious schemes, defining future policy, and especially placing bounds to it, in his dispatch of 19 August, which read as follows:

Carnarvon to Jervois.

Downing Street.
August 19, 1876.

Sir,

I have to acknowledge the receipt of your despatches, of the numbers and dates noted in the margin.

2. Two have reference to the late disturbances in those Malay States which are adjacent to Sungei Ujong, and to the policy which you recommend should be adopted for their future government under British protection, the first having been written before you received my telegram of the 29th April, in which I informed you that I was not prepared to sanction any line of policy which would involve the British Government in the government or protection of these States; the second, written after the receipt of that telegram, being merely in further elucidation of the plan which you had already submitted to me.

3. The plan, as I collect from your despatches, may shortly be stated as follows:—

4. That finding it impossible to retain Datu Sultan as Yam Tuan Besar, your proposal is that Rajah Ahmat should be placed as Malay Captain, apparently a new designation, over Sri Menanti, Ulu Moar, and Jumpole, and that these States should be placed under British protection, with a British Resident Agent, leaving Johole, Rambow, and Jellabu under their present Datus, who you say are friendly to British interests, and with whom we might conclude treaties framed in order to secure their proper government and to protect them from becoming a refuge for criminals and bad characters. Sungei Ujong you propose should remain as at present under British protection, and supported by the presence of a Resident, leaving the remaining States, as you anticipate would be the case, to place themselves under Rajah Ahmat.

5. I may here observe, that although you state that Rajah Ahmat would be acceptable to the people over whom you propose to place him, it is not clear in what way you anticipate he would be able to clear the country of freebooters who infest it, or maintain order or protect the person of the Resident, unless indeed troops are to be permanently stationed at certain points or a powerful police force organized such as is proposed for Perak.

6. I may also remark, that the proposed proclamation, of which you enclose a draft, appears to be open to the same objections as those which I felt it my duty to make respecting the conduct of affairs in Perak subsequent to the Pangkore engagement.

7. As Malacca is bounded by Sungei Ujong, which is quiet, and by Rambow, Johole, and Moar, States said to be adequately governed by their existing Datus, who are not therefore to be displaced, I do not clearly

understand how there can be dangers on the frontier of Malacca from free-booters coming down through these well governed States from the highlands of Sri Menanti, Jumpole, and Ulu Moar, or why it should be necessary in order to secure our frontier from the harassing incursions to which they may be liable, to adopt your proposal to extend the responsibility of the Colonial Government by taking under British protection these three States, governed by Rajah Ahmat, by the appointment of a Resident to advise and assist him.

8. You will, subsequently to the date of your despatches, have received mine of the 1st of June, in which, after mature consideration, I made known to you the decisions at which Her Majesty's Government had arrived as to the policy to be pursued towards the native States generally; and as Her Majesty's Government are unwilling to depart from that policy or to allow any further extension of the system of Residents until they have had further experience of the working of those already established, I shall wish you to reconsider the general question of the policy to be pursued towards the nine States, in accordance with the views contained in my despatch above referred to.

9. I have received, with much satisfaction, your despatch reporting the surrender of that turbulent chief Rajah Antar, and I see no reason to doubt that you were right in accepting his offer to use his endeavour to induce the various other disaffected chiefs to come in; and I trust that you will now be able to make such satisfactory arrangements as will enable the Government to disentangle itself from further complications with these States beyond what we are involved in in the case of Sungie Ujong, where I am of opinion it will be necessary to maintain a British Resident.

10. In conclusion, I would impress upon you the necessity of adhering to a line of policy which will, as far as possible, avoid a further and especially an undefined and uncertain extension of our political responsibilities in the Malay Peninsula, as it cannot be doubted that for a long time to come the task of bringing those States with which we are connected by the presence of Residents into a state of peace and order, will tax the utmost resources of the Colonial Government.

Working to this new brief, Sir William Jervois was able to report in September 1876 that he had discussed the whole question with the chiefs and reached agreement with them.

The arrangement I have made with them is, that the states of Sri Menanti, Ulu Moar, Jumpole and Johole, together with the districts of Terrachee, Gunong Passir and Eenas, shall form a confederacy under an 'Eam Tuan', who will reside at Sri Menanti, each district and state being governed by its own Datu, under the 'Eam Tuan'. Sungei Ujong, Rambowe, and Jellabu will be independent States under their present rulers. . . . Moar will, as heretofore, be under Sultan Ali.[1]

[1] S.S. No. 429, 13 Dec. 1876.

Rajah Antah was not to become 'Yam Tuan Besar' over the Nine States but merely 'Yam Tuan' over four, with British protection extended only to Sungei Ujong.

Details of this compromise plan were submitted to Lord Carnarvon on 13 December, and his approval was conveyed in a dispatch dated 27 February 1877.

I have read your Despatch and its enclosures with great interest, and considering the complicated and difficult questions with which you have to deal, I agree with you in hoping that a simple as well as a satisfactory conclusion has been arrived at. I am the more persuaded to take this view because not only was your language in the negotiations and meetings with the chiefs judicious and conciliatory, but the agreement made with them on the 23rd of November appears to have been desired by both the chiefs and the people of the nine States concerned, and to have been unanimously entered into by them.

Its success will mainly depend on a right choice having been made in Tunku Antar as Eam Tuan of the Confederation. It is desirable that there should be a full and clear knowledge of the temper of the chiefs, the feeling of the people, the state of the country. . . .

Although Jervois's settlement of the western Malay States left Muar under the rule of the old Sultan Ali, that ruler died soon afterwards on 20 June, leaving a disputed succession. Colonel Anson (officer administering the Government at that time) invited the Maharajah of Johore to take charge of the territory until its fate should be decided. The Maharajah accepted this task with alacrity on 30 June 1877. Tunku Alam claimed the succession in a letter to Anson dated 4 July, and he was supported by Read. The result, however, of a visit paid by the Colonial Secretary to Muar in July was that the headmen of Muar decided that the Maharajah was in fact their proper ruler. Lord Carnarvon was rightly suspicious about the whole affair, warning Anson on 3 September that he was not to impose a ruler upon the disputed territory 'in order to reward political services'. There was renewed agreement, however, of the chiefs and headmen in October. Carnarvon still objected to the proposed annexation but went out of office while the question was still undecided. It was another Secretary of State, Sir Michael M. E. Hicks Beach, Bart., who uttered the last protest to a different governor, querying the propriety of all that had been done to favour the Maharajah of Johore's candidature. By then, however, the question had been settled and he could only conclude, on 20 April 1878, that 'I have no option but to acquiesce in what I trust is the true choice of the people of Muar'. True choice or not, the thing had been done, rounding off the process by which the whole of western Malaya was brought, at least indirectly, under British influence.

Neither Lord Carnarvon nor Sir William Jervois were in office by the time this last step was taken. Sir William's removal was brought about by a telegram from Lord Carnarvon, received on 13 February 1877, asking him to inspect fortifications in Australia. He agreed to do so and to leave for Australia on 2 April.[1] Colonel Anson left Penang on about 18 March so as to discuss policy with the Governor before taking over from him as Administrator. Anson was accordingly in Singapore when Jervois, whose wife and two daughters had already left for Europe, was told by the Colonial Office that he could not take his private secretary, Captain McCallum, R.E., to Australia. What followed is best told in Anson's words:

. . . he was much annoyed at the refusal, and said to me, 'Look here, Anson, I have a great mind to follow my family to England'. I said 'I don't know whether you care for the G. (he was a K.C.M.G.), because if you do, you will probably get it. Besides, the Government of South Australia is vacant on account of Cairns's health, and it is not unlikely it might be offered to you, in order that you might remain in Australia to see your recommendations regarding the fortifications carried out. Besides, if you do not go, you will see Colonel A.B.'s name mentioned, as having done the work, and then you will feel sorry you had not done it yourself'. He replied, 'I believe you are right' . . . and, as I had predicted, he was offered, and accepted, the Government of South Australia.

In a letter Sir William wrote to Anson from Government House, Melbourne, on 4 July, he said: 'When I embarked on board the *Normandy*, on the 3rd April last, and you took up the administration of the Straits Government, I had no more idea that I should become Governor of one of the Australian Colonies than that I should be appointed Emperor of the Chinese, but the sudden resignation of Cairns, and my presence in these parts, have resulted in my being deposited, for a few years, in South Australia. . . .'[2]

Whether Jervois expected the Australian governorship, as Anson asserts, or whether the offer took him by surprise, as he himself alleges, there are good reasons for supposing that his period in the Straits was in any case finished. His family had already gone and his inclination, when thwarted by the Colonial Office, was to return to

---

[1] Owing to 'a recent family bereavement' there was no farewell banquet for Sir William. *Straits Times*, 7 Apr. 1877.   [2] Anson, op. cit., p. 353.

England; not merely to stay where he was. And, granted that his ability was beyond question, Lord Carnarvon might well have feared that his continuance in the Straits would bring about too rapid an extension of British influence in the eastern States. These had been visited by Jervois when he first arrived (see p. 209 above) and he returned to them in 1876, indicating on his return the sort of interest which the Colonial Office wished, at that moment, to discourage. For talents such as his, Australia was clearly the place, with scope for energetic government but none for encroachment on foreign territory. In the Straits the immediate need was for a Governor who would do as he was told; preferably a man from the Colonial Office itself.

With the departure of Sir William Jervois a phase in Malayan history comes to an end. Another extensive territory had been added, for all practical purposes, to the British Empire. Still further extension was probable, but the next phase would be one, rather, of consolidation. Lord Stanley of Alderley, that persistent critic of colonial policy, pointed out in the House of Lords that the further development of the Malay States would depend upon the character of the Residents.

in order to succeed it will be necessary for the Noble Earl to appoint a higher class of men than those that have been hitherto employed: they must be directly responsible to himself and be independent of the Singapore Council and indifferent to the favour of the Singapore Press and mercantile body.[1]

The search for men of such high character was not to be wholly without success.

---

[1] Hansard, vol. ccxxx, June–July 1876, cols. 825–6.

APPENDIX A

Engagement entered into by the Chiefs of Perak at Pulo Pangkor.
Dated 20 January 1874

WHEREAS, a state of anarchy exists in the Kingdom of Perak owing to the want of settled government in the Country, and no efficient power exists for the protection of the people and for securing to them the fruits of their industry, and

Whereas, large numbers of Chinese are employed and large sums of money invested in Tin mining in Perak by British subjects and others residing in Her Majesty's Possessions, and the said mines and property are not adequately protected, and piracy, murder and arson are rife in the said country, whereby British trade and interests greatly suffer, and the peace and good order of the neighbouring British Settlements are sometimes menaced, and

Whereas, certain Chiefs for the time being of the said Kingdom of Perak have stated their inability to cope with the present difficulties, and together with those interested in the industry of the country have requested assistance, and

Whereas, Her Majesty's Government is bound by Treaty Stipulations to protect the said Kingdom and to assist its rulers, now,

His Excellency Sir Andrew Clarke, K.C.M.G., C.B., Governor of the Colony of the Straits Settlements, in compliance with the said request, and with a view of assisting the said rulers and of effecting a permanent settlement of affairs in Perak, has proposed the following Articles of arrangement as mutually beneficial to the Independent Rulers of Perak, their subjects, the subjects of Her Majesty, and others residing in or trading with Perak, that is to say:

I. *First*. That the Rajah Muda Abdullah be recognised as the Sultan of Perak.

II. *Second*. That the Rajah Bandahara Ismail, now acting Sultan, be allowed to retain the title of Sultan Muda with a pension and a certain small Territory assigned to him.

III. *Third*. That all the other nominations of great Officers made at the time the Rajah Bandahara Ismail received the regalia be confirmed.

IV. *Fourth*. That the power given to the Orang Kayah Mantri over Larut by the late Sultan be confirmed.

V. *Fifth*. That all Revenues be collected and all appointments made in the name of the Sultan.

VI. *Sixth*. That the Sultan receive and provide a suitable residence for a British Officer to be called Resident, who shall be accredited to his Court, and whose advice must be asked and acted upon on all questions other than those touching Malay Religion and Custom.

VII. *Seventh.* That the Governor of Larut shall have attached to him as Assistant Resident, a British Officer acting under the Resident of Perak, with similar power and subordinate only to the said Resident.

VIII. *Eighth.* That the cost of these Residents with their Establishments be determined by the Government of the Straits Settlements and be a first charge on the Revenues of Perak.

IX. *Ninth.* That a Civil list regulating the income to be received by the Sultan, by the Bandahara, by the Mantri, and by the other Officers be the next charge on the said Revenue.

X. *Tenth.* That the collection and control of all Revenues and the general administration of the Country be regulated under the advice of these Residents.

XI. *Eleventh.* That the Treaty under which the Pulo Dinding and the islands of Pangkor were ceded to Great Britain having been misunderstood and it being desirable to re-adjust the same, so as to carry into effect the intention of the Framers thereof, it is hereby declared that the Boundaries of the said Territory so ceded shall be rectified as follows, that is to say:

From Bukit Sigari, as laid down in the Chart Sheet No. 1, Straits of Malacca, a tracing of which is annexed, marked A, in a straight line to the sea, thence along the sea coast to the south, to Pulo Katta on the West, and from Pulo Katta a line running North East about five miles, and thence North to Bukit Sigari.

XII. *Twelfth.* That the Southern watershed of the Krean River, that is to say, the portion of land draining into that River from the South be declared British Territory, as a rectification of the Southern Boundary of Province Wellesley. Such Boundary to be marked out by Commissioners; one named by the Government of the Straits Settlements, and the other by the Sultan of Perak.

XIII. *Thirteenth.* That on the cessation of the present disturbances in Perak and the re-establishment of peace and amity among the contending factions in that Country, immediate measures under the control and supervision of one or more British Officers shall be taken for restoring as far as practicable the occupation of the Mines, and the possession of Machinery etc., as held previous to the commencement of these disturbances, and for the payment of compensation for damages, the decision of such officer or officers shall be final in such case.

XIV. *Fourteenth.* The Mantri of Larut engages to acknowledge as a debt due by him to the Government of the Straits Settlements, the charges and expenses incurred by this investigation, as well as the charges and expenses to which the Colony of the Straits Settlements and Great Britain have been put or may be put by their efforts to secure the tranquility of Perak and the safety of trade.

The above Articles having been severally read and explained to the undersigned who having understood the same, have severally agreed to and accepted them as binding on them and their Heirs and Successors.

. This done and concluded at Pulo Pangkor in the British Possessions, this Twentieth day of January, in the year of the Christian Era, one thousand eight hundred and seventy-four.

Executed before me,

ANDREW CLARKE

Governor, Commander-in-Chief

and Vice-Admiral of the Straits

Settlements

Chop of the Sultan of Perak

   „   „ „ Bandahara of Perak

   „   „ „ Tumongong of Perak

   „   „ „ Mantri of Perak

   „   „ „ Shahbander of Perak

   „   „ „ Raja Mahkota of Perak

   „   „ „ Laxamana of Perak

   „   „ „ Datoh Sa'gor

APPENDIX B

Agreement entered into by certain Chiefs of the Nine States on 23 November 1876

WE, the undersigned, have appeared before His Excellency the Governor of the Straits Settlements, with a view to making an agreement for securing the peace and tranquility of the countries over which we govern, or which we represent. We give this paper as a token of our good faith, and promise as follows:

2. We desire to live in peace in our own States, and to recognise Tuanko Antar as Eam Tuan of Sri Menanti, having authority over Sri Menanti, Johole, Moar, Jompole, Terachi, Gunong Passir, and Eenas.

3. We promise that we will in no way molest the neighbouring States, Rumbowe, Sunghie Ujong and Jellabu, who do not desire to form part of the confederation under the Eam Tuan Besar, and it is understood that these three States are wholly distinct.

4. We promise that peaceful persons, whether Malays or Chinese or others, desirous of trading in our countries shall have full liberty to do so, and shall be unmolested.

5. We further express our regret at the late disturbances which have happened in the Nine States, and we promise that those persons who have been friendly to the British Government during or since these disturbances shall be in no way molested.

6. And we agree that in case of any dispute or difficulty arising among our States which we are unable to settle, we will refer for advice to His Highness the Maharajah of Johore.

7. We agree that from this time the Eam Tuan will use no other chop than one worded as follows:

'Alwathick Birabil Ghafoor, Eam Tuan Tunku Antar Sri Menanti ebu Almurham Eam Tuan Rajah Radin, Sonat, 1293'

except on the present occasion, the chop not being ready.

Mark of Datu Jumpole
Mark of Datu Terrachi
Mark of representative of Datu Gunong Passir
Mark of representative of Datu Eenas
Chop of Datu Moar
Chop of Datu Johole
Chop of Tunku Antar

APPENDIX C

Despatch No. 62

Singapore,
10th February, 1876.

My Lord,

In despatch No. 218 of the 10th December 1875 Your Lordship, whilst asking for explanations, expresses strong opinions on some points connected with the course of action which I considered it necessary to adopt with reference to the affairs of the state of Perak, as communicated in my despatch No. 291 dated 16th October last.

2. In expressing the opinions which Your Lordship had then formed on the subject, you stated that I made a serious departure from the Policy which had been sanctioned by H.M. Government, and which, until you received the news of the murder of Mr. Birch, you still fully believed to be in force in Perak as well as in other neighbouring states. You also remark that upon that change of policy, disastrous consequences ensued, and that it was the signal for resistance and attack. Your Lordship proceeds to bring to my notice some extracts from despatches, with a view of showing that the policy of H.M. Government was to appoint British Officers as Residents, whose duty it would be solely to advise the Native Rulers in matters relating to the Government of their respective states.

3. In order that a fair judgement may be formed as to the nature of the change which I made with respect to the administration of affairs in Perak, I beg that Your Lordship will refer firstly to the Pangkore Treaty itself, and to the injunctions laid down by Your Lordship with reference thereto, and, secondly, will permit me to draw therefrom the deductions which under the circumstances which I shall detail, it seems to me necessarily follow as to the course of action which it was imperative to adopt in order to give effect to the engagements contained in the Treaty and to your strongly expressed injunction, that the Sultan and Chiefs of Perak were to be informed, that Her Majesty's Government would look to the exact fulfilments of their pledges and would hold responsible those of whom had violated the engagement which they had solemnly agreed upon.

The extracts which you quote from despatches addressed to me in July last, more than 18 months after the Pangkore Engagement was entered into, and 2 months after Sir A. Clarke had left the Government, could not, I considered, be held to enjoin me to take the retrograde step of reversing the course of action which, under that engagement and under your strict injunctions, had been adopted by my Predecessor.

4. I believe that I can show Your Lordship that the policy as pursued since the date of the Pangkore Treaty has been really not at all what you

seem to have considered it to have been, and that you are under a mis-apprehension as to the line of action which you have approved, and does not do justice to that which you now condemn. The step which I have taken appears to you to be a great one in advance because you have believed that a policy of advice only was in operation, whereas, in fact, from the commencement of British intervention the Government of the Malayan states to which British Residents have been accredited, has been in greater or less degree, exercised by those Officers themselves.

5. Even if it were ever contemplated by this Govt. that the Residents should confine their attention to merely giving advice, it has been found from the very commencement that such a course has been impossible.

6. There has been really no ruler, neither in Perak, Salangore or Sungie Ujong, in each of which states we have had Residents, who ever has had the power to carry out the advice of the Resident.

7. The power of the recognised ruler has been more or less nominal, and any of the petty chiefs and usurpers of local power could set this authority at defiance with impunity.

True, the Resident as a matter of course always would have advised the Ruler that it is his duty to preserve peace and order in his state, to maintain a pure dispensation of justice regardless of the rank of criminals, to place the collections of Revenue on a satisfactory footing and generally to secure good administration. The Rulers, however, would have been powerless, even had they been willing to carry out this advice, and the very fact of their attempting to do so would have raised up enemies amongst the Chiefs, whose unjustifiable practices have been denounced, and amongst robber bands whose source of livelihood depends upon the maladministration of the Country.

8. Under these circumstances the Resident has not only had to give advice but also to render active assistance and take the control of public affairs. He has had to organize an armed force, to take into his own hands the collection of the revenues, to listen to all complaints made, to punish evildoers, to repress armed gangs of robbers and murderers, to apprehend criminals, and to see that justice was done.

9. When I arrived here in May last, I found that each Resident was practically administering the Govt. of the state to which he was accredited and I certainly always considered that this was understood to be the case in the Colonial Office, as it certainly was by every one out here, from the very commencement of the Residential system.

10. These remarks apply to all the states to which Residents have been accredited, and, in the case of Perak, the necessity for this course was considerably enhanced by the anarchy in the country caused by Ismail's claims, which led to a division of parties and by the weak obstinate be-haviour of Sultan Abdullah to whom a Resident had been appointed. I will discuss hereafter this question of the division of parties and in what manner it affected the position of the Resident.

11. I would now beg to point out to you that, in addition to the general considerations which as I have shown in para. 6, 7 and 8, rendered the Residential system as a system of advice, if such were ever contemplated, a practical impossibility, that the very terms of the Pangkore Treaty contained the elements of control, and that a system of virtual administration in Perak, either covertly or openly, was but the logical sequence of the terms of the Treaty, especially when regarded in connection with those considerations before alluded to.

12. Upon turning to the Treaty, we find that all revenues were to be collected in the name of the Sultan, but that the collection and control of such revenues and the general administration of the country were to be regulated under the advice of the Resident, and it is stated in the Treaty itself that this advice 'must be acted upon' by the Sultan. Such an engagement to which the Sultan and Chiefs of Perak were held bound virtually threw the Govt. of the country into the hands of the Resident, and committed Her Majesty's Govt. to this policy.

13. I may remark that this was pointed out to Your Lordship at the time in the House of Lords, by Lord Stanley of Alderley, when he said that he 'felt it to be his duty to warn H.M. Govt. against giving its sanction to the plans of the Straits Govt. by which it would not only be entering into equivocal and entangling engagements, but embarking in a course which must inevitably lead to the invasion and conquest of the whole of the Malay Peninsula. The object was in reality to impose upon the Sultan of Perak two British Officials to be called Resident and Assistant Resident to be paid out of the Perak Revenues and with powers which would make them the virtual rulers of the country'. Now I would beg to observe that although Your Lordship, when replying, reminded Lord Stanley that the Residents had not been imposed upon the Sultan, but that they had been appointed at the distinct request and entreaty of the Rajahs to whose courts they had been sent, Your Lordship did not contradict the very grave assertion made by him that the engagements entered into would make the Residents the virtual rulers of the country.

14. That it was early recognised by my predecessor that a system of mere advice was impossible is shown by the following extract from the instructions issued to Mr. Birch on the 26th October 1874 prior to his taking up the duties of Resident, from which you will observe that the power therein conferred upon him is not at all compatible with such system.

'The subject of the future revenue relations of Perak remains. His Excellency in the absence of any reliable information on this important matter is not now prepared to give you any distinct instructions, further than to allow the existing system to go on when not of such an irregular character as to require immediate alteration, but you will use your best exertions to put down by force if necessary, all unlawful exactions of whatever nature, so as to secure that whatever revenue is collected shall be for the state alone, and that freebooters, leviers of blackmail, and Chiefs pretending authority to levy duties may be hindered in their extortions, and all revenue collected may be paid into the General Treasury of the country.'

15. Nor were such instructions confined to the Resident accredited to Perak. I find that, in the case of Salangore also, Mr. Davidson received such instructions as virtually authorized him to administer the affairs of that state. The following extracts bear upon this point:

'His Excellency desires that you will proceed at once to Klang where you will establish yourself, at first making such arrangement for your personal accommodation as the nature of the case will admit of, and proceeding as soon as possible to organize a Resident's guard and Police of such force as you may think proper. His Excellency desires that you will at once publish notices far and wide, recalling all fugitives, promising them protection and taking special steps for having such of them as possessed property restored to the possession of that property and providing them all with waste land to cultivate if they wish to cultivate. The system of collecting revenue on imports should occupy your early attention.

'You will send in a regular monthly report of progress and a monthly statement showing the revenue and expenses of the country which you will take under your special charge being assisted by such officers, clerks etc. as may be sanctioned by His Excellency on your representation after arrival at Klang. A steam launch will be provided for your use at once to enable you to visit the several places of trade and population in Salangore and His Excellency desires that you will take an early opportunity of seeing the Sultan of Salangore at Laroot, and that you will enter upon such relations with His Highness as will enable you in gaining his confidence to be of real service in securing the peace and prosperity of his country.'

16. Your Lordship will observe that these instructions are so couched that the Resident became the Agent of the Governor rather than the Adviser of the Sultan and Viceroy, in fact I may say, that the latter position was never taken up and that the entire control of the affairs of this state of Salangore has been concentrated in the Resident.

17. Upon referring to para. 10 of your despatch under acknowledgement you stated that you have always understood that the British Officers confined themselves to advising and assisting the Native Authorities, and that until the receipt of the intelligence of Mr. Birch's death, Your Lordship fully believed that such a system was in force in Perak as well as in the neighbouring territories.

With all deference I think that you have misconceived the position of affairs, for both from despatches and reports which were forwarded to you before my arrival in the Colony, it appears to me to be clearly shewn that the position which the Resident assumed towards the States was not merely that of an adviser. I will confine the following remarks to the State of Perak.

18. In Sir A. Clarke's despatch to Your Lordship dated December 30th

1874, he pointed out that Mr. Birch was in every way eminently qualified for undertaking the task of initiating all the practical measures essential for the future administration of a semi-civilized country. He further states that Mr. Birch possessed in a remarkable degree untiring physical energy and endurance of infinite value to one whose duties will necessarily entail upon him constant exposure to climate and weather.

Assuming that it was the duty of the Resident practically to take upon himself the administration of the affairs of the country, such qualifications were doubtless invaluable for the work which had to be done, and which had been more or less done, in all the states to which Residents have been appointed, but they are not the qualifications for which an officer would be selected if he were only intended to be a passive adviser.

19. But it is to Mr. Birch's report on Perak dated 2nd April and forwarded to you with despatch No. 121 of 26th April 1875, that I would beg especially to call Your Lordship's attention as shewing that, in his position as Resident and nominal adviser, Mr. Birch really performed all those duties which in para. 8 of this despatch I have stated must be performed by a Resident when the Ruler is powerless, even if willing, to carry out the advice tendered to him.

From para. 2 and 74, you will observe that after having made the acquaintance of the Sultan Mr. Birch was travelling in various parts of Perak for some five months. In para. 11, there is not mention of any advice tendered to the Sultan, but a hope is expressed that when the Sultan has a new house that he would give up opium-smoking and think for himself.

In para. 16, 17, 18, he mentions that the complaints of illegal fining and and oppression which came before *him* (Mr. Birch) were on the decrease. In para. 19 and 20 he mentions that *he* had reorganized the system of collecting the imports and exports and that it was now under the supervision of one of *his* officers who kept the accounts.

In para. 27 he states that *he* had submitted a scale of duties to the Governor who had approved of the same. In para. 30 and 31, he states that *he* hopes to have a short code of laws ready for the Datus, and that the Datus and Sultans in many cases referred the ryots to *him* for the settlement of complaints.

In para. 40 he states *he* is unable to deal with the appointments of Panghulus and Datus until he had become personally acquainted with the topography of the country. In para. 62, 72, and 73, he states that *he* intended or proposed to have Police stations at various points.

Finally in para. 90 he states that the *British Administration* in Laroot has been very successful.

20. Now, My Lord, I would beg to observe that, although this report admits of no doubt that the Resident (backed by the terms of the Pangkore engagement which as I have stated in para. 12 virtually threw the Govt. of the country into his hands) had assumed powers far beyond that of an adviser and counsellor, Your Lordship, in acknowledging the receipt of the

report states that you had read it with much interest and that you trusted that peace and prosperity will be still further developed.

21. I certainly always considered, as I have stated in para. 9, that the Colonial Office understood that the relation of the Resident to the Ruler was far beyond that of a mere adviser, and I was strengthened in that belief by the apparent acquiescence of your Lordship in reports such as that to which I have referred. When, therefore, I arrived here and found, as I have stated in para. 9, that each Resident was practically administering the Govt. of the State to which he was accredited, I considered that I should only be carrying out the views of the Colonial Office in supporting such system and endeavouring, if possible, to bring it to a successful issue. I would beg to point out to you that this system was not introduced by me, but that I found it in operation, and, as I have explained, I considered it, under the circumstances of the case, a logical consequence of our intervention.

22. Soon after my arrival here, I recognized that the success of the system as it existed was, amongst other conditions, dependent upon the amenability of the Ruler. When the Resident and the central authority acted in harmony, and when the views of the former were cordially supported by the latter, comparative success accrued. But when their mutual relations were distinguished by disunion and discord rather than by harmony and unanimity and when the central authority would not submit to be strengthened by the moral and material force which the Resident could bring to bear, failure, either total or partial, was the inevitable result.

23. Now I beg you to observe that, on my arrival here I found that the success of the Residential system in the states of Salangore and Perak presented a very marked contrast. In both these states, as well as in that of Sungie Ujong, the Residents had the conduct of affairs in their own hands, but different results had ensued, for the reason that the relations between the Resident and the Ruler were marked respectively by the opposite features which the system is capable of presenting and which I have explained in the previous paragraph.

24. In Salangore as you remark in para. 15 of your despatch under acknowledgement, comparative success had attended the system. This is to be accounted for by the fact that Tunku Kudin, Viceroy of Salangore, recognizing that his position as ruler of a Malay state is that which I have described the position of such rulers to be generally (in paragraph 7) has trusted implicitly in Mr. Davidson, the Resident, and has, together with the Sultan who is also amenable, immediately ratified any measures proposed by Mr. Davidson, knowing that such measures were for the good of the country. Mr. Davidson has felt himself obliged to take all the duties of the Administration of the country as stated in para. 8 into his own hands but in this also Tunku Kudin gives him all the assistance he can and co-operates with him to the utmost of his ability.

25. But, I would, however, observe that this condition of affairs in

Salangore does not possess the elements of permanency. In the event of anything happening to the central native authority there is a possibility that his successor would not follow in his footsteps and would not submit to be guided by the decisions of the Resident. In that case, a state of things would ensue somewhat similar to that which I found existing in Perak. And here I may remark that Mr. Davidson has had considerable difficulties to contend with in Salangore and that he has been successful in putting down and preventing disturbance by the cordial support he had received from the Viceroy whilst acting in his name.

26. I have previously stated that the necessity for a British Resident adopting a course of control was considerably enhanced in Perak by the division of parties in that state and by the fact that the treaty of Pangkore itself contained the elements of control, insomuch that the Sultan was bound thereby to act upon the Resident's advice in matters concerning the general administration of the country and the collection of revenue and, indeed, in all matters except such as referred to Malay religion and custom. A Proclamation had been issued in consequence of your despatch of the 4th September holding inviolable the engagements which the Sultan and Chiefs made at Pangkore. However, notwithstanding these engagements to which Sultan Abdullah had solemnly agreed, and for the keeping of which he was held responsible by Her Majesty's Govt., I found that he was thwarting the Resident, and that, in consequence, the conduct of public business was rendered well nigh impossible.

In fact the relations between Abdullah and the Resident were marked by disunion and discord. The situation was rendered still more difficult by the position which was assumed by Ex-Sultan Ismail in the matter.

27. Under the Pangkore Treaty, Ismail was dethroned and Abdullah was recognized as Sultan. A Resident was attached to the Court of Abdullah and an Assistant Resident was appointed for Laroot. Ismail, who was not present at Pangkore did not assent to the arrangements, and not unnaturally so. Rightly or wrongly, he had been elected Sultan by a certain number of Chiefs, and in virtue of such election, held the Regalia of the country in his possession. He was acknowledged as Sultan throughout the greater part of the country, extending from Passir Sala on the Perak River, upwards.

28. Although Abdullah, therefore, the nominal ruler of the lower portion of the River, was the rightful heir to the throne, according to the principles of Perak succession, and although we recognized him as such at Pangkore, it by no means followed that the deposed Ismail would acquiesce in the terms of an engagement which would deprive him of the important power which he possessed in the upper country, especially as that engagement was entered into by his rival Abdullah, and by Chiefs, many of whom had previously installed him (Ismail) as Sultan. In my opinion it seems unreasonable to suppose that Ismail would have surrendered his power under such an engagement in which he had not even been consulted, yet I am

given to understand that the idea was entertained at Pangkore. Your Lordship will observe from letter to Ismail, p. 157 of Blue Book, that it was assumed that he would at once peaceably surrender the Regalia. It appears also from para. 111 of enclosure 7 despatch No. 43, dated February 24th 1874, that the new Sultan was to send to Ismail for the Regalia and that the Governor promised to attend the ceremony of Coronation, and thus certify to the people of Perak and the surrounding states that the Kingdom of Perak was finally and peacefully settled under Sultan Abdullah.

29. To my mind, it admits of no argument that such an engagement could scarcely have failed to have exasperated Ismail. It appears to me that, with the obstinacy and dogged determination, which recent events have proved he possesses, added to his sense of wounded dignity, he would have at once decided not to yield the important position which he held in the upper country, as long as he could avoid doing so. He must have regarded Abdullah as well as those chiefs who supported him, with very bitter feelings. He must also have looked upon the Resident, the Agent of the British Govt. who had supplanted him in favor of his rival Abdullah, with peculiar animosity, and must have been anxious for an opportunity to gratify his wounded pride.

30. But, even supposing Ismail had no personal feeling in the matter, the position of the Resident in Perak was a most peculiar one. It would be as well to review the situation under the most favourable circumstances and presume that Abdullah was as amenable to the counsels of the Resident, as is Tunku [Kudin] in Salangore and the Datu Klana in Sungie Ujong.

31. Even in that case, the Residential system as carried on in those states and as described in para. 24 could not have succeeded in Perak as it did in Salangore and Sungie Ujong, because Abdullah did not fill in Perak a similar position to that of the two rulers to whom I have referred and who are regarded, each in their respective states, as a central authority in whose name the Resident can carry on the administration of the country.

32. When Mr. Birch, who was appointed Resident with Abdullah some ten months after the Pangkore engagement had been entered upon, arrived in Perak, he found that Ismail, during this interval, had had time to strengthen his position and that there were practically two Sultans in Perak, each supported by a particular division of the country, as stated in para. 27 and that great jealousy existed between the people of the Ulu (up-country) and those of the Hiler (down country). Ismail, whose party outnumbered that of Abdullah, had never acknowledged Abdullah as Sultan, nor the engagement as a Treaty, by which he was bound, or even in which he was concerned. He also still retained possession of the Regalia, and, by so doing, secured the allegiance of a great many subjects who regarded such possession as symbolic of sovereignty, and without which, in the eyes of Malays, complete regal power could not be assumed.

33. Besides this dual head, Mr. Birch also found that from the weakness of the ruling powers the minor chiefs were more powerful in this state,

than in any other part of the Peninsula, and that, although owning nominal allegiance to one or other of the two Sultans, they were practically independent in their several districts, that they oppressed the ryots (many of whom were slave debtors) residing therein, and that they levied blackmail and illegal taxes on all who happened to pass through their particular district.

34. Thus, my Lord, you will otherwise observe that instead of having one central authority in Perak in whose name and through whose amehability all orders could be given and requisite reforms effected, two Sultans each antagonistic to the other, divided this central authority between them, the Sultan as recognised by us under the Pangkore Treaty, being the weaker of the two and powerless to act. Besides this dual head, a number of semi-independent Chiefs, over whom neither Sultan possessed any practical control, and who had thus to be dealt with directly, completed a division of authority which rendered the conduct of public business nearly impossible. I would here beg to remark that Your Lordship in your despatch of the 25th May last, to which you call my attention in para. 11 of the despatch under acknowledgement, appears to infer that there was a central authority in Perak, whereas, as I have just demonstrated, there was really no such authority through whom our influence could be exerted either in respect to the abolition of debt-slavery, which forms the subject of the despatch in question, or indeed to any other matter.

35. Such was the condition of affairs in which Mr. Birch found the State of Perak in November 1874, when he arrived to carry out a system which as stated in para. 12 committed us to the control of the country. One of the first duties of Mr. Birch was to impress upon the Sultan and chiefs that the treaty would be carried out in its entirety and that those who violated it would be held responsible for so doing.

I find that, on appointment, injunctions on this point were issued to Mr. Birch in the following terms:

'You will explain clearly to all, with whom you come into contact in Perak, that the terms of the Engagement have been approved by Her Majesty's Government in England and will be strictly enforced. On this subject a number of copies of a Proclamation recently issued here in English and Malay giving the effect of a despatch from the Secretary of State for the Colonies are sent to you for distribution where you think they will be useful, and you will clearly explain the meaning and effect of the language used by Lord Carnarvon in that despatch, so that there may be no misunderstanding on this subject.'

36. I have hitherto presumed that Abdullah was perfectly amenable to the counsels of the Resident, so that under the virtual control exercised by the latter, the district, over which Abdullah held sway, was progressing favourably. In that case there still remained for the Resident three important duties to perform.

(1) To induce Ismail to agree to the terms of the Pangkore engagement

and to surrender the Regalia to Abdullah who had been elected in his stead. Also to induce those chiefs who had not already signed the engagement to do so, in order that the whole state of Perak might come under the dominion of Abdullah and be brought to the same condition, and by the same means, as that portion of the country which was already held by him.

(2) To put an end to unlawful exactions and to hinder free-booters, leviers of blackmail and chiefs pretending authority, from indulging in their extortions, so that all the revenue could be paid into the general treasury of the state.

(3) To be especially careful that Your Lordship's injunctions were firmly carried out, and that the Chiefs who had signed the engagement were strictly held to the terms they solemnly agreed upon, to investigate any violation thereof, and to warn them of the consequence of such violation.

37. As regards the first point, Ismail, impelled doubtless by motives and feelings such as I have stated in para. 29 and recognizing that his position was even stronger than it was at the time of the Pangkore engagement, received Mr. Birch as the Agent of the British Govt. attached to Abdullah. An apparent civility, a well disguised courtesy of manner and a pretended acquiescence concealed a strength of purpose, a feeling of injury, and a stern resolution not to part with that which he had acquired. As intractable as he was civil, as obstinate as he was courteous, and as firm as he was seemingly acquiescent, he could not be induced by any persuasion or argument to adopt the decisions of the British Govt. nor to yield the high position which he occupied. His very ignorance and dependence upon his counsellors rendered him even still more difficult to deal with.

38. Notwithstanding, however, that the resistance made by Ismail was strictly passive in its nature, Mr. Birch found that, in the large district in which Ismail was acknowledged, he was unable in his capacity as Resident to initiate reforms and to effect changes in the name of a Sultan, who was not recognized therein as such, but who was rather regarded with jealousy and dislike. Nor could he do so in the name of the Ex-Sultan, for he would then have confirmed the position to which Ismail was aspiring and would have acted in opposition to the general purpose of the Pangkore engagement and to the expressed injunctions of Her Majesty's Govt. Nevertheless he had his duties as Resident to perform in this district, to repress disorder and to bring about a more settled state of things and this he had to endeavour to do without augmenting the jealousy which existed between the two parties.

39. It must, moreover, be borne in mind, that, in endeavouring to effect these objects, he found that the chiefs, although owning nominal allegiance to one or other of the two Sultans who divided the head authority between them, were semi-independent and had to be dealt with directly. Had the ruling power been a strong one, or had the Resident been able to act in the name of one central authority there is no doubt that this semi-independence would have disappeared.

40. By taking up the position assigned to him by his instructions, Mr. Birch was enabled to do much towards carrying out the second duty which as Resident he had to perform and to his credit, I may say that in the 12 months during which he held the post of Resident illegal extortion and exaction and the levying of the blackmail greatly diminished. Now although the ryots could not fail to recognise the protection which they gained from the presence of a British Officer, and in the course adopted by him in putting down extortion and blackmail a relief from a.burden against which they dared not complain, the chiefs on the other hand doubtless regarded such proceedings as encroachments on the power which they have exercised.

It is not to be wondered at, that they were loath to surrender their power, and that Mr. Birch in virtue of the instructions issued to him was often obliged on failure of persuasion, to have recourse to threats of force. Nor is it to be wondered at, that in consequence, Mr. Birch was regarded by some of the chiefs whose power he had curbed, with ill feeling and distrust.

41. And to none of these chiefs did the new order of things prove probably more distasteful than to the Maharajah Lela. He had not been concerned in the Pangkore Treaty, and holding as head of the 'eight' a most important position in the state, he doubtless felt annoyed and slighted that other chiefs of Perak had entered into this engagement without consulting him. For 10 months, however, British intervention, confined as it was to Laroot, was not brought to bear upon him. Impelled doubtless by feelings of annoyance and pique, he had, during this time, the opportunity of cementing a friendship with Ismail, although in February 1872 he had been one of the chiefs who addressed a letter to the Governor, urging the claims of Abdullah to the throne.

42. I have twice mentioned that Ismail's position was stronger in November 1874, than it was at the time of the Pangkore engagement. This is mainly due to the fact that no step was taken to establish Abdullah in his position nor to strengthen that position by the presence of a Resident for some 10 months. Had the Pangkore engagement been immediately acted upon and had Abdullah then received the moral support of a Resident, perhaps many subsequent difficulties would never have arisen, whilst, as it was, the delay which ensued detracted from the solemn importance with which the engagement should have been regarded by the chiefs who had contracted it. During this interval, the Bandahara, the Tumonggong and the Mantri, neither of whom had been very warm supporters of Abdullah, practically abandoned the cause of Abdullah and espoused that of Ismail, whilst the Datu Sagor wavered between the two Sultans. Rajah Muda Yusuf, who until 1874 had never even met Ismail, whilst declaring himself to be the rightful Sultan, repudiated Abdullah and associated himself with Ismail. There remained therefore but the Laxamana, the Shahbandar and the Rajah Makota as supporters of Abdullah.

43. Such was the position of the chiefs as regards the nominal allegiance

which they owed to the two heads who, together, constituted the central authority. I may remark that such allegiance did not necessitate active support, in fact during recent events Rajah Muda Yusuf has actively supported us, and the Bandahara, the Tumonggong and the Mantri have afforded us assistance in more or less degree.

44. Ismail's position was still strengthened by the declared allegiance of the Maharajah Lela. Living as the latter did at Passir Sala, the point of division of the upper and lower districts, he was the first to feel the presence and power of the Resident when British intervention was brought to bear in Perak. He also doubtless felt some contempt for the position of Abdullah supported as he was by these chiefs, each of whom were inferior in rank to himself. He probably regarded Mr. Birch as an intruder and as an agent of Abdullah, and, no doubt he viewed the abolition of illegal taxes and blackmail as practised at Passir Sala with exasperated feelings. Exasperation gave rise to insolence, and Mr. Birch, who, from the Residency at Bandar Bahru, could always keep a watch over his actions, experienced greater trouble and obstruction from him than from any other chief in Perak. I shall allude again to this point when considering Your Lordship's observation that my proceedings in Perak were the signal for resistance and attack.

45. In para. 40 I have stated that Mr. Birch was in a considerable measure successful in putting down illegal extortion and exaction in Perak, and that he was, in consequence, regarded with ill feeling and distrust by the chiefs whose power he had curbed. But any resistance to his proceedings was, as a rule, similar to that offered by Ismail, in his relations with the Resident, viz. passive.

This was probably due more to the jealousy which existed between the several chiefs and their followers, and the almost impossibility of their uniting for a common object, rather than to any individual feeling in the matter.

Arrangements had not been perfected for indemnifying the principal Chiefs and rulers for loss of power and profit, and many of them no doubt feared that British intervention which brought gain to the ryots meant loss to them. At the same time they probably did not individually feel themselves in a position openly to oppose the reformatory measures effected by the Resident.

46. It is to be observed that the Resident could only carry out the measures necessary for the good government of the country in the name of Abdullah and with his consent and approval. Now as I have mentioned in para. 32, Abdullah was not recognised as Sultan in the Ulu, and any measure introduced therein, in his name, had naturally the effect of increasing the jealousy between the two parties and of encountering opposition from Ex-Sultan Ismail and his chiefs. Mr. Birch was naturally anxious to carry out such measures in the Ulu as is shown by some of the extracts from his report to which I have alluded in para. 19 but, at the same time,

it would have been a task of great difficulty, and one in which the name of Abdullah would have had to be used as sparingly as possible.

47. Thus, even had Abdullah, as hitherto presumed, been perfectly amenable to the counsels of the Resident, you will observe that the division of the parties in the state of Perak was fatal to the successful working of the Residential system as carried on in the states of Salangore and Sungie Ujong, in whose name the Residents can practically carry on the administration of affairs. In Perak, such action was rendered impossible by the absence of this necessary central authority, one division of the country, and that the most considerable one, recognizing neither the Sultan as elected at Pangkore, nor his authority to sanction the introduction of the reforms and changes, necessary for the improvement of the country and the welfare of its inhabitants.

48. And here, I would observe that the failure of the Residential system in Perak so far as it arose from the division of parties, was quite independent of any action or general line of conduct of either the Resident or of Abdullah, but that it arose purely from the fact of there being this division of parties, with their mutual jealousy, distrust and antagonism. This disturbing element was peculiar to the state of Perak and it is therefore, I submit, unfair to make a comparison of the working of the Residential system in this state with the working of that system in Salangore and Sungie Ujong, where success has been due to the amenability of the central authority as previously explained.

49. In the para. to which I have just referred, I have endeavoured to explain to Your Lordship in general terms, that when the relations of the Resident and the Ruler were not distinguished by perfect harmony, failure, either total or partial, was certain to ensue. In order to show the fatal effects of the division of central authority in Perak, I have presumed that the Sultan, as elected at Pangkore, was amenable to the decisions of the Resident, but upon descending from hypothesis to facts, Your Lordship will recognise that this second disturbing element of want of harmony between the Resident and the Ruler was certain to bring about a complete collapse of the Residential system in Perak.

Extremely difficult as it would have been to have brought this system to a successful issue in this state, even had Abdullah been perfectly amenable, the difficulty became an impossibility when Abdullah adopted a position antagonistic to the Counsels of the Resident.

50. The difficulty of conducting public business was not, therefore, confined to the Ulu, it was wellnigh impossible to effect progress or to establish reforms, even in the Hilir, on account of the duplicity and folly of Abdullah, who instead of uniting with the Resident for the public good, took every opportunity to thwart him in his endeavour. The schemes matured by Mr. Birch for the improvement of the country and to which I have referred in para. 46 required Abdullah's signature or chop in order that the Resident might be vested with the necessary powers for carrying them into effect.

But Abdullah, with the intractability which has distinguished him throughout, would not ratify these schemes, but postponed doing so, upon the most frivolous excuse, and shewed a general desire to break all the engagements into which he had entered at Pangkore.

51. These and many other matters which I found existing in Perak on my arrival here in May last, I reported to Your Lordship in detail in my previous despatch No. 291 of the 16th October last. In my despatch No. 298, transmitted by the same mail as the despatch to which I have just referred, I stated the difference that existed in the working of the Residential system in the states of Salangore and Sungie Ujong, as distinguished from Perak, and I based my despatch No. 291 upon the unsatisfactory condition of affairs which I found existing in Perak, and therein stated the measures which I had adopted with a view of obviating the difficulties experienced in carrying out the Residential system in that state.

52. As mentioned in para. 9, I certainly thought that the relations which existed between Resident and Ruler in the states to which the Residential system had been applied were understood at the Colonial Office and met with general approval. It was not until I received Your Lordship's despatch No. 218 that I perceived that you had misconceived the position which the Residents have occupied, and have been obliged to occupy, in the Native States of the Malayan Peninsula. I have therefore endeavoured to make you acquainted with these relations and with the difficulties by which the working of the Residential system in Perak was surrounded.

53. And here, I beg leave to take exception to Your remark in para. 2 of your despatch under acknowledgement, that the policy as inaugurated in 1874 in the Malay States was of the nature of an experiment. My Lord, British intervention once entered upon, there could, I submit, be no withdrawal until, yielding in course of time to British Influence, these states like that of Johore, possessed a Govt. founded on just and enlightened principles. As the leading European nation in these waters and in the East generally, I conceive we could not experiment with these States. Adjacent as they are to our own settlements, the interests of civilization and the safety of our own possessions demanded that we should release them from the anarchy and confusion into which they had fallen, and restore order and good government. But we could not possibly intervene for this purpose only to retire upon the appearance of any difficulty. I submit that such a course would be unjust to the states, dangerous to our own settlements and prejudicial to our interests in this part of the world. We could not leave to their fate those who had been induced to give us their support in introducing a new order of things, nor abandon the country to a state of confusion which after our withdrawal, would become more distracted than before we undertook the settlement of affairs, without incurring, throughout the East, a charge of injustice and vacillation, the result, moreover, being that we should only have again to undertake the settlement of affairs in the states, but with the difficulties and expense of intervention enormously increased.

54. And, as regards the state of Perak, I did not for a moment imagine that it could ever be contemplated on our part to break the Pangkore Treaty, and ourselves refuse to carry out engagements which Her Majesty's Govt. decided should be strictly fulfilled by the Sultan and Chiefs of that State. I conceived that in affairs of this solemn character we were equally bound by our engagements as they, and that there was no withdrawal from the position we have assumed in relation to Perak. I well understand that Residents and Assistant Residents, at the so-called 'Native Courts' held their appointments provisionally and that so far they were being tried experimentally, but as regards the policy itself being of the nature of an experiment, I submit that, taking the facts into consideration this expression can only mean that if the system as introduced did not succeed, recourse must be had to some other plan to secure the object in view.

55. I venture to say that the proper course for anyone, who desired loyally to carry out the engagements which H.M. Govt. desired should be held inviolate was to endeavour as far as possible to put into working order the system they had approved. Upon reviewing the question with the additional acquaintance of facts which, as stated in para. 52, I have endeavoured to bring to Your Lordship's notice, you will readily perceive that there were considerations which weighed with me when adopting the course I did in Perak, other than those which I have fully discussed in my despatch No. 291 of the 16th October last, to which I must beg Your Lordship to give further consideration.

56. Upon my arrival here, I made it my duty to investigate Native States affairs, and I soon perceived that in Perak there was a deadlock and that I should have to cope with a double difficulty before any progress could be effected, viz. the want of amenability in the Ruler, and the absence of a central authority, both of which conflicting causes I have demonstrated to be fatal to the success of the Residential system. So serious were these difficulties that when I viewed them in connection with the other circumstances enumerated in para. 26 of the despatch just referred to I can only repeat that I at first inclined to the opinion that the best course to adopt would be to declare Perak British territory and govern it accordingly, though such a step of course, could not have been taken without the authority of H.M. Government.

57. I believed that this step would have removed the jealousy which existed between Ismail and Abdullah and their respective adherents, that the former would prefer the govt. of the country being in the hands of the British, whilst the latter, having broken through all his engagements and powerless in himself, could have made no opposition, and that such a step would meet with favour from the Ryots who would be benefitted by the change, especially from the Chinese who would have sure protection for life and property and upon the immigration of whom the country depends for further developments.

58. But I was anxious if possible not to reverse the policy as approved

by H.M. Govt. but rather to endeavour to bring it to a successful issue by overcoming the difficulties with which its workings were surrounded. To do so, two points required to be kept in view, both of which had to be satisfied, namely, firstly, to endeavour to conciliate Ismail and his party and thus to unite the present divided authority and secondly, to adopt such a plan as would prevent the measures proposed by the Resident from being rendered of no effect on account of the intractability of Abdullah.

59. It was after much consideration, therefore, that I thought I should be able to secure this double end, by adopting the course I proposed instead of that of annexation, and I still think that this course of administrating the affairs of the country in the name of the Sultan with the assistance of a Malay Council, was, at the time, the wisest one which could have been adopted. I was prepared to deal liberally with those whose pecuniary interests would be affected by the change, and I considered that by getting the chiefs on both sides to accept seats in the Council, I should be able to bring them together on friendly terms, and, by giving them a share in the Government of the country break down the jealousy which existed from the idea that Abdullah only was consulted by the Resident.

60. Had this course been carried out, it would have conferred upon the Resident or Commissioner powers similar to those exercised with such good effect by Mr. Davidson and Captain Murray in Salangore and Sungie Ujong, modified, however, by his first having to consult with the leading men in the country on any important subject, and by his having to obtain the assent of the Governor in any action proposed to be taken in opposition to the feelings of the Council. Thus, my Lord, the powers secured to the Resident or Commissioner by the course which I adopted were less authoritative than those exercised by the Residents in Salangore and Sungie Ujong.

61. With regard to the opinion expressed by Your Lordship in para. 14 of despatch No. 218 that this course was an entire reversal of existing policy, I do not think, now that you have been made acquainted with the relations which exist between our Residents and the Malay Rulers in Malay states, that you will continue of this opinion but will recognise that the step was taken by me with a view to making the policy, as approved of by H.M. Govt., workable in Perak. Finding that British intervention had committed us to the policy inaugurated in 1874, and to take an active interest in the Native states, and looking at the strict injunctions of H.M. Govt. that the Sultan and Chiefs of Perak were to be held bound by their engagements, I certainly thought that I should earn the thanks of H.M. Govt. by removing the deadlock which existed in Perak, especially when I was able to do so by a comparatively slight modification of the system which had met with their approval.

62. You refer, in para. 12 of the despatch under reply, to your despatch of 15th July last, as defining the extent of the policy as approved of by H.M. Govt. When I regarded the circumstances attending our interven-

tion, the introduction of a system which necessitated the power of control, the irretrievable step that was taken by the introduction of that system, the binding nature of the Pangkore engagement and the precise and definite injunctions issued in consequence thereof, I could not suppose that the course which had been adopted from the very commencement could be reversed by the apparent withdrawal which the despatch in question might be construed to convey. It would have been dangerous to have shown symptoms of vacillation which would have been taken for weakness, and especially in those states where the system was being successfully conducted. Moreover, as I have just mentioned and previously demonstrated, the course which had been adopted had been one of necessity, and had not the Residents directed the Government of the states to which they had been appointed, their position would have become untenable and their presence with the native Rulers neither advantageous nor consistent with the respect with which the Malays regard the officers of the British Govt. The same remarks refer to Your Lordship's despatch of the 27th July last, alluded to in para. 13 of the despatch under reply.

63. Instead of altering the working of the system which I found necessarily in force and which had met with comparative success in Salangore and Sungie Ujong, I rather considered it to be an imperative duty to endeavour to remove the dual conflicting element in Perak and to bring the system in that state to a similar successful issue. This was the more necessary as, by the folly of Abdullah, the obstinacy and intractability of Ismail, the jealousy of parties and the consequent inability of the Resident to improve the condition of the country or people, Perak was fast becoming a source of anxiety even to its chiefs. In September therefore, as fully stated in my despatch No. 291 I put the case before the Rajas and Chiefs of Perak, with the result that Raja Muda Yusuf, the heir-apparent to the Sultanship and one of Ismail's principal supporters, together with Raja Dris of blood-royal and next in order for the Bandaharaship, stated in writing their conviction that, unless the British Govt. would further assist them, Perak affairs could never be put on a satisfactory footing. After instancing some of the obstacles to a settled state of affairs, such as the fact of there being two Sultans, the improper levying of taxes and fines and the total absence of justice, they begged me, as Her Majesty's representative, to take over the country.

64. Abdullah, to whom I spoke fully on the subject, thinking no doubt how best to consult his own interests and having seen the document above referred to, sent me a similar one, coupled with a request that he might remain Sultan, and in a separate letter, he expressed contrition for the past and promised amendment for the future. Abdullah also handed to Mr. Birch two Notifications for publication, giving the Resident power to act in his name, without obtaining a separate chop or seal for each separate document which the Resident, in the interests of the country, and in the ordinary course of business, might have to execute. Thus one great

conflicting element which was experienced in carrying out the Residential system in Perak was overcome by this voluntary act of Abdullah who conferred powers on the Resident or Commissioner very similar to those possessed by the Residents in Salangore and Sungie Ujong, who have never had any difficulty in obtaining the chops and seals of the Rulers, and in their names respectively have thus been able to administer the Government of those states.

65. The second conflicting element was met by the establishment of the Malay Council. The nucleus of this Council was formed by the action of Sultan Abdullah, Raja Muda Yusuf and Raja Dris, and it remained but to invite, and I did invite, Ex-Sultan Ismail and the Raja Bandahara to complete the Council of the 'Waris Negri', or princes of the blood-royal who would be consulted by the Residents or other British Officers on all important state affairs.

66. By adopting this course, I considered that the difficulties which had brought about in Perak a collapse of the Residential system, would be met, and that with but a comparatively small step in advance, as explained in para. 60. Sultan Abdullah's offer to confer more power on the Resident was accepted and the fact that the Sultan and chiefs had for certain reasons given certain powers to the British Officers in Perak was set forth in the Proclamation issued by me. It may be, that in stating my action in the matter, I considered it less in connection with the Residential system as a whole, and as practised where successful than as an important change for the state of Perak, and that by laying therefore, undue weight on its introduction, I inadvertently gave Your Lordship a wrong impression on the subject.

67. In para. 17, Your Lordship infers that the course which I adopted of governing the country in the name of the Sultan was not practically likely to succeed. You will, however, observe, as I have explained, that this course is virtually that which exists in those states where the Residential system has been more or less successful. Hence there is no logical reason why it should not have met with a similar success in Perak. The establishment of a Malay Council to assist the Resident in important state affairs was calculated to remove the jealousies which existed and to give the members an interest in the Govt. which they had never before enjoyed. The example set by the Brookes in Sarawak and the course adopted by the Maharajah of Johore, in both of which states the Ruler is assisted by a Council, showed it to be a perfectly feasible scheme.

68. In the same para. you infer also that this course does not differ from annexation. I beg to refer you to para. 61 of this despatch where I explain that this course is not a reversal of the policy approved by H.M. Government. When governing in the name of the Sultan, the revenues of the country are paid into an independent Treasury and applied entirely to public purposes in the state. Again this course may be either temporary or permanent—permanent if upon further experience we found that it was desirable to maintain it in order to preserve peace and good government,

temporary if in the course of events we found any chief, like the Maharajah of Johore who had the necessary strength of character and who could and would undertake the Govt. of the state, when it would be easy to hand over the Govt. to him. The difference between the plan I proposed and that of the Pangkore Treaty was this:—

The one provided for a Commissioner to act in the name of the Sultan, the other for a Resident where advice must be taken and acted upon by the Sultan. If the course adopted by me amounted to annexation, I submit that the Pangkore Treaty practically amounted to annexation too.

69. When I wrote my despatch No. 291, I considered that if you disapproved of the step taken by me, we could revert to the old order of things, strongly as I condemned it as inapplicable to the circumstances of Perak. You call my attention to this point in para. 17 of No. 218. I am still of opinion that had the recent disturbances in Perak not broken out, we could if desired have receded to the old position. I do not think that we could possibly do so now. I could not foresee the murder of Mr. Birch nor the events which have followed since in rapid succession. To abandon the present position would now be construed as weakness and would have the worst possible effect on the Malay Peninsula and, as I submit for the reasons mentioned in my despatch of the 3rd December last, prejudicial to our interests in the East.

70. You express a very strong opinion that I had no authority for acting as I did, and that I had no ground for supposing that Her Majesty's Govt. would approve of the course which I adopted. On this point I beg to call your attention to the following facts.

71. My predecessor having been requested by Lord Kimberley to consider whether it would be advisable to appoint a British Officer to reside in any of the Malay states, not only engaged to place a Resident in Perak and an Assistant Resident in Laroot, but, in opposition to the views expressed by Lord Kimberley, who stated that Her Majesty's Govt. had no desire to interfere in the internal affairs of the Malayan states, intervened in a very decided manner in the internal affairs of Perak. He collected together a majority of the chiefs of that state and entered into a Treaty by which one Sultan was deposed and another set up, and that Treaty, moreover, provided that that Government of the country should practically be placed in the hands of the Resident. The treaty, if confirmed, really committed the British Govt. to a decided policy of intervention in the internal affairs of Perak. It may be said that the Laroot difficulty rendered prompt action necessary and so indeed, it did, but there was certainly not so much reason for immediate action in the case of the Sultan of Perak or for the practical assumption of the Govt. of that state by a British Officer, as there was for the step I took with a view of removing difficulties, which increased in proportion to the time they were permitted to remain, in the working of the system which I found in existence in Perak. I submit that the steps taken by my predecessor, without authority, in January 1874 were

infinitely more vital and important than the step which I took in October, 1875.

72. My Lord, I do not advert to this action of my predecessor for the purpose of casting blame upon him, for I felt as he did that in dealing with Malay Chiefs, it is necessary to settle with them promptly. What I wish to point out to you is that the vastly important measures which were undertaken without any authority from Her Majesty's Govt. in January 1874, met with your unqualified approval and that in despatch to Sir A. Clarke, No. 64 of the 29th May, 1874, you did not delay the assurance that H.M. Govt. appreciated the ability and energy he had shown and on September 4th 1874, you commended him for the ability, zeal and tact which he had displayed, in bringing about the successful result which had been obtained.

73. Moreover, in replying to Lord Stanley of Alderley in the House of Lords, on the 19th May, 1874, you expressed an opinion that it could not be said, at the worst, that Sir A. Clarke had very far exceeded his duty as an English Governor.

74. You did not then state as in para. 22 of the despatch under reply that the 'Powers and responsibilities as the Governor of the Straits Settlements, cannot be held to apply to the relations of Her Majesty's Govt. with the Malay States, in the same manner and degree as to the internal affairs of the Colony'. Nor do I find in Your Lordship's despatches any mention of those observations on the subject of acting without authority and without specific instructions which you stated in para. 23 it would have been equally your duty to have made to me under any circumstances. I only find that most vital and important steps were taken by my predecessor without authority, that those steps met with your unqualified approval, and that H.M. Govt. ratified these proceedings by holding the chiefs personally responsible for the engagements which they had made.

75. These injunctions had been broken through and steps which I took were but with a view to making the policy, which had been approved of, workable and the engagements which had been infringed, respected. Such a step was, as I have shown, comparatively but a small one, and was but carrying out, in a modified form, the policy previously approved and commended. I considered it, moreover, a duty which I had to perform to give effect to that policy and I believed that I should secure the thanks of H.M. Govt. by thus relieving the system, as approved of by them, from the deadlock by which it was marked in Perak. Seeing that the first important step of intervention with its attendant engagement, which had been taken without instructions, had met with your approval, and that it was impossible to carry on negotiations with Abdullah and the chiefs unless I spoke and acted as if charged with full authority, I did not hesitate to assume the responsibility of taking this step which was necessary for the due fulfilment of that to which we were solemnly engaged. I could not but suppose that you would give me your full support in endeavouring to bring the system, as found to be workable in other Native states, to a successful

issue in Perak. As stated in para. 35 of my despatch No. 291, I took upon myself to do what, under the circumstances, I considered you would wish to have done, and I hoped that you would have given full consideration to the statements made in that despatch, and that those statements would have convinced you of the necessity of the action taken by me.

76. As to consulting you by telegraph which you suggest in para. 21, it was my obvious duty to have done, I can only say that I considered whether I should telegraph, and I deliberately determined not to do so. A long despatch on the subject has apparently failed to convey a distinct view of the reasons for my action, and I considered at the time that it would have been impossible within the limits of telegraphic communication to have entered fully into the question. Considering the step which I contemplated taking as being absolutely necessary, and one which would be sure to meet with your approval upon you being made fully acquainted with the facts of the case, I deemed it the best course to act without delay. Regarding the matter firstly as a duty, and secondly as a means of bringing the system as approved of by you to a workable shape, I felt certain that I was not stepping far beyond the bounds of my instructions as Governor, and I had reason to believe that my action would meet with your unqualified approbation.

77. I now pass on to consider the statement that the course which I adopted was the signal for resistance and attack. With regard to the view expressed by you that the murder of Mr. Birch and other disastrous consequences ensued upon the modification of the policy which I adopted, such an inference cannot justly be drawn from the facts which have come to my knowledge. It was unfortunate for the success and the due appreciation of the policy as modified by me that Mr. Birch's murder should have followed so soon after the change had been publicly announced, but it by no means follows that even if there had been no such modification of policy that Mr. Birch would not have been murdered when he exposed himself in the way he did at Passir Salah.

78. You will observe that I felt that the view might be entertained that my action resulted in Mr. Birch's murder when in para. 11 of despatch No. 327 of 16th November 1875, and in para. 3–10 of despatch No. 335 of 2nd December 1875, I pointed out reasons for the conclusion that such an inference would be unjust and inconsistent with a true appreciation of the facts of the case. I am more than ever convinced, and recent events appear to me to demonstrate, that the consequences to which you refer, were caused by a dislike on the part of the Chiefs to our intervention in any shape in the affairs of the State of Perak. A similar dislike of our intervention has shewn itself in some of the states about Malacca and culminated, as you are aware, in active hostility.

It cannot possibly be held that the attack upon Sungie Ujong was caused by the step I took in Perak, for there is no connection or sympathy whatever between that state and the small states of Sri Menanti, Ulu Moar and

Jumpole, which are about 150 miles from Perak and are separated from Perak by the state of Salangore.

There seems to be abundant reason to believe that, even previous to the modification of policy which I adopted in Perak, some of the chiefs there were considering whether they could not unite to get rid of the interference of the Resident.

79. In one of the letters found in the boat of Hajee Ali purporting to be written by Hajee Mahomed Ali to Rajah Hajee Yahyah (a grandson of Ismail) there is this passage—'Your Slave beg to inform Your Highness regarding the arrangement of what we are going to do is that Your Highness must come down quickly and your slave hopes that the money Your Highness must bring with him without delay, for the Rajah Abdullah has given his power to Mr. Birch and Captain Kim Ching. Also I beg to inform Your Highness that in my opinion that is if Your Highness is late, it is almost impossible to carry out the arrangement of what we are going to do.' No date is given to this letter, but as Mr. Kim Ching (who had obtained a concession from Abdullah previous to our interference in Perak) had been in Perak having interviews with Abdullah about the end of July last, it would seem from internal evidence to have been written about the month of August.

80. In another letter found in Hajee Ali's possession, purporting to come from two Chinamen and addressed to Tunku Panglima Besar Abdul Galeel (Rajah Ngah, one of Ismail's chief fighting men) dated 18th Rajah 1292, August 1875, they state, 'a trustworthy man from our friend Hajee Mahomed Saleh came and brought a certifying letter from our friend to receive money from us, we are much surprised to hear it without any cause to receive this money, what is our friend going to do with this money, if we are not sure on what business this money is how can we send the money for our money is put out, if there is a way that we can make more profit than we can do now, then we remove the money, if we are not sure of the business we dare not remove the money from Penang so many thousands. This is what we inform our friend.'

81. In another letter purporting to be written by Hajee Ali to Rajah Yahyah the following occurs:—

'Your slave informs you that regarding the arrangement of what we are going to do is do not be late about it, come down quick with the money, you must get them and come down as soon as possible. About Hajee Mahomed Saleh he has gone to Penang, now Mr. Birch has had the power given by Rajah Abdullah, this is what your slave informs Your Highness, do not Your Highness trust the money which we sent for by Hajee Mahomed Salleh, Your Highness knows better. Do not Your Highness fail of what your slave informs, and hopes to God and his messenger that you will come down as soon as possible.' There is no date given to this letter, but from the reference made to Hajee Mahomed Saleh, who was in Penang about the end of July or beginning of August, it would seem to have been written about the same time, namely August 1875.

82. Another paper was found in Hajee Ali's boat. This was a draft letter apparently coming from several people whose names are not mentioned to Mr. Birch. A translation of this by Mr. Swettenham is enclosed. This paper is undated, but, as will be gathered therefrom, would seem to have been written shortly after Mr. Birch first went to reside in Perak, consequent on the Pangkore engagement.

83. From another paper found in Hajee Ali's possession it would appear that he had made an agreement with Tunku Panglima Besar Abdul Galeel (Rajah Ngah) and Hajee Mahomed Yassin for mutual support and assistance in the strongest terms, and in pursuance of their arrangement it would appear that while the Panglima Besar resided with Ismail, and Hajee Mahomed Yassin with Abdullah, Hajee Ali went from one to the other and was constantly at the Residency with Mr. Birch. This document throws light upon Hajee Ali's position, and will account for his possession of the papers referred to.

84. Since I last wrote Mr. Swettenham has taken down a statement made by Syed Masahore who joined Mr. Swettenham immediately upon the commencement of hostilities and has been employed in our service since. From this statement it will be observed that about 21st September Maharajah Lelah was engaged in placing a stockade round his house and that on that day he held the conversation therein reported and produced the paper which if it contained the chops therein mentioned, must have been written some time previously. If there is any truth in this statement then it would appear that long before any action was taken by me, preparation for resistance was made.

85. I left Perak on 16th September. The letters of Rajah Yusuf and Rajah Dris before referred to were respectively dated the 19th September. Abdullah's letter was dated 1st October. The Proclamation was sent to Perak on the 23rd October and the first copy was posted at the Residency on the 26th. The dates are important as from the statement last referred to, the Maharajah Lelah and his people were building his stockade on the 21st September and had then the paper with the chops referred to.

86. Between the 28th October and 4th November copies were given to Rajahs Ismail, Yusuf and Usman (the Bandahara) and posted at Blanja, Senggang, Sayung, Qualla Kangsa and Kota Lama, up the river by Mr. Swettenham and the bearers were nowhere molested in any way. Mr. Birch had also distributed the Proclamations without molestation from the mouth of the Perak River up to Passir Sala.

87. This statement of Syed Masahore is to some considerable extent borne out by statement of reports already forwarded to Your Lordship and if true, as in the main I believe it to be, I think I am justified in drawing this deduction that the attack on Mr. Birch at that time at Passir Sala was unpremeditated, that the Maharajah Lelah was exasperated and prepared to protect his followers who stabbed Arshad, and that he himself relied for assistance upon the leading men of Perak. Apart from the statement it

appears from the draft letter found in his house and which there can be no doubt now was intended for Ismail, Ismail himself having acknowledged the Maharajah Lelah as one of his great men, that he fully relied upon Ismail's assistance with men and money.

88. I think I may also safely draw this deduction that even had no proclamation been issued Mr. Birch could not have exposed himself at Passir Sala with safety and it is quite possible that had Mr. Birch not been murdered at Passir Sala an attack might have been made upon the Residency which might have been only too successful and led to a much greater loss of life than any we have yet had to deplore, and to a combination and confederacy which would probably have caused an obstinate war and still greater loss of life.

89. True I erred, in common with all concerned, in supposing we could intervene in the affairs of Perak without a display of military force. I now see that if the advice of the Residents was to be acted upon and the Sultan and chiefs held strictly bound to the engagements which they had made, military force must sooner or later, in greater or less degree, have become necessary to support the position which had been assumed.

90. When the proclamations which had been issued by Abdullah and by me were to be posted in Perak, it was considered whether it was advisable to station a small body of troops there, to give material support to the Resident, in case any refractory chief opposed this scheme for bringing the system to a workable footing. It was then decided that the Resident's Sikh Guard would be sufficient to meet with such a contingency. It was in reference to this question of sending a small body of troops that Mr. Birch telegraphed to me that all was well and that the proclamations had been posted without incident all the way down the river.

91. I trust that Your Lordship will consider that I have now fully replied to your despatch under acknowledgement. I trust that the explanations which I have supplied will be satisfactory to you and to Her Majesty's Government, but I would beg most respectfully to submit that it would have been more consistent with justice, had you refrained from expressing strong opinions upon my proceedings until after my explanations had been received.

92. It remains for me now to consider briefly what in my opinion should be the policy to be pursued in respect of this state of Perak. Doubtless H.M. Government have come to a decision on this point but I shall not be fulfilling my duty if I did not acquaint you with my views on the subject at the present time.

93. In para. 69 of this despatch, I have stated that I now consider it impossible to recede from the policy which has been adopted in Perak. The effect of such a step would be to induce the people in all the protected territories, as well as in our own settlements, to imagine that if they wanted to get rid of us, all that they would have to do would be to kill one of our officers and resist our troops, when we should immediately withdraw,

after inflicting some punishment on those upon whom we could lay our hands. The Chiefs and those who have been implicated in the murder of our Resident and in the subsequent outrages must be captured or prevented from returning to the country, and this could not be effected, if we receded from the position we occupy. If we did so, again, all those natives who have been friendly to us and affording us assistance during the outbreak, or at least have maintained a neutral attitude, would probably be murdered, and anarchy and civil war would once more ensue.

94. The only question as it seems to me with regard to Perak, is, whether we should adhere to the policy of governing by a British Officer in the name of the Sultan, or whether we should annex the country as a portion of Her Majesty's Dominions. As stated in para. 25 and 26 of my despatch No. 335 of the 2nd December, I am of opinion that under present circumstances complete annexation will now be the best course to adopt. The other alternative is, I still think, workable, but instead of a purely Malay Council, I should propose a mixed Council consisting of such British Officers, Malays, and Chinese as may from time to time be thought desirable.

95. Recent events, however, have so altered and strengthened our position that I believe we could take over and govern the country with a comparatively small establishment and with perfect facility. We can indemnify the chiefs who would be entitled to such consideration at our hands, and thus get rid of the conflicting interests with which we should have to deal if we allowed the chiefs to retain their power. We could modify the Malay laws and customs and still keep them in harmony with their religious ideas. A great opportunity would be presented for abolishing, upon equitable principles, the existing system of debt-slavery, and we should also not only secure the repayment of the advances of money made by the Government of the Straits Settlements, but hold a material guarantee for such portion of the expenditure as may be fairly incurred in consequence of the outrage that has been committed upon our Representative.

96. I know well all that can be urged that we should take no further responsibilities upon ourselves in respect to acquiring new territory, and that even where our subjects have been wronged that they have only themselves to thank for going into a country where its rulers are unable or unwilling to afford them protection. I know that it has also been urged that our army is not to be kept for the purpose of preserving peace in semi-civilized or barbarous states, but that the responsibility must rest on the constituted authorities.

97. If these Malayan States were not immediately upon our borders, if the preservation of the peace within those states were not of vital importance to the interests of our own settlements and to the maintenance of peace and good order therein, if we had assumed no responsibility connected therewith, I might with perfect consistency with the views I hold advise you that the proper course to pursue would be a policy of non-interference. But intimately connected as we are with them, that policy

has never been pursued and there has always been in a greater or less degree an intimate relationship between ourselves and the states in the neighbourhood of these settlements.

98. Looking at the close relationship which we have been obliged to assume in respect to these states, especially since we have actively intervened in their affairs, I submit that the true policy to adopt, not only with regard to Perak, but also with respect to the other states in our neighbourhood, and under our protection, is to look forward to the time when the annexation of some of them will probably become a necessity.

That period should be postponed as long as possible, but we should be prepared to assume the responsibility whenever it becomes absolutely necessary to do so in order to secure peace and good Government.

99. Upon considering the progress of recent events in Perak, and the arguments stated in para. 95 of this despatch, I have arrived at the conclusion that the time has come when it would be advisable to declare Perak a portion of H.M. Dominions. We already occupy the country and the people are rapidly returning to their homes. When, moreover, we have opened up communications from the sea-coast to the Perak River and to Kinta and when a well organised and disciplined Police force has been raised and taken the place of the Military force now in occupation I should, with the aid of a small body of troops for an emergency, have no more fear about carrying on the Government or of a rising against us. The police force should of course be well officered and provided with a sufficient number of reliable non-commissioned Officers.

100. It may be said that the occupation of Perak would be attended with expense without any adequate return and that it would therefore be unwise to occupy it. Doubtless Perak is now covered with jungle, but its present aspect is no criterion of its powers of production. Laroot, at present the most thickly populated portion of the state, already yields a revenue of $20,000 a month, the important import and export farms at the mouth of the Perak River were recently let for $7,000 a month, so that without any scheme of taxation except royalty on minerals and taxes on the imports and exports, Perak even now raises a revenue of over $300,000 per annum. This will be sufficient to cover any allowance to chiefs that may be determined upon, and the cost of the necessary establishments, and still leave a balance for opening up roads and communications and for the payment of interest on debt.

101. There is every prospect that the revenue would considerably increase if the country became a British possession. I am assured by influential and wealthy Chinamen that if Perak were under British rule, swarms of industrious Chinese would flock in, and these with the Chinese and British capital which would soon be invested in the state, would completely change the face of the country. Province Wellesley was once a jungle, it is now covered with fine plantations, employing many thousands of Indian, Chinese and other Coolies.

The agricultural and mineral wealth of Perak is very great and with the certain introduction of immigration and coolie labour the Malays would soon be outnumbered and all difficulties respecting them would cease.

102. I trust that nothing I have written in this despatch will lead you to believe that I do not entertain the highest respect for the views which you have expressed. I have felt it my duty, however, to explain that many of the conclusions apparently arrived at by your Lordship have been based on an imperfect acquaintance with facts, and without realizing the difficulties of the position in which I have been placed. If in doing so, I have appeared at all to step beyond proper bounds, I trust Your Lordship will take into account the fact that you have expressed very strong opinions for the special purpose of eliciting explanations from me with respect to the course which I felt it my duty to adopt in the matter now under consideration.

(Signed) F. D. JERVOIS.

APPENDIX D

Earl of Carnarvon to Sir William Jervois, Governor. No. 127.

Downing Street,
May, 20th, 1876.

Sir,

In my Despatch No. 218 of the 10th of December, while inviting explanations from you on various points which seemed to me to require them, I intimated that I would defer pronouncing any final decision on the course of action which you took with respect to the affairs of Perak in October last.

2. I am now in receipt of your reply, being your Despatch No. 62 of the 10th of February last. I could have wished on all grounds to avoid the necessity of further pursuing the question of your conduct in relation to these transactions; but it seems to me that I can hardly allow much of this last communication from you to remain unanswered. I will make no comment on the general tone and language of your despatch, which in an unusual manner reflects on the justice and fairness of my decision, because I am quite content that it should be judged by the plain facts of the case, and because I desire to leave every possible freedom of expression to an officer who, however mistakenly, conceives himself to have been subjected to undeserved censure. I shall simply allude, as briefly as the subject admits, to some of the principal points in your despatch which, if unanswered, would be perhaps open to misconception.

3. The matters treated of in this correspondence may be conveniently divided under three heads:—

(A) The condition of affairs in Perak from the time of the Pangkore Treaty in January 1874 up to October 1875.

(B) The nature of the action taken by you at the latter date.

(C) The future policy of the British Government with reference to Perak and the Malay Peninsula.

4. The representations made by you under these three heads may be thus summarised:—

(A) That there were practically two Sultans in Perak, of whom the one not recognised by our Government, Ismail, was acknowledged throughout the greater part of the country, while the other, Abdullah was the weaker of the two and powerless to act; that there were besides a number of powerful minor chiefs, practically independent in their districts; that owing to the absence of an efficient central authority and the impracticable character of Abdullah, it would have been impossible in any case for the Resident accredited to him to confine himself to advising and assisting; but that the Residents in Perak as well as in Salangore and Sungie Ujong, have practically been administrators of the Government; and that this was contemplated by, and was the logical sequence of, the Pangkore Treaty, as had been understood by the Colonial Office.

(B) That the action taken by you with respect to the Proclamation issued in October was but a slight modification of the policy already approved and commended, and that it was not to this change of policy that Mr. Birch's murder and other recent events could be attributed.

(C) That though the alternative policy of governing by a British Officer in the name of the Sultan, assisted by a Council, is still capable of being worked, in your opinion complete annexation is the best course to adopt.

5. I will proceed at once to state in general terms the reasons for which it is impossible for Her Majesty's Government to assent to your explanations of past transactions, alluding incidentally to various arguments and expressions used by you which require more special notice. The future policy to be pursued I shall reserve for separate treatment hereafter.

6. In commenting upon your present description of the state of affairs in Perak, and the position which it was intended the Resident should there occupy, it will be necessary to revert at some length to the information supplied by your predecessor and yourself during the period now under review.

7. My predecessor, Lord Kimberley, in his Despatch of the 20th September 1873, had given Sir Andrew Clarke, who was then proceeding to assume the government of the colony, special instructions as to the policy to be observed towards the native states; and in desiring him to consider the advisability of appointing British Officers to reside in any of those states, he expressly added that such appointments could only be made with the full consent of the native government.

8. Sir A. Clarke, in his Despatch of 26th January 1874, giving an account of his proceedings at the Dindings, and the conclusion of the Pangkore engagement, enclosed a letter which had been addressed to him by Sultan Abdullah requesting him, in the name of himself and his great men, to send 'A man of sufficient abilities to live in Perak, and show us a good system of government for our dominions.' And he stated that he had found Abdullah, who was the rightful heir to the throne, a man of considerable intelligence, and possessing perfect confidence that he would be able to maintain his position if he were once placed in Perak as its legitimate ruler; that all the chiefs except the Mantri of Laroot (who had previously set up a claim to be independent, which, however, he was then induced to abandon) and his party were prepared at once to receive him as their sovereign, and that it was these considerations that led him to propose the fourteen articles of the engagement which after a full discussion were finally accepted and ratified.

Of Ismail (who had been informally declared Sultan and possessed the regalia) he said little more than that he was an aged man, and he observed that though he was not present himself, the chiefs who were present had sufficient authority to act as they did in the full recognition of Abdullah as

Sultan. He deferred entering fully into the policy which he proposed should be pursued as regards the duties of the Residents, but in a separate Despatch of the same date explaining the very critical position of affairs in Laroot, which had induced him to go beyond his instructions and at once place a British officer in that district, he spoke of Captain Speedy as possessing the confidence of the chiefs of the Malay Government, and said that he would assist that government in destroying stockades, disarming the Chinese factions, and restoring peace.

9. In his subsequent Despatch of the 24th of February Sir A. Clarke forwarded additional information as to the past history and present state of Perak, and explained more fully his views with reference to the question of the appointment of Residents. In that despatch he stated that he had been unofficially informed that Ismail had expressed his adherence to the engagement of the other Chiefs, and, with special reference to Lord Kimberley's stipulation as to the consent of the native government being a necessary condition of the appointment of Residents, he had no hesitation in saying that 'the proposal met with the fullest concurrence from the native chiefs'; a statement which, I may here remark, it is obviously impossible to reconcile with the conviction you now entertain (par. 78) that the recent outbreak was 'caused by dislike on the part of the Chiefs to our intervention in any shape in the affairs of Perak'.

The views which your predecessor then entertained as to the nature of the position to be assumed by the Residents may be gathered from the following extracts from the same Despatch: 'This proposal of appointing British Officers to reside in the Malay States is not a new one; it was first proposed to appoint them for the purpose of assisting the legitimate rulers of the Country, with a view to teaching them the great and simple principles of good government, of showing them the most feasible or practical methods of opening up their countries' etc. etc.

'The Malays, like every other Eastern nation, require to be treated much more like children and to be taught, and this especially in the matters of improvement etc.'

'Such teaching can only be effected by an officer living on the spot whose time should be devoted to carefully studying the wants and capabilities of each State, the character of the Sultan and his Chiefs, and to making himself personally acquainted with every portion of the country, and thus fitting himself for the post of counsellor when the time for opening up the country arrives.'

'This watching the collection of the revenue and controlling the expenditure will form no insignificant part of a Resident's duties, and as far as bringing about a good system of Government is concerned, will be about the most important portion of them.'

'To check squeezing, and to induce the Sultan to select proper men for the collection will be the Resident's special care.'

All this clearly indicates that the true functions of the Resident were to be those of an influential adviser, and not as you now suppose, a direct administrator of the district.

10. In another Despatch of the same date Sir A. Clarke forwarded Minutes by Members of his Executive Council, on the general subject of the policy to be pursued towards the native states, which are material as showing the objects which they contemplated would be obtained by the appointment of Residents.

Major McNair gave as his opinion 'that a closer influence must be brought to bear on the Native States. That he was in favour of a Resident Officer being nominated to dwell in their country, as it was by daily intercourse that the European could acquire and maintain their confidence.' 'Many of the Malay Chiefs,' he continues, 'have represented to me that what they want is an officer who would reside near them to give them confidence and support, who would teach them to collect and spend their revenue, to administer a better form of justice, and to maintain order.'

Mr. Willans, an old and experienced officer of the local Government, wrote—'From a long experience of the natives, I am satisfied that they are amenable to reason, and will follow the advice of any European they respect, and I believe if Residents were appointed they would be readily received, and if properly chosen be looked up to, and exert a great and beneficial influence; they would argue with the Chiefs in a pleasant not domineering way, and point out to them the advantages of the European system.' Etc., etc.

Mr. Braddell wrote 'Such is the influence of the British Government in the neighbouring Malay States that the mere fact of the residence in any State of a representative of the Great Government would of itself give stability to the rule of the Chiefs and establish order in the country.' 'Their duties would at first be not merely to advise the Chiefs, but to show them practically what they have to do in the way of ruling the country.' 'It only requires that the wishes of Government should be made known to the native rulers to secure implicit obedience.' 'The end can I believe be gained by Government without involving itself in responsibilities.'

Mr. Birch recorded his entire assent to Mr. Braddell's views.

Mr. C. J. Irving, who alone of Sir A. Clarke's Council dissented from the proposed policy of appointing permanent Residents, after describing the Malays generally, added, 'Given such a people, and put down among them any European Officer whose sole duty it would be to be giving good advice, etc:' and further, 'If the policy of Her Majesty's Government were to keep pushing our influence in those countries, and becoming virtually the governing power, the appointment of permanent Residents would probably be a step in the right direction. But this I understand from the Secretary of State's Despatch is not the course that is designed.'

11. The above extracts are amply sufficient to show that the essence of the scheme of appointing Residents as originally proposed was that the native Chiefs were willing and desirous to receive British officers who would

advise and assist them in the Government of the country. It was no doubt expected that such an officer would exercise very great influence in the country, but, seeing that the Chiefs are continually spoken of as quite ready to carry out whatever measures of reform or improvement were pointed but to them, and seeing that the appointment of Officers in Perak for this purpose had originated in a voluntary compact and had not been accepted under compulsion, the position a Resident was to occupy would be very different from that of a Controller, still less would it be equivalent to that of an administrator of a government as you now describe them to have been.

12. The nature of the advice to be given by an officer in such a position would obviously be determined by considerations of a practical and local nature, such as, the extent of the authority of the recognised ruler, the position of the petty Chiefs, and the characteristic habits of the people, and therefore it appears to me to be beside the point to argue, as you apparently do, in the fifth, sixth and seventh paragraphs of your Despatch under reply that because the Government was weak it was therefore impossible for the Resident to confine his attention to giving advice.

13. You cite indeed the provision in the Pangkore Treaty that the advice 'was to be acted upon' in justification of your view that the engagement contained in it 'the element of control,' but, bearing in mind the assumed readiness of the Sultan to accept advice, it is impossible to consider that particular provision, except in connection with the circumstances under which the engagement was entered into, and I am by no means prepared to admit the correctness of your statement that the Pangkore engagement virtually threw the government of the country into the hands of the Resident. It is at all events beyond question that you are under a complete misapprehension in maintaining as you have done that it was fully understood at the Colonial Office that the system pursued towards these Native States, though nominally one of advice, was really one of direct or actual government.

14. It was on the contrary after full consideration of the Despatches from which I have quoted, and in the belief that they had before them a complete and accurate account of the position of affairs in Perak, and of the proposed residential system, that Her Majesty's Government gave a general approval to the action of Sir Andrew Clarke, and eventually assented to his provisionally stationing Residents with the Chiefs in the districts of Salangore, Perak and Sungei Ujong.

15. The Despatches above mentioned were received in this Department on the 30th of March 1874: my approval of his proceedings was conveyed to Sir A. Clarke in the Despatch of the 29th of May, which was supplemented by a telegram of the 1st June giving a conditional authority to proceed with the appointment of a Resident at Perak which you allude to in the 42nd paragraph of your Despatch (and I doubt not that your predecessor could give a satisfactory explanation on the point,) the subject was disposed of, so far as this Department was concerned, without any unnecessary loss of time.

16. The next information which I received from Sir A. Clarke bearing on the present question is that contained in his despatch of the 16th of June, 1874 reporting a visit of Mr. Birch to several of the Native States. The following extracts relate to Perak.

'Mr. Birch and his party proceeded down the river by boat to Blanja where the ex-Sultan Ismail dwells. The ex-Sultan was absent at one of his mines, but returned as soon as he heard of the arrival of the Colonial Secretary, and several interviews took place at which he professed perfect readiness to give over the regalia to Sultan Abdullah, if the latter will only come to receive them. This, it is rumoured, Sultan Abdullah hesitates at present to do, feeling probably that their newly established relations are not sufficiently cordial to induce him to seek for the present a closer intimacy, but I do not anticipate that I shall find any difficulty when I have eventually to deal with the question. At Blanja Mr. Birch was not received very cordially, this village having become the refuge of several freebooting chiefs, who, driven from other States thought that in the probable grievances of the ex-Sultan they saw a chance of future difficulties by which they could benefit.

'The party then proceeded to Batarabit where the Sultan Abdullah accorded them most hospitable reception.' Sir Andrew Clarke continues as follows: 'For the appointment of a British Resident the Sultan Abdullah is most anxious, and in this desire he is supported by his principal Chiefs. At present every Chief has a "squeezing" place on the river where he levies black mail from passing boats, and no sort of real government exists. The Sultan and his Chiefs honestly wish to remedy this state of affairs, but they do not know how to set about any reform, and having no confidence in themselves or in each other, they require a guiding hand to lead them. The results of this tour may be considered to be satisfactory. The greatest courtesy and kindness were exhibited by the Chiefs and inhabitants of all the villages except Blanja. The whole country traversed was at peace, and there is reason to anticipate that the appointment of British Residents will foster the feeling of security that now prevails.'

17. In his Despatch of the 4th of November, enclosing the proclamation issued under the authority of my Despatch of 4th September 1874, relative to the Pangkore engagement, Sir A. Clarke did not furnish any fresh information as to the state of affairs in Perak.

But in his speech to the Legislative Council, which he forwarded by the same mail, he spoke of 'the moderate, and I may say fair, success which I have reason to believe has attended our interference in Perak,' and after describing at some length the past history of the troubles in Perak, and the policy of Sir H. Ord, and having explained 'that it was necessary to determine and then recognise who was the true bona fide and legitimate ruler of the whole country' he continued, with reference to the engagement of Pangkore, 'I was enabled to come to a just and satisfactory decision, and to place in the supreme Government of that country a man who, whether fitted for it or not, is to my mind the legitimate ruler. So far that decision has been hitherto satisfactory and with regard to the displaced ruler, the Chief who had been temporarily elected, I am confident in my own mind and all the evidence proves it, that that was only a temporary sovereignty which had been given to Ismail. But I am only dealing with results, and though 8 or 10 months have passed since that, and there has been naturally an amount of soreness among the people whose head man had been actually sovereign, there has been no outbreak, and I am inclined to hope that with a little watchfulness on our part, the people of Perak will cheerfully accept the sovereignty of Abdullah, and especially if his rule is assisted by the advice and assistance of an English officer.' He then described the improvements which had already taken place in Larut and Perak subsequently on his intervention, and added, 'This is a general sketch of the condition of affairs there, and although Ismail and Abdullah have not yet come together, I hope and believe that they will, and that beyond the intrigues of a few disappointed petty Rajahs, who are interested in keeping the sore alive, there is no ground for anxiety or for not thinking that in that large native state we have now established a condition of things which will bear favourably and well upon our own interests here.'

18. The next communications which I received from Sir A. Clarke relating to Perak matters were his Despatches of the 23rd and 24th December, in which he reported that he had sent Mr. Birch on two missions, one having reference to riots at the Salama Mines, which threatened to be serious, and the other to the settlement of the Krian boundary question. In the first he says that on the arrival of Mr. Birch, accompanied by a small escort of police, and Captain Speedy with his own native guard, 'The pirates, although they vaunted up to the last moment that they would fight, escaped into the jungle, where they were hotly pursued by the native police, and sixty were captured and forwarded to the Sultan of Perak for punishment;' and that Mr. Birch, after a few days, having seen that the country was tranquil, and that the miners had returned to their work, was enabled to return to Penang.

In the second he says 'I am glad to be able to inform your Lordship that Mr. Birch's mission has been successful, and that I have received a communication from him reporting that acting as the Representative of this Government he had held a most satisfactory interview with the ex-Sultan Ismail, who had agreed to sign the engagement of Pangkore above referred to, but wished that the Sultan Abdullah should meet him first.' He then describes the preparations which were being made for the meeting between the two Princes, which was arranged to take place in a few days, and was to be attended by all the Chiefs of Perak, except two of no importance, and concluded 'I have little doubt that the reconciliation now effected between the Ruler and ex-Ruler of Perak will prevent any further complication in that State.'

19. And it was with an allusion to the success which had attended these missions that Sir A. Clarke announced about this date (30th December

1874) that after long and anxious considerations he had nominated Mr. Birch to be Resident at Perak. Nor is there anything in his Despatches of this date to show that the nature of the position to be occupied by the Residents was other than that which had been entertained ten months before.

20. You quote at some length in your present Despatch the instructions issued to Mr. Birch and to Mr. Davidson prior to their assumption of the duties of Resident. But these instructions were never sent home and have consequently never been under my eye. They may possibly give a somewhat different complexion to the Residential Schemes proposed by Sir Andrew Clarke in the Despatches to which I have already referred, but as, whatever may be the cause, complete copies have never been furnished to this Department, I am not in a position to criticise with any advantage the extracts you now bring to my notice; and it is obviously impossible to draw any inference as to the effect they might have produced on my mind or that of any other Secretary of State in the same position.

21. It was at this period that you were appointed to succeed Sir A. Clarke in the government of the Straits Settlements, and on your departure you were furnished with my Despatch of the 8th of April, announcing my decisions 'not to confirm the appointments made by him until you had an opportunity of considering the whole subject,' with an allusion to the peculiar nature of the duties to be discharged, and the special qualifications required. You were informed that the appointments were to be treated as 'temporary, and of an experimental character,' and it was thus open to you, should you see occasion, to point out to her Majesty's Government any difficulties that had arisen in the working of the Residential system not foreseen by your predecessor, or any want of success attendant on his selection of individuals.

22. During the interval between your departure and assumption of the Government Sir Andrew Clarke forwarded to this Department several reports made by the officers acting as Residents. That of Mr. Birch was enclosed in his Despatch of the 26th of April, and with reference to it your predecessor said 'Mr. Birch appears already to have secured considerable ascendancy over many of the Chiefs of Perak, and has been courteously received by all, but in a country which has been for so many years misgoverned by petty Rajahs progress must necessarily be slow. Mr. Birch hardly describes Perak as being in so flourishing a condition as some previous Despatches might perhaps lead me to suppose; but I observe that he mentions the jealousies of the Chiefs amongst themselves, which alone had prevented a reconciliation between Abdullah and Ismail, as disappearing and that the future of Perak might safely be looked upon as a prosperous one. He adds that under his influence there had been already decided improvement in respect to the oppression that had been practised by the more troublesome Rajahs, and that he had visited Ismail and the other Chiefs, and had everywhere been treated with respect.'

23. I have referred at length to these Despatches, (and they contain all the information which Her Majesty's Government had before them on the subject), to show that their general tenour was to the effect that though difficulties had arisen such as might have been expected, still these were in course of being surmounted, and that the system of acting on the Native Chiefs by advice was working well, and promised to be ultimately successful.

The general aspect of affairs in Perak as thus presented differs materially from the entirely new and complicated political situation now sketched in paragraphs 26 to 29 of your Despatch. I find but little evidence of 'relations between Abdullah and the Resident marked by disunion and discord,' or of a second Sultan acknowledged throughout the greater part of the country, or of difficulties arising from the personal character of the ruler necessarily precluding success.

The Maharaja Lela's name occurs incidentally on various occasions, but I nowhere find him occupying that peculiar and obstructive position attributed to him in the 44th paragraph of your present Despatch.

There is nothing in all this correspondence tending to show that Her Majesty's Government would in any circumstances have sanctioned a forcible intervention in the affairs of these States. On the contrary I should have thought it sufficiently obvious that they would be averse to a policy under which it was likely to arise; but, assuming the situation of Perak to have been as critical as you now represent it, and assuming that it was contemplated that the Residents were to control the Government of the country, it is clear that a resort to force would sooner or later have been inevitable, and that it must be inexpedient if not actually fatal to place such officers in isolated positions, and to leave them without proper support.

24. I may here allude to the 19th paragraph of your Despatch, in which you quote various extracts from Mr. Birch's report of 2nd April 1873 as showing the position which in your opinion he occupied. In emphasising the word 'he' as you do, you appear to me to be giving it a meaning which the context does not bear. Mr. Birch, who expresses his hope that 'this Report will show how I have employed my time during the five months I have been at Perak,' in rendering an account of his proceedings to the superior officer from whom his authority was derived would naturally give prominence to his own doings and the influence which he had himself been enabled to exercise for the benefit of Perak, and his expressions cannot be construed as if they were intended to define the exact relations between the Sultan and himself, which would be well known to the persons he addressed.

25. It was, however, precisely because this and other reports received about this time, when the Residential system had been in operation for a few months, were not free from indications of a liability to danger arising out of an assumption by the Resident of duties in excess of their position as counsellors, that I expressly cautioned you in the three Despatches of 25th

May, 13th July and 27th July quoted in my Despatch of 10th December, as to the great care which was requisite with respect to the nature of the advice to be given and the possible assumption of a right to direct the policy of the Chiefs.

As I have already shown, the scheme at first proposed by your predecessor was a system of acting by advice, and there was therefore nothing to induce Her Majesty's Government to lay down any express instructions against undue interference until the occasion had shown that additional precautions were necessary to guard against the growth of this tendency. But granting that on your assumption of the Government you did not rightly apprehend the views and intentions of Her Majesty's Government, the Despatches to which I have just referred at all events clearly showed that the policy which had been approved was not one involving the actual Government of these States, and I am compelled therefore to consider unsatisfactory the statement in the 52nd paragraph of your present Despatch, that until you were in receipt of mine of the 10th December you had not perceived the alleged misconception on the subject.

26. You assumed the Government of the Straits Settlements on the 10th May, 1875, and the only Despatches which I received from you between that date and those of the 16th October, bearing upon the affairs of Perak were (1) that of the 8th of July relative to the Krean boundary question, a delicate matter; as to which, far from intimating that any serious difficulties had arisen with Abdullah, you implied that the course you proposed would remove a possible source of dissatisfaction; and (2) your Despatch of the 18th of September reporting your visit to the Perak Chiefs and promising to furnish full information in a general report on the affairs of the Native States.

It is clear, however, from the enclosures to your Despatch of the 16th of October (e.g. Mr. Birch's letter of 13th May), that you were very early in possession of information tending to show the unsatisfactory working of the Residential system at least in the case of Abdullah; and it would have been well if you had put Her Majesty's Government in possession of the facts, together with any inference which, with your necessarily large means of acquiring local knowledge, you might draw on so important a question.

27. And here I think it right to point out that, even in your Despatch of the 16th of October, there are expressions which are not altogether consistent with portions of that which I am now considering. You then wrote of the Residential system generally 'The position of a Resident at the Court of a Malay State is in many respects a peculiar one. If his advice be followed, he is in a position to be of great benefit to the State. . . . When, however, as has been the case in Perak, his advice is for the most part not followed, his power of usefulness must obviously be very restricted.'

These remarks could hardly prepare me for a state of affairs now described as follows: 'From the commencement of British intervention the Government of the Malayan States to which British Residents have been accredited has been in greater or lesser degree exercised by those officers themselves. There has been really no ruler, neither in Perak, Salangore or Sungei Ujong who has ever had the power to carry out the advice of the Resident. Under these circumstances the Resident has not only had to give advice, but also to render active assistance, and take the control of public affairs.'

Again, your description of Ismail in the former Despatch as 'without an idea of his own,' 'completely in the hands of the Mantri and other minor chiefs,' 'unable to read or write,' and probably not alive to the contents of a letter he had addressed to you, hardly corresponds with that of the somewhat remarkable character thus graphically delineated in the 37th paragraph of your present Despatch 'An apparent civility, a well-disguised courtesy of manner and a pretended acquiescence concealed a strength of purpose, a feeling of injury, and a stern resolution not to part with that which he had acquired. As intractable as he was civil, as obstinate as he was courteous and as firm as he was seemingly acquiescent, he could not be induced by any persuasion or argument. . . .'

28. Before concluding this portion of my subject, I cannot omit to notice the 13th paragraph of your Despatch in which you allude to a speech made by me in the House of Lords as a further proof that it was understood in the Colonial Office from the commencement of the Residential system that the Residents were practically the administrators of the Government. Without expressing any opinion as to the propriety of criticisms founded in this way on the report of a parliamentary debate, I may observe that, even assuming the report to be complete and accurate, it is neither reasonable nor customary to rest an important argument on the mere omission on the part of a minister to contradict a particular assertion of another speaker when replying to a speech into which a great number and variety of details were introduced.

I find, however, on referring to the debate (which I would remind you occurred on the 19th May 1874, previous to the date on which I authorised Sir A. Clarke conditionally to proceed with the appointment of Residents, and some months before Residents were actually accredited either to the Sultan of Perak or of Salangore), that there are other portions besides those quoted by you which are material as showing the ideas which I then entertained as to the future position of the Residents. Thus, with reference to the observations of Lord Stanley of Alderley, 'If it were merely desired to assist the States of Salangore and Perak to maintain order and improve their government, it would have been as easy to do so without committing this country to the possibility of war and annexation by sending to these States a British official of some experience to act under their authority,' and that 'it would be preferable to appoint officials with the title of consuls,' I am reported to have said that I did not object to the title of 'Residents,' and that I thought that if they confined themselves to their proper and legitimate duties they would be of the highest service both to the country and the Rajahs; and it was at this point that I called special attention to the fact that these Residents were to be sent at the distinct request and entreaty of the Rajahs themselves.

29. Leaving this point, however, I ought to notice the 18th, 20th and 21st paragraphs of your Despatch. In the first you quote Sir A. Clarke's description of Mr. Birch's qualification for the office of Resident. I cannot admit that the question of the nature of the office to be assumed is affected by the fact that Mr. Birch possessed in an eminent degree qualities which would be equally valuable to a ruler as to the adviser of a ruler in a country like Perak. In the 20th and 21st paragraphs you refer to my 'apparent acquiescence' in the reports of the Residents, which you find in my expressions that 'I had read them with interest and trusted that peace and prosperity might be further developed.' I own here to some surprise. The language which you quote in evidence of my opinion on so grave and important a matter is little more than an ordinary acknowledgement; but it was immediately followed by two other paragraphs which you omit to notice, reminding you that the appointments had not been confirmed, and that the character of all advice required to be carefully considered, and it is obvious that these passages preclude the inference you draw.

30. Having shown in the previous portion of this Despatch that the Residential scheme as approved by Her Majesty's Government was very far from being what you have supposed, it is of course impossible for me to admit that the system you introduced when the proclamations were issued, providing for the government of Perak in the name of the Sultan by British Commissioners responsible to you, was merely a slight modification of the existing system as already approved. An essential difference of policy has indeed been admitted in the colony, for I find in the report of the debate in the Legislative Council of the Straits Settlements of 5th November last, which you have transmitted to me, it was then said that, unfortunately, events had proved the policy which 12 months since was considered the best that could possibly be adopted, to be barren of results, because its strength consisted only in what might be called moral force. It had been found impossible to carry out that principle, and it must give place to the more vigorous policy which His Excellency had now entered upon, and of which the speaker had no doubt the result would be greater, at the same time that moral force must give place to physical force.

I have, however, said enough as to the incorrectness of your present contention; and it remains for me to point out the objections to which Her Majesty's Government consider that your policy would in any case have been open and the reasons which compel me, having regard to the disastrous consequences that ensued on its adoption, to convey to you their disapproval of it.

31. It is hardly possible to maintain that the system you proposed to introduce was adopted with the full assent of the Native Chiefs. You do indeed in your Despatch of 16th October say that you had been informed

that 'some of the Chiefs, anxious for a better system, and desirous of putting an end to the divided state of Perak, wished the British Government to take the country altogether under their control,' and that you found this representation was quite correct in the case of Yusuf; but I find that when you made this suggestion to Ismail and to Abdullah, they both, so far from readily assenting, put you off in the first instance by asking to consult other Chiefs before giving a definite reply; and though Abdullah subsequently wrote you a letter expressing concurrence in the arrangement, it was after you had distinctly threatened him in the letter of 27th September with the following ultimatum: 'Now we propose to our friend that officers of the British Government shall govern the country in the name of our friend. If our friend agrees to this, our friend will still be recognised as Sultan and receive a large allowance, but if our friend does not agree to this, we cannot help our friend, and our friend will be no longer Sultan.'

In another place you state 'I determined, if the Sultan could be induced to agree, to adopt the policy of governing Perak by means of British officers in his name;' and I cannot but conclude that, with a view to getting a nominal assent to a system which deprived the Chiefs of the last semblance of power, and was naturally repulsive to them, you exercised a pressure which was obviously inexpedient unless it was to be supported by something more than moral force, and which could not have been justified unless you had been previously instructed that Her Majesty's Government would sanction a forcible intervention.

In the 89th paragraph of your present Despatch you admit that you 'erred in common with all concerned in supposing you could have intervened in the affairs of Perak without a display of force, and that a military force must, sooner or later in greater or lesser degree have been necessary to support the position which had been assumed;' but a careful perusal of your description of the general aspect of affairs in Perak, with its divided sovereignty and the powerful semi-independent Chiefs such as the Maharaja Lela clearly shows that the result might have been earlier anticipated, and consequently that the precautions which you took against resistance as mentioned in the 90th paragraph of your Despatch were altogether inadequate.

32. But a further objection that I have to take to the policy you decided on adopting arises from the fact that it could only have been possible to recede from it with extreme difficulty.

You say 'This course may be temporary if in the course of events we found any Chief like the Maharajah of Johore who had the necessary strength of character, and who could and would undertake the government of the State, when it would be easy to hand over the government to him;' but I do not find that there was any reasonable probability of such an event occurring and to point to possible results in the event of certain improbable contingencies is not a sufficient justification of a doubtful policy. On the other hand it is quite certain that grave responsibilities must be incurred from the moment that a country is professedly governed by British Commissioners. Supposing British capital and Chinese labour to have been thereby attracted to Perak, powerful interests would certainly have protested in the event of the British Government subsequently determining as you contemplate to withdraw from these responsibilities.

33. It is, moreover, impossible for me to concur in the view expressed in the 77th and following paragraphs of your Despatch as to the absence of connection between the adoption of your policy and the occurrence of Mr. Birch's death and the subsequent events. Whether or no there was such an amount of disaffection that some struggle was ultimately inevitable, I cannot, with the facts before me, pretend to say, but the evidence you bring forward to show that in any case an outbreak was to be anticipated appears to me far from conclusive. The erection of a stockade in a Malay country is not of such rare occurrence that I can accept your deductions from this and other similar evidence that even if no proclamation had been issued, 'An attack might have been made upon the Residency which might have led to a combination and confederacy which would probably have caused an obstinate war and still greater loss of life.' But if it were clear that discontent existed in various quarters it seems strange that you should have entered upon so serious a policy as that involved in the issue of the Proclamation except after adopting full and well considered precautions.

After a complete review of all the circumstances of the case, I can come to no other conclusion than that the existing discontent, which probably had its origin in the assumption by the Resident of an authority in excess of that which had been contemplated by Her Majesty's Government when the Pangkore engagement was approved, was materially increased by the mode in which you induced the Perak Chiefs to give an involuntary assent to a system which deprived them of their privilege and powers; while the issue of the proclamation in an ill-advised manner at an isolated place would seem to have been the more immediate provocation of the outrage from which the present crisis has arisen.

34. And here it may be as well to allude to the argument which in several places in your recent Despatches you have drawn from the warning which I instructed you to convey to the Chiefs who entered into the Perak engagement that H.M. Government would look to the exact fulfilment of the pledges voluntarily given and would hold responsible those who violated their solemn engagements. This was simply a message to be delivered by you to the Chiefs, and cannot be construed as giving you authority to modify the system which had been contemplated in the treaty, in the event of that system not being successful, still less as giving you an extraordinary discretion to enforce certain provisions of the engagement in a mode which, as I have already pointed out to you, necessarily involved the support of the Resident by material force, and was consequently diametrically opposed to the policy which had been approved by Her Majesty's Government.

35. If the system introduced by your predecessor had in your opinion failed, 'from causes fatal to its successful working' as the 17th and 56th paragraphs of your present Despatch would imply, your first duty was to consult Her Majesty's Government explaining fully the state of affairs as they presented themselves to you, before deciding on the immediate adoption of another system designed to meet the same object; and I cannot but remark in passing, with reference to the 66th paragraph of your Despatch, that, if the Residential system had collapsed, it is not easy to perceive how you could have brought yourself to believe that 'a comparatively small step in advance' or 'a slight modification of the system' would be likely to remove 'the dead-lock' you have described.

36. In justification of your decision to carry this policy into immediate effect, you in the main urge your own belief that the course of action would meet with unqualified approbation.

In the third paragraph of your Despatch you speak of the course of action 'which it was imperative to adopt,' and you appear to assume, as you do also in the 53rd and 54th paragraphs, that the course you adopted was the only alternative to an abandonment of the position that had been occupied by the British Government since the ratification of the Pangkore engagement. I cannot admit that this dilemma was a necessary one. On the one hand Her Majesty's Government were not free lightly to recede upon the appearance of difficulty from their endeavour to terminate the anarchy which had long prevailed; on the other hand, if a change of policy had become necessary, the nature of that policy could only be finally determined by them, and a decision on the point ought not to have been anticipated by the Government of the Straits Settlements.

37. But you acted on the assumption that your proceedings would meet with my approval, and you justify this in the 71st and 72nd paragraphs by a comparison of the action of Sir A. Clarke in January 1874 with your own in October last. I do not perceive, however, that the circumstances of the two cases are similar. In the former case the serious disorders in Laroot had reached a point requiring immediate action, and the plea of urgency could fairly be brought forward. My predecessor, in view of those disorders and the injury to trade and British interests consequent on the prevailing anarchy, had previously instructed Sir A. Clarke to consider what steps could be taken to restore peace, admitting that it was incumbent on Her Majesty's Government to employ their influence to this end; and with the exception of Captain Speedy's appointment to Laroot, Sir A. Clarke took no other immediate action consequent on the treaty until after the subject had been finally brought before Her Majesty's Government.

Nor did Sir A. Clarke pretend to speak and act 'as if charged with full authority', for he expressly states in the Despatch reporting his proceedings, 'I trust your Lordship will understand that by so giving my assent I have in no way bound Her Majesty's Government to any particular course, and that it is perfectly possible now to withdraw from the position

I have temporarily assumed.' In so acting he no doubt incurred a serious responsibility and because I gave him a qualified approval in the unusual circumstances of the case it by no means follows that I can approve a complete change of policy, made without authority, not conceived with due regard to the necessity it involved of providing against resistance, and disastrous in its consequences.

38. Assuming, however, all and everything that you have urged in justification of the course which you have adopted, assuming further the imperative need of immediate action, it was absolutely incumbent on you to communicate with me in the ordinary manner. The telegraph was available, and the difficult position in which you have placed both yourself and Her Majesty's Government is in fact directly due to your omission to consult me in that manner, for which I do not find in your Despatch any other justification than that contained in the 76th paragraph, where you state that you deliberately determined not to do so as you felt it impossible to enter with sufficient fulness into the question, and so to convey a distinct view of the reasons for your action. This explanation I need only remark is of itself sufficient to show that you were conscious of the complicated position of affairs, of the absence of complete information on the subject in this Department, and of the magnitude of the change which you were making; and these considerations alone should have been sufficient to induce you, in the absence of any urgent grounds for immediate action, to submit your proposals for approval instead of relying upon your own judgment.

39. With reference to the question of the future policy which ought to govern the relations of Her Majesty's Government towards Perak, I purpose to address you in a separate Despatch; and I will now add only the expression of the sincere reluctance and pain with which I have felt myself constrained to express an unfavourable opinion of some part of your proceedings.

It is not my object to convey censure, and indeed, I have already highly approved the conspicuous ability and determination with which you acted subsequently to the outbreak of these disorders. I am glad to take this opportunity of repeating my appreciation of your conduct during this period, but I am confident that your long experience as a distinguished servant of the Crown will make you fully aware on reflection, that an officer representing Her Majesty in a distant dependency must be most careful to assure himself that the Government to which he is responsible not only understands but approves any important administrative or political changes which he may contemplate; that he is not at liberty of his own motion to initiate such measures; and that the necessity for obtaining a distinct assurance of approval is so great as to outweigh any advantage which might appear to him likely to ensue from more immediate action. I am equally confident that I can rely as fully upon your cordial and unreserved co-operation in that policy which will be announced to you as if it had not unfortunately been my duty to disapprove of some of your recent acts and opinions.

I have etc.

(signed) CARNARVON

Governor Sir W. Jervois.
   K.C.M.G., C.B.

APPENDIX E

THE documents concerning this controversy of 1876 are in the Public Record Office, C.O. 273, No. 83, Vol. I (Jan. to Apr. 1876). Lord Carnarvon's first reactions to the dispatch here reprinted as Appendix C are still to be read in his own words, of which the following extracts deserve quotation:

Ref. Paragraph 4. 'One of the strongest charges ever brought against a Secretary of State by a Colonial Governor.'

Ref. Paragraph 5. 'An outrageous doctrine if it really means anything.'

Ref. Paragraph 11. 'Monstrous!'

Ref. Paragraph 34. 'The insolence of this expression can hardly be matched in any Colonial Dispatch.'

Ref. Paragraph 89. 'It is very late to perceive this. It should have been foreseen. . . .'

APPENDIX F

Chinese Secret Societies

FOR the following details the author is indebted to Mr. W. L. Blythe, C.M.G., who has allowed him to see the typescript of a forthcoming work in which the origin and nature of these societies is fully explained. *Triad and Tabut* by M. L. Wynne (Singapore, 1941) is the work upon which historians have so far relied but Mr. Blythe has been able to show that Wynne's central theory is fallacious. This theory postulates the original existence of two organizations in China, the Hung League and the Han League, from which the rival factions in Malaya respectively derived. It is now sufficiently clear that all these societies had the same origin. All had a common ancestry in the Hung Brotherhood. This had two branches, the Ko Lao Hui of northern China and the Triad or Ghee Hin society of southern China. As the Chinese in Malaya came from the south their societies were all originally branches of the Triad. Groups seceded from the original society as a result of racial conflict or an internal struggle for power. Within the Brotherhood there were different groups or lodges, sometimes formed from a particular language-group, sometimes from people engaged in a particular occupation or with similar interests. For example, the Toh Peh Kong society of Penang was an offshoot of the local Triad society, the Ghee Hin, formed by the Hokkiens who wanted their own organization separate from that of the Cantonese. There was no ideological opposition between the different societies. Their origins, objects, customs, and ritual were all much alike. But they often found themselves opposed in commercial matters, in the tendering for revenue farms, the preservation of a monopoly, the right to mine in a certain area, and so forth, each society being called upon to support the undertakings of its own members.

In Larut in 1872 the dispute was between the miners of Klian Bahru who came from the Four Districts (Sz Yip) of south-western Kwangtung, and the miners of Klian Pau who came from the district of Chen Shang in central Kwangtung, and these last were expelled from the mines in February–March 1872. They turned for help to an association in Penang known as the 'Five Large Districts Kongsee' which was composed of people from five districts in Central Kwantung province adjacent to the district of Chen Shang from which the dispossessed miners came. This faction, the Chen Shang miners and their supporters, now became known as the Five Districts, Go Kwan (Ng Yuen) in opposition to their enemies the Four Districts. The Four District faction was supported by the Ghee Hin society and the Ho Hup Seah, while the Five District faction was supported by the Hai San society of which many of the Chen Shang miners were members.

APPENDIX G

Vessels of the Royal Navy stationed in the Straits during the period 1867–77

THE warships which appear in this story belong to a period during which sail was slowly being replaced by steam. They were still rigged as ships or barks, and their sails were frequently in use. They were no longer dependent, however, on the wind. They were becoming dependent, instead, on coal. At the same time, the old line of gun-ports, the broadside battery, had given place to a different type of armament, mounted on the centre line of the ship. In some ships, not all, the clipper bow had been replaced by that almost vertical stem which was to be a warship characteristic for many years to come. These Victorian men-of-war represented a half-way stage between the old sailing-ship fleet and the navy of World War I. So far as the shores of Malaya were concerned, the vessels to be seen mostly fell into one or other of the following categories:

    (1) *Ironclad battleship* (14 guns)
    (2) *Screw sloop* (7 guns)
    (3) *Screw corvette* (6 guns)
    (4) *Screw gun vessel, 1st class* (4 guns)
    (5) *Screw gun vessel, 2nd class* (4 guns)

Most of these mounted their relatively few but heavy guns on the centre line. Almost the only vessel of the old broadside type was the *Charybdis* (17 guns).

The only battleship to visit Malayan waters was the flagship, *Iron Duke*. She was a twin-screw ironclad of 6,034 tons, 280 feet between perpendiculars, with 3,500 h.p. engines and a speed on trials of 13·6 knots. Her crew numbered 450. She was built at Pembroke to the design of Mr. E. J. Reed, launched in 1869 and completed in 1870. In September 1871 she was chosen as flagship for Vice-Admiral Shadwell, then appointed Commander-in-Chief on the China Station. Drawing 22 ft. 11 in., she was the first capital ship to pass the Suez Canal, then 24 ft. deep. Even with her fuel unloaded, it was as much as three tugs could do. The fuel carried was insufficient for so long a voyage and *Iron Duke* reached Galle with only one day's fuel in hand after steaming for three weeks at four knots. *Iron Duke* and *Audacious* were henceforward to be the alternate flagships on the China Station for the next eighteen years. She was relieved by *Audacious* about a year later and this time tried to *steam* through the Suez Canal, scraping both sides and grounding on four separate occasions. The year 1875, begun thus inauspiciously, brought still worse luck in September. On manœuvres off the Wicklow coast the *Iron Duke* rammed and sank the *Vanguard*, a sister ship of the same class. *Iron Duke* was on the China Station again in 1878 and did useful service until 1890, being sold for scrap in 1906.

The screw sloop class was represented on the Malayan coast by the *Rinaldo* and the *Zebra*. *Rinaldo*, of seven guns and built of wood, with 200 h.p. engines, measured 1,365 tons, 185 ft. 1 in. between perpendiculars, and drew 15 ft. 8 in. of water. She was completed in 1860 and served on the China Station where she was recommissioned on 10 May 1870 with a new crew brought from England in the *Donegal*. *Rinaldo*'s armament comprised five 64-pounders on the quarter-deck, one 64-pounder gun on the forecastle, and a 7-inch gun amidships. This last weapon could fire shot, shell, shrapnel, or case-shot. Her crew comprised:

Officers . . .	18
Petty officers . .	30
Seamen . . .	82
Boys, 1st and 2nd class .	23
Marines . . .	24
Total	177

The *Rinaldo*'s sister ship *Zebra* was also at one time in the Straits: a vessel which was paid off at Hong Kong in April 1873 and subsequently scrapped.

Screw corvettes were less in evidence but the *Thalia* of six guns makes an occasional appearance. She was completed in 1869 at Woolwich, measuring 2,216 tons and 200 ft. 1 in. between perpendiculars. She drew 18 ft. 7 in. and was a bigger ship than *Rinaldo*. *Thalia* had a complement of:

Officers . . .	26
Petty officers . .	48
Seamen . . .	102
Boys, 1st and 2nd class .	30
Marines . . .	29
Total	235

Far commoner than the sloop or corvette, however, was the screw gun vessel. The larger class in this category was represented by the *Nassau*, of four guns (originally of fourteen). She was built of wood at Pembroke, and launched in 1866. Measuring 877 tons and 185 ft. between perpendiculars, she drew 12 ft. 4 in. She was armed with two 20-pounder Armstrong cannon on the quarter-deck and two on the forecastle. Her complement comprised:

Officers . . .	15
Petty officers . .	23
Seamen and stokers .	43
Boys, 1st and 2nd class .	6
Marines . . .	11
Total	98

Commonest of the men-of-war to be seen in the Straits were the screw gun vessels, 2nd class. Their shallow draught made them particularly suitable for this service. Mention is thus made in these pages of the *Avon*,

Hornet, Teazer, Midge, Frolic, Rifleman, Hart, and *Fly.* These were composite twin-screw vessels built in about 1867-8 at Portsmouth, Birkenhead, or Stockton-on-Tees. They were all of 584 tons and 155 ft. 0 in. between perpendiculars, drawing between 8 ft. 7 in. and 10 ft. 0 in. of water and fitted with 120 h.p. engines. They theoretically mounted four guns but the *Avon* in 1873-4 was armed with seven 64-pounders and two 20-pounder guns, the last used as bow- and stern-chasers. For crew they carried about eighty officers and men. As a class they seem to have been regarded as worn out or obsolete by 1888 or 1890.

INDEX

(Names of ships are listed separately under 'Ships')

DATE DUE

5-5			
APR 1 5 1971			
MAY 1 9 1976			
GAYLORD			PRINTED IN U.S.A.